Microsoft® Windows Server® 2008: A Beginner's Guide

MARTY **MATTHEWS**

New York   Chicago   San Francisco
Lisbon   London   Madrid   Mexico City   Milan
New Delhi   San Juan   Seoul   Singapore   Sydney   Toronto

The *McGraw·Hill* Companies

Cataloging-in-Publication Data is on file with the Library of Congress

Microsoft® Windows Server® 2008: A Beginner's Guide

34567890   DOC DOC   1 5 4 3 2 1

ISBN   978-0-07-226351-0
MHID   0-07-226351-2

Sponsoring Editor	**Technical Editor**	**Production Supervisor**
Jane K. Brownlow	John Cronan	Jean Bodeaux
Editorial Supervisor	**Copy Editor**	**Composition**
Jody McKenzie	Jan Jue	International Typesetting and Composition
Project Manager	**Proofreader**	
Vastavikta Sharma (International Typesetting and Composition)	Megha Roy Chowdhury	**Illustration**
	Indexer	International Typesetting and Composition
Acquisitions Coordinator	Steve Ingle	**Art Director, Cover**
Jennifer Housh		Jeff Weeks

To Dick and Pat Shepard,
The world's greatest neighbors and wonderful friends.
Thanks Dick and Pat, for always being there, no matter what the need.

ABOUT THE AUTHOR

Martin (Marty) Matthews has used computers for more than 40 years, from some of the early mainframe computers to recent personal computers. He has done this as a programmer, systems analyst, manager, vice president, and president of a software firm. As a result, he has firsthand knowledge of not only how to program and use a computer, but also how to make the best use of the information a computer can produce.

Over 25 years ago, Marty wrote his first computer book, on how to buy minicomputers. Twenty-three years ago, Marty and his wife, Carole, began writing books as a major part of their occupation. In the intervening years, they have written over 70 books, including ones on desktop publishing, web publishing, Microsoft Office, and Microsoft operating systems from MS-DOS through Windows Server 2003 and Windows Vista. Recent books published by McGraw-Hill include *Windows Server 2003: A Beginner's Guide* and a number of volumes in the best-selling QuickSteps series, of which he is the co-creator.

CONTENTS

Part I

The Windows Server 2008 Environment

Part II

Deploying Windows Server 2008

Part IV

Communications and the Internet

Part V

Administering Windows Server 2008

ACKNOWLEDGMENTS

It takes a number of people to create a book like this and especially to make it a really good book. The following people, and others I do not know, have added much to the book and have made my job manageable.

Jane Brownlow, executive editor, provided the needed support, as well as a lot of latitude. Thanks, Jane!

John Cronan, technical editor, corrected many errors, added many tips and notes, and generally improved the book. John is also a great friend. Thanks, John!

Jan Jue, copy editor, added to the readability and understandability of the book while listening to my considerations and being great to work with. Thanks, Jan!

Carole Matthews, my life partner for over 35 years, my very best friend, and sharer of our parenting adventure, provided the necessary support without which this book would not have been possible. Thanks, my love!

INTRODUCTION

Windows Server 2008 is now a fully mature server operating system. What began as Windows NT went through major transition in Windows 2000 Server and Windows Server 2003 to become in Windows Server 2008 a full-featured, fully capable server operating system. The net result is a server operating system that is more reliable, easier to install, and more scalable. It also has an excellent directory service, is easier to manage, provides better security, and delivers exceptional web support.

The purpose of this book is to show you how to use these features and many others, and how to get the attendant benefits.

How This Book Is Organized

Windows Server 2008: A Beginner's Guide is written the way many people learn. It starts by reviewing the basic concepts and then uses a learn-by-doing method to demonstrate the major features of the product. Throughout, the book uses detailed examples and clear explanations with many line drawings and screenshots to give you the insight needed to make the fullest use of Windows Server 2008. *Windows Server 2008: A Beginner's Guide* has five parts, each providing a complete discussion of one major aspect of Windows Server 2008.

Part I: The Windows Server 2008 Environment

Part I introduces you to the Windows Server 2008 environment and to what's new about it. This part establishes the foundation for the rest of the book.

▼ **Chapter 1, Exploring Windows Server 2008,** provides an overview of Windows Server 2008 and serves as a guide to the more in-depth discussions that take place in the later chapters.

Part II: Deploying Windows Server 2008

Part II covers planning for and deploying Windows Server 2008 across an organization. The purpose of this part is to assist you in going through the planning process and then actually doing a detailed installation.

▼ **Chapter 2, Preparing for Installation,** looks at all the steps that must be carried out prior to installing Windows Server 2008, including the possible pitfalls to stay clear of.

■ **Chapter 3, Installing Windows Server 2008,** takes you through the various steps necessary to install the Server from different starting points, for both upgrading and doing a clean install.

▲ **Chapter 4, Windows Deployment Services,** describes how to use the Windows Deployment Services to automate the installation of Windows Server 2008.

Part III: Networking Windows Server 2008

Part III devotes three chapters to networking, the single most important function within Windows Server 2008.

▼ **Chapter 5, Windows Server 2008 Networking Environment,** provides a comprehensive foundation on networking by describing the schemes, hardware, and protocols or standards that are used to make it function.

■ **Chapter 6, Setting Up and Managing a Network,** describes how networking is set up and managed in Windows Server 2008.

▲ **Chapter 7, Using Active Directory and Domains,** looks at how domains are used in Windows Server 2008 and the central role that Active Directory plays in managing networking.

Part IV: Communications and the Internet

Part IV covers the ways that you and your organization can reach out from your LAN to connect to others or allow others to connect to you, both on the Internet and through direct communications.

▼ **Chapter 8, Communications and Internet Services,** provides an overview of communications and how to set it up, including using a dial-up connection with the Remote Access Service (RAS) and using an Internet connection with Internet Explorer.

- ■ **Chapter 9, Internet Information Services Version 7**, describes Internet Information Services (IIS) and how it is set up and managed.

- ■ **Chapter 10, Virtual Private Networking**, explains VPN: how it works; how it is set up with PPTP, L2TP, and SSTP; and how it is used.

- ▲ **Chapter 11, Terminal Services and Remote Desktop**, describes the significantly enhanced Terminal Services, how it is set up, and then how to use Application Server Mode, Remote Administration Mode, and Remote Desktop Connection.

Part V: Administering Windows Server 2008

The purpose of Part V is to explore the numerous administrative tools that are available within Windows Server 2008 and to discuss how they can best be used.

- ▼ **Chapter 12, Managing Storage and File Systems**, looks at the extensive set of tools that are available in Windows Server 2008 to handle the various types of storage systems and the files and folders they contain.

- ■ **Chapter 13, Setting Up and Managing Printing and Faxing**, describes what constitutes Windows Server 2008 printing and Print Services, how to set it up, how to manage it, how to manage the fonts that are required for it, and how to use the Fax Server and faxing.

- ■ **Chapter 14, Managing Windows Server 2008**, discusses the system management tools and user management tools that are not part of setting up, networking, file management, and printing.

- ▲ **Chapter 15, Controlling Windows Server 2008 Security**, describes each of the security demands and the Windows Server 2008 facilities that address that demand, as well as the ways to implement those facilities.

Conventions Used in This Book

Windows Server 2008: A Beginner's Guide uses several conventions designed to make the book easier for you to follow:

- ▼ **Bold type** is used for text that you are to type from the keyboard.

- ■ *Italic type* is used for a word or phrase that is being defined or otherwise deserves special emphasis.

- ■ A `monospaced typeface` is used for command listings either produced by Windows Server 2008 or entered by the user.

- ■ SMALL CAPITAL LETTERS are used for keys on the keyboard such as ENTER and SHIFT.

- ▲ When you are expected to enter a command, you are told to press the key(s). If you are to enter text or numbers, you are told to type them.

PART I

The Windows Server 2008 Environment

CHAPTER 1

Exploring Windows Server 2008

Windows Server 2008 is the latest Microsoft Windows operating system for servers in a client/server network. It comes in several editions, ranging from simple web servers to complex datacenter servers. All editions include extensive built-in web and local area networking technologies. They all provide many features, especially in the areas of management and security that allow the secure connection among people, systems, and devices for the exchange of information and the sharing of computer resources. These features support the integration of people and computers working together in a single organization as well as across many organizations to provide a high level of connectedness, collaboration, and interoperability.

REASONS FOR WINDOWS SERVER 2008

Windows Server 2008 is a significant upgrade from Windows Server 2003, and most especially from Windows 2000 Server. There are many reasons for saying this, but here are some of the outstanding ones:

▼ *It is easier to configure and manage.* Windows Server 2008 has added Server Manager to replace several tools in prior versions of Windows Server to create a single, unified management interface to install, configure, and control all the roles on the server.

■ *It offers better security.* Windows Server 2008 considerably enhances security to protect the entire network through improvements in authenticating the user, controlling user access, securing stored data, securing data transmission, and managing security.

■ *It is a more powerful web server.* Internet Information Services Version 7 (IIS 7) provides a comprehensive platform with new and enhanced web services for building, delivering, and managing web applications with improved security.

■ *It offers easier and more secure remote access.* Terminal Services in Windows Server 2008 has added two new modules, Terminal Services Gateway and Terminal Services RemoteApps, that increase the security with which a remote computer can access a local area network (LAN) and that greatly improve the experience of remotely executing an application.

■ *It substantially enhances the ability to customize a server.* The Server Manager's role selection allows you to specify only those roles, role services, and features that you want installed, thereby shrinking the components that require computer resources and management and that can be attacked.

▲ *It provides a new command-line environment.* Windows Server 2008's PowerShell allows you a much greater and more powerful ability to configure and control the operating system without using the graphical user interface (GUI). This allows Windows Server 2008 to have an installation option of just the server core without the GUI and with only some of the roles.

The purpose of this book is to show you how to use many of these features plus a number of others. This chapter will provide a quick overview of Windows Server 2008, looking briefly at the major areas of the product, including a description of its function and how it relates to the rest of the product.

COMPARE WINDOWS SERVER 2008 EDITIONS

Windows Server 2008 comprises five independent and separately sold editions:

▼ **Windows Server 2008 Standard Edition**   A full network server operating system that is meant for small-to moderate-sized organizations and handles most server roles and features. It is an upgrade for Windows Server 2003 Standard Edition and Windows 2000 Server and is available in Server Core and full server installations for both 32-bit (called "x86" because of its origin with Intel 8086, 386, and 486 chip sets) and 64-bit (called "x64" using the AMD chip sets) processors.

■ **Windows Server 2008 Enterprise Edition**   A full network server operating system that is meant for larger organizations, especially those involved in e-commerce. In addition to the features in the Standard Edition, the Enterprise Edition provides failover clustering and Active Directory Federation Services, as well as improved scalability and availability. It is an upgrade for Windows server 2003 Enterprise Edition and Windows 2000 Advanced Server and is available in Server Core and full server installation options for both 32-bit and 64-bit processors.

■ **Windows Server 2008 Datacenter Edition**   A full network server operating system that is meant for the largest organizations, especially those involved in data warehousing and online transaction processing. It provides all of the Enterprise Edition capabilities with support for additional processors and unlimited virtual image use rights. It is an upgrade for Windows Server 2003 Datacenter Edition and Windows 2000 Datacenter Server and is available in Server Core and full server installation for both 32-bit and 64-bit processors.

■ **Windows Web Server 2008**   A limited server operating system solely for hosting web sites and delivering web applications using Internet Information Services (IIS) for both 32-bit and 64-bit processors.

▲ **Windows Server 2008 for Itanium-based Systems**   A limited server operating system for the Intel Itanium 2 64-bit processor. Only some of the server roles are available on this platform, but the IIS web server and application delivery are included. Further discussion of the Itanium-based edition is outside the scope of this book.

Hardware Considerations

The hardware considerations for the Windows Server 2008 editions have a consistent set of minimum and recommended requirements, as shown in Table 1-1, and a mixture of maximum values, as shown in Table 1-2.

System Component	Minimum	Recommended
x86 processor speed	1GHz	2GHz
x64 processor speed	1.4GHz	2GHz
Memory (RAM)	512MB	2GB
Disk space	10GB	40GB
Peripherals	DVD-ROM, Super VGA monitor, keyboard, and mouse	DVD-ROM, Super VGA monitor, keyboard, and mouse

Table 1-1. Minimum Requirements for All Versions of Windows Server 2008

NOTE The meaning of the abbreviations in Tables 1-1 and 1-2 are as follows: GHz (gigahertz) is a measure of processor speed in billions of cycles per second; MB, GB, and TB (megabyte, gigabyte, and terabyte) are measures of memory and disk space in millions, billions, and trillions of bytes (each of which is eight bits [a 0 or 1] and is roughly equivalent to an English language character); RAM (random access memory) is the primary solid-state memory in the computer; ROM (read only memory) can be solid-state devices in the computer or CD (compact disc) or DVD (digital video disc) devices that cannot be written to by the user; VGA (video graphics array) is a type of video display.

2008 Server Edition	Platforms	Physical Processors	Maximum Memory	Failover Clustering
Standard	32-bit	4	4GB	None
Standard	64-bit	4	32GB	None
Enterprise	32-bit	8	64GB	8-node
Enterprise	64-bit	8	2TB	16-node
Datacenter	32-bit	32	64GB	8-node
Datacenter	64-bit	64	2TB	16-node
Web Server	32-bit	4	4GB	None
Web Server	64-bit	4	32GB	None

Table 1-2. Hardware Maximums among Windows Server 2008 Editions

This book will focus on the Windows Server 2008 Standard Edition and touch a bit on the Web Server and the Enterprise Edition.

The remaining sections in this chapter provide an introductory look at the major areas of Windows Server 2008 that provide for the following functions:

▼ Deploying Windows Server 2008

■ Networking Windows Server 2008

■ Communicating and Using the Internet with Windows Server 2008

▲ Administering Windows Server 2008

The sections discussed here correspond to the remaining parts of this book, so you can easily jump from this overview to the details later in the book.

DEPLOY WINDOWS SERVER 2008

Successfully bringing Windows Server 2008 into an organization means that not only the operating system is installed, but also that the appropriate planning has taken place before the installation, and that the desired customization and optimization has taken place after the installation. To meet this objective, you must plan and then completely carry out the deployment.

Prepare for Windows Server 2008

To prepare for Windows Server 2008, you must assure that:

▼ Your computers meet the requirements of Windows Server 2008.

■ Windows Server 2008 supports all the hardware you need that is attached to your computers.

■ You know the installation decisions and have made the choices that provide the best operating environment for you.

■ Your computers have been prepared for an operating system installation.

▲ You have a solid plan for carrying out the installation.

Chapter 2 helps you to prepare for installation by looking at each of these areas, and it discusses what you need to know to make the installation as smooth as possible.

Install Windows Server 2008

Windows Server 2008 can be installed and customized in a variety of ways, which fall into three categories:

▼ **Manually**   Someone sits in front of the computer to be installed and, in real time, installs and configures the software on that machine.

■ **Automated**   A script or answer file is used to carry out the installation, so a person has only to start the installation on a computer and can then let the script finish it.

▲ **Remotely**   A person sits in front of a server and performs the installation on another computer across the network. This installation can be manual or automated.

Chapter 3 explains in detail how to use the manual approach for installing Windows Server 2008 with many variations. Chapter 4 describes the automated approach for installing Windows Server 2008.

Configure Windows Server 2008

The initial installation of Windows Server 2008, the steps that get you to a running Windows Server 2008 as shown in Figure 1-1, does not install many of the major server

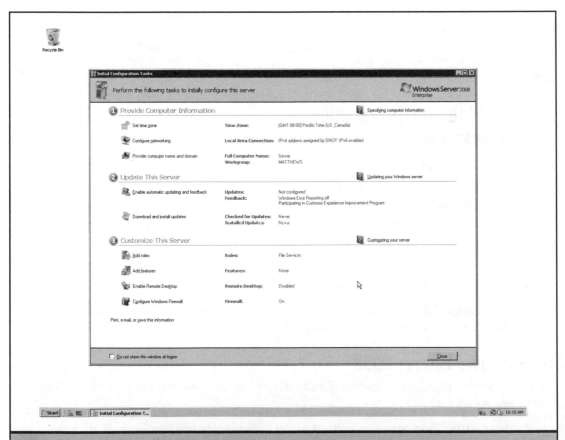

Figure 1-1.   When Windows Server 2008 completes installation, most server roles have not been installed.

components, called "roles" in Windows Server 2008, which were automatically installed in prior versions of Windows Server. The installation of server roles, as well as role services and features, is the job of the Server Manager.

The Server Manager window provides the means to install up to 16 different server roles such as Active Directory Domain Services, Application Server, File Services, and Web Server (IIS); as well as up to 36 features such as BitLocker Drive Encryption, Failover Clustering, and Remote Assistance. Once the roles and features are installed, the same Server Manager window gives you information about a role and provides the means to configure and control it, as shown in Figure 1-2 for the File Services role.

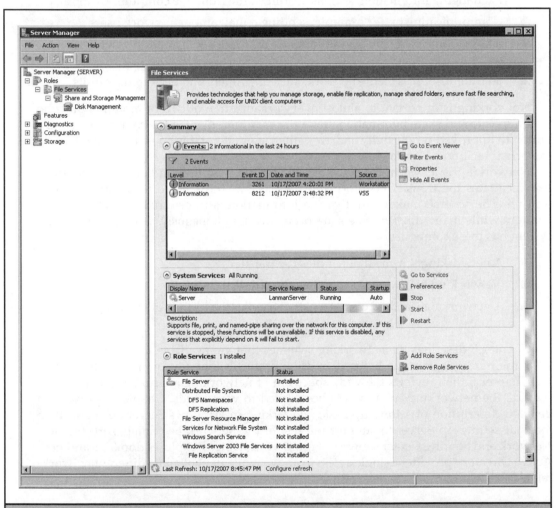

Figure 1-2.   In the Server Manager, you can get information and control a role, as well as install it.

Using Server Manager is introduced in Chapter 3 and is discussed throughout this book as it is used to install and manage the many roles and features.

NETWORK WINDOWS SERVER 2008

Windows Server 2008 is a network operating system and it exists for its networking ability. This allows it to connect with other computers for the purpose of performing the following functions:

▼ Exchanging information, such as sending a file from one computer to another

■ Communicating by, for example, sending e-mail among network users

■ Sharing information by having common files accessed by multiple network users

▲ Sharing resources on the network, such as printers and backup disk units

Networking is important to almost every organization of two or more people who communicate and share information. It is a primary ingredient in the computer's contribution to improved productivity and, from the viewpoint of this book, is the single most important facility in Windows Server 2008.

Networking is a system that includes the physical connection between computers that facilitates the transfer of information, as well as the scheme for controlling that transfer. The scheme makes sure that the information is transferred correctly and accurately while many other transfers are occurring simultaneously. Thus, a networking system has these components:

▼ A networking scheme that handles the transfer

■ Networking hardware that handles the physical connection

▲ A networking standard or protocol that handles the identification and addressing

Chapter 5 describes the networking schemes that are available in Windows Server 2008, the hardware that can be used, and the protocols that are common in the industry. Chapter 5 then reviews the wide spectrum of networking alternatives available to provide the networking environment best suited to your needs. Chapter 6 provides a detailed description of setting up basic networking in Windows Server 2008 and then looks at setting up Server to support the rest of the network beginning with the new Network and Sharing Center shown in Figure 1-3. Chapter 7 explores domains and how Active Directory provides a single access to and management of many different network-related functions.

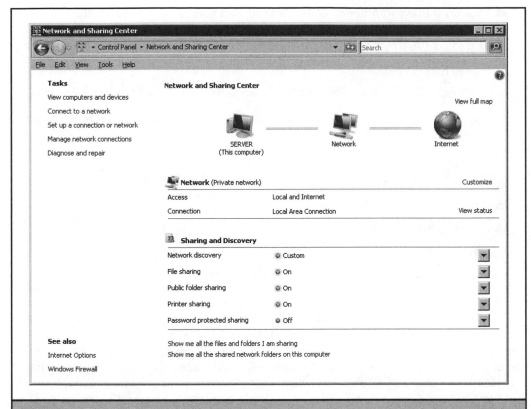

Figure 1-3.   The new Network and Sharing Center provides the gateway to setting up and controlling networking.

COMMUNICATE AND USE THE INTERNET
WITH WINDOWS SERVER 2008

"Networking" is often thought of as using a LAN. In this age of the Internet, Windows Server 2008 networking has a much broader meaning that includes all the types of connections that you make outside of your LAN using what was classically called "communications." The Network and Sharing Center, just described, provides the entry point for working with both LAN and external connections.

The types of external connections include:

▼   Direct connection to the Internet from the LAN through a digital subscriber line (DSL) or cable connection

■   Broadband wireless connections

- Dial-up line computer-to-computer communications using a modem
- Leased-line and private-line wide area network (WAN)
- Remote Access Service (RAS) for accessing a LAN over a direct, dial-up, leased, or private line
- ▲ Virtual private networking (VPN) to securely access a LAN over the Internet

Windows Server 2008's communications ability includes the following possible ways to exchange information:

- ▼ Computer or LAN to the Internet
- Computer to LAN
- LAN to LAN
- ▲ Computer or LAN to WAN

Communication may include a modem, wireless adapter, or other device to connect a single computer to a method of transmission, or it may use a router or other device to connect a network to the method of transmission. Communications can be over copper wires, fiber-optic cable, microwave, ground wireless, infrared, or satellite transmission.

Windows Server 2008 includes a number of roles, features, and applications (see the Server Manager's role selection in Figure 1-4) that control and/or utilize communications or an external networking capability. In addition, Windows Server 2008 networking includes programs to set up and manage Remote Access Service (RAS) and virtual private networking (VPN) forms of networking over a major distance, as well as the Remote Desktop Connection to link to a remote computer. Finally, IIS can be used to publish web pages and web applications on either the Internet or an intranet.

Chapter 8 provides an overview of communications and how to set up the various Windows Server 2008 roles and features that support it. Chapter 8 also discusses establishing an Internet connection and using Internet Explorer over the Internet. Chapter 9 looks at IIS, how it's set up, and how it's managed. Chapter 10 describes how to set up and use VPN, while Chapter 11 discusses Terminal Services, the foundation for Remote Desktop Connection and other remote operations.

ADMINISTER WINDOWS SERVER 2008

The job of administering a Windows Server 2008 network, even one as small as a single server and a few workstations, is a significant task. To assist in this, Windows Server 2008 has a number of system management tools that can be used to monitor and tune the system's performance, both locally and remotely. These tools can be categorized into the following areas:

- ▼ Overall server management
- File system management

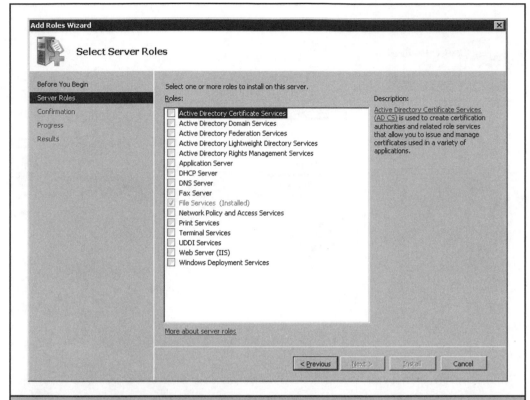

Figure 1-4.   The Server Manager role selection provides for the installation of the primary server components like Active Directory Domain Services and Web Server (IIS).

- ■ Printing management
- ■ Security management
- ▲ Other system management

Overall Server Management

As you have already read, the primary overall server management tool in Windows Server 2008 is the Server Manager. The Server Manager is often the single tool needed to install, monitor, and manage both major and minor server components, as described earlier in this chapter, as well as throughout this book. Many of the other facilities for administering Windows Server 2008 described in the following sections are also installed and can be managed from Server Manager. Figure 1-4 showed the major roles that can be installed from Server Manager. For many of these major roles, a number of optional role services

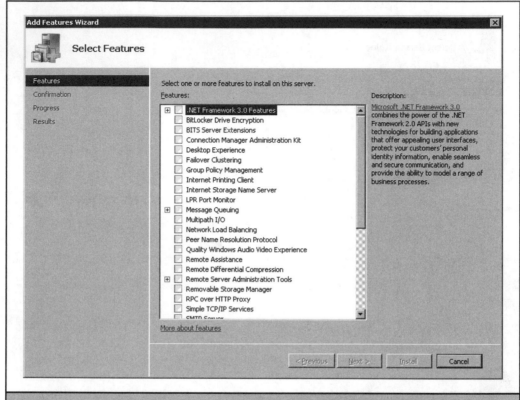

Figure 1-5.   In addition to the roles that can be installed and managed with Server Manager, a number of independent features can also be installed there.

also can be installed. In addition to the roles, a large number of independent server features can be installed with the Server Manager, some of which are shown in Figure 1-5.

File System Management

Windows Server 2008 is designed to work in a wide range of computing environments and with several other operating systems. As a result, the structure of its file storage has to be flexible. This is manifest in the types of storage that are available and in the file systems that Windows Server 2008 can utilize.

Prior to Windows 2000 Server, only one type of storage was available, called *basic storage*, which allowed a drive to be divided into partitions or volumes only before it was reformatted. Windows 2000 Server and Windows Server 2003 added *dynamic storage*, which allows the dynamic creation of and changes to volumes. In Windows Server 2008, you can shrink and extend volumes within a basic storage drive, which has the same effect as repartitioning the drive, but there are other advanced features, such as a volume spanning two or more drives that require dynamic storage. When you first install Windows Server 2008, all drives are basic storage. You can then choose to convert a given drive to dynamic storage and have both types in a computer, or convert all drives to dynamic storage.

The Windows Server 2008 file system can extend well beyond a single drive, or even beyond all the drives in a single machine, to all the drives in a network, and it even includes volumes stored offline. The management of this system is significant, and Windows Server 2008 thus has a significant set of tools to handle file system management, which is described in Chapter 12. Among these tools are:

▼ Disk Management

■ Dynamic Volume Management

■ Distributed File System

▲ Disk Backup and Recovery

Figure 1-6 shows the Disk Management pane within the Server Manager window. It is also available within Computer Management.

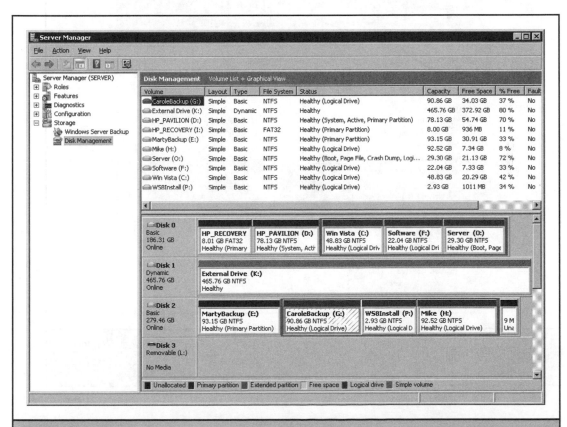

Figure 1-6. Disk management can be handled in either the Server Manager or Computer Management.

Printing Management

The ability to transfer computer information to paper or other media is still important, and the ability to share printers is a major network function, as you can see in Figure 1-7. Both Windows Server 2008 and Windows Vista can share their printers and therefore serve as print servers. In addition, Windows Server 2008 has a Print Services role that can be installed and managed in Server Manager. This role allows you to manage all the printers on the network. Chapter 13 describes what constitutes Windows Server 2008 printing, how to set it up, how to manage it, and how to manage the fonts that are required for printing.

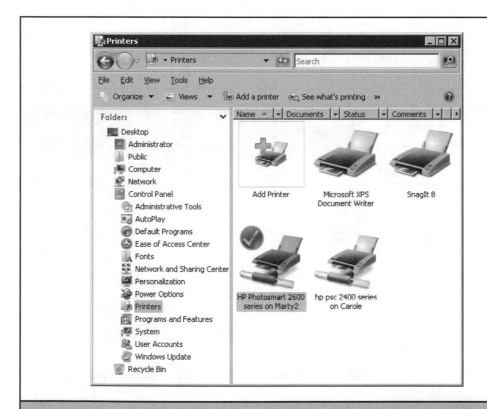

Figure 1-7. Most recent versions of Windows can share printers across the network. Windows Server 2008 can manage them all.

Security Management

The demands for security in a computer network include:

▼ **Authenticating the user**   Knowing who is trying to use a computer or network connection

■ **Controlling access**   Placing and maintaining limits on what a user can do

■ **Securing stored data**   Keeping stored data from being used even with access

■ **Securing data transmission**   Keeping data in a network from being misused

▲ **Managing security**   Establishing security policies and auditing their compliance

Windows Server 2008 uses a multilayered approach to implementing security and provides a number of facilities that are used to handle security demands, such as policies for logging on and accessing resources. Central to Windows Server 2008's security strategy is the use of permissions to control what users can do, as shown in Figure 1-8. Other security features are available with Active Directory, which provides a network centralization of security management that is beneficial to strong security. Chapter 15 describes each of the security demands and the Windows Server 2008 facilities that address each demand, as well as the ways to implement those facilities.

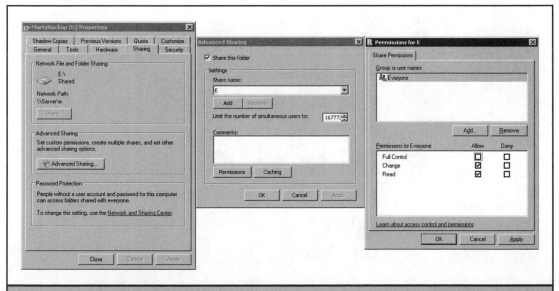

Figure 1-8.   One aspect of security is to set what a group can do on a drive.

Other System Management

Windows Server 2008 has a variety of other system management tools to control many facets of the operating system. Chapter 14 looks at the system management tools and user management tools that are not covered elsewhere. These tools include:

▼   The Control Panel (see Figure 1-9)

■   The Task Manager

■   The Microsoft Management Console

■   The Registry

▲   The boot process

Figure 1-9.   The Control Panel provides the means to control many basic functions within Windows Server 2008.

PART II

Deploying Windows Server 2008

CHAPTER 2

Preparing for Installation

D eploying Windows Server 2008 is a significant undertaking that requires thorough planning and careful attention to details. The purpose of this and the next two chapters is to assist you in going through the planning process and then carrying out the detailed installation. Chapter 2 looks at the steps that must be carried out prior to installing this newest Windows server, including ways to handle possible pitfalls. Chapter 3 takes you through installing Windows Server 2008 from different starting points, including upgrading and performing a clean install. Chapter 4 shows how Windows Deployment Services can be used to automate the installation of Windows Server 2008.

CONSIDER INSTALLATION NEEDS

The installation of Windows Server 2008 is, on the surface, a simple procedure: you put the Microsoft distribution DVD in the drive or access the files over a network and follow the instructions on the screen. However, below the surface, the installation isn't necessarily that simple. Before you can actually install the software, you must consider the following:

▼ Your computers must meet the requirements of Windows Server 2008.

■ You must be sure that Windows Server 2008 supports all the hardware in your system.

■ You must know the choices that provide the best operating environment for each of the installation decisions.

■ Your computers must be prepared for the operating system (OS) installation.

▲ You must have a solid plan for carrying out the installation.

This chapter helps you prepare for installation by looking at each of these areas for Windows Server 2008. I'll discuss what you need to know to make the installation as smooth as possible.

CHECK SYSTEM REQUIREMENTS

Windows Server 2008 has significant hardware requirements. Review Table 2-1 to make sure your systems meet the minimum requirements.

NOTE In this and the remaining chapters of this book, when you see Windows Server 2008 without an identifying edition, I am speaking about Standard Edition in the few instances where it makes a factual difference. Chapter 1 shows the differences in hardware requirements among the five editions, and additional information is provided in the following sections.

System Component	Processor Type	Requirements
Processor	x86 (32-bits)	1GHz minimum, 2GHz recommended
	x64 (64-bits)	1.4GHz minimum 2GHz recommended
RAM		512MB minimum, 2GB recommended
Hard disk free space		10GB minimum, 40GB recommended
CD/DVD drive		DVD drive required unless a network is installed
Video display system		Super VGA or higher resolution monitor
Input devices		Keyboard and mouse (both optional)
Network device		Compatible network card

Table 2-1.   Minimum and Recommended System Requirements for Windows Server 2008

About System Requirements

The requirements in Table 2-1 are generalized; special situations do exist for which various requirements apply. These special situations are noted in the following paragraphs.

Processors

Windows Server 2008 Standard Edition supports up to four processors in a single computer, in what is known as *symmetric multiprocessing (SMP)*. Windows Server 2008 Enterprise Edition supports up to eight processors in a single computer. Windows Server 2008 Datacenter Edition supports up to 32 processors in the 32-bit version and up to 64 processors in the 64-bit version. This allows a wide range of scaling in a Windows Server 2008 installation, from a single computer with a single processor to many computers, each with a number of processors.

Random Access Memory (RAM)

Windows Server 2008 Standard Edition with an x86 processor supports up to 4GB (gigabytes) of memory, while an x64 processor can support up to 32GB. Windows Server 2008 Enterprise and Datacenter editions with an x86 processor support up to 64GB, while an x64 processor can support up to 2TB (terabytes).

Hard Disk Space

The amount of free hard disk space required is dependent on a number of factors, especially in Windows Server 2008. Among these factors are the following:

▼ The Windows components that are installed. Different components require different amounts of space, and they are *additive,* so depending on what you choose to install, the amounts of necessary disk space will vary.

■ A network-based installation requires approximately 3GB of additional free disk space to store additional files.

▲ An upgrade requires more space than a new installation to expand an existing user account's database into *Active Directory,* which consolidates the access to all the resources on a network into a single hierarchical view and a single point of administration.

DVD-ROM

A DVD-ROM drive is required if the Microsoft distribution disc is used. It is not required with a network-based installation.

Networking

A network card is not required if networking is not desired (unlikely) and if a network-based installation is not used. If a network-based installation is used, it requires a suitable server to deliver the files and a means of booting the computer on which the installation is to be done.

Check System Compatibility

After you have checked and determined that your system meets the minimum requirements for installing Windows Server 2008, you need to determine whether the particular hardware and software used across the network are compatible with the OS. You can do this using two Microsoft tools, described in the next two sections, that assess the hardware readiness and application compatibility. In addition, .txt files in the root folder on the Windows Server 2008 DVD may contain late-breaking information on hardware and software compatibility and other information you need before you install.

TIP You can save a lot of problem-resolution time by checking for hardware compatibility and making any necessary adjustments before installing Windows Server 2008.

Use the Hardware Assessment Wizard

The Hardware Assessment Wizard checks all of the computers on a network, creates an inventory of their hardware components, and prepares reports using Excel spreadsheets that assess the readiness of the computers to support Windows Server 2008. To use this program, you need the following minimum hardware and software on the computer where the Hardware Assessment Wizard will run:

▼ **Hardware**: 1.6GHz processor, 1GB of memory, 1GB of disk space, network adapter card

▲ **Software**: 32-bit Windows OS including XP SP2 or later, Vista, Server 2003 R2, or Server 2008; .Net Framework V 2; Excel 2007 or 2003 SP2; Word 2007 or 2003 SP2

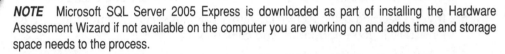

NOTE Microsoft SQL Server 2005 Express is downloaded as part of installing the Hardware Assessment Wizard if not available on the computer you are working on and adds time and storage space needs to the process.

The Hardware Assessment Wizard can be downloaded from the following Microsoft site:

http://www.microsoft.com/technet/solutionaccelerators/hardwareassessment/wv/ default.mspx

Once you have downloaded and installed the Hardware Assessment Wizard, it should start automatically, but you can start it by:

1. Click Start | All Programs, scroll to the bottom of the menu, and click Windows Hardware Assessment.

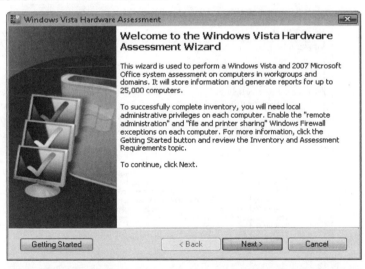

NOTE At the time this book was written, only the Windows Vista version of the Hardware Assessment Wizard was available. I believe that there will be a Windows Server 2008 version available by the time this book reaches you.

2. Click Getting Started and, as desired, read the Help document displayed. After closing Help, click Next.

3. Enter a name for the database to be built and click Next. Accept the default actions to perform and click Next.

4. Select the methods you want to use to find the computers on your network. This depends on the type of network you have. The first two options are the defaults and work in most cases. The last option is the manual fallback. Make your selection and click Next.

5. If you specified using the Windows networking protocols, select the workgroups in the network that you want included in the inventory and click Next.

6. If you specified using Active Directory domain services, enter the Active Directory logon information and click Next.

7. Select, or enter after clicking New Account, the local or domain accounts and their passwords to access the computers to be inventories.

8. Review the actions you have selected, click Back to make any needed changes. When the actions are the way you want them, click Start. You will see a series of thermometer bars that will display the progress of the assessment.

9. When the assessment is complete, click View Summary Details Of The Wizard Operations. View the results in the Details Summary. This will tell you the computers that were found and how many inventories were completed. It will also list the Microsoft Word and Excel reports that have been generated.

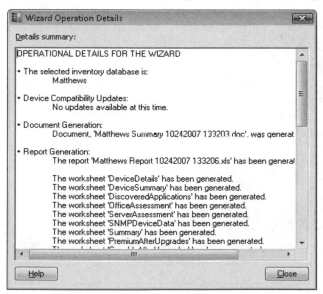

10. When you are ready, click Close. Click Open The Reports Folder. Double-click each of the reports to open them in their applications. These reports provide a wealth of information, as you can see in Figure 2-1.

11. After you have completed reading and/or printing the reports, close the applications and then click Finish to close the Hardware Assessment Wizard.

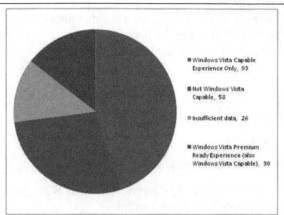

Figure 3: Windows Vista Ready Computers (without hardware upgrades)

Table 1: Windows Vista Ready Computers (without hardware upgrades)

Windows Vista Ready Computers (without recommended hardware upgrades	Computer Count	Percentage
Windows Vista Premium Ready Computers	30	14%
Windows Vista Capable Experience Only	93	45%
Not Windows Vista Capable	58	28%
Insufficient Data	26	13%
Total	207	100%

Windows Vista Ready Computers with Hardware Upgrades

The hardware of some computers can be upgraded in relatively simple ways to make them Windows Vista Capable or improve the Windows Vista experience. The following table provides information about the potential Windows Vista readiness of your organization's computers after performing the recommended hardware upgrades.

	Current Operating System (E)	Service Pack Level (F)	Current Windows Vista Experience (G)	Reasons Not Capable (H)
5	Windows XP Tablet PC Edition	Service Pack 2	Capable	
6	Windows Server 2003	Service Pack 2	Capable	
7	Windows XP Tablet PC Edition	Service Pack 2	Not Capable	RAM less than 512MB
8	Windows Vista™ Ultimate	Service Pack 2	Capable	
9	Windows Vista™ Ultimate		Capable	
10	Windows Server 2003	Service Pack 2	Premium Ready	
11	Windows Vista™ Ultimate	Service Pack 2	Premium Ready	
12	Windows Vista™ Enterprise		Capable	
13	Windows XP Professional	Service Pack 2	Not Capable	CD-ROM drive not found
14	Windows XP Professional		Not Capable	Free disk space less than 15 GB
15	Windows Server 2003	Insufficient Data	Insufficient Data	CPU Unknown Hard Disk Unknown Memory Unknown
16	Windows XP Professional		Not Capable	CPU less than 800 MHz

Summary / ClientAssessment \ **ServerAssessment** / OfficeAssessment / SN

Figure 2-1.   The Hardware Assessment Wizard provides both written and tabular information about the ability of your network computers to handle Windows Server 2008.

Check Application Compatibility

Microsoft provides a web site on application compatibility that references several documents and a downloadable toolkit that checks for application compatibility. The Application Compatibility Toolkit (ACT) can be run on:

▼   Windows Vista

■   Windows XP SP2

■   Window Server 2008

■   Windows Server 2003 SP1

▲   Windows 2000 Server SP4 and Update Rollup 1

ACT requires that SQL Server 2000, SQL Server 2005, or SQL Server 2005 Express Edition be running on the computer ACT will run on.

NOTE   Once again, the application compatibility discussion, figures, and illustrations are for Windows Vista because those items for Windows Server 2008 are not ready as this is written.

1. Begin by opening the web site http://go.microsoft.com/fwlink/?linkid=29880, reading the overview, and then right-clicking the top link, Enterprise Guidance: Getting Started With Application Compatibility, and clicking Open. Scroll down and click Getting Started With Windows *Vista* Application Compatibility card (this requires Microsoft Office PowerPoint 2007; you can get a free PowerPoint 2007 viewer by downloading it from Microsoft at http://www .microsoft.com/downloads/ and scrolling down to PowerPoint Viewer 2007).

    This is a pair of tightly packed PowerPoint slides with lots of detailed application compatibility information, as you can see in Figure 2-2.

2. When you have completed looking at the application compatibility card, close PowerPoint, click Application Compatibility Toolkit Deployment Guide And Step By Step Guides, click Save, choose the drive and folder where you want it saved, and click Save.

3. Open the drive and folder containing the Application Compatibility Toolkit Deployment Guide, unzip the files, and review those that are of interest. When you are done, close the application used to view the files.

4. On the third page of the Application Compatibility site, click Download ACT 5.0, click Download, click Run, click Run again, click Next, accept the license, click Next twice, click Install, and click Finish. A presentation will start and explain ACT. A presentation will start and explain ACT, as shown in Figure 2-3.

5. When the presentation is finished, click Start | All Programs | Microsoft Application Compatibility Toolkit | Application Compatibility Manager. The ACT Configuration Wizard will open.

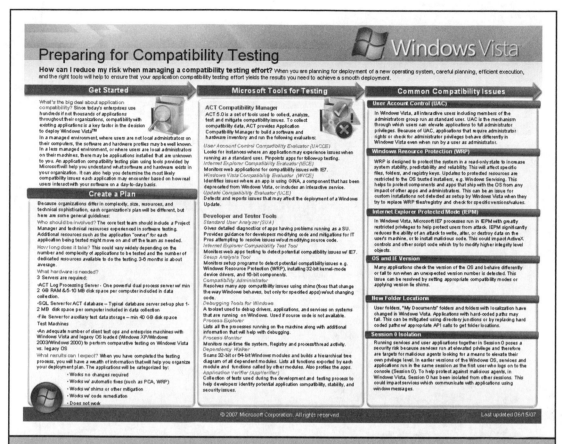

Figure 2-2. Microsoft provides a lot of information and a powerful toolkit to test for application compatibility.

6. Click Next and select the configuration options that are correct for you. When you have completed the configuration settings, use the instructions in the ACT Step-by-Step Guide to perform the application compatibility testing that you want.

MAKE CORRECT INSTALLATION CHOICES

During the Windows Server 2008 installation process, you have a number of choices about how you want to install the software. If you consider these choices before you perform the installation and take the time to determine which choices will be best for your operation, you will probably end up better satisfying your needs. Some of the choices

Figure 2-3. ACT includes a presentation to get you started.

depend on earlier decisions and may not be available on certain decision paths. The choices that you will have during a Windows Server 2008 installation are whether to:

▼ Upgrade an existing Windows installation or do a clean installation

■ Dual-boot Windows Server 2008 with another version of Windows or not

■ Choose the partition in which to do the installation or use the default

■ Start Setup from an existing Windows installation or by booting from the installation DVD

▲ Install the full version of Windows or install only the Server Core

Decide to Upgrade or Do a Clean Installation

The first decision that you must make for a Windows Server 2008 installation is deciding which type of installation you want to perform, as shown in the Install Windows screen in Figure 2-4. Although the actual choice takes place later in the installation process, you need to make the decision before you start the installation because it affects how you start the installation. An *upgrade,* in this case, means replacing a currently installed OS with Windows Server 2008 in the same disk partition. A *new installation,* on the other hand, will install Windows Server 2008 in a newly formatted disk or in a separate disk partition without an OS, where either the OS has been removed or the partition has never had one (this is also called a *clean install*).

You can upgrade to the various Windows Server 2008 editions as shown next:

▼   **To Windows Server 2008 Standard Edition from:**
Windows Server 2003 Standard Edition (all Service Packs and R2)

■   **To Windows Server 2008 Enterprise Edition from:**
Windows Server 2003 Standard Edition (all Service Packs and R2)
Windows Server 2003 Enterprise Edition (all Service Packs and R2)

▲   **To Windows Server 2008 Datacenter Edition from:**
Windows Server 2003 Datacenter Edition (all Service Packs and R2)

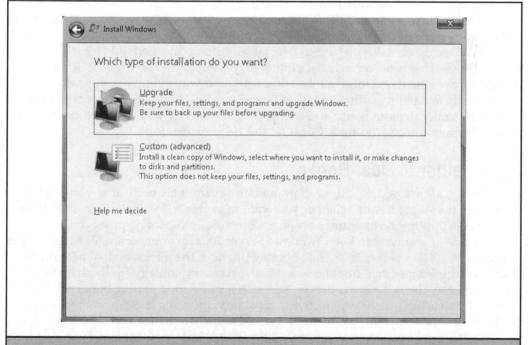

Figure 2-4.   The primary installation decision is whether to upgrade or to do a clean install.

If you are not currently running one of the identified upgradeable products, you can either upgrade to one of those products and then upgrade to Windows Server 2008, or you can perform a clean install.

The major reasons to upgrade, if you can, are the following:

▼ To preserve all the current settings (such as users, rights, and permissions), applications, and data on your computer. Your current environment is preserved intact while upgrading to a new OS.

▲ To make the installation of Windows Server 2008 simpler. Many of the installation decisions are made for you, using the settings in the current OS.

The major reasons to do a clean install are these:

▼ To get around an OS that cannot be upgraded.

■ To dual-boot into both the old OS and Windows Server 2008. This allows you to use either OS. Windows Server 2008 would be in its own partition.

▲ To clean up your hard disks, which makes them more efficient, gets rid of unused files, and gives you back a lot of disk space.

If you can either upgrade or do a clean install (setting aside dual-booting for a moment, which will be discussed in the next section), this decision is between preserving your current system with all of its settings, applications, and inefficient and wasted space, and doing a clean install. The clean install gives your new OS an environment not hampered by all that has been done on the computer in the past, *but* it is a *lot* more work. With a clean install, you have to reinstall all your applications and reestablish all of your settings. This is not an easy decision. It may seem like a "no-brainer" to keep your current environment and forgo all the extra work, but you should ask yourself whether you're really *that* happy with your current environment. Installing a new OS is an excellent opportunity to clean house and set up your system the way it should be, even if it takes a fair amount of extra time. Consider this decision carefully.

Decide Whether to Dual-Boot

Dual-booting allows you to choose from among several OSs each time you start your computer. If you are unsure whether you want to switch to Windows Server 2008, or if you have an application that runs only on another OS, dual-booting gives you a solution. For example, if you want to keep Windows Server 2003 on your computer to use it after installing Windows Server 2008, dual-booting provides the means to do what you want. If you are thinking of dual-booting as a disaster recovery strategy for those instances in which you can't boot Windows Server 2008, that is not a good reason, because Windows Server 2008 has built-in disaster recovery capability including backup and recovery, key recovery, and booting into safe mode, discussed elsewhere in this book.

You can dual-boot Windows Server 2008 with Windows 2000 and later Windows OSs, both client and server. In all cases, you must have installed the other OS before installing Windows Server 2008. If you are installing Windows Server 2008 on a computer that already has a dual-boot environment, Windows Server 2008 Setup will create a third boot environment in which you can boot all three OSs.

Dual-booting also has significant drawbacks:

▼   You must install Windows Server 2008 in a separate partition so that it doesn't overwrite any of the files belonging to the original OS. This means that you must reinstall all the applications you want to run under Windows Server 2008 and you must reestablish all your settings, as you do in a clean install.

■   You may have to handle some complex file-system compatibility issues. See the discussion following this list of bulleted items.

■   In a dual-booting situation, the Plug and Play features of prior OSs and Windows Server 2008 could cause a device not to work properly in one OS because the other OS reconfigured it.

■   Dual-booting takes up additional disk space with two complete OSs.

▲   Dual-booting makes the operating environment more complex than it would be otherwise.

When you dual-boot, both OSs must be able to read the files that you want to share between them. This means that the shared files must be stored in a file system that both OSs can use. When you install Windows Server 2008, you will use the New Technology File System (NTFS). NTFS has significant features in Windows Server 2008, such as Active Directory, improved security, and file encryption, but these features may not be usable by earlier versions of Window with NTFS or by those OSs that use the FAT and FAT32 file systems. Therefore, you run the risk of earlier OSs not being able to access the files created in Windows Server 2008.

Dual-booting is a compromise and doesn't give you all that you can get out of Windows Server 2008. It is therefore not recommended unless you have a need that is not handled any other way, such as a needed application that does not run under Windows Server 2008—and even in this case, you might leave the application on a dedicated server and move most of your work to another server running just Windows Server 2008.

NOTE   Although earlier OSs may not be able to access some NTFS files on the same computer in a dual-boot situation, all OSs can access those same files if the access is over a network (the server translates the files as they are passed to the network).

Decide on Partitioning

Partitioning divides a single hard disk into two or more partitions, or *volumes*. These partitions are given drive letters, such as *D, E,* or *F,* and so are called *logical drives*. When you do a clean install of Windows Server 2008, you are shown the current partitioning of the boot disk and asked to select the partition you want to use to install Windows Server 2008, as shown in Figure 2-5.

When you boot from the Windows Server 2008 distribution DVD, the partition dialog box, shown in Figure 2-5, looks slightly different. In the lower right, there is Drive

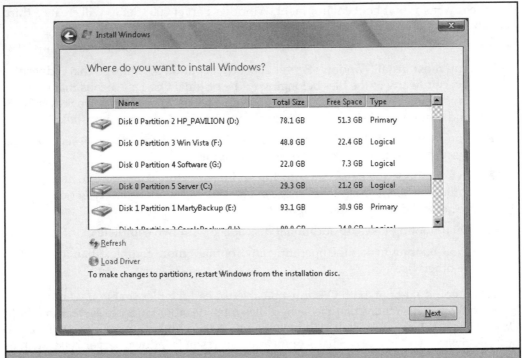

Figure 2-5.   To dual-boot, you must partition a drive to divide it between the OSs.

Options (Advanced). If you click this option, you see several options for working with partitions. You can:

▼ **Delete** an existing partition, creating free space on a drive

■ **Extend** an existing partition if there is free space to extend into

■ **Create** a new partition if there is free space in which to do it

▲ **Format** an existing or new partition

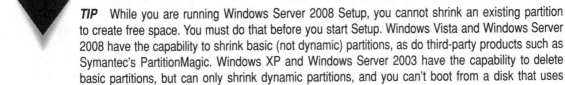

TIP   While you are running Windows Server 2008 Setup, you cannot shrink an existing partition to create free space. You must do that before you start Setup. Windows Vista and Windows Server 2008 have the capability to shrink basic (not dynamic) partitions, as do third-party products such as Symantec's PartitionMagic. Windows XP and Windows Server 2003 have the capability to delete basic partitions, but can only shrink dynamic partitions, and you can't boot from a disk that uses dynamic partitions.

There are two main reasons for partitioning: to have two different file systems on the same drive, and to provide a logical separation of information or files. If you dual-boot, you need to use at least two different partitions to keep the two OSs separate so that the

Windows Server 2008 installation does not replace any of the original OS's files. Another reason for a separate partition is if you want to use the Remote Installation Service (RIS) to remotely install Windows Vista on workstations.

When you are considering the partitioning options, you also need to consider the size of each partition. You need to allocate at least 10GB for Windows Server 2008 by itself, and it is wise to leave yourself some extra space. If you are working with an active server, you should allocate around 40GB for such things as Active Directory information, user accounts, RAM swap files, optional components, and future Service Packs.

Under many circumstances, you'll want only a single partition on a hard disk to give yourself the maximum flexibility to use up to the entire disk. You can also manage your partitioning after you complete installation (see Chapter 12).

Decide How to Start Setup

You can start Windows Server 2008 Setup from within an existing Windows installation or by booting from the Microsoft distribution DVD. If you start from an existing Windows installation, you can do either an upgrade or a clean install. The considerations are:

▼ If you start by booting the DVD, you can only do a clean install, and, of course, you need the DVD.

■ If you start from an existing installation, you can do so either from a DVD or from a folder on your network that has Setup in it.

▲ If you want to make any changes to the partitioning of a drive, or to format a partition, you must boot from the distribution DVD to do so.

To start from an existing Windows installation:

1. Start the existing Windows installation.

2. When the existing Windows has completed booting, insert the Windows Server 2008 DVD in its drive. The AutoPlay dialog box will open.

Click Run Setup.exe.

Or, click Start, click Computer, navigate to the drive and folder containing Windows Server 2008 Setup, and double-click Setup.

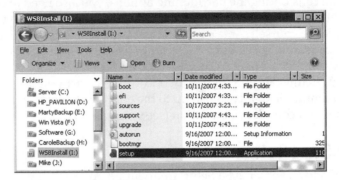

To start by booting from the DVD:

1. Insert the Windows Server 2008 DVD in its drive and restart the computer.

2. Immediately after the manufacturer's splash screen, press any key when you see "Press Any Key To Boot From CD Or DVD."

In all cases, after some preliminary messages, you'll see the Install Windows screen shown in Figure 2-6.

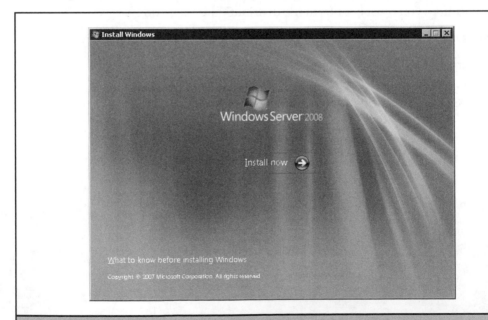

Figure 2-6. How you start Setup determines the options you will have.

Decide on Full or Core Options

The major editions of Windows Server 2008 (Standard, Enterprise, and Datacenter) can be installed in either a full installation or a Server Core installation, as shown in Figure 2-7.

▼ **Full installation** includes all the components (roles and features) that are available in the edition of Windows Server 2008 being installed, as well as the full user interface.

▲ **Server Core installation** is a minimal installation with only a subset of the components and without the user interface. A Server Core installation can be managed from the command prompt, either locally from the computer on which it is installed, or remotely from a Terminal Services remote desktop connection.

The Server Core installation cannot run most third-party applications because of the lack of the user interface, but it reduces the management overhead, as well as the areas of the server that can be attacked. The Server Core will run the following roles and features.

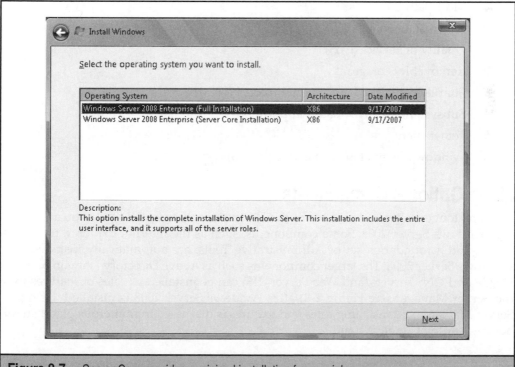

Figure 2-7. Server Core provides a minimal installation for special-purpose servers.

Roles:

- ▼ Active Directory Domain Services
- ■ Active Directory Lightweight Directory Services
- ■ Dynamic Host Configuration Protocol (DHCP) Server
- ■ Domain Name Service (DNS) Server
- ■ File Services
- ■ Print Server
- ■ Streaming Media Services
- ▲ Web Server (IIS)

Features:

- ▼ Backup
- ■ BitLocker Drive Encryption
- ■ Failover Clustering
- ■ Multipath IO
- ■ Network Load Balancing
- ■ Quality of Service (QoS)
- ■ Removable Storage
- ■ Simple Network Management Protocol (SNMP)
- ■ Subsystem for UNIX-based applications
- ■ Telnet client
- ▲ Windows Internet Name Service (WINS)

Installing Optional Components

Setup no longer asks you to choose optional components to install while you are installing Windows Server 2008. Some components, such as the Internet Explorer, the Accessories, and a foundation set of Administrative Tools, are automatically installed with Windows Server 2008. The larger components such as Active Directory Domain Services, DHCP and DNS servers, and Web Server (IIS) can be installed as roles or features from the Server Manager (see Figure 2-8) after Windows Server 2008 is installed. Using the Server Manager and installing roles and features is discussed in numerous places in this book including Chapters 1 and 3.

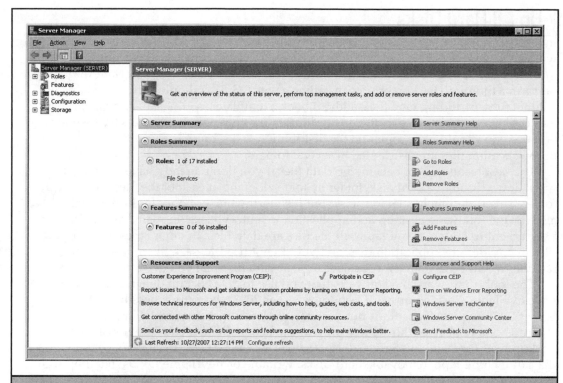

Figure 2-8.   Most major components of Windows Server 2008 are installed from the Server Manager after Windows Server 2008 is installed.

PREPARE FOR INSTALLATION

Installing an OS entails a moderate risk that you could lose some or all the information on the computer, which makes it a good idea to back up the hard disks before the installation. Installing an OS is also a great opportunity to clean up and make the system more efficient. In addition, you need to make certain adjustments to the system to make sure that the installation runs smoothly. All of these tasks are included in the following steps to prepare for an OS installation:

▼   Back up all hard disks

■   Inventory current software

■   Clean up current files

■   Upgrade hardware

▲   Disable conflicting hardware and software

Back Up All Hard Disks

In a server environment, backing up is probably better disciplined than it is for a client workstation, unless the server also takes charge of backing up the workstation. Therefore, backing up may or may not be a routine task. In any case, it is important that you perform a thorough backup prior to installing a new OS. This should include backing up all data files, including mail files, address books, templates, settings, documents, favorites, cookies, and history. Backing up application files not only is unnecessary (usually), because you should have copies on the distribution disks, but it is also difficult, because the application files are distributed in several folders.

The best technique for backing up data files if you don't already have a file list is to work down through a hard disk, folder by folder, looking at each of the files within each folder. This is definitely a tedious task, but it's worthwhile not only for backing up, but also for the following cleanup and application inventory tasks. In many cases, you can back up entire folders if you know all the files are data files. In other cases, many of the files in a folder are application files, and you do not need to back them up—although a few files might be custom templates, settings, or data files that you do want to preserve.

The tools (hardware and software) that you use to do a backup depend on what you have available. Backing up with Windows Server 2003's backup is possible. (Windows Server 2008 has new capability, but you need to back up before installing it.) The best choice is one of several third-party programs, such as Symantec's (previously Veritas) Backup Exec for Windows Servers (http://www.Symantec.com/Business/). Backup media can include tape, removable hard disks, writable or rewritable DVDs, fixed optical drives, or spare fixed hard disks on another system. Whatever you use, make sure that you can read it back in your Windows Server 2008 system.

 TIP With the low cost of large hard disks, it might be worthwhile to get one or more just to hold the latest backup of one or more systems, although you should still also use removable media so that you can store a copy of your data away from the computer in a fireproof container.

Inventory Current Software

As you are going through the hard disks to back them up, you should also take an inventory of the applications on the disk, in case you need to reinstall anything. Separately from the disk review, note what is on the Desktop, the Start menu, the All Programs menu, and the taskbar. Additionally, open Add Or Remove Programs (Programs And Features in Windows Vista and Server 2008) on the Control Panel, and note what programs it shows as currently installed, as well as the Windows components that are currently installed. For each application, note the installed version, whether it is still used, what its supporting files are (such as templates and settings), and where the files are stored on the hard disk. (This latter information needs to be fed back to the backup process to make sure these files are included.) Finally, you need to make sure you still have the distribution disks for each application and note where they are kept. These steps will assure that you have the knowledge, application files, and data files necessary to restore the applications that were running on the computer before Windows Server 2008 was installed.

Clean Up Current Files

Most of us intend to clean up the disks we are responsible for, to get rid of the files and applications that are no longer used, but few of us get around to it. It is a difficult chore, and who is to say that an application or file will never be needed again? Also, we have all had the experience of either needing a file we recently removed or finding a file that has gone unused for some time.

Given that you have done a thorough job of backing up your data files and have a complete inventory of applications, the question of whether a file will be needed again is moot, because you can always restore the file or application if you need it. That leaves only the objection that it is a long, arduous task—and it is.

The best way to clean up a hard disk is also the easiest and the scariest because it is so final—reformatting the hard drive and reloading only the applications and files that you know will be immediately used. This puts a lot of pressure on backing up well and making sure you have a good application inventory, but given that you do, reformatting the hard drive is a good solution. Still, it is a fair amount of work because of the time to reload what you want on the hard drive.

Cleaning up a server adds another dimension covering the entire user- and permission-related information. Basically, the users and permissions database must be audited, and unused and duplicate entries must be removed. Even harder is cleaning up the user and shared folders on the server. Again, these are the kinds of tasks that often get put off, but they are truly necessary if you are going to have a clean and efficient system. Explaining to users that you have a safe backup, and that if they really need a file you'll add it back, helps convince them that it is okay to remove from the server the *lightly used* (no one will admit it is *never* used) information.

Upgrade Hardware

Like cleaning up a hard disk, performing hardware upgrades often gets put off because it can disrupt a system. So again, use the "new OS" excuse to get it done. Use the inventory that you took earlier to determine what hardware you need or want to upgrade, and purchase and install the hardware before installing Windows Server 2008, so the new OS has the benefit of the new hardware. In doing this, consider upgrading the BIOS on the motherboard by checking the manufacturer's web site to determine whether an upgrade is available and, if so, whether it would benefit you.

Disable Conflicting Hardware and Software

Certain hardware and software, if it is running, can cause Setup to fail. For that reason, you need to take the following steps on each computer to prepare for a Windows Server 2008 installation:

▼ Disable any UPS (uninterruptible power supply) device connected to the computer's serial port by removing the serial cable from the computer. The UPS can cause problems with Setup's device-detection process. You can reconnect the cable after Setup is complete.

■ If you are using disk mirroring, it needs to be disabled prior to starting Setup. You can restart disk mirroring when Setup completes.

▲ Stop all programs that are running, especially any virus-detection programs, before starting Setup. These programs may give you spurious virus warning messages while Setup is writing to the disk. Sometimes these programs are automatically started when the system is booted, so you may have to go to some lengths to find and stop them. Here's how:

1. Click Start | All Programs | Startup, and remove any programs you see there. Similarly, remove any program in the Autoexec.bat file.

2. Restart your computer, right-click any icons on the right side of the taskbar, and select Close, Disable, or Exit if one of those options exists.

3. Press CTRL-ALT-DEL, and click Task Manager (or Start Task Manager in Windows Vista and Server 2008) to open the Windows Task Manager shown in Figure 2-9.

4. Select each of the programs in the Applications tab that are running and click End Task. You may also want to go to the Control Panel Add Or Remove Programs (or Programs And Features in Windows Vista and Server 2008) and remove any remaining programs that automatically start.

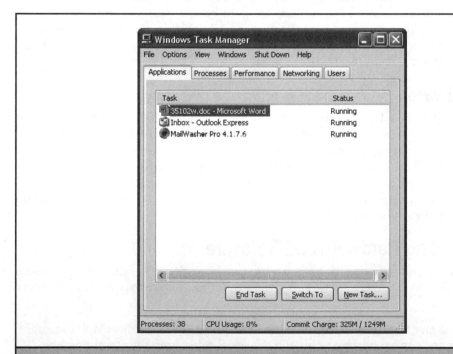

Figure 2-9. Applications can be stopped in the Task Manager.

PLAN A WINDOWS SERVER 2008 MIGRATION

Going through the tasks described so far in this chapter for a server and several workstations is a fair amount of work; doing it for a number of servers and many workstations is a major undertaking. In both cases, having a solid plan for how it will be accomplished is most helpful, and in the large installation case, it is mandatory.

A migration plan must reflect the organization it is designed for, but most plans should cover the following steps:

1. Identify what computers are to be upgraded or installed with Windows Server 2008 or Windows Vista and the order in which their upgrades will be completed.

2. Identify the hardware that needs to be acquired and installed so that Step 1 can be accomplished.

3. Assign someone the task of developing a detailed list of tasks needed to complete Steps 1 and 2.

4. Develop a timeline for completing the tasks in Step 3.

5. Determine a set of installation dates that will provide the minimum amount of disruption to the company's normal activities. A long weekend is often a good idea for everyone except those doing the changeover.

6. Develop a budget for the software, hardware, and labor specified in the preceding steps.

7. Identify realistically the possible disruptions to the company's business and the cost of such disruptions.

8. Identify the benefits of changing over to Windows Server 2008 and how those benefits translate into reduced costs and improved revenues.

Most organizations of any size require a plan such as this, and upper management will look long and hard at the results of Steps 6–8. It is, of course, not a simple numerical comparison. The dollars in Step 6 are hard, out-of-pocket funds, and the dollars in Steps 7 and 8 may be hard to identify. The real question is whether the benefits of Windows Server 2008 are worth the costs, and how well could the company get along without the changeover. Every organization has to answer that question for itself.

Carrying out a changeover from one OS to another is a serious undertaking. Companies have been significantly harmed when upgrades were poorly done, and they have benefited greatly when they were done correctly. Here are the three key elements to success:

▼ Have a detailed knowledge of your current computers and networking system and what you want to achieve with Windows Server 2008.

■ Create a detailed plan of how you are going to carry out the conversion with minimal cost and disruption to the organization.

▲ Communicate continually and exhaustively with everyone involved.

CHAPTER 3

Installing Windows Server 2008

The physical process of installing the Windows Server 2008 software on a server has become much simpler than with Windows Server 2003 and is almost trivial. The setup and configuration of the server, once the operating system (OS) is installed, while not much harder than with Windows Server 2003, is a much more substantial process. With the preparation described in Chapter 2 completed, you are ready to start the actual installation of Windows Server 2008. If you have not read Chapter 2 and completed its preparatory steps, I strongly recommend you do that before continuing here.

PREPARE WINDOWS SERVER 2003 FOR UPGRADE

To upgrade Windows Server 2003, you must first update it to at least Service Pack 1 (SP1), and it is recommended that you update it to Service Pack 2 (SP2). In addition, you need to update the Active Directory domain structure to support Windows Server 2008.

Update Windows Server 2003 to SP1 or 2

The easiest way to update Windows Server 2003 so you can install Windows Server 2008 is to use the online Windows Update.

1. While you are in Windows Server 2003, click Start | All Programs | Windows Update. You are connected to the Microsoft Windows Update site. Follow the instructions to determine the updates you need, and to download and install them. This can take over an hour for SP2.

2. When the update is finished, you are told that the computer must be restarted. Do so.

Update Active Directory

To update the Active Directory domain structure, you need to be on the domain infrastructure operations master computer and run a program on the Windows Server 2008 DVD.

1. To identify the domain infrastructure operations master computer, click Start | Administrative Tools | Active Directory Users And Computers to open the Active Directory Users And Computers window.

2. Right-click the domain object and click Operations Masters. In the Operations Masters dialog box, click the Infrastructure tab. Note the name of the Operations Master computer and close both the dialog box and the Active Directory Users And Computers window.

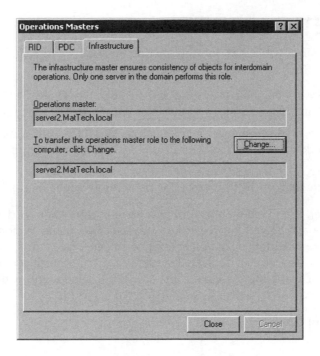

3. Log onto the infrastructure operations master computer with permissions for a domain administrator and insert the Windows Server 2008 DVD in the DVD drive. In the Windows Explorer, locate the \sources\adprep\ folder and drag it to a hard drive on the computer.

4. Click Start | Command Prompt. Type **cd \adprep** to open the folder.

5. Type **adprep /forestprep** and press ENTER to update the forest information. You are warned that any Windows 2000 Active Directory Domain Controllers must be upgraded to SP4.

6. Type **c** and press ENTER. After several minutes (depending on the size of your forest, it could be several hours), you'll get a message that the forestwide information has been successfully updated.

7. Type **adprep /domainprep /gpprep** and press ENTER to update the domainwide information and the group policy information.

8. When you get the message that Adprep successfully completed the update, close the Command Prompt and the Active Directory Users And Computers window.

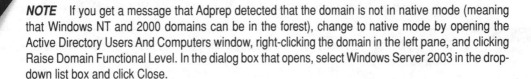

NOTE   If you get a message that Adprep detected that the domain is not in native mode (meaning that Windows NT and 2000 domains can be in the forest), change to native mode by opening the Active Directory Users And Computers window, right-clicking the domain in the left pane, and clicking Raise Domain Functional Level. In the dialog box that opens, select Windows Server 2003 in the drop-down list box and click Close.

CHOOSE A SETUP METHOD

There are a number of ways that Windows Server 2008 can be installed, but they fall into three categories:

▼ **Manually**   A person sits in front of the computer where the OS is to be installed and, in real time, does the installation on that machine.

■ **Automated**   A script or answer file is used to carry out the installation, so a person does not have to stay in front of the computer being installed.

▲ **Remotely**   A person sits in front of a server and performs the installation on a computer across the network. The installation can be manual or automated.

In this chapter, the manual approach, with several variations, is described in detail. In Chapter 4, the automated approach will be described using Windows Deployment Services, which require remotely bootable network interface cards and motherboards that support them, as well as a dedicated server or volume (partition) on a server.

The process of installing Windows Server 2008, independent of the approach, has three distinct phases, each of which needs its own discussion:

▼ Start Setup

■ Run Setup

▲ Configure a server

START SETUP

Setup can be started either by directly booting the Windows Server 2008 Installation DVD or from an existing Windows installation where the Windows Server 2008 installation files can be available either locally or over a network. Both methods have a lot in common.

NOTE   Installing over a network is different than installing remotely. Installing over a network reverses the positions. You are in front of the machine being installed, accessing the network to get the installation files. With remote installation, you are in front of the server installing on a machine across the network.

Starting by Directly Booting Setup

You can directly boot Setup with a new unformatted hard drive or one that has any other OS on it. The only question is whether you can boot from a DVD, which is required.

NOTE   If you directly boot Setup, you cannot do an upgrade. You must start Setup from the product you are upgrading.

If the system on which you want to do the installation can boot from a DVD, then you can start Setup simply by following these steps:

1. Insert the Windows Server 2008 DVD in the DVD drive.

2. Restart the computer.

3. Immediately after the initial startup screen, in the upper left you should see the message "Press Any Key To Boot From CD Or DVD." Press any key.

4. Windows Server 2008 Setup will load and ask you to select the language, time and currency format, and keyboard you want to use. When you are ready, click Next.

5. The Install Windows dialog box will appear as shown in Figure 3-1. Click Install Now.

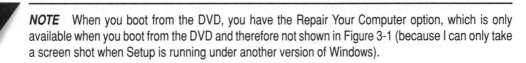

NOTE When you boot from the DVD, you have the Repair Your Computer option, which is only available when you boot from the DVD and therefore not shown in Figure 3-1 (because I can only take a screen shot when Setup is running under another version of Windows).

Figure 3-1.   The initial Install window will look slightly different, depending on whether you booted from the DVD or started in a newer version of Windows. This figure shows the latter.

Can't Boot from a DVD?

If you can't boot from a DVD but believe you should be able to (most recent computers can boot from a DVD if there is a DVD drive installed), you may need to change one or more settings in the system BIOS (basic input/output system), which is entered at the very beginning of the boot process. How you enter the BIOS is usually identified in the first startup screen. Often you press and hold the F1 or F2 function keys. Also, both the DEL and the ESC keys are sometimes used for this purpose. Once you have entered the BIOS, you need to change the boot sequence to boot from the DVD drive first, before the hard drive. In the BIOS:

1. Look for an option, a menu, or a tab that says "Boot" or "Boot Sequence" and click it, or use the arrow or other keys to select or open it to see the boot options.

2. You should see a sequential list showing the priority in which boot devices are accessed. Like this:

    ▼ Internal Hard Disk Drive (or HDD)

    ■ CD/DVD Drive

    ■ Floppy Drive

    ▲ Internal Network Card

3. You want to change the order so the DVD drive is first; otherwise, some higher-priority device, like the hard drive, will be used to start the computer.

4. How you change the order varies on different computers, but in most cases the instructions for doing it are on the screen. Generally, you use the arrow keys to select an option, use the SPACEBAR to enable or disable an option, use the + and – keys or the U or D keys to move an option up or down, use ENTER or a function key to complete and/or save a change, and press ESC or another function key to cancel any changes.

TIP   If you have two DVD drives, such as a DVD-ROM and DVD-RW, try them both; one may work and the other not.

If you can't boot from a DVD, then the only other alternative is to start Windows Server 2008 Setup from a newer version of Windows (see the next section).

Starting from a Newer Windows Version

You can start Windows Server 2008 Setup from a newer version of Windows, beginning with Windows 2000 ("starting" Setup from these OSs doesn't mean you can "upgrade" from them). This startup can be done by inserting the DVD while Windows is running, or by locating the set of install files on a hard disk or DVD drive either locally or across the network.

NOTE   You can upgrade to Windows Server 2008 Standard Edition from Windows Server 2003 Standard Edition (Service Pack 1 and later), and you can upgrade to Windows Server 2008 Enterprise Edition from Windows Server 2003 Standard or Enterprise Edition (Service Pack 1 and later).

Start from a Local DVD Drive

With a newer version of Windows running on the computer with a DVD drive available where you want to install Windows Server 2008:

1. Insert the Windows Server 2008 DVD into its drive.

2. The AutoPlay feature, if active, will load the DVD, and the AutoPlay dialog box will appear. Click Run Setup.exe to start Setup and see the initial Install dialog box, as shown earlier in Figure 3-1.

3. It may be that your AutoPlay feature will automatically run Setup, and the initial Install dialog box is the first thing you see.

4. When you see the initial Install dialog box, click Install Now.

5. If the AutoPlay dialog box doesn't appear or doesn't function as expected and you don't see the initial Install dialog box, use the instructions in the following section, "Start From a Local or Network Drive."

Start from a Local or Network Drive

The Setup files can be copied from the DVD to a hard drive, either on the local or networked computer. You can then start Setup from that computer, including, with the appropriate permissions, from a remote DVD drive—given, of course, that you are connected to that network.

1. On any computer on the network (call this the "Setup Server"), insert the Windows Server 2008 distribution DVD into the DVD-ROM drive.

2. Either copy the contents of the Windows Server 2008 distribution DVD to a new folder on the hard disk on the Setup Server and then share that folder, or share the DVD-ROM drive on that computer.

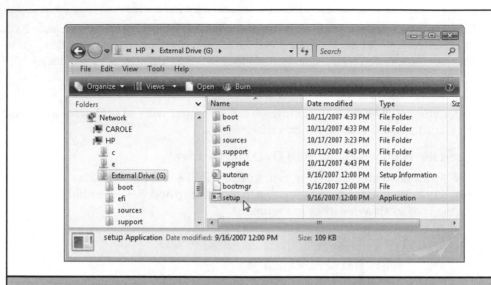

Figure 3-2. Setup can be started from a computer and drive across a network.

NOTE To share a drive, either a hard drive or a DVD drive, click Start | Computer. Locate the hard drive or DVD drive, right-click it, and click Share. Click Advanced Sharing; click Continue in User Account Control; click the Share This folder; click Permissions, with Everyone selected in the top; click Full Control under Allow in the bottom. Click OK three times (or two OKs and a Close, depending what OS you are starting from).

3. On the computer where you want to install Windows Server 2008 (call this the "Install" computer), click Start | Computer. Locate the Setup Server and the drive and folder in which the Windows Server 2008 DVD resides.

4. Double-click Setup.exe, as shown in Figure 3-2 to start Setup. If you start from Windows Vista, you will see a User Account Control dialog box asking if you want to allow Setup.exe to run. Click Allow.

5. The initial Install dialog box will open. Click Install Now.

RUN SETUP

Running Windows Server 2008 Setup is straightforward and has only slight variations depending on whether you are:

▼ Running an upgrade started from Windows Server 2003

■ Running a clean install started from a newer Windows version

▲ Running a clean install started by booting the DVD

Running an Upgrade

An upgrade to Windows Server 2008 must be done from Windows Server 2003 for the same or lesser edition (in the case of Standard to Enterprise). That means that Setup must be started from the product being upgraded. Also, some of the settings for Windows Server 2008 are taken from the earlier system.

CAUTION   If you install Windows Server 2008 as an upgrade, you cannot uninstall it, although if Setup fails, the system will be rolled back to Windows Server 2003.

NOTE   You cannot upgrade to Windows Server 2008 Server Core.

Having started from Windows Server 2003 and clicked Install Now, if you have an Internet connection and the appropriate services, you should have the Get Important Updates For Installation dialog box on your screen (see Figure 3-3). If so, go to Step 1. Otherwise, you will see the product key entry screen and need to start with Step 2.

1. While it will take a little longer, I strongly recommend that you click Go Online To Get The Latest Updates…, which, after getting the updates, will display the product key entry dialog box.

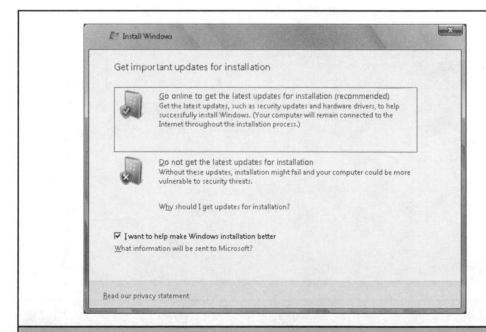

Figure 3-3.   It is recommended that you get the latest updates for Setup before starting the installation process.

2. Enter the product key that is shown on the Windows Server 2008 DVD envelope or case and click Next.

3. In the choice between Full Installation and a Server Core Installation, if you want to do an upgrade, you must choose Full Installation and then click Next.

4. Click I Accept The License Terms (or forget about installing Windows Server 2008) and then click Next.

5. In the Upgrade or Custom dialog box, shown in Figure 3-4, click Upgrade.

NOTE   If you have not installed at least Service Pack 1 (SP1) for Windows Server 2003, you'll be reminded that you need to do so before doing the upgrade to Windows Server 2008.

6. You are reminded that you need to check to make sure that your current programs are compatible with Windows Server 2008. This is discussed in Chapter 2. When you are ready, click Next.

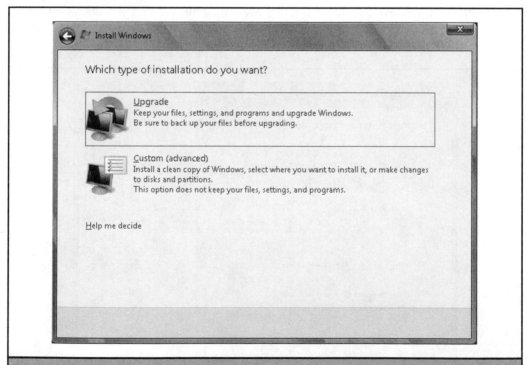

Figure 3-4.   Doing an upgrade preserves your current programs and settings.

7. Setup will begin by copying and gathering files. It will continue with expanding files and installing features and updates, and then will complete the upgrade. During this process, the computer will reboot several times and you may need to click OK to facilitate that. After a final reboot, Windows Server 2008 will start.

8. Press CTRL-ALT-DEL and enter the administrator's password to log on. The Windows Server 2008 desktop will display along with the Server Manager window (see Figure 3-5). This window and the steps to configure Windows Server 2008 are discussed later in this chapter under "Configure a Server."

NOTE   The time to do a clean install is quite fast, in the neighborhood of 15 to 20 minutes. An upgrade, though, can take one to several hours, depending on the complexity of the server being upgraded.

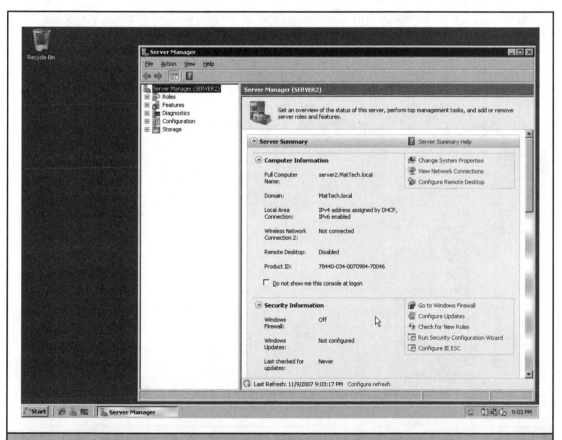

Figure 3-5.   When doing an upgrade, the Initial Configuration Tasks window is skipped.

Run a Clean Install Started from a Newer Windows Version

CAUTION By definition, a clean install means that anything that was previously on the hard disk partition or volume has been or will be removed and therefore lost, to give you a clean hard disk partition.

Having started from a newer Windows version and clicked Install Now, you should have the Get Important Updates For Installation dialog box on your screen.

1. As with an upgrade, I recommend that you click Go Online To Get The Latest Updates…, which, after getting the updates, will display the product key entry dialog box, as shown in Figure 3-6.

2. Enter the product key that is shown on the Windows Server 2008 DVD envelope or case, or on a separate document, and click Next.

3. In the choice between Full Installation and a Server Core Installation, you must decide if you want a limited-purpose server where you can use the Server Core (see the discussion in Chapter 2), or if you need all of the server features, in which case you should choose Full Installation and then click Next.

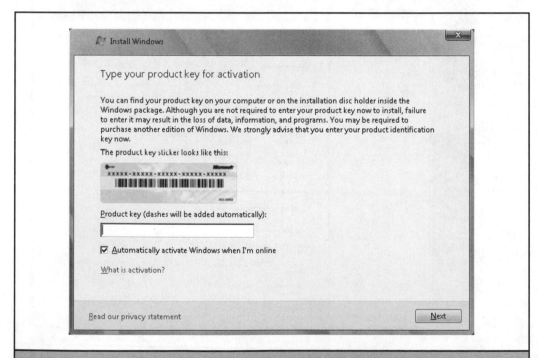

Figure 3-6. If you or your company buys a number of Windows Server 2008 licenses, you'll get the product keys on a document separate from the disc.

4. Click I Accept The License Terms (or forget about installing Windows Server 2008) and then click Next.

5. In the Upgrade or Custom dialog box, shown earlier in Figure 3-4 unless you started from Windows Server 2003, your only choice will be to click Custom. Do that and click Next.

6. You are asked where you want to install Windows Server 2008. Select the desired partition (see Figure 3-7), and click Next.

7. Setup will begin copying and expanding files, installing features and updates, rebooting a couple of times during the process. When it is complete, you will be told the user's password must be changed. Click OK.

8. Enter and then confirm a new password, and click OK. The Windows desktop will appear and display the Initial Configuration Tasks window, as shown in Figure 3-8. This window and the steps to configure Windows Server 2008 are discussed later in this chapter under "Configure a Server."

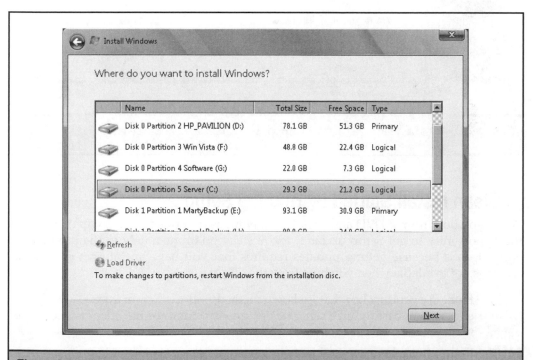

Figure 3-7. You need to have a partition in which to install Windows Server 2008 and that is formatted with NTFS.

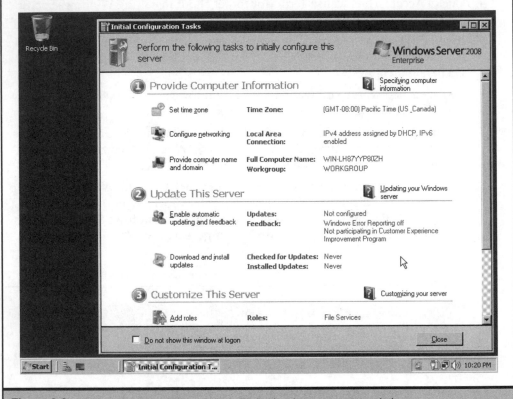

Figure 3-8. After a clean install, the default display is a lower screen resolution.

Run a Clean Install Started by Booting Setup

When you boot from a DVD and click Install Now, as described earlier, you do not have the opportunity to get Setup updates, and instead go immediately to the product key entry. This is because getting updates requires that you have an Internet connection, which is not available when you boot from the DVD.

1. Enter the product key that is shown on the Windows Server 2008 DVD envelope or case, or on a separate document; under normal circumstances you want to automatically activate Windows and click Next.

2. In the choice between Full Installation and a Server Core Installation, you must decide if you want a limited-purpose server where you can use the Server Core (see the discussion in Chapter 2), or if you need all of the server features, in which case you should choose Full Installation; then click Next.

3. Click I Accept The License Terms (or forget about installing Windows Server 2008) and then click Next.

4. In the Upgrade or Custom dialog box, shown earlier in Figure 3-4, your only choice will be to click Custom. Do that and click Next.

5. You are asked where you want to install Windows Server 2008. Select the desired partition. If you wish to extend or delete that partition, or to create a new partition (extend and create are only possible if you have unused space on the hard drive, and/or format a partition), click Drive Options (Advanced). Otherwise, click Next.

   If you clicked Drive Options with the partition you want to operate on selected, click one of the options. You are given any needed warning messages; click OK or Cancel. When your partitioning work is complete, click Next.

TIP Formatting a partition from Setup is very fast, much more so than the normal formatting.

6. Setup will begin copying and expanding files, installing features and updates, rebooting a couple of times during the process. When it is complete, you will be told the user's password must be changed. Click OK.

NOTE With Windows Server 2008 you need to use a "strong" password, which is at least eight characters long and contains upper- and lowercase characters as well as numbers and special characters.

7. Enter and then confirm a new password, press ENTER, and then click OK when you are told the password has been changed. The Windows desktop will appear and display the Initial Configuration Tasks window, as shown earlier in Figure 3-8. This window and the steps to configure Windows Server 2008 are discussed in the next section.

CONFIGURE A SERVER

Configuring a server in various ways is really the subject of most of this book. The purpose here is to do the initial configuration needed to get a usable server. The rest of the book discusses about fine-tuning these and many other settings. For that reason, the discussion here is brief and limited to what is necessary to do an initial configuration of a server.

Initialization and Personalization

The first steps that most people want to take after installing a new OS are to initialize and personalize it, so it looks and operates the way they want it. If you did an upgrade, many of these steps are not needed because your or your organization's preferences have been carried over from Windows Server 2003. Even with an upgrade, it is still useful to go through the steps so you can make sure that nothing has changed.

Initial Configuration Tasks

The Initial Configuration Tasks (ICT) window shown earlier in Figure 3-8, the first window that is opened after a clean install, is a good place to start configuring a server (if you did an upgrade, you won't see the ICT window, and most of the settings are brought over from Windows Server 2003). Work through the ICT window with these steps:

1. In the ICT window, look at the time and time zone that are displayed, and if they are not correct, click Set Time Zone. Make the needed changes and close the dialog boxes that are opened.

2. Skip Configure Networking, for that section is described next, and click Provide Computer Name And Domain. Enter a computer description if you wish and click Change.

3. Enter the computer name that will be used across the network, and then select either a domain or a workgroup, and enter a name of the domain or workgroup of which the computer will be a member. You will be welcomed to the domain or workgroup. Click OK. You will be told that you need to restart the computer.

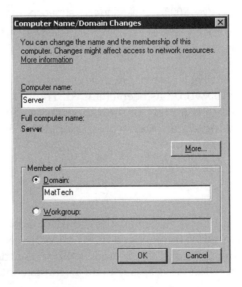

4. If you want to enable automatic updating, and I recommend that, click that option and click Enable Windows Automatic Updating And Feedback.

5. If you want to check for and download the latest updates for Windows Server 2008, again recommended, click that option and follow the instructions. When you are done, close Internet Explorer and return to the ICT window.

6. Leave the settings of roles and features for the discussion that begins later in this chapter under "Install Server Roles," and is continued in a number of other chapters in this book.

7. You probably do not need the ICT window in the future, having made the preceding settings. All of the settings in the ICT window can be made in other places in Windows Server 2008. If you don't want to see the ICT window every time you start Windows, click Do Not Show This Window At Logon.

8. When you are finished with the ICT window, click Close. The Server Manager window will open. This window will be discussed in depth later in this chapter under "Install Server Roles." For now, click Minimize to allow you to do some other preparatory tasks.

Personalize the Desktop

It is important that Windows look and respond the way you want it to, so that you can be as efficient as possible. To do that, you want to start by personalizing the desktop.

1. Right-click the desktop and click Personalize. The Personalization window will open, as shown in Figure 3-9.

2. Click Display Settings, drag the Resolution slider and set the color density to where you want them, click OK, and click Yes to Do You Want To Keep These Display Settings.

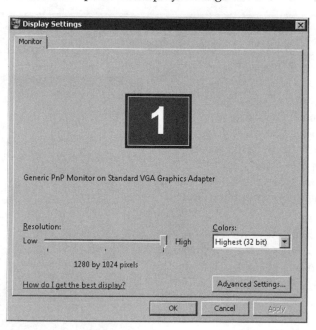

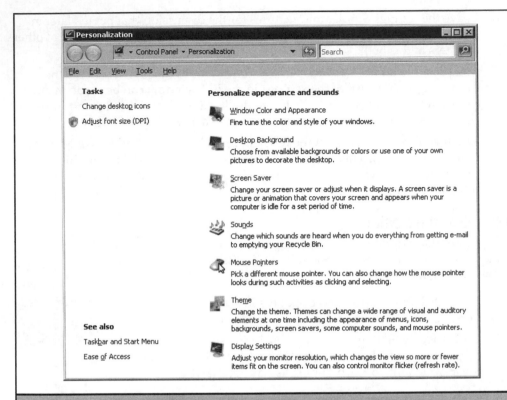

Figure 3-9. Personalizing the desktop keeps little things from being bothersome.

3. Click Window Color And Appearance. Click Effects, make any changes you want (ClearType is very helpful with flat screen LCD displays), and click OK. Click Advanced, again make any desired changes, and click OK twice.

4. Click Change Desktop Icons in the Tasks column. Click any additional icons you want on the desktop, such as Computer, and click OK.

5. Click Taskbar And Start Menu Properties, look at each of the tabs and their options, make the changes you want, and click OK.

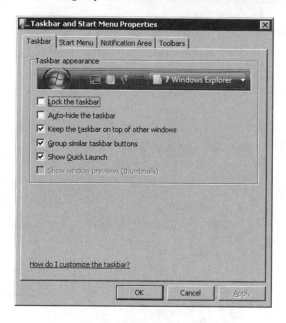

6. Similarly look at the remaining options on the Personalization window and make the desired changes. When you are ready, close the Personalization window.

7. To Personalize the Quick Launch toolbar next to the Start menu, for example, by adding Computer there, click Start, and drag the word *Computer* to the Quick Launch toolbar. Here, you see that I've added both Computer and Internet Explorer to it.

Configure Networking

Considerable space is spent in this book on networking and setting it up in a way that is best for your organization. In this chapter, we just want to make sure it is working and possibly make some quick setting changes to accomplish that.

1. Click Start | Control Panel. In the Control Panel window that opens, double-click Network And Sharing Center. The Network And Sharing Center window opens, as you can see in Figure 3-10.

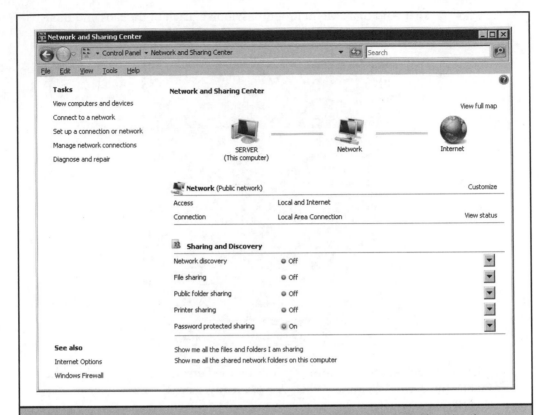

Figure 3-10. The Network And Sharing Center is a true control panel that provides a lot of information and control in one window.

You can see from the diagram at the top of Figure 3-10 that the server in this figure is part of a network that in turn is connected to the Internet and that those connections are working as expected (if your Network And Sharing Center does not show your computer is connected to a network, see "Connecting to a Network" later in this chapter). Depending on whether you did an upgrade or a clean install and, if an upgrade, whether the previous system was on a domain and possibly a domain controller, your Network And Sharing Center may look different from Figure 3-10, which is for a clean install on a standard server.

2. Given that this server is part of a local area network (LAN) within an organization, you may want to change the type of network you are connected to, from the default Public Network (with a clean install),

to a Private Network with greater sharing and discovery to facilitate a greater exchange of information. To do that:

a. Click Customize, click Private, click Next, and click Close.

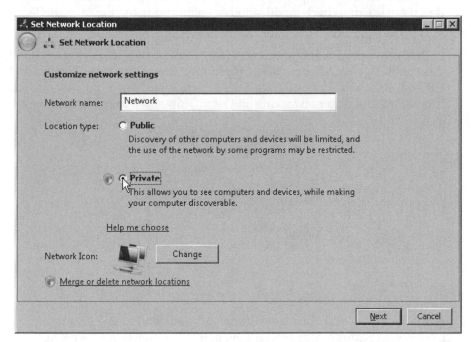

b. Click the down arrow opposite Network Discovery, click Turn On Network Discovery, and click Apply.

c. Click the down arrow opposite File Sharing, click Turn On File Sharing, and click Apply.

d. Click the down arrow opposite Public Folder Sharing, click Turn On Sharing So Anyone With Network Access Can Open Files or, if you wish, Open, Change, And Create Files, and click Apply.

e. Click the down arrow opposite Printer Sharing, click Turn On Printer Sharing (this is only available if you have a printer connected), and click Apply.

f. At your option, click the down arrow opposite Password Protected Sharing, click Turn Off Password Protected Sharing, and click Apply.

3. When you are ready, close the Network And Sharing Center.

Connecting to a Network

On most servers that are five years old or less, Windows Server 2008 Setup will be able to establish a network connection and, if it is available, an Internet connection. If your

Network And Sharing Center does not show that you have a connection, then follow these steps:

1. Make sure that the computer has a good physical connection to the network. If you are unsure, check it with another computer using the same cable.

2. Make sure that other computers on the network are working properly.

3. In the Network And Sharing Center (see "Configure Networking" earlier in this chapter), click Manage Network Connections in the Tasks column on the left. You should see a Local Area Connection. If you don't, you need to look at Chapters 5 and 6 on networking and setting up and managing a network.

4. Right-click the Local Area Connection and click Status. The Local Area Connection Status dialog box will open. If the connection is working properly, you should see activity (in bytes) being sent and received.

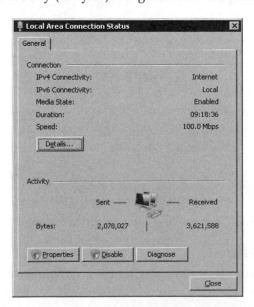

5. If you don't see network activity, click Properties to open the Local Area Connection Properties dialog box. Click Internet Protocol Version 4 (TCP/IPv4) and click Properties.

6. If Obtain An IP Address Automatically is checked, click Advanced. In the Advanced TCP/IP Settings dialog box, you should see DHCP Enabled, indicating that a Dynamic Host Configuration Protocol (DHCP) server on the network is providing the Internet Protocol (IP) address. Click OK.

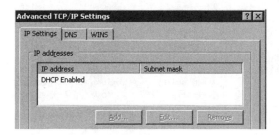

7. If you don't see DHCP Enabled, then, back in the Internet Protocol Version 4 Properties dialog box, you need to click Use The Following IP Address, and enter an address. This server will also need to be a DHCP server. Both addressing and enabling the DHCP Server role are described under "Install Server Roles" later in this chapter.

8. Close all open dialog boxes and windows and click Start | Shut Down arrow | Restart. Enter something in the Shut Down Windows Comment text box and click OK.

9. When Windows Server 2008 restarts, click Start | Control Panel. In the Control Panel, double-click Network And Sharing Center. If the Network And Sharing Center window still shows that you are not connected to a network, then you need to go through Chapters 5 and 6 and set up networking.

Explore Your Server

Before you continue configuring the server, take a quick look at how the server is configured coming out of the Setup. The amount of initial configuration that you have to do will depend on whether you did a clean install or an upgrade. Since an upgrade maintains many of the previous settings, and even Active Directory is set up if the server is a domain controller, there may be very little for you to do in the next several sections. To check that out, take a quick look at the system before starting into the configuration, with the following steps:

1. Click Start and click Computer. When it appears, click Folders in the left column and drag Folders to the top of the column. Open the Computer and Network for a view of your system similar to Figure 3-11.

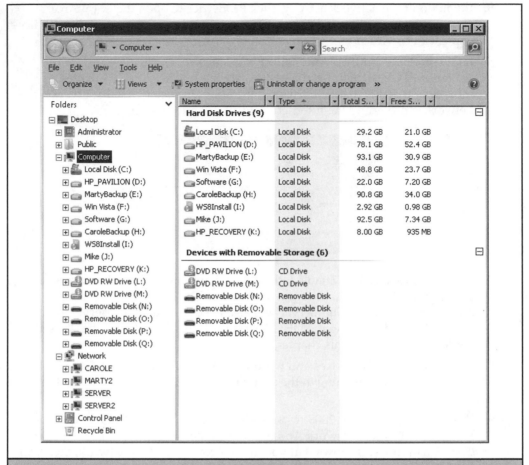

Figure 3-11.   Opening Computer and Network lets you see what is available on and can be seen from the server.

2. Open the hard drives and the folders on those drives by double-clicking them to see what is on the disks.

3. Right-click your boot drive or volume (probably C:—it should have a Windows flag on it) and click Properties to see how much room you have after installing Windows Server 2008.

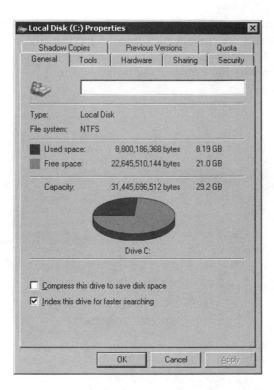

4. Open a computer on your network and then open one of its drives to see if you are connected to the network and if you can see other computers to which you can link.

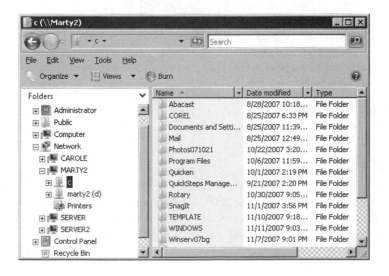

5. Click Start and point at Administrative Tools. Note that you can restart Server Manager in the Start menu, Quick Launch toolbar, and in Administrative Tools. (Your Administrative Tools menu may be different than that shown next, depending on whether you did an upgrade or not.)

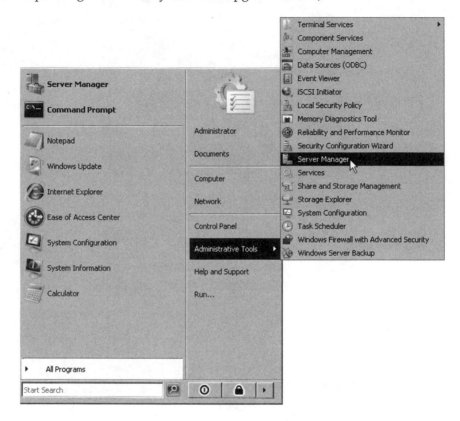

6. Look around at anything else that you want to explore. When you are done, close all dialog boxes.

This gives you a very brief overview of your server, but it should give you an idea of what needs to be done to configure it.

Install Server Roles

The Server Manager is a new facility in Windows Server 2008. While it replaces Manage Your Server in Windows Server 2003, it provides a more complete server management capability as well as more information. Figure 3-5, earlier in this chapter, shows a Server Manager window for an upgrade of an Active Directory domain controller.

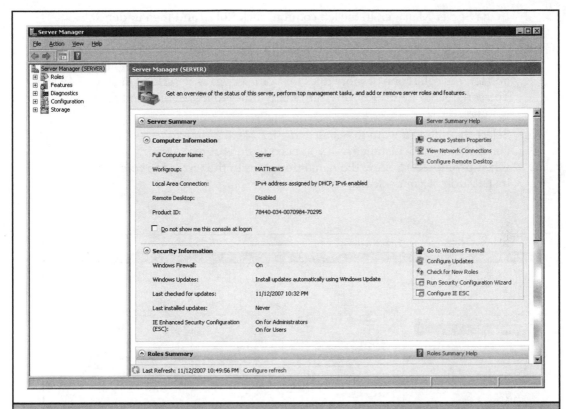

Figure 3-12. Server Manager is the primary management facility in Windows Server 2008.

Figure 3-12 shows a Server Manager window for a clean install after the preceding Initialization and Personalization steps.

1. Reopen Server Manager (it should be on your taskbar; if not, click Start | Server Manager) and review your Server Manager window. At the top are computer and security information and a number of links to manage those areas.

2. Scroll down and you'll see the roles and features summaries and links to add and remove both. At the bottom are links for various resources and support.

   If you did a clean install and the initialization and personalization steps earlier in this chapter, you'll have one role, File Services, installed and no features. If you did an upgrade, you may have a number of roles and features that were carried over from Windows Server 2003. Here we'll discuss installing several roles and in the remainder of the book we'll come back to Server Manager often to install a number of the roles and features.

3. In the Server Manager, in the left column, click Roles, and then under Roles Summary, click Add Roles on the right to see the roles that are available for you. After verifying that the server has been properly set up, click Next. The Add Roles Wizard Select Server Roles dialog box will open, as shown in Figure 3-13, and let you select one or more roles for your server, as described in Table 3-1. You can open the Add Roles Wizard many times to install different roles and features.

4. Select the role you want to install and click Next. (Some roles require ancillary components to be installed. All you need to do is agree to their installation when prompted.) Follow the remaining steps in the wizard to complete installation of your selected role.

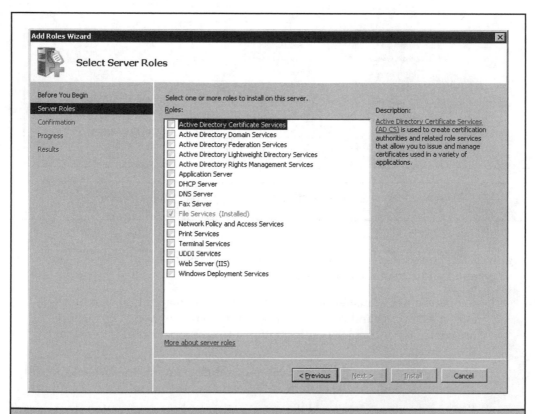

Figure 3-13.　Windows Server 2008 starts out offering 16 roles, but Microsoft may add others you can download.

Server Roles	Description
Active Directory Certificate Services	Issues and manages security certificates needed in many applications
Active Directory Domain Services	Sets up Active Directory service and creates a domain controller to store and manage directory information and logon processes (abbreviated AD DS)
Active Directory Federation Services	Provides single sign on (SSO) and customized client access for web-based and network applications
Active Directory Lightweight Directory Services	An alternative to AD DS for the storing of application data across a network
Active Directory Rights Management Services	Provides licenses to identify users and give them specific rights to use information
Application Server	Provides access and management services to .NET Framework and other web applications that clients with a license can use
DHCP Server	Sets up the Dynamic Host Configuration Protocol to assign IP addresses to clients on the network
DNS Server	Sets up the Domain Name System to translate computer names and their domains to Internet Protocol (IP) addresses
Fax Server	Provides for the sending and receiving of faxes and for management of faxing on a network
File Services	Stores and manages files that can be accessed by clients
Network Policy and Access Services	Installs the Network Policy Server that provides for Routing and Remote Access Services and the necessary security for that
Print Services	Provides access to and management of network printers
Terminal Services	Installs a service that allows a client to run an application on the server as if it were on that client computer
UDDI Services	Provides for sharing information on an intranet using Universal Description, Discovery, and Integration (UDDI)
Web Server (IIS)	Provides for the hosting of web pages and web applications
Windows Deployment Services	Provides for the deployment of Windows operating systems over a network

Table 3-1.   Server Roles Available from Server Manager

Decide to Use Domains or Workgroups

Installing AD DS assumes that you have made the decision to use domains across your network in place of workgroups. A *workgroup* is a simple networking structure used to share folders and printers with a minimum of security. In a workgroup, there is no server structure and little difference between servers and clients. Workgroups are used only in the smallest networks.

A *domain* has a much more sophisticated structure that groups networking resources and user accounts under a domain name, provides for multiple levels of servers that can keep automatically replicated copies of the same information, and generally provides a high level of security. Windows Server 2008's Active Directory requires one or more domains.

Unless you have a very small network, fewer than ten users, and little potential for growth, choosing to use a domain is strongly recommended.

Installing a DNS Server

The Domain Name System (DNS) is used to translate or "resolve" a computer name to an IP address and the reverse. DNS is required by AD DS and DHCP and if it isn't already installed on the network, it will be automatically installed when you install AD DS. See Chapter 6 for more information on installing and using DNS. Here we'll install it with AD DS.

Installing Active Directory Domain Services

When you choose to set up AD DS, you are also choosing to set up a domain controller. Active Directory, which consolidates the access to all resources on a network into a single hierarchical view and a single point of administration, is a large part of Windows Server 2008 and a topic this book spends most of a chapter on (Chapter 7). Here, suffice it to say that if you have multiple servers, you will want to use Active Directory, if for no other reason than that it consolidates the username and password logon for the entire network. Active Directory must reside on a domain controller and requires a DNS server. Part of configuring Active Directory will mean checking for these requirements and setting up the domain controller. This process is done in two steps:

▼   Use the Server Manager's Add Roles Wizard to install AD DS.

▲   Use the AD DS Installation Wizard to configure AD DS, which can be either a new domain or an existing one.

Install Active Directory Domain Services

1. In the Server Manager, click Roles in the left column, click Add Roles on the right, and then click Next.

2. In the Add Roles Wizard Select Server Roles dialog box, click Active Directory Domain Services; click Next; read the introduction, notes, and some of the other information; and then click Next. Note the messages and click Install.

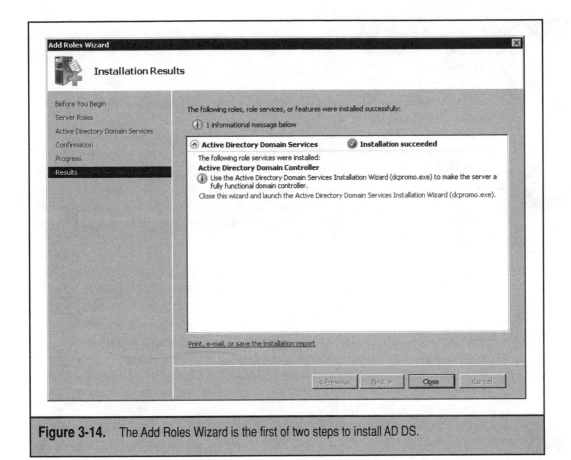

Figure 3-14. The Add Roles Wizard is the first of two steps to install AD DS.

3. The installation will start. You can see the progress in a thermometer bar. When it is complete, you are told that the installation succeeded, as you see in Figure 3-14. Click Close.

Configure Active Directory Domain Services in a New Domain

1. In the Server Manager's Roles Summary, click Active Directory Domain Services. In the AD DS pane that opens, in the information bar, click Run The Active Directory Domain Services Installation Wizard.

2. Click Next in the AD DS Installation Wizard that opens. Choose whether to use an existing forest, in which case you need to choose between a new domain and an existing one, or whether you want to create a new domain in a new forest. Click Next.

NOTE If you choose to create a domain and are not using a strong password (at least eight characters with both upper- and lowercase characters, numbers, and special characters), then you need to create one.

3. Having chosen to create a new domain, enter the fully qualified domain name (FQDN) for the new domain (for example, acme.org or acme.local) and click Next. Select the Forest Functional level from among Windows 2000, Windows Server 2003, and Windows Server 2008, depending on what you have on your network. (The higher the level, the more features that are available.) Click Next.

TIP If you choose a simple name such as "Sales," which is certainly acceptable, you will be warned that the name does not appear to be a FQDN. It is nonetheless acceptable. Click Yes to go ahead and use it, or No to go back and change it.

4. If the current server is the first domain controller for a domain and is not a DNS server, you will be told that under those circumstances it is recommended that this server be a DNS server and that option will be checked. Leave that and click Next.

5. If the server has a dynamically assigned IP address, you will be told that you should assign it a static address. Choose whether to assign a static address (recommended) or not. If you choose to assign an address, you must click No, quit the AD DS Installation Wizard, assign an address (see the accompanying Note), and come back here.

NOTE To assign a static IP address, click Start | Control Panel and double-click Network And Sharing Center. In the Network And Sharing Center, click Manage Network Connections in the left column. Right-click the Local Area Connection and click Properties. Click Internet Protocol Version 4 (TCP/IPv4) and click Properties. Click Use The Following IP Address and enter an IP address. If you don't have an IP address, you can make one up using the number range 192.168.0.0 through 192.168.255.255. For example, 192.168.1.9 is a legitimate number, and if it isn't used by another computer on your network, it will work fine. Press TAB to go to Subnet Mask. Subnet mask 255.255.255.0 should be filled in for you. Press TAB and enter your default gateway. This is the router that connects you to the Internet. If you are using the 192.168.0.0 schema, 192.168.1.1 is often the default gateway. Click OK to close the Internet Protocol Version 4 (TCP/IPv4) Properties dialog box. Click Close to close the Local Area Connection Properties dialog box, and click Close twice more to close Network Connections and the Network And Sharing Center.

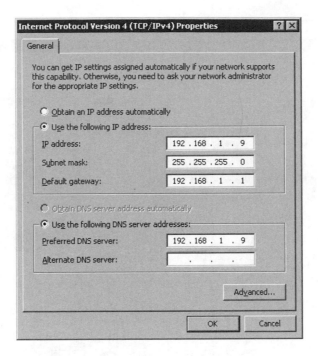

6. If this is the second or more DNS server and the parent zone cannot be found, you will be told that you need to manually create a delegation to this server if you want to integrate it with the existing DNS infrastructure. If that is what you want, you need to quit the AD DS Installation Wizard, create the delegation, and come back here. Otherwise, click Yes to continue with a stand-alone DNS server.

7. You will be shown the default Database and Log Folders locations, which you can change. It is suggested that they be kept on separate volumes or partitions. Make the necessary corrections to these paths and click Next.

8. Enter and confirm the password for the Directory Service Restore Mode Administrator. This is the password that is used when this domain controller is started in Directory Service Restore Mode. Click Next.

9. Review the summary of actions you have chosen, which should resemble Figure 3-15 if you chose to create a new domain in a new forest. If you want to change anything, use Back to go back and make the changes. When you are ready, click Next. The domain controller and Active Directory will be configured. This can take up to several hours if there is a complex domain.

> **Active Directory Domain Services Installation Wizard**
>
> **Summary**
>
> Review your selections:
>
> Configure this server as the first Active Directory domain controller in a new forest.
>
> The new domain name is Marty.local. This is also the name of the new forest.
>
> The NetBIOS name of the domain is MARTY
>
> Forest Functional Level: Windows Server 2003
>
> Domain Functional Level: Windows Server 2003
>
> Site: Default-First-Site-Name
>
> Additional Options:
>
> To change an option, click Back. To begin the operation, click Next.
>
> These settings can be exported to an answer file for use with other unattended operations.
> More about using an answer file
>
> [Export settings...]
>
> [< Back]   [Next >]   [Cancel]

Figure 3-15. Creating a new domain in a new forest should include creating a DNS server.

10. When you are told the AD DS is installed on this server, click Finish and restart your computer. For further AD DS options and management, see Chapter 7.

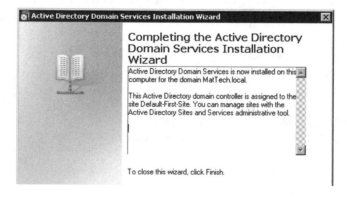

> **Active Directory Domain Services Installation Wizard**
>
> **Completing the Active Directory Domain Services Installation Wizard**
>
> Active Directory Domain Services is now installed on this computer for the domain MatTech.local.
>
> This Active Directory domain controller is assigned to the site Default-First-Site. You can manage sites with the Active Directory Sites and Services administrative tool.
>
> To close this wizard, click Finish.

Configure Active Directory Domain Services in an Existing Domain

1. In the Server Manager's Roles Summary, click Active Directory Domain Services. In the AD DS pane that opens, in the information bar, click Run The Active Directory Domain Services Installation Wizard.

2. Click Next in the AD DS Installation Wizard that opens. Choose whether to use an existing forest, in which case you need to choose between a new domain and an existing one, or whether you want to create a new domain in a new forest. Click Next.

3. Having chosen to add a domain controller to an existing domain, enter the name of the existing domain if it is not entered for you and click Set. Enter the username and password of an account in the domain, click OK, and click Next.

4. Select the domain this new server will be a part of and click Next. Select a site for the new domain controller and click Next.

5. Since this is not the first domain controller, you may not want this server to be a DNS server, in which case click that check box to uncheck it. It is a good idea to have at least two or more domain controllers be Global Catalog masters for replication purposes, so it is often advisable to keep that option checked. Click Next.

6. You will be shown the default Database and Log Folders locations, which you can change. It is suggested that they be kept on separate volumes or partitions. Make the necessary corrections to these paths and click Next.

7. Enter and confirm the password for the Directory Service Restore Mode Administrator. This is the password that is used when this domain controller is started in Directory Service Restore Mode. Click Next.

8. Review the summary of actions you have chosen, which should look like Figure 3-16 if you choose to add a domain controller to an existing domain. If you want to change anything, use Back to go back and make the changes. When you are ready, click Next. The domain controller and Active Directory will be configured. This can take up to several hours depending on the complexity of your domain.

9. When you are told the AD DS is installed on this server, click Finish and restart your computer. For further AD DS options and management, see Chapter 7.

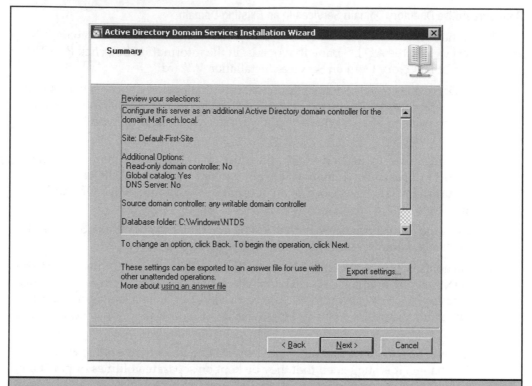

Figure 3-16. Adding a domain controller to an existing domain is simpler then creating a new domain, but getting the new controller to talk to the existing domain may be frustrating.

Installing a DHCP Server

If the server that you are setting up is the first server in a network and you don't want to manually assign IP addresses to all the computers in the network, you need to set up the Dynamic Host Configuration Protocol (DHCP) to automatically assign and manage IP addresses for all the other computers on the network. See Chapter 6 on how to do this.

CHAPTER 4

Windows Deployment Services

Windows Deployment Services (WDS) is used to install Windows Vista or Windows Server 2008, as well as Office 2007, on clients from a server running WDS. This allows you to set up a server to install these products on clients. This is a substantial improvement over having to spend time in front of each computer on which the products are being installed.

Several requirements must be met to run WDS:

▼ You must have Administrator privileges.

■ The server must meet the minimum requirements for running Windows Server 2008, either Standard or Enterprise Edition, as described in Chapter 2.

■ The server must have a separate New Technology File System (NTFS) drive or partition (volume) with at least 10GB free (recommended) where WDS can be installed. The WDS volume cannot be the boot volume and cannot have any of the system files stored on it (normally kept in the \Windows\System32\ folder).

■ Either the WDS server or other servers on the network must have Domain Name Service (DNS), Dynamic Host Configuration Protocol (DHCP), and Active Directory Domain Services (AD DS) running.

■ The Windows files and applications programs that you want to install on the client computer must be on the WDS server.

■ The client that will be installed by WDS must meet the minimum requirements for the operating system (OS) and applications being installed.

■ The client must have an NTFS-formatted volume on which WDS will install the OS and other desired software. This drive cannot use the Encrypted File System (EFS) or the Distributed File System (DFS), and all previous information on the drive will be lost (you can only do a clean install with WDS).

■ The client computer's networking facility (network interface card [NIC] or onboard networking) must support the Preboot Execution Environment (PXE) protocol to allow it to be booted over the network.

▲ Each client computer will need to have a license for each installation of a particular OS image. This can be an individual license or one install on a volume license.

NOTE   If you are not comfortable with the concepts and operation of DNS, DHCP, and AD, it is recommended that you read Part III of this book on networking (Chapters 5, 6, and 7) first and then return to this chapter.

INSTALL AND SET UP WINDOWS DEPLOYMENT SERVICES

WDS is a Server Manager role that must be separately installed and then configured.

Install Windows Deployment Services

WDS is installed with the Server Manager:

1. On the server that you want to contain WDS, click Start | Server Manager. In the Server Manager, click Roles in the left column and click Add Roles on the right.

2. Click Next to display the list of roles, as shown in Figure 4-1. Click Windows Deployment Services, click Next, and read the introduction and notes.

3. Click Next. You are asked if you want to install a Transport Server by itself, which is a subset of the full WDS, or the combination of a Transport Server and a Deployment Server, which provides the full functionality of WDS. The Transport Server alone is used only in a limited situation where you want to transmit information to a number of servers. This chapter will discuss the full WDS.

4. Leave the default in which both the Transport Server and the Deployment Server are selected, click Next, and click Install.

5. When you are told the installation is complete, click Close, and then close the Server Manager.

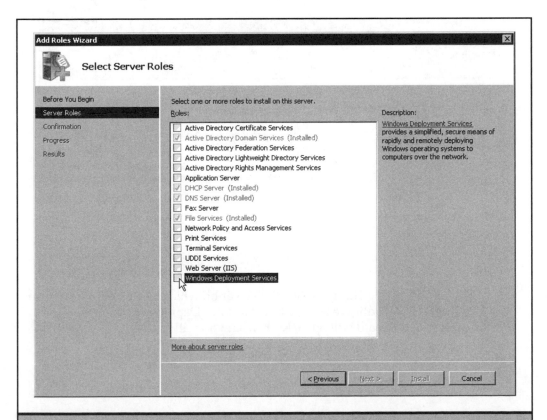

Figure 4-1.   Windows Deployment Services is a role in Server Manager.

Configure Windows Deployment Services

To make a server a Windows Deployment Services server, you must configure it, add the default boot image, and add the default install image. The boot image is used to boot a client computer with PXE so that the OS can be installed. The install image is the image of the OS to be installed.

Configure WDS

The configuration of WDS tells it the volume and folder it will use on the server and the options that will be enabled.

1. Begin by identifying and possibly formatting a volume and creating a folder on that volume (you can't use the root directory) that will be used with WDS. The volume cannot contain any files used by the server's existing OS and should be at least 10GB. The folder that will contain the images to be installed must have a name without spaces.

2. Click Start | Administrative Tools | Windows Deployment Services. The Windows Deployment Services management console (window) will open.

3. Click Servers to open it, right-click the server on which you want to configure WDS, and click Configure Server. The Windows Deployment Services Configuration Wizard will open. Read what you will need.

TIP   If you need to format a volume, a quick way is to click Start | Server Manager, click Storage | Disk Management, right-click the volume to be formatted, and click Format. You can also create a partition from free space as well as format a drive/partition. See Chapter 12 for more details on creating and formatting volumes and partitioning drives.

4.   Click Next. Enter the path to the NTFS volume that will be used for WDS and the name of a folder within that volume. Click Next.

5.   If DHCP is running on the same server as WDS, then you need to click both options on the DHCP Option 60 dialog box and click Next.

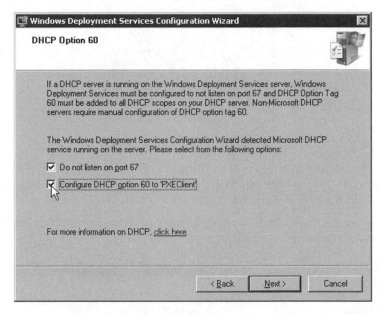

6.   Leave the default of not immediately responding to any client computer and click Finish. Click Add Images To The Windows Deployment Server Now to remove the check mark, and click Finish again.

Add a Boot Image

When a client computer is booted using a PXE network boot, WDS on the server will answer the request for a boot image and supply one that starts the install image. If there are two or more boot images, for example, to start several different install images, WDS will provide a boot menu that is similar to the Boot Configuration Data (BCD) menu used by Windows Vista and Windows Server 2008.

> **NOTE** You should use the boot.wim file on the Windows Server 2008 DVD and not the one on the Windows Vista DVD if you want the full functionality of WDS.

1. In the WDS window, open the server to which you have just configured WDS, right-click Boot Images, and click Add Boot Image.

2. Click Browse and navigate to the location of the Windows installation files and folders (those that originated on the Windows Setup DVD) that you want to install on the client computers.

3. Open the /Sources/ folder, double-click on Boot.wim, and click Next. Enter an image name and description, and click Next.

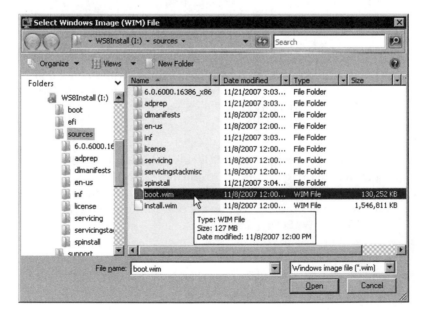

4.   You are shown a list of the settings you have chosen. If these are not correct, click Back and make the necessary changes. When the list is correct, click Next. The WDS Add Image Wizard will add the boot image to the WDS volume you identified in "Configure WDS" immediately preceding.

5.   When the WDS Add Image Wizard has completed the operation, click Finish.

Add an Install Image

The install image, which is started by the boot image, is a single large file (approximately 1.5GB for the x86 version of Windows Server 2008) that performs the full install of Windows Server 2008 or Windows Vista (the example here will be Windows Server 2008, but the steps apply equally well to Windows Vista).

1.   In the WDS window, open the server to which you have configured WDS, right-click Install Images, and click Add Install Image.

2.   If this is the first image you are adding to the server, accept the default Create A New Image Group, enter a group name or accept the default, and click Next.

3.   Click Browse and navigate to the location of the Windows installation files and folders (those that originated on the Windows Setup CD) that you want to install on the client computers.

4.   Open the /Sources/ folder, double-click Install.wim, and click Next. Select the images you want to add, and click Next.

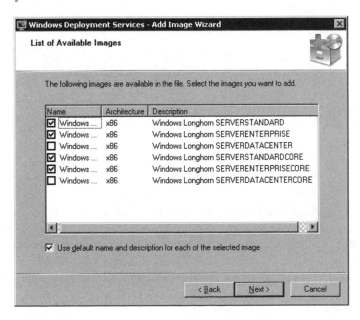

5. You are shown a list of the settings you have chosen. If these are not correct, click Back and make the necessary changes. When the list is correct, click Next. The WDS Add Image Wizard will add the install images to the WDS volume you identified in "Configure WDS" earlier in this chapter.

6. When the WDS Add Image Wizard has completed the operation, click Finish.

Configure a PXE Bootable Client

To do a PXE network boot, you will need to change the boot sequence in the computer's BIOS (basic input/output system), which is entered at the very beginning of the boot process. How you enter the BIOS is usually identified in the first startup screen. Often you press and hold the F1 or F2 function keys. Also, both the DEL and the ESC keys are sometimes used for this purpose. Once you have entered the BIOS, you need to change the boot sequence to do a PXE network boot first, before the hard drive. In the BIOS:

1. Look for an option, a menu, or a tab that says "Boot" or "Boot Sequence" and click it, or use the arrow or other keys to select or open it to see the boot options.

2. You should see a list showing the sequence in which boot devices are accessed, like this:

   ▼ Internal Hard Disk Drive (or HDD)

   ■ CD/DVD Drive

   ■ Floppy Drive

   ▲ Internal Network Card (or NIC)

3. You want to change the order so Internal Network Card (or NIC) is first; otherwise, some higher device, like the hard drive, will be used to start the computer.

4. How you change the order varies on different computers, but in most cases the instructions for doing it are on the screen. Generally, you use the arrow keys to select an option, use the SPACEBAR to enable or disable an option, use the + and – keys or the U or D keys to move an option up or down, use ENTER or a function key to complete and/or save a change, and press ESC or another function key to cancel any changes.

5. You may also need to separately enable the NIC with PXE booting. You need to look for an option or menu item that lets you change the settings for the computer's networking card or integrated facility. It may be under another option such as "Onboard Devices."

6. When you get to the settings for the NIC, you need to enable booting or PXE booting. Once you have done that, you need to save your changes and close your BIOS.

TEST AND TROUBLESHOOT WINDOWS DEPLOYMENT SERVICES

With a PXE bootable client; DHCP, DNS, and Active Directory all running and properly configured; and a valid domain username and password available; you are ready to test WDS and if necessary troubleshoot it.

Test Windows Deployment Services

Test the ability of WDS to install Windows Server 2008:

1. Restart the client computer with PXE network booting on which you want to use WDS to install Windows Server 2008 or Vista. You'll see a statement that the computer is booting from the NIC and that DHCP is being searched.

2. When the WDS server is found, you will be told to press F12 to do a network boot. Do so quickly or you will get a message that you are exiting network booting. In that case, simply reboot and more quickly press F12.

3. If you press F12 in time, and have more than one boot image, you will see a menu of available images. Use the arrow keys to select one and press ENTER. In either case, WDS will start.

4. Select the locale and keyboard you want to use and click Next. Enter a domain username (in the form domain\user) and password with administrative privileges to log on to the network. Click OK.

5. If more than one installation image is available, you will be given the choice of which to install. Make your choice and click Next. Windows Setup should start.

6. If you are given a choice, select the disk partition in which to install Windows. You can click Drive Options (Advanced) to work with and format the partitions. Click Next when ready. Setup will begin copying and expanding files, and installing features and updates.

7. The system will be restarted twice (make sure *not* to press F12) and you will be asked to select the country, time and currency, and keyboard layout. Click Next.

8. When asked, enter the product key and click Next. Click I Accept The License Terms and click Next. Enter a computer name and click Start. Setup will complete the installation, you'll be asked to enter and confirm a password, and Windows Server 2008 will be started for the first time.

Troubleshoot Windows Deployment Services

There are obviously a number of things that can go wrong during the WDS test. The most common problems:

▼   Not being able to do a PXE network boot

▲   Not being able to connect to the WDS server

Look at each of these next.

Not Able to Do a PXE Network Boot

The first step is to be sure that the client computer can do a PXE network boot. Most computers, especially computers used in business that have been produced in the last several years, have this capability. If you are not sure, look in the BIOS (see "Configure a PXE Bootable Client" earlier in this chapter) for any mention of this. You can also look at the documentation that came with the computer, or look at the manufacturer's web site for any information.

Not Able to Connect

If you see an indication that a network boot is being attempted (you should see several lines of text that mention the version of PXE and both a MAC [media access control] address and GUID [Globally Unique Identifier] followed by "DHCP" and a series of dots), but you get a message "No Boot Filename Received" followed by a message that network booting is being terminated, then for some reason the server is not replying to the queries from the network boot ROM (read-only memory chip). This normally occurs because Active Directory, DNS, and DHCP are not installed or configured properly, or because the policies and permissions are getting in your way. Chapter 6 talks in detail about setting up DNS and DHCP, as well as introducing policies and permissions, and Chapter 7 talks about Active Directory. Overall, the tasks are these:

▼ Set up networking, making sure that TCP/IP is installed and that the DNS and DHCP server(s) have a fixed IP address.

■ Set up DNS and DHCP, making sure that DHCP is running on a domain controller, that it is authorized for the WDS server, and that a scope has been created covering the clients to be installed by WDS. A correctly set up DHCP server should have the components shown here:

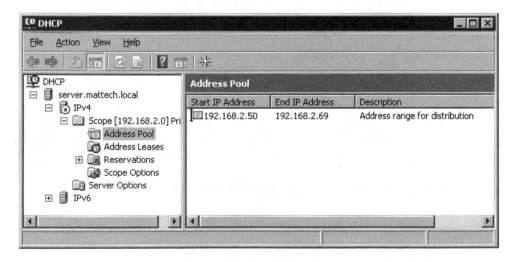

■ Set up Active Directory such that the WDS server is a domain controller in the same domain in which the clients to be installed are members.

■ Review the policies and permissions for the WDS server and for the client(s), and make sure that nothing stands in the way of doing the remote installation.

■ Make sure the person logged on to do the WDS installation (you) has domain administrator privileges.

▲ Make sure that the client and server can see each other and exchange files over the network.

PART III

Networking Windows Server 2008

CHAPTER 5

Windows Server 2008 Networking Environment

etworking is the single most important function within Windows Server 2008. It is its reason for being. The ability to connect computers and allow them to share information and resources with a high degree of security and control is at the forefront of the push for improved productivity. In line with that importance, this part devotes three chapters to networking. Chapter 5 provides a comprehensive foundation on networking by describing the schemes, hardware, and protocols or standards that are used to make it function. Chapter 6 describes how networking is set up and managed in Windows Server 2008. Chapter 7 looks at how domains are used in Windows Server 2008 and the central role that Active Directory plays in managing networking.

NETWORKING

Windows Server 2008 is a *network operating system.* This allows the interconnection of multiple computers for the purpose of:

▼ Exchanging information, such as by sending a file from one computer to another

■ Communicating, for example, by sending e-mail among network users

■ Sharing information by having common files accessed by network users

■ Sharing resources on the network, such as printers, backup devices, and a broadband Internet connection

▲ Providing a high degree of security and control for both data and its communication, and for the users of the network

Networking is important to almost every organization of two or more people who communicate and share information. Exchanging information allows multiple people to easily work from and utilize the same data and prevents errors caused by not having the latest information. E-mail communications facilitate the fast and easy coordination among people of current information, such as meeting arrangements. Sharing information allows multiple people to update and maintain a large database. Sharing resources allows an organization to purchase better (more capable and expensive) devices (for example, a color laser printer) than if they were to purchase one for each user. Networking is a primary ingredient in the computer's contribution to improved productivity, and from the viewpoint of this book, networking is the single most important facility in Windows Server 2008.

Networking is a system that includes the connection between computers that facilitates the transfer of information, as well as the scheme for controlling that transfer. The scheme makes sure that the information is transferred correctly (to the correct recipient) and accurately (the data is exactly the same on both the receiving and sending ends) while many other transfers are occurring simultaneously. To accomplish these objectives while other information is being transferred—generally, a lot of other information—there must be a standard way to correctly identify and address each transfer, and to stop one transfer while another is taking place. A networking system then has these components:

▼ A networking scheme that handles the transfer

■ Networking hardware that handles the connection

▲ A networking standard or protocol that handles the identification and addressing

Windows Server 2008 supports several different networking schemes, works with a variety of hardware, and handles several protocols. The purpose of this chapter is to look at the possible networking options provided for in Windows Server 2008 in enough detail for you to choose which of these options is best for your installation. Chapter 6 will then look at how to set up and manage networking with Windows Server 2008, and Chapter 7 will look at Active Directory and domains in greater depth.

NOTE   While this section of the book provides a great deal of networking information, it pales in comparison with Tom Sheldon's Encyclopedia of Networking & Telecommunications (McGraw-Hill, 2001). If you find you need more information than is presented here, see Tom's book. He also maintains an active web site at http://www.linktionary.com.

NETWORKING SCHEMES

The schemes used to transfer information in a network substantially determine the hardware that is used, are integral to the software, and must implement the standards or protocols desired. It is therefore difficult to talk about just the schemes, just the hardware, or just the protocols. They are very interrelated. This is further complicated by the networking scheme being a function of both the type of networking and the technology it employs.

Network Types

The network type is determined by whether the network is confined to a single location or is spread over a wide geographic area.

A network that is spread over a wide geographic area is called a *wide area network (WAN)*. WANs can use both shared and private telephone lines, satellite links, microwave links, and both shared and dedicated fiber-optic or copper cabling to connect nodes across a street or on the other side of the world. WANs with reasonable amounts of bandwidth handle 1 million bits (megabits) per second (Mbps) and above. They are expensive, on the order of one to several thousand dollars per month, and demand sophisticated technology. WANs are therefore a major undertaking for a larger organization. A simpler and less expensive, although still not cheap, use of WANs is to interconnect smaller networks within a building or within a campus of closely located buildings. This use of intracampus WANs is discussed in several other places in this chapter.

NOTE   Many companies are using the Internet to do what WANs once handled, such as e-mail and private information exchange using virtual private networking or VPN, which is discussed in Chapter 10, so the growth in WANs is very modest.

A network that is confined to a single location is called a *local area network (LAN)*. LANs use dedicated cabling or wireless channels and generally do not go outside of a single building; they may be limited to a single floor of a building or to a department within a company. LANs are much more common than WANs and are the type of network primarily discussed in this and the next two chapters. LANs have two subcategories, peer-to-peer LANs and client/server LANs, which are distinguished by how they distribute networking tasks.

Peer-to-Peer LANs

All computers in a peer-to-peer LAN are both servers and clients and therefore share in both providing and using resources. Any computer in the network may store information and provide resources, such as a printer, for the use of any other computer in the network. Peer-to-peer networking is an easy first step to networking, accomplished simply by joining existing computers together, as shown in Figure 5-1. It does not require the purchase of new computers or significant changes to the way an organization is using computers, yet resources can be shared (as in the printer in Figure 5-1), files and communications can be transferred, and common information can be accessed by all.

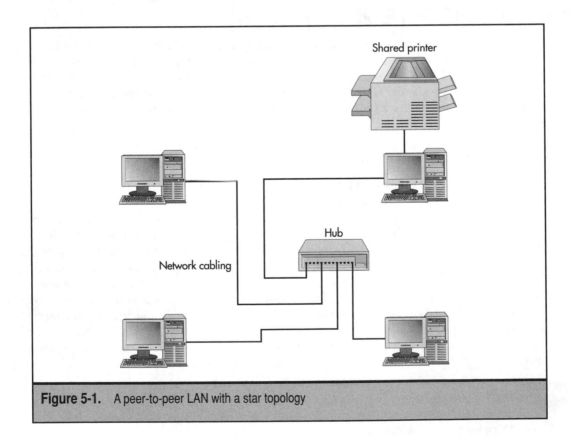

Figure 5-1.   A peer-to-peer LAN with a star topology

Peer-to-peer LANs tend to be used in smaller organizations that neither need to share a large central resource, such as a database, nor need a high degree of security or central control. Each computer in a peer-to-peer LAN is autonomous and often is joined together with other computers simply to transfer files and share expensive equipment. As you'll read later in the chapter, under "Networking Hardware," putting together a peer-to-peer LAN with existing computers is fairly easy and can be inexpensive (less than $30 per station).

Client/Server LANs

The computers in a client/server LAN perform one of two functions: they are either servers or clients. *Servers* manage the network, centrally store information that is to be shared on the network, and provide the shared resources to the network. *Clients,* or workstations, are the users of the network and are normal desktop or laptop computers. To create a network, the clients and server(s) are connected together, possibly with stand-alone network resources such as a printer, as shown in Figure 5-2.

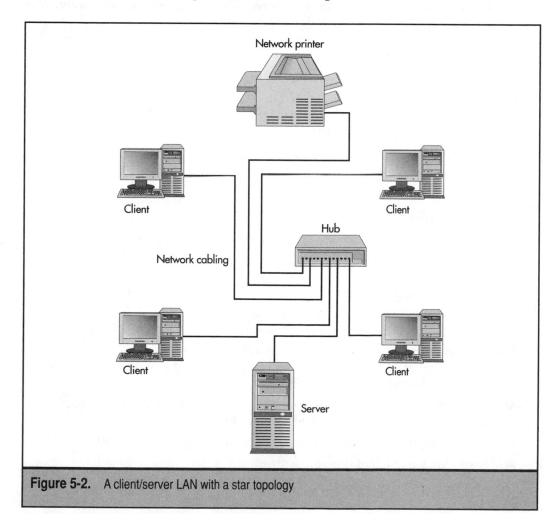

Figure 5-2.   A client/server LAN with a star topology

The management functions provided by the server include network security and managing the permissions needed to implement security, communications among network users, and management of shared files on the network. Servers generally are more capable than clients in terms of having more memory, faster (and possibly more) processors, larger (and maybe more) disks, and more special peripherals, such as large, high-speed tape drives. Servers generally are dedicated to their function and are infrequently used for normal computer tasks, such as word processing.

Clients generally are less capable than servers and, infrequently, may not even have a disk. Clients usually are normal desktop and laptop computers that perform the normal functions for those types of machines, in addition to being part of a network. Clients can also be "miniservers," by sharing out some or all of their disk drives or other resources. Therefore, the principal difference between peer-to-peer networks and client/server networks is the addition of a dedicated server.

Windows Vista and Windows Server 2008 work together to form a client/server network operating environment, with Windows Server 2008 performing its function and Windows Vista being the client. Several Windows Vista computers can operate in a peer-to-peer network, but the general assumption throughout this book is that you are principally interested in client/server networking using Windows Server 2008 and Windows Vista clients.

The Networking Task

The task performed by the networking system is substantial and complex. At a minimum, the task includes these elements:

- ▼ Identifying each of the computers in a network
- Identifying the information to be transferred as an individual *message*
- Adding to each message a unique identification and the address of the sending and receiving computers
- Enclosing the message in one or more moderate-sized *packets*, similar to envelopes, with the sending and receiving addresses and where the packet belongs within a message
- Encapsulating packets into *frames* that are transferred over the network
- Monitoring network traffic to know when to send a frame so as to avoid colliding with other frames on the network
- Transmitting a frame over the network (depending on the interconnection devices that are used, the frame may be opened and the packets put in new frames while en route)
- Providing the physical means, including cabling and wireless electronic devices, to carry the frame between computers
- Monitoring network traffic to know when a frame is to be received
- Receiving a frame that is on the network

■ Extracting the packets in one or more frames and combining the packets into the original message

▲ Determining whether the message belongs to the receiving computer and then either sending the message into the computer for further processing if it belongs to the computer, or ignoring the message if it doesn't belong to the computer

NOTE Names for pieces of information, such as messages, packets, and frames, are discussed further under "TCP" later in this chapter; Figure 5-20 in that section shows these pieces of information pictorially.

To better describe the networking task, the International Organization for Standardization, or ISO (a U.N. organization incorrectly referred to as the "International Standards Organization"; the acronym "ISO" comes from the Greek word *isos,* meaning equal), developed a reference model for networking. This model is called the Open Systems Interconnection (OSI) model.

NOTE The OSI model is useful for describing networking and for relating its various components. It does not necessarily represent Windows Server 2008 or any other networking implementation, but it is a widely known and accepted reference.

The OSI Model

The OSI model describes how information in one computer moves through a network to another computer. It defines networking in terms of seven layers, each of which performs a particular set of functions within the networking task, breaking the networking task into seven smaller tasks. Each layer can communicate with the layers above and below it and with its opposite layer in another networked computer, as shown in Figure 5-3. The communication between computers goes down through the lower layers, across the physical connection, and back up the layers in the other computer.

In the OSI model, the lower two layers are implemented in a combination of hardware and software, while the upper five layers are all implemented in software. The software in the lower layers is dedicated to networking and may be burned into silicon. The software in upper layers is a part of the operating system or an application for which networking is only one of its tasks. For example, an e-mail client application wishing to get its mail off the server passes its request to the Application layer of the network system in its computer. This information is passed down through the layers until it reaches the Physical layer, where the information is placed on the physical network. The Physical layer in the server takes the information off the physical network and passes it up through the layers until it reaches the Application layer, which passes the request to the e-mail server application.

Each of the OSI layers can add, if necessary, specific control information to information being transferred over the network. The control information can be for other layers in its own stack or for its opposite layer in the other computer and can be either requests or instructions. The control information can be added either as a header at the beginning of information being transferred or as a trailer at the end. The header or trailer added at

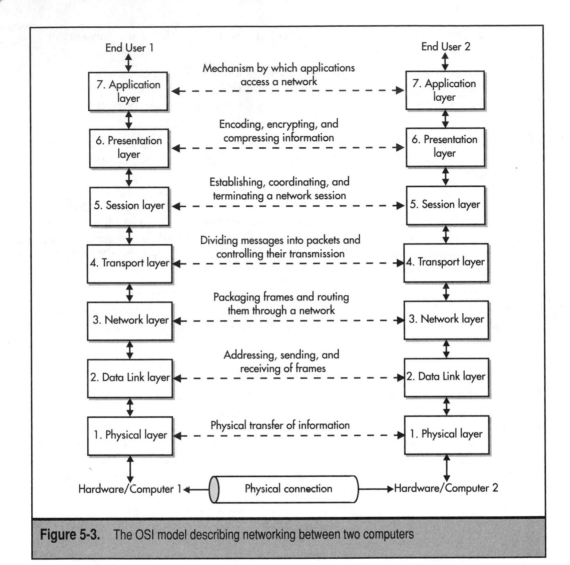

Figure 5-3. The OSI model describing networking between two computers

one layer becomes part of the basic information being transferred at another layer. The next layer may add another header or trailer or, if an existing header or trailer is intended for that layer, remove the header or trailer. The following lists the type of control information and function defined for each layer:

▼ **Physical layer** Defines the physical specifications, such as voltages and timing, to make the network interface function as intended. These specifications are implemented in networking hardware.

■ **Data Link layer** Defines the addressing of frames and the sending and receiving of frames between two linked computers. After passing a frame to the

Physical layer to be sent, the Data Link layer waits for acknowledgment that the frame has been received before it sends another frame; if the acknowledgment is not received, the Data Link layer resends the first frame. The Data Link layer provides point-to-point linkage between itself and the receiving computer by using physical addresses. The physical address at the Data Link layer is called the *media access control (MAC)* address. The Data Link specifications are implemented in a combination of hardware and dedicated networking software.

■ **Network layer**   Defines the packaging of packets into frames and the logical addressing (as opposed to the physical addressing used in the Data Link layer) necessary to provide internetwork routing through multiple, connected networks. Packets, which may be larger or smaller than frames, are broken up or combined to create a frame in the sending computer, and are reassembled or disassembled in the receiving computer to reproduce the original packets. The Network layer's internetworking commonly uses the Internet Protocol (IP) addressing to identify where frames should be sent. The Network layer specifications are implemented in dedicated networking software.

■ **Transport layer**   Defines the division of a message into packets, the identification of the packets, and the control of the packet transmission to know whether the packets are being sent and received correctly, and if not, to pause and resend a transmission. The Transport layer creates, regulates, and terminates a flow of packets by using a *virtual circuit* between the sending and receiving computers (the flow is still down through the other layers, across the connection, and up the other side, but it occurs as if the two Transport layers were directly talking to each other). The Transport layer commonly uses the Transmission Control Protocol (TCP) to start, regulate, and terminate the flow of packets. The Transport layer specifications are implemented in networking-related operating system (OS) software, such as Windows Server 2008, using networking protocols.

■ **Session layer**   Defines the dialog between computers so that they know both when to start and stop transmission, creating a *session,* and when to repeat a session if it is not correctly received. The Session layer also handles security-related issues and has its roots in the mainframe/terminal timesharing environment. The Session layer specifications are implemented in network-related OS software.

■ **Presentation layer**   Defines the encoding of information so that it is easily and securely transmitted and read by the receiving computer. This includes the conversion of character, graphic, audio, and video information into common data representation, the encryption and compression of information, and the return of the information to its native form upon receipt. The Presentation layer specifications are implemented in OS software.

▲ **Application layer**   Defines the mechanism by which applications access the network to send and receive information. This includes the two-way handling of information, as well as the identifying, locating, and determining of the availability of the partner for an information exchange. The Application layer specifications are implemented in OS and application software.

Keep the OSI model in mind as you read the remainder of this and the next several chapters. It will help you relate the various components used in networking. Later in this chapter, under "Interconnection Device Summary," you'll see how the OSI model relates to hardware devices such as hubs and switches, and under "Networking Protocols," you'll see how the OSI model relates to networking protocols and data-naming conventions.

LAN Technologies

LAN technologies are standards that span hardware and software, to handle a large part of the dedicated networking task. LAN technologies handle the entire Data Link layer and some of both the Physical and Network layers. Almost all new networks and a large majority of existing networks use either the wired Ethernet networking technology or a wireless technology that interfaces with Ethernet, and so the discussion here will be on those.

Ethernet

Ethernet was developed in the early 1970s at Xerox PARC (Palo Alto Research Center) by Bob Metcalfe and others, and was made into a standard (called the DIX standard) by Digital Equipment, Intel, and Xerox about ten years later. The Institute of Electrical and Electronics Engineers (IEEE, pronounced "eye, triple e") made slight modifications to the DIX standard and came out with its IEEE 802.3 standard for Ethernet. This is often referred to as "Ethernet 802.3." Since Ethernet 802.3 has been adopted by ISO, making it a worldwide standard, and has become what most people and vendors mean when they say "Ethernet," it is what this book means by the term. Now three IEEE 802.3 Ethernet standards are in common use: IEEE 802.3, the original Ethernet standard operating at 10 Mbps; IEEE 802.3u Fast Ethernet, operating at 100 Mbps; and IEEE 802.3z Gigabit Ethernet, operating at 1,000 Mbps. These will be referred to as "Ethernet," "Fast Ethernet," and "Gigabit Ethernet," respectively. In addition, two Ethernet standards are just emerging: IEEE 803.3an 10 Gigabit Ethernet (10GbE), operating at 10,000 Mbps, which is just becoming available on the market, and 100 Gigabit Ethernet (100GbE), operating at 100,000 Mbps, which was still under development in mid-2007.

Ethernet is relatively inexpensive, works well interconnecting many different computer systems, and is easy to expand to very large networks. It therefore has become the dominant LAN technology by a wide margin, completely eclipsing some other early technologies, such as ARCnet, and significantly overshadowing Token Ring (an early LAN technology developed by IBM that had wide usage in larger organizations). As a result, Ethernet-related equipment and Ethernet support in software, including Windows Server 2008 and Windows Vista, has become pervasive. This has brought many vendors into the market to supply equipment, causing the pricing to become most reasonable. As a result, Ethernet (and more recently, Fast Ethernet and Gigabit Ethernet) has become the technology of choice for almost all wired networking.

Ethernet technology covers three specifications:

▼ A media-access method that describes how multiple computers share a single Ethernet channel without getting in each other's way

■ An Ethernet frame that describes a standardized bit structure for transferring information over an Ethernet network

▲ A hardware specification that describes the cabling and electronics used with Ethernet

Ethernet Media Access Method The objective of Ethernet is to have multiple computers operate independently of each other over a single connecting channel without interference. This is accomplished using a media-access method called *Carrier Sense Multiple Access with Collision Detection (CSMA/CD)*. CSMA/CD works like this:

1. A networked computer wishing to transmit information listens to the network to determine when it is idle.

2. When the computer determines the network is idle, it puts its information on the network with the destination address, making it available to all other computers on the network.

3. Each computer on the network checks whether the address is its own, and if it is, that computer pulls the information off the network.

4. When the network is again idle, all other computers have an equal chance of being the next one to transmit information.

5. If two computers simultaneously begin transmission, a *collision* will occur and be detected. All information on the network is ignored, and the network will be returned to its idle status. The two sending computers then choose a random time to wait before resending their information, thereby minimizing the chance of repeated collisions.

Collisions are a normal and expected part of network transmission, even repeated collisions that result in data errors, which is why the higher levels of the OSI networking model put such emphasis on error detection and correction.

Ethernet Frame The Ethernet *frame* is the standard format used for transferring data over an Ethernet network. The frame defines a specific layout that positions header information, source and destination addressing, data, and trailer information, as shown next. The specific definition and use of each field is as follows:

Preamble	SFD	Destination	Source	Length	Data	Padding	CRC
62 bits	2 bits	6 bytes	6 bytes	2 bytes	0–1500 bytes	46–0 bytes	4 bytes

▼ **Preamble** A series of alternating 1's and 0's that is used by the receiving computer to synchronize the information in the frame.

■ **SFD (start of frame delimiter)** A pair of 1's that is used to mark the start of the frame.

■ **Destination and Source addresses** Two 48-bit numbers representing the MAC address of the receiving and sending computers. These numbers are assigned by the IEEE to manufacturers and contain a 24-bit unique manufacturer number and a 24-bit number unique to a specific network interface card (NIC) or adapter that connects a computer to the network. This means that every network adapter comes with a unique address, and the end user does not have to worry about it. If a message is to be broadcast to all stations on a network, the destination address must contain all 1's.

- **Length**   The number of bytes in the data field. In earlier Ethernet standards, this was a type code, which was greater than 1,500 to avoid getting in the way of the length, which is 0 to 1,500.

- **Data**   The data being transmitted, which can be from 0 to 1,500 bytes long.

- **Padding**   Required if the data is less than 46 bytes, so if the data field contained 38 bytes, 8 bytes of padding would be included.

- ▲ **CRC (cyclical redundancy check)**   Also called a Frame Check Sequence (FCS), it is a 32-bit (4-byte) number derived from all the bits in the transmission by using a complex formula. The sending computer calculates this number and stores it in the frame sent to the other computer. The receiving computer also calculates the number and compares it with the number in the frame. If the numbers are the same, it is assumed that the transmission was received without error. If the numbers are different, the transmission will be repeated.

The principal difference between the original DIX Ethernet standard (called Ethernet II—Ethernet I was the original specification prior to DIX) and Ethernet 802.3 is that Ethernet II has a type code in place of the length in the frame. The type code is used to adapt Ethernet to different computer environments, which is done outside of the frame in 802.3. In the Internet protocol TCP/IP (see "Networking Protocols" later in this chapter), the Ethernet frame is used with a type code that identifies the Internet protocol.

Ethernet Hardware   Ethernet LAN technology defines eight alternative hardware standards that can be used with Ethernet; a ninth is under development. Each hardware standard uses a specific type of cable and cable layout, or *topology*, and provides a rated speed on the network in Mbps, a maximum segment length, and a maximum number of computers on a single segment. The hardware standards are as follows:

NOTE   In the IEEE names for the Ethernet hardware standards, such as 10Base5, the "10" is the speed in Mbps; the "Base" is for baseband, a type of transmission; and the "5" is the maximum segment length in hundreds of meters. In more recent standards, such as 10BaseT, the "T" stands for the type of cabling (twisted-pair in this case).

- ▼ **10Base5 (also called Thicknet)**   The original hardware specification in the DIX standard. It uses a thick coaxial cable in a bus topology with a fairly complex connection at each computer to produce a 10-Mbps speed over a 500-meter (1,640-foot) maximum segment with up to 100 computers per segment and three segments. 10Base5 is expensive and cumbersome to use, and is seldom used today.

- **10Base2 (also called Thinnet or Cheapernet)**   Uses RG-58 A/U thin coaxial cable in a bus topology with a simple BNC barrel type of connector to produce a 10-Mbps speed over a 185-meter (606-foot) maximum segment with up to 30 computers per segment and three segments. Until the 1990s, Thinnet was the least expensive form of Ethernet networking for small (30 or fewer nodes) organizations.

- **10BaseT (also called Twisted-Pair)** Uses unshielded twisted-pair (UTP) telephone-like cable in a star topology (see Figure 5-2) with a very simple RJ-45 telephone-like connector to produce a 10-Mbps speed over a 100-meter (328-foot) segment with one computer per segment and 1,024 segments. In the 1990s, 10BaseT came down in price to that of 10Base2, and with its exceptional expandability, it became very attractive for most organizations.

- **10BaseF** Uses fiber-optic cable in a star topology running at 10 Mbps to connect two networks up to 4,000 meters (13,120 feet, or about 2.5 miles) apart. This was often used to connect two or more buildings on a campus.

- **100BaseT (also called Fast Ethernet)** Has the same specifications as 10BaseT except that the cabling requirements are a little more demanding (requires Category 5 cable in place of Category 3) and it goes ten times as fast. 100BaseT is now cheaper than 10BaseT, and with its significant added speed, it has become the Ethernet hardware standard of choice. With the appropriate connecting hardware (see "Networking Hardware" later in the chapter), you can mix 10BaseT and 100BaseT hardware in the same network to slowly upgrade a 10BaseT network. There are two subspecifications to 100BaseT: 100BaseTX, the most common, which runs over Category 5 UTP using two twisted pairs, and 100BaseT4, which runs over Category 3 UTP using four twisted pairs.

- **100BaseFX** Uses fiber-optic cable running at 100 Mbps to connect two networks up to 412 meters (1,351 feet) apart or, if full-duplex (separate fibers for sending and receiving) is used, up to 2 kilometers (over 6,500 feet, or a mile and a quarter). Like 10BaseF, 100BaseFX is primarily used to join two networks.

- **1000BaseT and F (also called Gigabit Ethernet)** Uses standard Category 5 or fiber-optic cable to run at 1,000 Mbps. Distance standards range from 25 meters (82 feet) to 100 meters (328 feet) for copper UTP, and 550 meters (1,800 feet) for fiber. In mid-2007, Gigabit Ethernet equipment was on the market for only slightly more than Fast Ethernet, with ten times the speed. Its price has dropped significantly in the five years it has been on the market.

- **10GBaseT and various fiber configurations (also called 10 Gigabit Ethernet or 10GbE)** Uses Category 6 copper and several fiber-optic cable schemes to run at 10,000 Mbps. The standard distance for copper is 100 meters (328 feet). A number of 10GBase fiber standards use different types of fiber-optic cable with distances ranging from 28 meters (92 feet) to 40 kilometers (25 miles). In mid-2007, 10GBase equipment was difficult to obtain and quite expensive, but following the patterns of 100Base and 1000Base Ethernet, it will drop significantly.

- ▲ **100GBase (also called 100 Gigabit Ethernet or 100GbE)** is in the early stages of development with the objective of a fiber-optic network link running at 100,000 Mbps, which approaches internal computer speeds. The final standard may not be available until 2010 or later and may be slower than 100,000 Mbps.

"Networking Hardware," later in this chapter, goes into more detail about the Ethernet hardware standards and the options that are available to connect Ethernet networks.

NOTE   With higher speeds the number of collisions does increase somewhat, but the speed at which they are corrected more than compensates for this, providing a significant speed increase at each step.

Wireless Networking Technologies

Wireless networking technologies cover a broad spectrum of networking capabilities without wires, including:

▼ Broadband wireless topologies used in WANs and metropolitan area networks (MANs)

■ Cellular wireless networking

■ Microwave communications used in WANs

■ Satellite communications systems

▲ Wireless LANs

Broadband wireless and microwave are used between buildings to connect LANs, are fairly expensive, and generally are used only by large organizations. MANs (metropolitan area networks) are becoming more common in many communities and provide wireless networking in a multiblock area. Satellite communications are relatively expensive, slower, and are principally used in rural areas, on the ocean, and in airplanes. Cellular systems are becoming widely used in cities, office complexes, and large buildings. For some time, cellular networking was very slow, beginning at 16 Kbps (kilobits per second) to 64 Kbps, with more recent offerings at 144 Kbps. Currently a number of carriers including Verizon, Sprint, AT&T/Cingular, and T-Mobile are offering what is called "third-generation (3G) technology" with data rates of up to 2.4 Mbps (megabits per second).

Wireless LANs or WLANs have become well implemented, widely available, and reasonably priced. They are based on three current and one emerging standard:

▼ **IEEE 802.11b** uses the 2.4GHz band, provides data transfer of up to 11 Mbps, uses complementary code keying (CCK) encoding, and was the original widely used wireless standard.

■ **IEEE 802.11g** uses the 2.4GHz band, provides data transfer of up to 54 Mbps, uses the more efficient orthogonal frequency-division multiplexing (OFDM), and is now the most widely used wireless standard. Most IEEE 802.11g access points and adapters can also work with IEEE 802.11b access points and adapters.

■ **IEEE 802.11a** uses the 5GHz band, provides data transfer of up to 54 Mbps, uses orthogonal frequency-division multiplexing (OFDM), but has seen little adoption because it requires unique hardware and has less range than the 2.4GHz 802.11b or 802.11g.

▲ **IEEE 802.11n** was in its second draft as a standard in mid-2007 with up to two
years before the final standard would be approved. The draft standard calls
for using either the 2.4GHz or 5GHz band with data rates in excess of 100
Mbps and as high as 300 Mbps using multiple input multiple output (MIMO)
technology to handle multiple data streams through two to four antennas each
for transmitting and receiving. Some "pre-n" equipment is on the market but is
not recommended until the standard is approved and the equipment is certified
to follow it. The one exception to the last statement is if you have a closed
organization where you can control all the equipment and do not expect visitors.

A WLAN uses a fixed *access point* that is connected to the wired network through, for
instance, a hub, a switch, or a DSL router. This access point is a *transceiver* (transmitter
and receiver) to communicate wirelessly with a card or wireless circuit that is added to
each computer wishing to use the WLAN (see Figure 5-4). These computers operate on
the network in exactly the same way as they would with a network adapter and a cable
connection. There are some significant benefits to a WLAN over a normal wired LAN:

Photos courtesy of Linksys®, a division of Cisco Systems, Inc., used with permission, http://www.linksys.com.

Figure 5-4. A selection of Linksys® 54 Mbps Wireless LAN products, including the Wireless-G Access
Point, Wireless-G PCI Adapter for desktops, Wireless-G Notebook Adapter, and the Wireless Compact
USB Adapter for either desktops or laptops*

NOTE   In addition to the WLAN standard, there is a WIFI (wireless fidelity) standard that makes sure that the hardware from different manufacturers is compatible; thus, you can walk into any office, airport, or other building with a WIFI-standard wireless system and be able to connect if you have the appropriate permissions.

▼ You do not have the expense of cabling and the even higher expense of installing and maintaining cabling.

■ It is extremely easy to add users to and remove them from the network.

■ It is very easy for users to move from office to office or from room to room.

■ Users can roam within an area, say, carrying their laptops to a meeting.

▲ Visitors can easily get on the network.

The cost and speed of wireless networking used to be a hindrance, but the cost has come down substantially and the speed has gone up. An inexpensive access point is now under $70 and, remembering that you are dividing up 11 or 54 Mbps of bandwidth, is good for seven to ten users or $10 per user. The adapters for each cost as little as $25 and are built into many new computers. As a result, the total wireless cost of connecting a computer to a network is less than $35, which may be less than the cost of a wired network. The speed difference, though, between wireless and wired networking is not just the difference between 54 Mbps wireless and 100 Mbps wired, it's the net rate of dividing the 54 Mbps wireless channel by the number of people trying to use it at any instant.

Wireless networking has several other disadvantages:

▼ A wireless access point or "hotspot" has a limited range of 30 to 45 meters or 100 to 150 feet, and this can be affected by walls, especially those with metal in them, plumbing and ductwork, and other objects. There are range extenders and repeaters that can extend this range for a price, but they also slow the signal.

■ The default installation of wireless networking generally does not have encryption and other security features turned on, making it easy for someone without a physical connection to get onto the network.

■ Multiple wireless networks in close proximity can interfere with one another, causing the networking traffic to slow down and even be unusable. This is called "wireless pollution."

▲ Wireless networking circuits can be a significant drain on the batteries in portable devices.

Despite these drawbacks, wireless networking is the fastest-growing form of networking, especially in homes and smaller organizations.

Home Networking Technologies

Home networking technologies (which can also be used in small offices, especially home offices) generally share one of two types of existing cabling in a home, either telephone cabling or power cabling. The speed provided in both cases is relatively slow and the costs are not advantageous. For both home networking technologies, the objective is to get around installing separate network cabling. Since wireless networking does this excellently, the home networking technologies are all but dead.

NETWORKING HARDWARE

In its simplest form, computer networking needs only a cable to join two computers, and two adapters that plug into the computers and into which the cable connects, as shown in Figure 5-5.

For both the adapters and the network cable, you have several choices of types and features, and when you go beyond two computers, there are additional components for which there are multiple choices. The first and major decision in making these choices is the LAN technology you are going to use, because that, in many cases, will determine your cabling (if any) and network adapter, or at least put you in a certain category of cabling and network adapters. Therefore, begin this look at hardware with a summary, shown in Table 5-1, of what has been described earlier in this chapter regarding the alternative LAN technologies.

In choosing an Ethernet LAN technology, Ethernet 100BaseT is the current predominant choice. Probably well over 98 percent of buyers choose it. There probably have been no new installations of 10Base5 or 10Base2 for a number of years, and very few legacy installations remain. While some 10BaseT installations remain, they are fast disappearing and no new ones are going in. 100BaseF, and increasingly 1000Base, fiber is being used to interconnect networks, buildings, and floors within a building. The following hardware alternatives focus on the needs of these technologies.

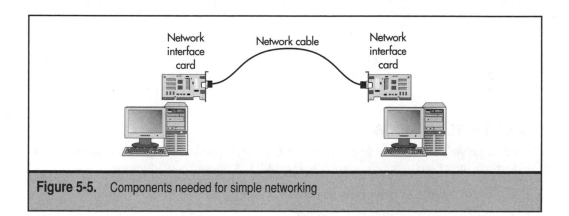

Figure 5-5.   Components needed for simple networking

Technology	Max. Speed (Mbps)	Type of Cabling (See Note)	Max. Network Nodes[1]	Max. Nodes/ Segment	Max. Segment Length	Min. Segment Length[2]	Max. Network Length[2]
10Base5	10	Thick coax	300	100	1,640 ft	8.5 ft	8,200 ft
10Base2	10	Thin coax	90	30	606 ft	2 ft	3,035 ft
10BaseT	10	UTP-Cat 3	1,024	2	328 ft		
10Base fiber	10	Fiber-optic		2	1.24 mi		
100BaseT	100	UTP-Cat 5	1,024	2	328 ft		
100Base fiber	100	Fiber-optic		2	1.24 mi		
1000BaseT	1,000	UTP-Cat5e	512	2	328 ft		
1000Base fiber	1,000	Fiber-optic		2	1,804 ft to 62 mi		
10GBaseT	10,000	STP-Cat6	512	2	328 ft		
10GBase fiber	10,000	Fiber-optic		2	108 ft to 25 mi		

[1] For the Ethernet technologies where the maximum number of nodes is not specified, there are subcategories with different maximums.
[2] Minimum segment length and maximum network length apply only to coaxial cable used in 10Base5 and 10Base2.

Table 5-1. Ethernet LAN Technology Specification Summary

NOTE UTP categories are further explained later in this chapter, under "UTP Categories." Also, a "node" is a workstation, a server, an interface device such as a switch or a router, or a stand-alone network printer.

Network Interface Cards

Even though you have probably decided on 100BaseT, if you are installing a wired network, the decision on which network adapter to buy still has several considerations:

▼ How will the adapter be connected?

■ What type of adapter will you use?

■ Do you want it to be able to wake up the computer?

▲ Which brand should you buy?

How Adapters Connect

Network adapters that are available today connect to a computer in one of four ways (see Figure 5-6):

▼   They plug into a PCI (Peripheral Component Interface) card slot inside a desktop or larger computer.

■   They plug a USB (Universal Serial Bus) port on the outside of either a desktop or laptop computer.

■   They plug into a PCMCIA (Personal Computer Memory Card International Association), or just "PC Card," slot or into an ExpressCard slot on the outside of most laptop computers and a few desktop computers.

▲   The ability to connect to a network is built into many new computers, both desktop and laptop, and does not need a separate adapter.

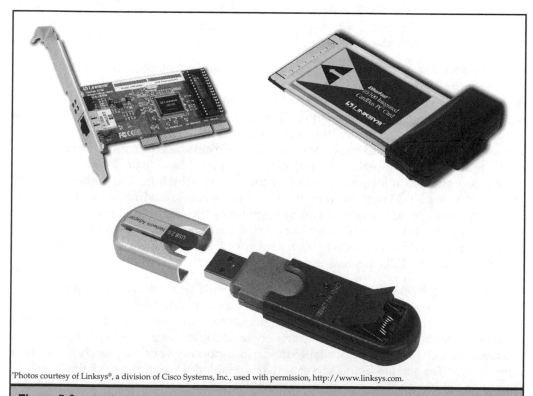

*Photos courtesy of Linksys®, a division of Cisco Systems, Inc., used with permission, http://www.linksys.com.

Figure 5-6.   A selection of Linksys® 10/100 Ethernet Wired Network Adapters, including the Managed Network PCI Adapter for desktops, EtherFast® 32-Bit PC Card Adapter for laptops, and the Compact USB 2.0 Adapter for either desktops or laptops*

Of course, if the ability to connect is built into a computer, you don't have to consider this further. If you do need to add an adapter, probably the easiest is a USB adapter, but it and the PC Card/ExpressCard adapter are considerably more expensive than the PCI card slot adapter. For the latter, though, you must open a desktop computer and plug the card into a PCI slot on the *motherboard* (the main system circuit board in a computer).

What Type of Card to Use

Most manufacturers, especially the larger name-brands, make several different types of 10/100BaseT PCI network adapters. These differences include whether a network adapter is full-duplex or half-duplex, whether it is made for a server, and whether it is multiport. All of these features add to the speed and efficiency of the board, but they also add to the cost, so you need to give them some consideration.

Half-Duplex vs. Full-Duplex Adapters   *Half-duplex* means that when a card is receiving it can't transmit, and vice versa. *Full-duplex* allows the card to transmit and receive at the same time. Obviously, full-duplex is faster, but it does not double the speed as you might expect; rather, it offers 30–50 percent improvement over half-duplex. Currently, most name-brand 10/100 network adapters are full-duplex, but it wouldn't hurt to check this factor when you are researching which ones to buy.

Server Network Adapters   Server network adapters are developed for use in servers, and they supply several features to support that role. Among these features are higher reliability and greater intelligence. The higher reliability is usually a combination of better parts and higher quality control. The greater intelligence means that there is a processor and even memory on the network adapter so that it doesn't have to go out to the computer's CPU and memory to handle its processes. This makes the card faster, allowing it to handle a higher volume of information. These features, of course, cost money, so you need to determine whether they are worthwhile. The higher-reliability cards cost about 30–50 percent more than a normal name-brand network adapter. The intelligent network adapters cost two to three times the cost of a normal name-brand network adapter. While that sounds like a lot, it translates to less than $100 additional per card, and you do not have to buy very many of them. When you compare this to the cost of upgrading a CPU, it's reasonable.

Multiport Network Adapters   Network adapters are available for servers that have two or four ports, the equivalent of two or four network adapters in the server. Given that PCI card slots are generally at a premium in most servers, these multiport boards may be attractive. The problem is that a dual-port network adapter costs over two times as much as a name-brand server network adapter, and a four-port network adapter costs over four times as much as a name-brand server network adapter. If you don't have the PCI slots, then this might be a solution, but another solution is to use an interconnection device in front of the network adapter (see "Interconnection Devices" later in this chapter). This is one of those situations in which there is no one right answer. It depends on the network design you are trying to construct.

Wake on LAN and Other Special Features

Several manufacturers, 3Com and Intel among them, have network adapters with a "Wake on LAN" feature that will power up a computer to full operating status after it has been turned off. This allows a network administrator or support person to update a computer after hours. Wake on LAN requires a motherboard that implements the PCI bus standard 2.2 or later. Most computers produced since around 1995 use this standard.

Two other special features some network adapters offer may prove useful: remote management and remote booting. Remote management allows a network administrator on a server with the appropriate software to monitor the activity and do remote management on a computer across a network. Remote booting allows a server to start a computer without depending on the operating system in the computer. This is important for diagnosing problems in the computer and for the remote installation of Windows and other applications (see Chapter 4 on Windows Deployment Services). Remote booting also requires PCI bus standard 2.2 or later.

If these features interest you, look carefully before buying a network adapter and make sure the motherboard you are intending to use it with supports the feature(s) you are getting on the network adapter. Remote booting in particular may require special support on the motherboard that is *not* included on some motherboards.

Which Brand

If you look at comparative shopping services (such as Yahoo! Shopping), you will see at least three approximate pricing levels of network adapters. For example, with wired 10/100 PCI adapters:

▼ Name-brand (3Com and Linksys are examples) with the special features previously mentioned: $50 to $350, depending on the features

■ Name-brand basic boards (without the special features): $10 to $50

▲ Generic basic boards (without the special features): $5 to $25

Although some of the price range in each of the three levels is caused by differences in features, much of the differential is caused by variations in what suppliers charge for the same board. You can see that by looking at Pricewatch (http://www.pricewatch .com) and PriceSCAN (http://www.pricescan.com), which compare the prices of the same item from different suppliers. In any case, make sure you know what you are buying and what the handling and freight charges are.

The pertinent question is whether the name-brand boards are worth the $5 to $25 differential. From my viewpoint, the answer is clearly yes. In the ten-plus years I have been working with PC networking, I have worked with approximately an equal number of generic and name-brand network adapters. I have had troubles with both, but I have had to throw away several of the generic boards, while I have always gotten the name-brand boards fixed or replaced. The backing and support of a name-brand is comforting (3Com's lifetime warranty in particular), and sometimes they have added features such as diagnostics that may be valuable. Granted, the lower prices of the generic boards are also attractive, but when a network goes down, that price may not look so good. If you buy a generic from a better supplier to get the supplier's support, your price is very close to the name-brand. My recommendation is to choose the name-brand board with the thought that it is going to be more easily recognized in software, such as Windows Server 2008, and will provide better support should it be needed.

Cabling

The primary networking technologies use one of two types of cabling, each of which has several considerations:

▼ Unshielded twisted-pair for 10BaseT, 100BaseT, and 1000BaseT

▲ Fiber-optic for 10BaseF, 100BaseF, and 1000BaseF

Unshielded Twisted-Pair (UTP)

UTP cable used in 10/100/1000BaseT is similar to, but generally not the same as, telephone wiring. For 10BaseT, this cable contains two pairs of wires, that is, four wires first twisted in pairs, and then the pairs are twisted together. An RJ-45 modular connector is placed on each end. Although only two pairs are used, the actual cable in both Category 3 and Category 4 cabling has four pairs, as shown in Figure 5-7. The RJ-45 connector, which

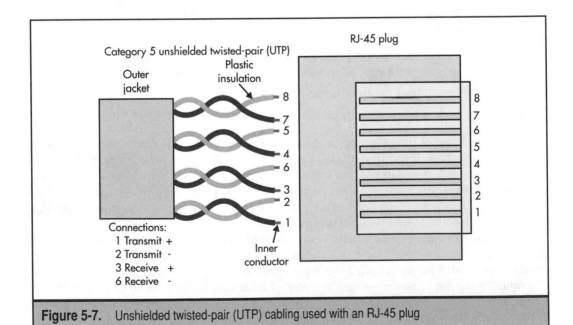

Figure 5-7.   Unshielded twisted-pair (UTP) cabling used with an RJ-45 plug

can handle four twisted pairs of wires, is similar to but slightly larger than the RJ-11 connector, which can handle two pairs of wires and is used in a normal phone connection. 100BaseT and 1000BaseT use four pairs or all eight wires in Category 5 cable and the same RJ-45 connector.

The pairs of wires in a UTP cable are twisted because that reduces the electrical interference that is picked up in the cable. The number of twists per foot has become a very exact science, and it is important to keep the cable properly twisted up close to the connector. An alternative to UTP is STP, with various degrees of shielding: shielding around each pair, shielding around all pairs, or shielding around both the individual pairs and around the combination. STP is considerably more expensive than UTP and is more difficult to handle. To handle the interference problem, follow these rules when running the cable:

▼   Don't run the cable near a fluorescent light fixture.

■   Don't run the cable near an electrical motor, such as those in machines, fans, water coolers, and copiers.

■   Don't run the cable alongside a power cable.

■   Don't make tight turns that can crimp the cable.

▲   Don't use a staple gun, which can crimp or short-circuit the cable.

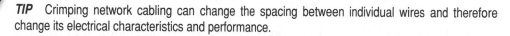

TIP   Crimping network cabling can change the spacing between individual wires and therefore change its electrical characteristics and performance.

Between voice and data (phone and network), a number of different types of UTP cable exist. The differences are in the degree of fire resistance, in the type of inner core, and in the grade or category of cable, which also specifies the number of twisted pairs.

Degree of Fire Resistance   UTP cables come in two degrees of fire resistance: *plenum* cable, marked "CMP" on the side of the cable, and *PVC* or *riser* cable, marked "CMR." Plenum cable, which often has a Teflon coating, is more fire resistant and doesn't give off dangerous fumes if it does burn. PVC or riser cable, while reasonably fire resistant, is made with polyvinyl chloride (PVC), which gives off potentially dangerous fumes if it does burn. Plenum cable costs roughly twice what PVC cable costs, but it can be used in air passages such as raised floors and suspended ceilings, while PVC cable can be used only in walls and out in the open (check your own local codes for the type of cable you should use).

Type of Inner Core   The inner core of UTP cable can be stranded or solid. Stranded wire is more flexible and less prone to breaking when bent a number of times. It is used in situations where it is frequently moved, such as in a patch panel and between a wall outlet and a computer. Solid wire has lower signal loss and therefore is better for longer runs where it won't be moved frequently, such as in walls and ceilings.

UTP Categories   The following are the seven categories of UTP cable that are used with voice and data communications:

▼   **Category 1**   Used in telephone installations prior to 1983, it has two twisted pairs.

■   **Category 2**   Used in telephone installations after 1982, it has four twisted pairs; it is used in some early data networks with speeds up to 4 Mbps.

■   **Category 3**   Used in many early data networks and most current phone systems. It normally has four twisted pairs, but can have as few as two twisted pairs and as many as 100. Generally it has three twists per foot (not in the specs), and easily handles network speeds of 10 Mbps with a bandwidth of 16 MHz.

■   **Category 4**   Used in Token Ring networks, it has four twisted pairs and can handle speeds up to 16 Mbps with a bandwidth of 20 MHz.

■   **Category 5**   Used in most networks until the mid-1990s, it has four twisted pairs, has eight twists per foot, and can handle 100 Mbps with a bandwidth of 100 MHz.

■   **Category 5e (enhanced Category 5)**   Used in almost all current networks, it has the same physical characteristics and bandwidth as Category 5 but with a lower error rate. It can be used with Gigabit Ethernet. Normally unshielded, it can also be shielded.

▲   **Category 6**   Built to go beyond Gigabit Ethernet and required for 10 Gigabit Ethernet, Category 6 has a bandwidth of 200 MHz, twice the bandwidth of Category 5e, with a lower error rate. It can be unshielded, but it is often shielded and used where electrical interference is a problem. Shielded Category 6 has four twisted pairs with a foil wrap around each pair and another foil wrap around all pairs.

Connect UTP   UTP cabling simply plugs into a network adapter and then into a wall outlet, hub, switch, or router, making 10/100/1000BaseT installation very simple, as you can see in Figure 5-8. For UTP to work between two computers without a hub or switch, the wires must be *crossed over*—the transmitting wires on one computer must become the receiving wires on the other computer. This is one of the functions of a hub, so the wires connecting a computer to a hub must be the same on both ends. When two computers are directly connected to each other, a special cable must be used that has the end connections reversed.

TIP   The rules of thumb used to stay within the 328-foot (100-meter) limit for a 10/100/1000BaseT segment are to keep the cable run from the wiring closet to the wall outlet at less than 300 feet, the run from the wall outlet to the computer at less than 20 feet, and the patch panel at less than 8 feet.

Fiber-Optic Cable

Fiber-optic cable transmits light over a very pure strand, or *fiber*, of glass less than the thickness of a human hair. The glass is so pure that there is very little loss of light in a very

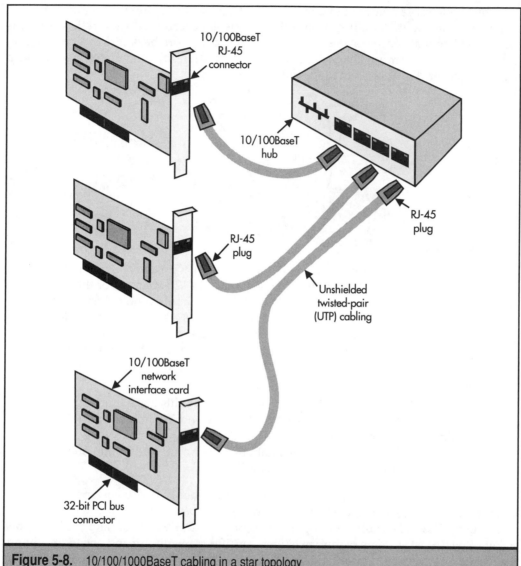

10/100BaseT
RJ-45
connector

10/100BaseT
hub

RJ-45
plug

RJ-45
plug

Unshielded
twisted-pair
(UTP) cabling

10/100BaseT
network
interface card

32-bit PCI bus
connector

Figure 5-8.   10/100/1000BaseT cabling in a star topology

long cable. The light source is either a light-emitting diode (LED) or a laser. Information is transmitted by turning the light source on and off to produce digital 1's and 0's. At the other end of the cable is a light detector that converts the light back to electrical pulses. Fiber-optic cable is immune to electrical and electromagnetic interference and does not radiate energy itself. This means that it is very hard for someone to tap undetected a fiber-optic cable and get the information it is carrying. The result is that fiber-optic cable is a very secure and efficient means of quickly carrying information over a long distance.

Fiber-optic cable, shown next, has a central core of transparent glass (or for short distances of a few meters, it can be plastic). This is surrounded by a reflecting glass called *cladding* that redirects any light coming out of the core back into it. The cladding is covered by one or more layers of plastic and other strengthening materials to make a sheath or jacket. There are two kinds of fiber-optic cable:

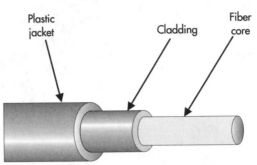

- ▼ **Single-mode or monomode fiber**   Uses a laser with a very small inner glass core (4 to 10 microns for the core and 75 to 125 microns for the core and cladding combined, written "4/75 to 10/125"). Single-mode fiber carries the light, in essence, straight down the fiber. This has a high efficiency, allowing for longer distances—as much as ten times the distance of multimode fiber—but it is also the most expensive, costing up to twice as much as multimode fiber. Single-mode fiber is used in long-distance WANs, in wiring campus networks, and less frequently in building backbones.

- ▲ **Multimode fiber**   Generally used with an LED, this has a much larger glass core (the standard is 62.5 microns for the core and 125 microns for the core and cladding). Multimode fiber allows the light to bounce off the walls, thus giving it a lower efficiency but at a substantially lower cost. Multimode fiber is used in *premise* wiring, wiring within a building.

The most common fiber-optic cable is multimode fiber with dimensions of 62.5/125. It comes with a single fiber (*simplex*); with two fibers (*duplex* or *zipcord*); or with 4, 6, 12, or more fibers. Like UTP cable, fiber-optic cable comes with PVC (riser) and plenum outer jackets. Since most systems require two fibers, one for transmitting and one for receiving, the two-fiber zipcord is encountered most often. At this time, PVC zipcord costs between 30 and 40 cents a foot, while plenum zipcord costs between 35 and 45 cents, both in 1,000-foot spools, plus the cost of connectors (see www.controlcable.com).

Gigabit over fiber (1000BaseF) requires the use of lasers (LEDs are not fast enough) and as a result has a longer maximum distance than 100BaseF (1,800 feet vs. 1,351 feet), which standard is based on LEDs. The standards for 1000BaseF are as follows:

Type of Fiber	Core Size	Maximum Distance
Multimode	50 or 62.5 microns	1,800 feet
Single-mode	8 to 10 microns	16,000 feet, or 3 miles

The cost of fiber-optic cabling has not decreased over the last couple of years, but nonetheless it is being used more and more frequently for the backbone and even some of the horizontal wiring in a building (see the following section).

TIA/EIA Cabling Standards

The Telecommunications Industry Association (TIA) and the Electronic Industries Association (EIA) together have defined a set of wiring standards for telecommunications and computer networking in a commercial building. The purpose of the standards is to provide a common set of specifications for cabling data, voice, and video in a building that provides the users and owners of the building quality, flexibility, value, and function in their telecommunications infrastructure while allowing diverse manufacturers to build equipment that will interoperate. The most applicable of these standards are the following:

▼ **TIA/EIA-587-A** For data, voice, and video cabling in a commercial building

■ **TIA/EIA-569** For the areas and pathways that hold telecommunications media in a building

■ **TIA/EIA-606** For the design and management of a telecommunications infrastructure

▲ **TIA/EIA-607** For the grounding and bonding requirements in telecommunications equipment and cabling

These standards define the rules and limitations for each part of the telecommunications and networking infrastructure in a building. The standards break this infrastructure into a defined set of areas and wiring types within a building, as shown in the next illustration, and defined as follows:

▼ **Entrance Facilities** Where the telecommunications services and/or a campus backbone enters a building

■ **Main Cross-Connects** The central facility within a building to which all the equipment rooms are connected with backbone wiring; there may also be a main cross-connect for a campus that ties together all the building main cross-connects

■ **Backbone Wiring** The fast, heavy-duty wiring that runs, generally vertically, from the main cross-connects to the equipment rooms in a building or between main cross-connects on a campus

■ **Equipment Rooms** The areas located on each floor of a building that provide the connection between the backbone wiring going to the main cross-connect and the horizontal wiring going to the telecommunications closets

■ **Horizontal Wiring** The second-level wiring that runs, generally across a drop ceiling, from the equipment rooms to the telecommunications closets, as well as the third-level wiring that runs across a ceiling and down a wall from the telecommunications closets to the wall outlets

- ■ **Telecommunications Closets** The areas located in several places on a floor of a building that serve a contiguous group of offices and provide a connection between the horizontal wiring running to the equipment rooms and the horizontal wiring running to individual wall outlets

- ▲ **Work Area Wiring** The external (not in a wall or ceiling) wiring that provides a connection between the termination of the horizontal wiring in a wall outlet and the computer or other device connected to the network

NOTE The TIA/EIA standards discuss both telecommunications and computer networking, and in reading them, you need to make sure what a given topic is discussing. For example, UTP for voice can run up to 800 meters, or 2,624 feet, whereas UTP for data can only run up to 100 meters, or 328 feet.

You can get more information on the TIA/EIA standards from the TIA web site at http://www.tiaonline.org or from Hubbell (a connector manufacturer) at http://www .hubbell- premise.com/standards.asp, which has a series of papers on cabling standards.

Cabling Cost Comparison

Table 5-2 provides a comparison of the cost of various types of network cables. This should be used only as a relative comparison between types and not as an indication of the current cost, which changes frequently. Also, there are significant differences in suppliers and quantity discounts.

Interconnection Devices

If you have more than two computers in a 10/100/1000BaseT network, you need some device to which you connect the additional computers. The simplest of these devices is a hub, but you might also use a switch, a router, or a bridge, depending on what you want to do. Each of these devices has a particular use, although there is overlap, and each has

Cable Type (1,000-foot prices 5/07)	Cost/Foot for PVC	Cost/Foot for Plenum
Category 5e Solid	8 cents	16 cents
Category 5e Stranded	9.5 cents	NA
Category 6 Solid	11 cents	24 cents
Fiber-optic multimode 63.5/125 zipcord	30 cents	40 cents

Table 5-2. Cabling Cost Comparison

several variations. These devices act as building blocks that allow you to expand a network segment and interconnect multiple segments.

Hubs

Hubs are used to connect multiple devices on the network. Normally these are worksta-tions, but they can also be servers, printers, other hubs, and other interconnection de-vices. A hub is a repeater device that takes whatever comes in on one line and puts it out on all other lines without any filtering or intelligence applied to the information stream or where it is going. This means that every station can hear what every other station has put on the network. As the traffic grows, the number of collisions between frames will increase, causing significant degradation in the network throughput. Hubs operate at the Physical layer of the OSI model, simply repeating the information they receive.

Today, hubs are all but extinct except for home use and have been replaced with switches and routers that have intelligence built into them and cost virtually the same or even less.

Switches

A *switch*, like a hub, has a number of ports, from 4 to 48 or more, and takes information that comes into one port and sends it out to one or more other ports. Unlike a hub, which does no filtering or processing of the information that flows through it, a switch is an intelligent device that looks at the physical destination address of the frame flowing into it and directs the frame to the correct port for that destination. This removes that frame from the rest of the network, since the frame goes over only the part of the network that connects the sending and receiving devices. This is similar to the maturing of the tele-phone system from the original party-line system to the current direct-dial system.

Switches, like bridges and routers, segment a network to reduce the traffic and colli-sions, and ultimately improve the throughput. Switch segmentation can be done at any level where you would otherwise have a hub, a bridge, or a router. Such a switch func-tions as a multiport bridge and is therefore operating at the Data Link layer or Layer 2 of the OSI model. Further intelligence can be added to some switches so that they become multiport switching routers that unpack frames and operate on the logical address in the packets. Such switching routers operate at the Network layer of the OSI model. For this reason, they are called "Layer 3 switches."

There are three types of switches: stand-alone switches, stackable switches, and mod-ular switches. The simplest switches cost under $5 a port, whereas a Layer 3 switching router may approach $200 a port.

Stand-Alone Switches *Stand-alone* switches, as shown in Figure 5-9, are used throughout most networks of four or more computers. Stand-alone switches come with 4 to 48 ports for 10/100BaseT, 100BaseT, 10/100/1000BaseT, 1000BaseT, 10GBaseT, and a number of fiber-optic and fiber/copper varieties and combinations. The 10/100BaseT switches cost from under $5 to as much as $10 per port, and 10/100/1000BaseT switches cost from under $8 to as much as $15 per port. There is a lot of variability in this pricing, but generally speaking, the price per port goes down with more ports in the switch.

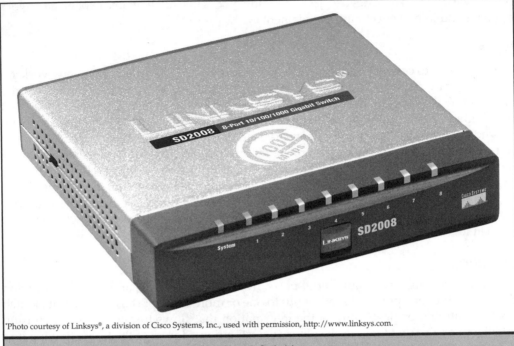

'Photo courtesy of Linksys®, a division of Cisco Systems, Inc., used with permission, http://www.linksys.com.

Figure 5-9. Linksys 8-port 10/100/1000 Gigabit Switch*

TIP Buying switches with Gigabit Ethernet capability does not add a lot more to the cost and gives you upgrade capability in the future.

Most stand-alone switches are just devices into which you plug in the 4 to 48 other devices you want to interconnect and that's it. If you want to make a change in the configuration, you have to physically unplug and replug the devices as needed to make the change. You can get smart stand-alone switches with management capability, like the one shown in Figure 5-10. This allows a switch to be monitored and configured remotely using a software package that normally comes with the switch. The software generally works with only one brand of switch, so it might be worthwhile to standardize on one brand if you are getting the additional management capability. Stand-alone switches with management capability cost $10 to $40 more per port and can even go higher depending on the capabilities.

Stackable Switches   In constructing a larger network, one with 100 or more workstations and a number of servers, you can do so with either a flat or a hierarchical structure, as shown in Figure 5-11. In using stand-alone switches, the only real difference is where the switches are located. When you daisy-chain one stand-alone switch to another to attach more workstations, the cable connecting the switches is another link to slow down the overall speed, and as the switches are spread out they become more difficult to physically manage. To get around this limitation, *stackable* switches were developed, which add ports

*Photo courtesy of Linksys®, a division of Cisco Systems, Inc., used with permission, http://www.linksys.com.

Figure 5-10.   Linksys ProConnect® II 2224 Layer 2 Management 24-port 10/100 Ethernet Switch*

in one location by joining the backplanes of the switches with extremely fast connections as if they were one switch. Therefore, any two devices connected anywhere in the stack have only a single switch between them.

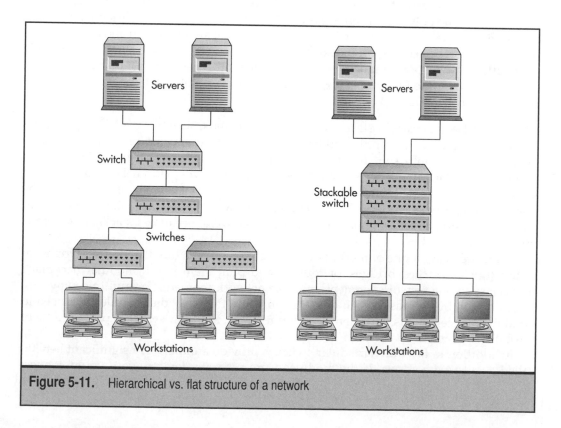

Figure 5-11.   Hierarchical vs. flat structure of a network

'Photo courtesy of 3Com® Corporation, used with permission, http://www.3com.com.

Figure 5-12.   3Com® Stackable Switch 5500 G 10/100/1000 (24- and 48-port models)*

Stackable switches, shown in Figure 5-12, are similar in appearance to stand-alone switches, and the only real difference is that the backplanes of stackable switches can be connected. Stackable switches can be stacked six to eight switches high and cost from $30 to $150 per port depending on the speeds and features they include, such as fiber-optic ports, 10G Ethernet ports, management, Power over Ethernet (PoE) for distributing electrical power over the Ethernet cable, OSI Layer 3 and even 4 functionality, and various built-in security features.

Modular Switches   A *modular switch,* also called an *enterprise switch,* is really a large chassis or cabinet with a power supply and backplane into which you can plug many different boards, including hubs, switches, bridges, and routers, as shown in Figure 5-13. By using a single backplane, modular switches get around the two- or four-layer limit, as do stackable switches. Modular switches actually preceded stackable switches, and in the less-demanding roles (where all you need are the switch functions), stackable switches are now being used where modular switches once were, because a stackable switch is much cheaper.

There are many forms of modular units, because you can buy the modules you want to use (hubs, switches, bridges, or routers) and plug them into a modular backplane that can span one network segment, multiple network segments, or multiple networks. Basically, you buy a chassis with power supply and then buy the modules you need to build the device that fits your network requirements. Modular switches provide a lot of flexibility, but at a steep price.

In addition to flexibility, modular switches provide another very significant benefit, called a *collapsed backbone.* If the modules were separate devices, you would connect

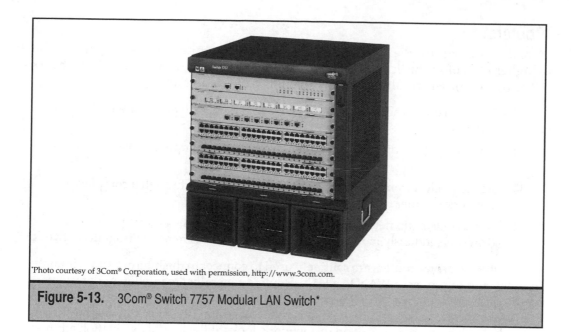

Photo courtesy of 3Com® Corporation, used with permission, http://www.3com.com.

Figure 5-13.   3Com® Switch 7757 Modular LAN Switch*

them with a high-speed backbone running at a minimum of 100 Mbps, often 1 Gbps, and now 10 Gbps, and maybe double those figures if you run at full-duplex. If you move all of these devices into a single modular switch where they are connected by the backplane, what in a stackable switch is a backbone connection is now collapsed onto the backplane and runs at between 100 Gbps and 600 Gbps.

Bridges

A *bridge* is used to either segment a network or join two networks. A bridge looks at the physical or MAC address in a frame on one side of the bridge, and if the frame has an address on the other side of the bridge, the frame is passed on to the other side. If the frame has an address on the originating side of the bridge, the bridge ignores the frame, because all devices on the originating side already can see the frame. Since a bridge looks at a frame's physical address, it is operating at the Data Link layer or Layer 2 of the OSI model, one layer above where a hub operates, but on the same layer as the simplest switches.

The purpose of the bridge is to reduce the traffic in a network by segmenting it, although it is still one network. When you join two networks with a bridge, the result is one network with two segments, but only the traffic that is addressed to the other segment gets through the bridge. Traffic that is addressed within the originating segment stays within its segment.

Bridges are basically simple devices and have for the most part been replaced with routers and switches, which can perform the same functions plus others for the same or even lower prices.

Routers

A *router* can perform the same segmenting and joining functions as a bridge, but at a higher level of sophistication, using the logical address of the OSI model's Network layer (Layer 3). The resulting added capabilities of a router are significant:

▼   Routers connect separate networks, leaving them independent with their own addressing.

■   Routers connect different types of networks; for example, 100BaseF and 100BaseT.

■   Routers select from among alternative routes a path through a complex network in order to get to an end destination.

▲   Routers clean up network traffic by checking if a frame is corrupted or lost (traveling endlessly in the network); if so, the frame is removed from the network.

For these reasons, routers are routinely used to connect to the Internet and within the Internet, and to connect a WAN to a LAN. Routers generally are intelligent devices with a processor and memory. With this capability, a router unpacks every frame that comes to it, looks at each packet within the frame, recalculates its CRC, checks to see how many times the packets have been around the network, looks at the logical destination address, determines the best path to get there, repackages the packets into a new frame with the new physical address, and sends the frame on its way. In addition, routers talk to other routers to determine the best path and to keep track of routes that have failed. Routers do all of this at amazing speeds. At the low end, routers process over 250,000 packets per second, and they go above several million packets a second on the upper end. Routers begin under $50 and go to over a thousand, depending on what they do.

Routers are being combined with both switches and wireless access point to join the Internet with either a wired or wireless network in one unit. Figure 5-14 show a Linksys unit that contains a router for connecting the Internet coming in from either a cable or DSL connection to a LAN, which is split out with an 8-port switch. This unit costs under $100.

*Photo courtesy of Linksys®, a division of Cisco Systems, Inc., used with permission, http://www.linksys.com.

Figure 5-14.   Linksys EtherFast® Cable/DSL Router with 8-port Switch*

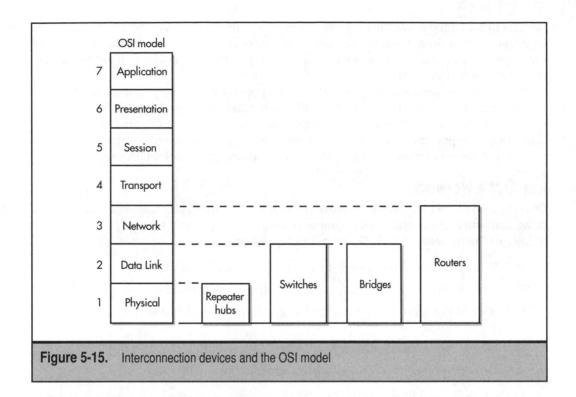

Figure 5-15. Interconnection devices and the OSI model

Interconnection Device Summary

When you are building a network, you have many choices regarding interconnection devices. You not only have the choice between hubs, bridges, routers, and switches, but you also have a number of choices within each of those categories, as well as combinations of these devices. You can get some insight into an answer by looking at where in the OSI model each of the devices operates, as shown in Figure 5-15. In almost all cases, you will be working with switches, and probably a router, to connect to the Internet. Beyond that, it will depend on how complex your network is.

NETWORKING TOPOLOGIES

Topology is the design of a network, the way it is laid out. In the figures in this chapter, you have seen several different topologies. 10Base2 and 10Base5 both used a *bus* topology, wherein all the network devices are attached to a single long cable. These forms of Ethernet, though, are dead. The 10/100/1000BaseT forms all use a *star* topology, where the network devices fan out on separate cables from a central switch, as you saw in Figures 5-1, 5-2, 5-8, and 5-11. When backbone cabling is added to a 10/100/1000BaseT network, you have a *star/bus* topology.

The bus topology was the original Ethernet topology, but it has the major disadvantage that a break in any part of the network brings the entire network down. In a star topology, a break in a line takes out only those parts of the network connected to the line, potentially only one station.

The cable for star topology is relatively inexpensive and is easy to manage. You can put the cable for a star topology in the wall and not connect it to a switch if it is not being used. Also, it is easy to move a station from one network segment to another simply by changing a jumper cable that connects the station from one switch to another. As a result, for wired networking, the star topology is the predominant topology in use.

Lay Out a Network

Once you have decided on the network technology and the type of network adapter, cabling, and interconnection devices that you want to use, you still have to figure out how to lay out the network. This includes a lot of questions, such as:

▼ Which workstations are grouped with which switches?

■ Do you stack several switches, or use a hierarchical structure?

■ Should the servers be centralized in one location or decentralized in each department?

■ When do you need a router?

▲ How do you connect two buildings separated by 1,500 feet or more?

There is no one right answer to any of these questions, and there is a lot of difference between the impact of the first question and that of the last question. You can easily alter the connections to change how workstations are grouped, but setting up a WAN is a job for professionals because you are talking about serious money to purchase the equipment and install it and significant expense if you want to change it.

In an Ethernet 100/1000BaseT network, several rules should be followed in a layout. These vary slightly with different manufacturers, but the general rules of thumb are shown in the following table:

Rule of Thumb	Fast Ethernet 100/1000BaseT
Maximum cable length between hub and workstation	100 meters, or 328 feet
Minimum cable type	Category 5e
Maximum number of hubs between two workstations or a switch and a workstation	Two hubs
Maximum number of cable segments between two workstations or a switch and a workstation	Three cable segments with a maximum total distance of 205 meters, or 672 feet

Microsoft Office Visio Professional is a good tool for both planning the layout of a network as you are building it and documenting the network after it is installed. With Visio, you can easily design the network layout that you want to use, quickly communicate that design to others, create a bill of material, and have a ready reference during installation. After a network is completed, Visio is a good tool for documenting changes in the network. Visio, a Microsoft Office product, can be found at http://office.microsoft.com/.

NETWORKING PROTOCOLS

Protocols are the standards or rules that allow many different systems and devices to interconnect and operate on a network, be it a small office network or the worldwide Internet. Protocols specify *how* and *when* something should happen, and *what* it is that should happen.

Protocols are developed in many different ways, but for one to become widely used, it must be accepted by a number of organizations, most importantly those building networking software and networking devices. To gain this acceptance, protocols are initially circulated as draft protocols, using documents called Requests for Comments (RFCs). If someone or some organization wants to change a protocol, a new RFC gets circulated with a higher number than the original RFC. The Information Sciences Institute (ISI) of the University of Southern California classifies RFCs as being approved Internet standards, proposed Internet standards, Internet best practices, and For Your Information (FYI). ISI also maintains a web site that lists RFCs and their classification (http://www .rfc-editor.org/) from which you can get copies of the RFCs. You can determine how a piece of software has implemented a protocol by looking at which RFCs are supported. For example, you can go to Microsoft's TechNet site (http://technet2.microsoft.com) and look up the topic "TCP/IP RFCs" and see a list of RFCs that are supported.

Numerous protocols deal with computer networking, but "networking protocols" normally refers to the logical addressing and transfer of information. These protocols deal with the Transport and Network layers of the OSI networking model, as shown in Figure 5-16. While several networking protocols were originally used, today almost all networking uses Transmission Control Protocol/Internet Protocol or TCP/IP.

TCP/IP

Transmission Control Protocol/Internet Protocol is a set of networking protocols that grew out of the Internet and has been refined over 25 years to be an excellent tool for transmitting large amounts of information reliably and quickly over a complex network. The two components, TCP and IP, were originally combined and later were separated to improve the efficiency of the system.

Until recently (around 2005), if someone said "IP" they automatically meant IPv4, the version of IP that had been in existence for over 25 years and provided 32-bit or 4-byte addressing. While 32-bit addressing provides for a large number of addresses (over 2 billion of them), IP addressing is used worldwide, and using IPv4, the world will run

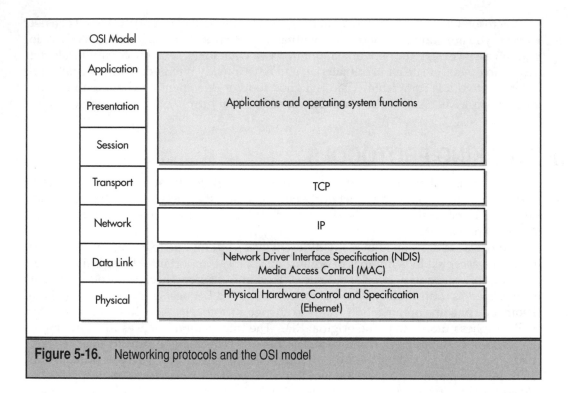

OSI Model

Application	
Presentation	Applications and operating system functions
Session	
Transport	TCP
Network	IP
Data Link	Network Driver Interface Specification (NDIS) Media Access Control (MAC)
Physical	Physical Hardware Control and Specification (Ethernet)

Figure 5-16.   Networking protocols and the OSI model

out of addresses. In addition a number of technological improvements have impacted
the Internet protocol. Therefore in the mid-1990s discussion began on a new Internet protocol, now called "IPv6," with a number of improvements including 128-bit or 16-byte
addressing. IPv6 has now become an official standard, and Windows Vista and Windows
Server 2008 support both IPv4 and IPv6. The worldwide implementation of IPv6 will
take a number of years, so IPv6 is made to work with IPv4, and systems for some time
will have to handle both.

IPv4

The Internet Protocol operates at the Network layer, Layer 3, of the OSI model controlling the assembly and routing of packets (sometimes called *datagrams* in IP). To send a
packet to a remote node across a complex network, such as the Internet, these are the
steps that take place:

1. The packet is assembled at the Network layer, and the IP address of the
    destination (which is a logical address, not a physical address) is added.

2. The packet is passed to the Data Link layer, which packages the packet in a
    frame and adds the physical address of the first router that starts the packet on
    its way to its destination.

3. The packet is passed to the closest router, which unpacks the frame, looks at the logical address on the packet, repackages the packet in a frame, and adds the physical address of the next router that continues the packet on its way to its destination.

4. Step 3 repeats for each router along the path.

5. At the last router before the destination, the destination physical address is added to the frame and the frame is sent to its destination.

This technique allows the information to follow any path through the network, with the decision on which path to take made by the local router, drawing on its knowledge of the local situation. IP is a connectionless service. It sends the packet on its way not knowing whether it is received or what route it took. Determining whether it is received and replacing the packet if it isn't is the function of TCP at the Transport layer. The route that the packet takes is a function of the routers at the Data Link layer. The packet that IP assembles has a maximum of up to 64KB, including a variable header with the source and destination addresses and other control information. The header, which is always a multiple of 4 bytes or 32 bits, is shown in Figure 5-17 and has these fields (each field shows the field length in bits):

▼ **Version**   Protocol version number, set to 4

■ **IHL**   Header length in terms of the number of 4-byte (32-bit) "words" (five-word minimum—in Figure 5-17 each row is a word, so the IHL is 6)

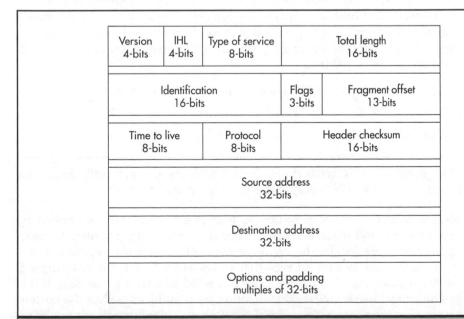

Figure 5-17.   IPv4 header

- **Type of Service**   The speed and reliability of service requested
- **Total Length**   Total packet length in bytes or "octets," with a maximum of 65,535
- **Identification**   Fragment identification, so it can be reconstructed
- **Flags**   Fragmentation indicator (DF: 0 = may fragment, 1 = don't fragment, MF: 0 = last fragments, 1 = more fragments)
- **Fragment Offset**   Number in a set of fragments; the first is 0
- **Time to Live**   The remaining number of times through a router before the packet is discarded
- **Protocol**   The protocol to use at the Transport layer
- **Header Checksum**   Number to check the integrity of the header only
- **Source Address**   The source computer's IP address
- **Destination Address**   The destination computer's IP address
- **Options**   Security, routing, and other optional information
- ▲ **Padding**   Ensures that header is in multiples of 4 bytes

IPv4 Addressing

The source and destination addresses in the IP header are the logical addresses assigned to particular computers, as compared with the physical address on a network card. These 32-bit or 4-byte numbers, called *IP addresses,* can have one of three formats, which vary the sizes of the network and host segments of the address. The leftmost ("high order") bits identify the particular format or "class." All of these classes have a network segment and a host segment that allow for locating a particular computer or router (*host*) within a particular network, as described here:

- ▼ Class A can identify up to 16,777,214 hosts in each of 126 networks.
- Class B can identify up to 65,534 hosts in each of 16,382 networks.
- ▲ Class C can identify up to 254 hosts in each of 2,097,150 networks.

NOTE   The general IP specification is in RFC 791, while addressing is additionally discussed in RFCs 790 and 796. All of these RFCs are available from http://www.ietf.org/rfc.html.

The IP address is commonly represented as four decimal numbers separated by periods, for example: 127.168.105.204. Each number is 1 byte in the address. To assist in identifying how to parse (or divide) an IP address into a network segment and a host segment, you must specify a *subnet mask* that serves as a template for this purpose. The subnet mask for class A is 255.0.0.0, for class B it is 255.255.0.0, and for class C it is 255.255.255.0. The subnet mask focuses the attention on local hosts within the current network. If you are working within the current network, the subnet mask can speed up the processing of the IP address.

IPv6

The biggest single change in IPv6 is the header and its huge address space. This address space not only allows for a very large number of additional addresses, but also provides for a more efficient hierarchical addressing that will make the job done by routers much easier. For example, if you are on the West Coast and wish to send an e-mail message to McGraw-Hill in New York City, with a hierarchical address, the early routers do not need to worry about the full path, only that you need to get to the Mid-Atlantic region.

Other changes in IPv6 include built-in security features, improved support for prioritization, and the ability to easily add new features to the header in the future.

The IPv6 header, shown in Figure 5-18, has the following fields:

▼ **Version** Protocol version number, set to 6

■ **Traffic Class** The speed and reliability of the service requested, similar to Type of Service in IPv4

■ **Flow Label** Allows the sequencing of packets between the source and destination

■ **Payload Length** Total packet length excluding the header, with a maximum of 65,535 bytes

■ **Next Header** The type of the first extension header (if present) or the protocol to use in the Transport layer, such as TCP, similar to Protocol in IPv4

■ **Hop Limit** The remaining number of links that can be transversed before the packet is discarded, similar to Time To Live in IPv4

■ **Source Address** The source computer's IP address

▲ **Destination Address** The destination computer's IP address; in some circumstances this may be temporarily set to the IP address of the next router

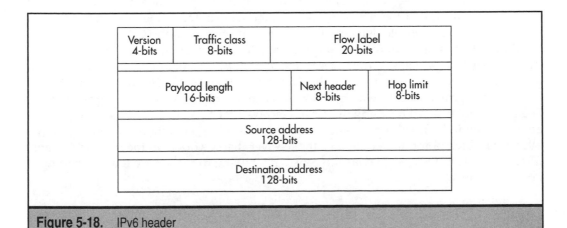

Figure 5-18. IPv6 header

Unlike IPv4, the IPv6 header is a fixed length of 40 bytes. Additional features are added to the IPv6 packet by using extension headers. Most IPv6 packets will not have an extension header, but the ones that have been defined are Hop-by-Hop Options header, Destination Options header, Routing header, Fragment header, Authentication header, and Encapsulating Security Payload header.

The one new field in the IPv6 header is the Flow Label for sequencing packets. The major field deleted in IPv6 is the Header Checksum, whose function is performed for the entire packet at the Data Link layer (Layer 2) when the packet is put within a frame.

IPv6 Addressing

A significant part of the IPv6 address space, which is defined in RFC 4291, is subdivided into hierarchical routing domains so that a particular address can carry not only its unique identity, but also the hierarchy of routers leading to it. To communicate the 128-bit or 16-byte address, it is divided into eight 16-bit blocks, each of which is converted into a four-digit hexadecimal (base 16) number separated by colons. Leading zeros are dropped, and if an entire block is zero, that zero can be dropped by having a double colon (::). For example, here is an IPv6 address:

    2001:DB8::2F3B:2AA:FF:FE28:9C5A

TCP

The Transmission Control Protocol operates at the Transport layer, which handles connections. Its purpose is to assure the reliable delivery of information to a specific destination. TCP is a connection-oriented service, in contrast with IP, which is connectionless. TCP makes the connection with the final destination and maintains contact with the destination to make sure that the information is correctly received. Once a connection is established, though, TCP depends on IP to handle the actual transfer. And because IP is connectionless, IP depends on TCP to assure delivery.

The sending and receiving TCPs (the protocols running in each machine) maintain an ongoing, full-duplex (both can be talking at the same time) dialog throughout a transmission to assure a reliable delivery. This begins with the sending TCP making sure that the destination is ready to receive information. Once an affirmative answer is received, the sending TCP packages a data message into a *segment* containing a header with control information and the first part of the data. This is then sent to IP, and TCP creates the remaining segments while watching for an acknowledgment that the segments have been received. If an acknowledgment is not received for a particular segment, it is re-created and handed off. This process continues until the final segment is sent and acknowledged, at which point the sender tells the receiver that it's done. In the process of transmission, the two Transport layers are constantly talking to make sure that everything is going smoothly.

NOTE Different and sometimes confusing names are used to refer to pieces of data being transferred through a network, depending on where you are in the OSI model and the protocol you are using. Using the TCP/IP protocol and Ethernet with the OSI model, as shown in Figure 5-19 at the top, applications create "messages" to be sent over a network. The message is handed down to the Transport level, where TCP divides the message into "segments" that include a segment header with port addresses. The segments are passed down to the Network layer, where IP packages the segments into "datagrams" with logical IP addresses. The datagrams are sent down to the Data Link layer, where Ethernet encapsulates them into a "frame" with a physical MAC address. The frames are passed to the Physical layer, which sends them over the network to the physical address, where the reverse process takes place. Alternatively, in the Transport and Network layers, a piece of information is generically called a "packet" of information.

The communication between the sending and receiving TCPs takes place in the segment header, which is shown in Figure 5-20 and explained in the following field list. The two protocols use the sequence number, the acknowledgment number, codes,

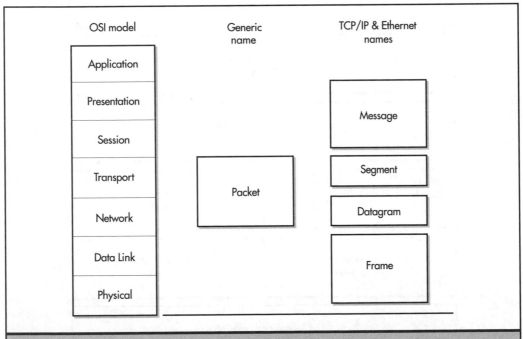

Figure 5-19.   The OSI model and the names used for pieces of information

sliding window size, urgent pointer, and options to carry on a very complex conversation about how a transmission is progressing. And all of it is happening in very small fractions of a second.

- ▼ **Source Port**   The port number in the Session layer, called a *socket,* that is sending the data

- ■ **Destination Port**   The port number in the Session layer, or socket, that is receiving the data

- ■ **Sequence Number**   A number sent to the receiver to tell it where the segment fits in the data stream

- ■ **Acknowledgment Number**   A number sent to the sender to tell it that a segment was received; the sequence number increments by 1

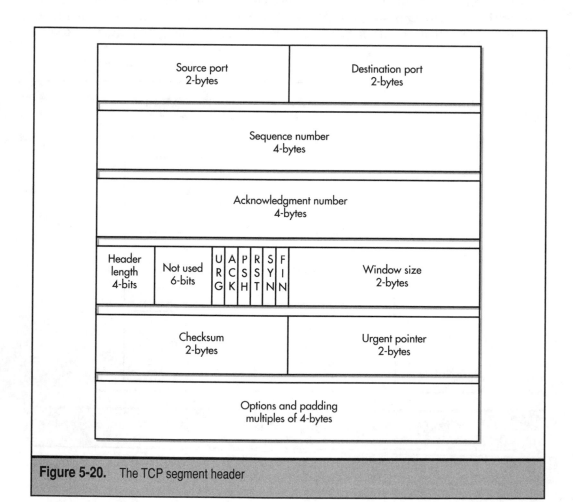

Figure 5-20.   The TCP segment header

- **Header Length** The length of the header and therefore the offset from the start of the header to the data
- **URG** The Urgent field; if 1, the Urgent Pointer is valid
- **ACK** The Acknowledgment field; if 1, the Acknowledgment Number is valid
- **PSH** The Push field; if 1, the receiver is not to buffer data, but instead to send it directly to the application, as with real-time audio and video
- **RST** The Reset field; if 1, the communication must be interrupted and the connection reset
- **SYN** The Synchronize field; if 1, a connection is requested by the sender; if accepted, the receiver leaves SYN = 1 and makes ACK = 1
- **FIN** The Finish field; if 1, the transmission is to be terminated
- **Window Size** The number of bytes that the receiver can accept in the next transmission
- **Checksum** A number with which to check the integrity of the segment
- **Urgent Pointer** If URG = 1, this is a number used as an offset to point to an urgent piece of information the receiver should look at
- **Options** Used for special circumstances; normally absent
- ▲ **Padding** Used to ensure that the header is in multiples of 4 bytes

TIP The general TCP specification is in RFC 793, which is available from http://www.ietf.org/rfc .html.

The functions performed by TCP and IP—the packaging, addressing, routing, transmission, and control of the networking process in a very complex environment—are mind-boggling. When you add to that the ease and reliability of networking, it is truly stunning. Now that you know all the networking ingredients presented in this chapter, isn't it amazing that networking works even in a small workgroup, let alone the Internet? That the Internet is such a worldwide success has to be one of the great wonders of the modern world.

At the beginning of this chapter, I stated that networking is the single most important facility in Windows Server 2008. Having read this chapter, you can see that the job of networking is a very complex task with many demands, and for Windows Server 2008 to handle it well is a tall order. In the next chapter, you'll see how Windows Server 2008 tackles these demands, and how to control what Windows Server 2008 does. I think you'll conclude that Windows Server 2008 is well suited to this most important function.

CHAPTER 6

Setting Up and Managing a Network

When you installed Windows Server 2008, a basic set of networking services was installed and configured using your input and system defaults. This setup may, but doesn't always, provide an operable networking system. In any case, you have a wide spectrum of networking alternatives to review and set to provide the networking environment best suited to your needs. The purpose of this chapter is to do just that, first by looking at how to set up basic networking in Windows Server 2008, and then by looking at how to set up Windows Server 2008 to support the rest of the network.

Basic networking means that the computer can communicate with other computers in the network. To do that, you must do the following:

▼   Assure the network adapter or interface card (NIC) is properly set up.

■   Install the networking functions that you want to perform.

▲   Click and configure a networking protocol.

SET UP NETWORK ADAPTERS

In a perfect world, the computer you are setting up would have a network adapter that is both supported by Windows Server 2008 and fully Plug and Play–compatible. If this describes your computer, then your network adapter was installed by Setup without incident and you don't need to read this section. As is known by anyone who has installed an operating system on more than two computers, this is an imperfect world. Therefore, this section looks at how to install a network adapter and what you need to do to make it fully operational.

NOTE   As described in Chapter 5, the term "network adapter" includes a number of devices that connect a computer to a network either by wire or wirelessly, such as PCI adapters for desktops, PC-Card and ExpressCard laptop adapters, USB adapters for either desktops or laptops, as well as wired and wireless network connections built into both desktops and laptops.

If you installed Windows Server 2008 using the instructions in Chapter 3, and if you went through the section "Configure a Server," then you can skip this section if you believe your network adapter is operating correctly. If you had problems with that section of Chapter 3 or did not go through it, then this section will be worthwhile to you.

Assuming that a network adapter *is* properly plugged into the computer, any of these three things could be causing it to not operate:

▼   The network adapter driver is either missing or not properly installed.

■   The required resources are not available.

▲   The network adapter is not functioning properly.

Look at each of these possibilities in turn in the next several sections.

Check the Network Adapter Driver

During installation, you may have gotten a message stating that a driver could not be found (although Setup may complete without telling you it skipped network setup because of the lack of a driver). Use the following steps to check whether you have a driver installed and, if you don't, try to install one:

1. Click Start | Control Panel, and double-click Network and Sharing Center. The Network and Sharing Center opens. If your window looks like Figure 6-1, then your network adapter and its driver are properly installed and working, and you can go on to the next major section. If that is not the case, then your Network and Sharing Center should look like Figure 6-2.

2. If your network does not appear in the Network and Sharing Center, you cannot get it there with one of the options in that window. Close the Network and Sharing Center window. You must first install the network adapter and its driver by using the Add Hardware Control Panel.

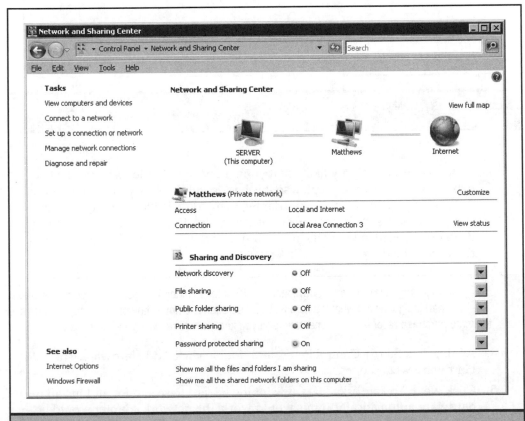

Figure 6-1. Networking installed and working properly

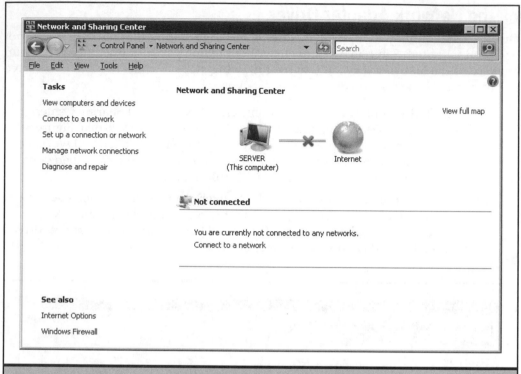

Figure 6-2.   Networking not working properly

3. At this point, it is highly likely that you will need a Windows Server 2008 driver for the network adapter, so it is best to get it before proceeding. If one did not come with the network adapter, then you need to get onto another computer, bring up the manufacturer's web site, locate and download the driver (you need to know the make and model of the network adapter), and then copy the driver onto a CD.

TIP   I went through the process of downloading a driver for an older 3Com card and found it painless. The hard part is figuring out what the card is, because often it is not written on the card, so you have to locate purchase records or documentation—if you know which records go with the card.

4. Again, click Start | Control Panel, and double-click Add Hardware. The Add Hardware wizard opens.

5. Click Next. You are asked if you want the wizard to search for and install the hardware automatically. If this would work, the network adapter would be installed already. Instead, click Install The Hardware That I Manually Select From A List.

6. Click Next. A list of common hardware types will appear. Scroll down, click Network Adapters, and click Next. A list of manufacturers and their network adapters is displayed. Scroll down the manufacturers and then the network adapters to see if yours is there. If it is, select it, click Next twice, and skip to Step 9.

7. If you didn't find your adapter (that is likely) and have a disk with the driver on it, click Have Disk. Click Browse, select a drive with the driver on it, locate and select the driver, and click Open. When it is displayed, click OK. When told that the device will be installed, click Next again.

8. You may get a message stating that the driver you are about to install does not have a Microsoft digital signature. Click Yes to install it anyway. The adapter and its necessary driver software will be installed.

9. Click Finish and restart your computer. Upon restarting, you should see a message in the lower right of your screen that the adapter and driver have been installed, as shown next.

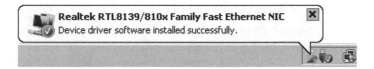

10. If you now click Start | Control Panel and double-click Network and Sharing Center, you should see the Local Area Connection option. If you see the Local Area Connection option, go to the next major section, "Install Network Functions and Configure Protocols."

11. If you still do not have a Local Area Connection, or some other problem occurred in the preceding process that does not point to an obvious solution, continue through the next two sections to see if a solution is presented.

TIP If your network adapter is not certified to run Windows Server 2008, it does not mean that it won't work with Windows Server 2008. It just means that Microsoft hasn't checked it out. Most older cards are not certified for the newer operating systems, but run just fine. Check with the manufacturer to see if they believe it works with Windows Server 2008.

Check the Network Adapter Resources

Most interface or adapter cards in a PC require dedicated resources in order to operate. The resources include interrupt request (IRQ) lines, I/O ports, and direct memory access (DMA) lines. Generally, two devices cannot share the same resources, except that PCI devices can share IRQs. Therefore, if two devices are assigned the same resource, a conflict occurs and the device will not operate properly. This will cause a network adapter to not function and the Local Area Connection icon to not appear. Check the resources used by the network adapter, with these steps:

1. Click Start | Control Panel, and double-click Device Manager. The Device Manager window opens and displays your network adapter as shown next. If you see a problem icon (an exclamation point) on your network adapter, then there may be a problem with the resource allocation. ──── Realtek RTL8139C+ Fast Ethernet NIC

2. Open the Network Adapters category and double-click the particular network adapter that is being researched. The Properties dialog box for that device will open and give you a device status. If there is a resource problem, then it should show up here.

3. Click the Resources tab. In the Conflicting Device List at the bottom of the dialog box, you will see the specifics of any resource conflicts.

4. If you have a conflict, click Use Automatic Settings to turn that setting off, and then go through each of the configurations in the Setting Based On drop-down list to see if any of them cures the problem.

5. If none of the canned configurations cures the problem, click the problem resource and click Change Setting. Click the up or down arrow to change the setting, and then click OK to see if that fixes the problem. Try several settings.

6. If you are having a hard time finding a solution, go back to the Device Manager (you can leave the network adapter Properties dialog box open), open the View menu, and click Resources By Type. Here, you can see all of the assignments for a given resource, as shown for interrupt request lines next, and find an empty resource to assign to the network adapter.

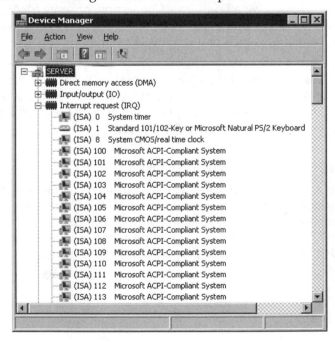

7. If you find an unassigned resource, go back to the network adapter Properties dialog box and assign it to the network adapter. If you cannot find an unassigned resource, you may have to make a tough choice between the network adapter and a conflicting device. Networking is a pretty important service, and if it is conflicting with a sound card, for example, you may have to remove the sound card to get networking.

8. If none of the previous suggestions works, return to the network adapter Properties dialog box, click the General tab, and then click Troubleshoot. Windows Server 2008 Help will open and lead you through a series of steps to try to resolve the problem.

9. When you have solved the resource problem as best you can, close the network adapter Properties dialog box and close the Device Manager. If you made changes in the resources, you may be told that you need to restart your computer and asked whether you want to do it now. Click Yes, and the computer will restart.

10. If you successfully made a change to the resources, you should now see a networking icon in the system tray in the lower right. If you do, go to the next major section, "Install Network Functions and Configure Protocols." If you don't see a Local Area Connection icon, continue with the following section.

Network Adapter Not Functioning

If neither installing a network adapter driver nor changing its resource allocation caused the networking icon to appear, it is very likely that the network adapter itself is not functioning properly. The easiest way to test that is to replace the network adapter with a known good one, ideally one that is both certified to run with Windows Server 2008 and Plug and Play–compatible. It is wise to have several spare network adapters; they are not terribly expensive (see Chapter 5), and switching out a suspected bad one can quickly solve problems.

INSTALL NETWORK FUNCTIONS AND CONFIGURE PROTOCOLS

Installing and checking out the network adapter is half of the equation; the other half has to do with setting up the networking functions within Windows Server 2008 as well as identifying and configuring the networking standards or protocols that will be used.

Install Network Functions

Networking functions provide the software for a computer to access other computers and, separately, for other computers to access the computer you are working on. In other words, the two primary functions allow the computer to be a client (it accesses other

computers) and to be a server (other computers access it). Make sure that these two services are installed by following these steps:

1. Click Start | Control Panel, double-click Network and Sharing Center, click
   Manage Network Connections on the left, and double-click Local Area
   Connection. The Local Area Connection Status dialog box opens, as shown
   next. In the particular case shown here, the computer thinks it is connected to
   the network and is sending and receiving information.

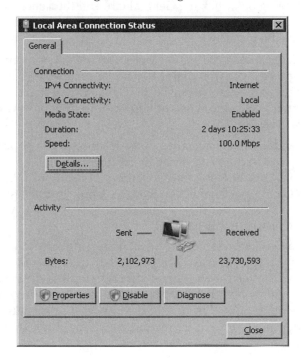

2. Click Properties. If the User account Control dialog box appears, click Continue.
   The Local Area Connection Properties dialog box, shown in Figure 6-3, opens
   and displays the services and protocols that have automatically been installed.
   Under the default circumstances, this includes three services—Client For
   Microsoft Networks, File And Printer Sharing For Microsoft Networks, and QoS
   (Quality of Service) Packet Scheduler—and four protocols—Internet Protocol
   (IPv4 and IPv6, see Chapter 5) and two for network discovery. If you have the
   first two services installed, you have achieved the objective of this section, but
   in any case, continue and explore the alternatives.

3. Click Install. The Select Network Feature Type dialog box opens, in which you
   can add clients, services, and protocols.

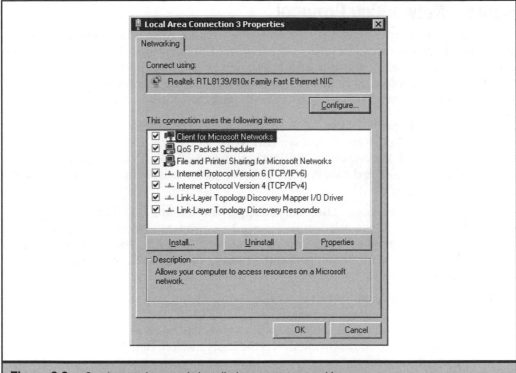

Figure 6-3. Services and protocols installed to support networking

4. Double-click Client. If you already have Client For Microsoft Networks installed, you will not have any further clients in the list without third-party software like NetWare.

5. If Client For Microsoft Networks is not installed, select it and click OK.

6. Back in the Select Network Feature Type dialog box, double-click Service. If you did a default installation, you already have File And Printer Sharing For Microsoft Networks and QoS (Quality of Service) Packet Scheduler installed, and you will not have any further services without third-party software.

7. If File And Printer Sharing For Microsoft Networks is not installed, select it and click OK.

This should assure that you have the two primary services installed.

Configure a Networking Protocol

As you read in Chapter 5, networking protocols are a set of standards used to package and transmit information over a network. The protocol determines how the information is divided into packets, how it is addressed, and what is done to assure it is reliably transferred. The protocol is therefore very important to the success of networking, but Windows Server 2008 makes the choices for you and by default installs five protocols:

▼ **TCP/IPv4** and **TCP/IPv6**   For use with LANs, the Internet, and most newer Apple Macintosh and Linux systems. Windows Server 2008 provides and installs both the original TCP/IPv4 and the new TCP/IPv6. Chapter 5 describes these in detail. Windows Server 2008 works with these two protocols interchangeably.

■ **Link-Layer Topology Discovery Mapper** and **Responder**   For searching a LAN for other network devices (computers, printers, and routers), and for responding to other devices that are searching the LAN. The searching is done at the "Link-Layer," described as the Data Link layer or Layer 2 in the OSI model in Chapter 5.

▲ **Reliable Multicast Protocol**   For use with the transmission of very large files, such as multimedia, especially video files. IPv4 by itself is not reliable for this type of file and requires TCP to confirm that data has been correctly received. This adds overhead, slowing down the transmission. Reliable Multicast Protocol provides the confirmation information with a much lower overhead, speeding up the transmission. Reliable Multicast Protocol is used by Microsoft Message Queuing (MSMQ).

Check and Change Protocols

Use the following instructions to check on and potentially change the protocols that have been installed and the settings that are being used.

NOTE   In the Local Area Connection Properties dialog box, you should see at least four and probably five protocols installed, as shown previously in Figure 6-3. In most cases, both TCP/IPv4 and TCP/IPv6 should already be installed, both Link-Layer (meaning the Data Link layer, Layer 2, in the OSI model) Topology Discovery Mapper and the Responder should be there, and probably the Reliable Multicast Protocol.

1. With the Select Network Feature Type dialog box still open (if it isn't, use the instructions in the last section to do that), double-click Protocol. The Select Network Protocol dialog box opens. This lists the available protocols (they may be all installed). If you want to install another protocol, do so now by double-clicking that protocol. Otherwise, click OK to close the Select Network Protocol dialog box, and click Cancel to close the Select Network Feature Type dialog box.

2. Select Internet Protocol Version 4 (TCP/IPv4) in the Local Area Connection Properties dialog box and click Properties. The Internet Protocol Version 4 (TCP/IPv4) Properties dialog box opens, as shown next. Here you can click to use either a dynamic IP address automatically assigned by a server running the Dynamic Host Configuration Protocol (DHCP), or a static IP address that you enter in this dialog box.

A server that is a DHCP and/or a Domain Name Service (DNS) server must have a static IP address; otherwise, all computers in a network cannot be automatically assigned an IP address from a DHCP server. If the DHCP server is down or nonexistent, Automatic Private IP Addressing (APIPA) assigns an IP address from the block of 65,000 numbers 169.254.0.0 through 169.254.255.255. It also generates a subnet mask of 255.255.0.0. APIPA is limited insofar as a computer using APIPA can talk only to other computers in the same subnet with an address in the same range of numbers. If all computers in a small network are using Windows 98/Me/2000/XP/Vista/Server 2003/Server 2008 (which all use APIPA) and have Obtain An IP Address Automatically selected, without a DHCP server they will automatically use the 169.254.0.0 through 169.254.255.255 range of IP numbers.

3. If you are working on a server that will be the DHCP server, the DNS server, or both, or if you know you must assign a static IP address to this computer, then do so by clicking Use The Following IP Address and entering an IP address. The IP address that you use should be from the block of IP addresses that your organization has been assigned by its Internet service provider (ISP) or other authority (see the discussion under "Get Blocks of IP Addresses," later in this chapter). If your organization is small and doesn't plan to access an outside network, then the static IP address can be from the block of APIPA numbers (but manually entered; refer to the number parameters in Step 2) or from several other blocks of private IP addresses (see "Get Blocks of IP Addresses").

4. If you entered a static IP address, you must also enter a subnet mask. This mask tells the IP which part of an IP address to consider a network address and which part to consider a computer or *host* address. If your organization was assigned a block of IP numbers, it was also given a subnet mask. If you used the APIPA range of addresses, then use 255.255.0.0 as the subnet mask.

5. If you don't have a specific reason to use a static IP address, click Obtain An IP Address Automatically, and use the addresses from either a DHCP server on the network or APIPA.

TIP   In very small networks (up to five or six workstations), IP addresses can be automatically obtained from a cable or DSL router.

6. Click OK to close the Internet Protocol Version 4 (TCP/IPv4) Properties dialog box and click Close to close the Local Area Connection Properties dialog box. You can leave open the Local Area Connection Status dialog box and the Network Connections and the Network and Sharing Center windows.

7. Click Start, click the Shut Down options arrow, and click Restart from the pop-up list that appears, click in the Comment box, enter a comment, and click OK.

8. When the computer restarts, reopen the Control Panel, the Network and Sharing Center, the Network Connections window, and the Local Area Connection Status dialog box as described in Step 1 under "Install Network Functions" earlier in this chapter. You should see activity on both the Sent and Received sides. Close this set of dialog boxes and windows.

9. If you did not see both send and receive activity, click Start and, in the Search text box at the bottom of the Start menu, type \\ and a computer name in your same subnet, and then press enter. The Windows Explorer should open and display the computer and its shared devices if networking is working. For example, if I type **martin** in the Search text box and press enter, I get what is shown next.

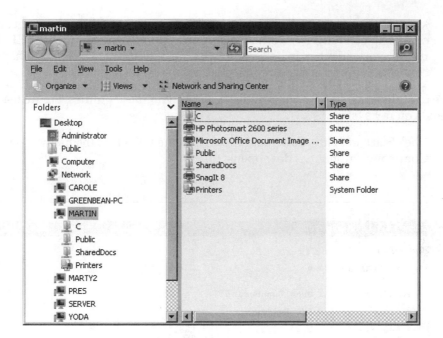

10. If you don't see any evidence of networking, double-check all the possible settings previously described. If you are using APIPA, make sure that the computer you are trying to contact is also using that range of numbers either as a static assigned address or with automatic assignment. If all the settings are correct, then check the cabling by making a simple connection of just several computers (if you do a direct UTP connection between two computers, remember that you need a special crossover cable with the transmit and receive wires reversed) and, finally, replace the network adapter. With a good network adapter, good cabling, and the correct settings, you'll be able to network.

TEST THE NETWORK

There are several command-line utilities that can be used to test a network installation. The more useful of these commands are the following:

▼ **Ipconfig**   Used to determine if a network configuration has been initialized and an IP address assigned. If an IP address and valid subnet mask are returned, then the configuration is initialized and there are no duplicates for the IP address. If a subnet mask of 0.0.0.0 is returned, then the IP address is a duplicate.

■ **Hostname**   Used to determine the computer name of the local computer.

▲ **Ping**   Used to query either the local computer or another computer on the network to see whether they respond. If the local computer responds, you know that TCP/IP is bound to the local network adapter and that both are operating correctly. If the other computer responds, you know that TCP/IP and the network adapters in both computers are operating correctly and that the connection between the computers is operable.

Use the following steps to test a network setup with these utilities. Figure 6-4 shows the results on my system.

1. Click Start and click Command Prompt on the top left of the menu. The Command Prompt window opens.

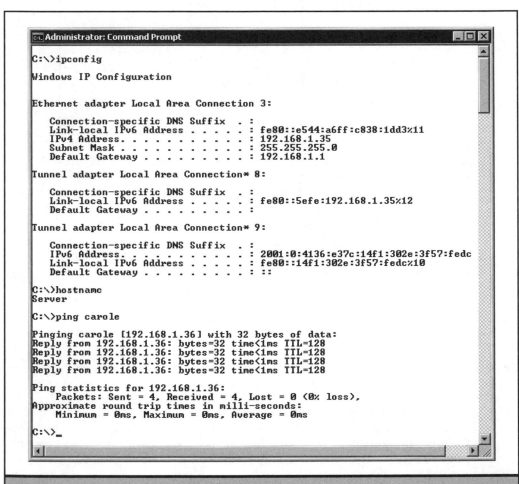

Figure 6-4. Testing a network with TCP/IP utilities

2. Type **ipconfig** and press ENTER. The IP address (both IPv4 and IPv6) and subnet mask of the current computer should be returned. If this did not happen, there is a problem with the current configuration.

TIP   If you type **ipconfig ?** at the command prompt, you will open Help for ipconfig and be able to see all the options that are available for this powerful command.

3. Type **hostname** and press ENTER. The computer name of the local computer should be returned.

4. Type **ping** *computer name* and press ENTER, where *computer name* is the name of another computer on your network. You should get four replies from the other computer.

5. If Ping did not work with a remote computer, try it on the current computer by typing **ping 127.0.0.1** and pressing ENTER. Again, you should get four replies, this time from the current computer. If you didn't get a reply here, then you have a problem with either the network setup or the network adapter. If you did get a reply here, but not in Step 4, then there is a problem either in the other computer or in the line connecting them.

6. When you are ready, type **Exit** and press ENTER to close the Command Prompt window.

NOTE   The 127.0.0.1 IP address is a special address set aside to refer to the computer on which it is entered, also called "localhost."

If you do find a problem here, use the steps in "Check and Change Protocols" earlier to isolate and fix the problem.

REVIEW SERVER SUPPORT AND NETWORK ADDRESSING

To set up Windows Server 2008 to support the rest of the network, the following services and facilities must be installed and configured:

▼ Dynamic Host Configuration Protocol (DHCP)
■ Domain Name System (DNS)
■ User accounts and group permissions
▲ Domains and Active Directory

In the process of determining the best settings for all of these elements, you'll also explore the elements themselves in greater depth. While it is not needed for Windows

Server 2008, Windows Server 2003, Windows Vista, or Windows XP, you may want to install Windows Internet Name Service (WINS) for connectivity to older Windows systems, so it will also be discussed. Domains and Active Directory are the subject of Chapter 7, but the remaining elements are discussed here.

Network Addressing

For networking to function, one computer must know how to address another. To do this, every computer has at least two, and probably three, addresses:

- **Physical address**   Address that the manufacturer builds onto each network device or network adapter (also called the *hardware address*). In Ethernet cards, this is the media access control (MAC) address.

- **Logical address**   Address assigned to a computer by a network administrator or a server and ultimately by an addressing authority. In TCP/IP, the IP address is the logical address and the Internet Assigned Numbers Authority (IANA) is the addressing authority that assigns a block of addresses, distributed as needed by a server or, less frequently, by an administrator. While the IANA is the ultimate naming authority, most companies and individuals get their IP address(es) from their Internet service provider (ISP).

- **Computer name**   Address used in most applications and in Windows Network. In earlier Microsoft Windows networking, this is the *NetBIOS name*. In TCP/IP, this can be a two-part name. The first and required part is for the current computer and is the *host name*; an example is "server." The second part is the *domain name* for the domain that contains the computer; for example, "matthews.com," making the complete name "server.matthews.com."

These three addresses operate at different layers of the OSI networking model (see the Chapter 5 section "The OSI Model"), as shown in Figure 6-5. The physical address operates at the Physical and Data Link layers, the logical address operates at the Network layer, and the computer name is used above the Network layer.

For all three of these addresses to work together, there must be a method of converting one to another. Given a computer name, it must be *resolved* to a logical address, and the logical address must be resolved to a physical address. The task of resolving a computer name into a logical address is the job of DNS or WINS, and resolving a logical address into a physical one is done by the networking protocol (for example, in TCP/IP, this is the Address Resolution Protocol, or ARP). In addition, with an ever-shorter supply of IP addresses, these addresses generally are distributed as needed by a server using DHCP. Choosing and setting up a networking protocol, as well as setting up DNS and DHCP, are major topics in this chapter, so the many tasks surrounding addressing are a connecting thread throughout the chapter.

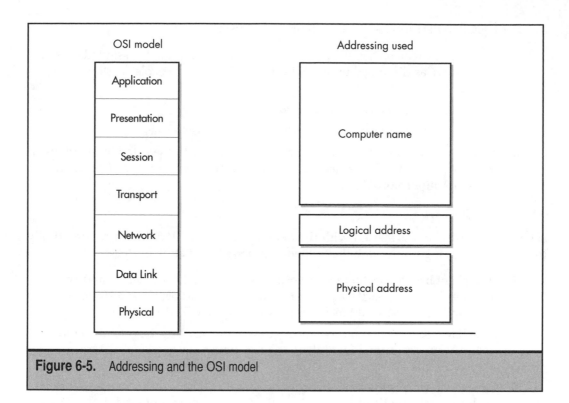

Figure 6-5. Addressing and the OSI model

IMPLEMENT DHCP, DNS, AND WINS

With a normal installation, DHCP, DNS, and WINS are not installed and are left as server roles (or in the case of WINS, a server feature) for you to select. The purpose of this section is to understand those services, install them, and configure them to your needs.

Understand the Dynamic Host Configuration Protocol

DHCP, which runs on one or more servers, has the job of assigning and managing IP addresses in a network. A *scope*, or range, of IP addresses is given to DHCP, which in turn *leases* (or assigns for a certain period) an IP address to a client. DHCP removes the possibility of errors inherent in manually assigning and entering IP addresses and also removes the management task of keeping track of who has what IP address. In an environment with many mobile users, the management task becomes all but impossible, and even in a fairly stable environment, this task is not easy.

For DHCP to perform its function, four steps must be taken:

▼ A server on which DHCP will be installed must be manually assigned a fixed IP address, as discussed under "Check and Change Protocols" earlier in this chapter.

■ DHCP must be enabled and authorized on the server.

■ DHCP must have a scope of IP addresses and a lease term.

▲ Clients must have Obtain An IP Address Automatically selected in the Internet Protocol (TCP/IP) Properties dialog box, as discussed earlier in "Configure a Networking Protocol."

How DHCP Works

The first time a client is started with the default Obtain An IP Address Automatically network setting, it goes through the following process to get an IP address:

▼ The client broadcasts on the network a request for a DHCP server and an IP address. It uses 0.0.0.0 as the source address, uses 255.255.255.255 as the destination address, and includes its physical (MAC) address.

■ All DHCP servers that receive the request broadcast a message that includes the MAC address, an offered IP address, a subnet mask, a length of lease, and the server's IP address.

■ The client accepts the first offer that reaches it and broadcasts that acceptance, including its new IP address and the IP of the server that offered it.

▲ This acceptance is acknowledged by the offering server.

Each time the client is started after receiving an IP address, it attempts to use the same IP address from the same server. The server can accept this or not, but during the lease term, it normally is accepted. Halfway through the lease term, the client will automatically ask for the lease to be extended, and under most circumstances it is extended. If the lease isn't extended, the client will continue to use the IP address and broadcast a request for any other server to renew the current IP address. If this is refused, the client will broadcast a request for any IP address, as it did at the start.

Configure DHCP

Configuring DHCP is the process of defining IP addresses, both individually and in blocks, or scopes. To do that, you will need the following items:

▼ A block of IP addresses to use in a scope

■ Scope name

■ Starting IP address in the scope range

■ Ending IP address in the scope range

- Subnet mask to be used with this range of IP addresses
- Starting and ending addresses of the ranges to exclude from the scope
- DHCP client lease duration
- ▲ Settings for server, scope, and client options

Get Blocks of IP Addresses

Which block of IP addresses is used in a scope depends on whether the computers to be assigned the addresses will be public or private. If the computers will be interfacing directly with the Internet, they are *public* and thus need a globally unique IP number. If the computers will be operating only on an internal network, where they are separated from the public network by a router, bridge, and/or firewall, they are *private* and need only organizational uniqueness. IANA has set aside three blocks of IP addresses that can be used by any organization for its private, internal needs without any coordination with any other organization, but these blocks should not be used for connecting to the Internet. These private-use blocks of IP addresses are as follows:

- ▼ 10.0.0.0 through 10.255.255.255
- 172.16.0.0 through 172.31.255.255
- ▲ 192.168.0.0 through 192.168.255.255

In addition, the APIPA range from 169.254.0.0 through 169.254.255.255 is discussed earlier in this chapter. Remember, though, that APIPA works only with computers within its own subnet and with IP addresses from the same range. In a small network, though, you can mix DHCP and APIPA addressing and always be assured that an IP number will be available independent of DHCP.

If you want a block of public IP addresses, you must request it from one of several organizations, depending on the size of the block that you want. At the local level for a small to moderate-sized block of IP addresses, your local ISP can assign it to you out of a block they have been assigned. For a larger block, a regional ISP may be able to handle the request. If not, you have to go to one of three international Internet registries:

- ▼ American Registry for Internet Numbers (ARIN), at http://www.arin.net/, which covers North and South America, the Caribbean, and sub-Saharan Africa
- Réseaux IP Européens (RIPE), at http://www.ripe.net/, which covers Europe, the Middle East, and northern Africa
- ▲ Asia Pacific Network Information Center (APNIC), at http://www.apnic.net/, which covers Asia and the Pacific

The coordination of these three organizations is performed by IANA, at http://www.iana.com/. In December 1997, IP addressing authority for the Americas was transferred from Network Solutions, Inc. (InterNIC) to ARIN. ARIN, RIPE, APNIC, and IANA are all nonprofit organizations representing a broad membership of ISPs, communications companies, manufacturers, other organizations, and individuals. The smallest block that ARIN will allocate (to ISPs for reassignment) or assign (to organizations and individuals) is 4,096 addresses, for which they currently charge $2,250 per year. Larger blocks can cost up to $18,000 per year. ISPs will allocate smaller blocks using their own fee structure. The ARIN minimum block size and fee apply to the current Internet Protocol version 4 (IPv4). IPv6 is in the early stages of being assigned and has its own rules for allocation and assignment. At the time this is written, blocks of IPv6 numbers were being allocated for free through December 31, 2007.

Understand the Domain Name System

DNS has the job of resolving or converting an easy-to-remember user-friendly name into an IP address. It does this by maintaining a database of name–IP address pairs. DNS is an application in the TCP/IP protocol suite that was developed to handle the name resolution needed on the Internet. As a result, it uses a hierarchical *domain name space* that you use on the Internet. For example, the name *server1.editorial.osborne.com* has the following structure:

Root domain	.
Top-level domain	Com
Second-level domain	Osborne
Third-level domain	Editorial
Host name	server1

A host name is always the leftmost portion of a name and refers to a specific computer. Within a specific domain, you need to only use the host name. It is only as you move outside of a domain that you need to use the domain names.

TIP   When creating a domain name space, keep it simple. Use short, simple, unique names and keep the number of levels to a minimum.

To make a domain name space easier to manage, it can be broken into *zones,* or discrete segments. A separate name database is kept for each zone, giving a network administrator a more manageable task. A DNS server, or a *name server,* can contain one or more zones, and multiple servers may contain the database for the same zone. In the latter case, one server is designated as the *primary server,* and the other name servers within that zone periodically query the primary server for a *zone transfer* to update the database. As a result, all zone maintenance must be performed on the primary server.

DNS can resolve a name to an IP address, in what is called a *forward lookup,* as well as resolve an IP address into a name, in what is called a *reverse lookup.* In the process of name resolution, if a local name server cannot resolve a name, it passes it on to the other name servers the local server knows about, including accessing the Internet to query name servers there. As a name server queries for a name, it caches the results, so that it does not have to do the query again in the near future. This caching is done for a finite period, called the *time to live (TTL)*, which you can set; the default time is 60 minutes.

Install DNS and DHCP

NOTE To install DHCP on your server and have it work properly, you'll have to disable any DHCP servicing you might have from a router (like a DSL connection) on your network.

As a normal part of installing Windows Server 2008, as described in Chapter 3, DNS and DHCP are not installed. Since DNS and DHCP are optional networking roles, you'll look at how to install them and then look at how to set up each.

NOTE Unlike with previous versions of Windows Server, you can install DNS and DHCP and other components of Windows Server 2008 in only one way—by using the Server Manager Add Roles to do so. The Control Panel | Programs And Features | Turn Windows Features On Or Off option simply opens the Server Manager.

Begin by setting a static IP address for the server if you didn't do it earlier; then if DNS and DHCP are not installed or you are not sure whether they are, check that and, if necessary, install them:

1. Click Start | Command Prompt. In the Command Prompt window type **ipconfig** and press ENTER. Write down (or just leave the Command Prompt window open and refer to it when needed) the IPv6 and IPv4 addresses, the subnet mask, and the default gateway. If you have any problems in the following steps and sections, you'll be able to return to these settings. Type **Exit** and press ENTER to close the Command Prompt window.

2. Click Start | Server Manager. The Server Manager window opens. Look at the bottom of the Server Manager window. If the last refresh isn't very current, click Configure Refresh, select Refresh Every, select 2 Minutes, and click OK.

> Last Refresh: 5/17/2007 11:14:58 AM   Configure refresh

TIP In Windows Server 2008 you can also start the Server Manager's icon, which by default is on the left of the Quick Launch toolbar.

3. In the Server Summary Computer Information section of the Server Manager, click View Network Connections, and in the Control Panel\Network Connections window that opens, double-click Local Area Connection. In the Local Area Connection Status dialog box, click Properties. If the User account Control dialog box appears, click Continue.

4. In the Local Area Connection Properties dialog box, click Internet Protocol Version 4 and click Properties. In the Internet Protocol Version 4 Properties dialog box, click Use The Following IP Address.

5. Unless you have a specifically assigned IP address for the server you are working on, enter the IP address, subnet mask, and default gateway that you got from Ipconfig. Once again enter the IP address of the current server as the Preferred DNS Server, and enter the IP address of a second server if applicable (use Ping to acquire this—get the IPv6 address for future use), as shown in Figure 6-6.

6. Click OK and Close to close several dialog boxes and windows, restart the server, and reopen the Server Manager.

7. In the Roles Summary section, if DHCP and DNS are installed, you'll see their roles listed. If you do, you can skip to the next major section. Otherwise, if your

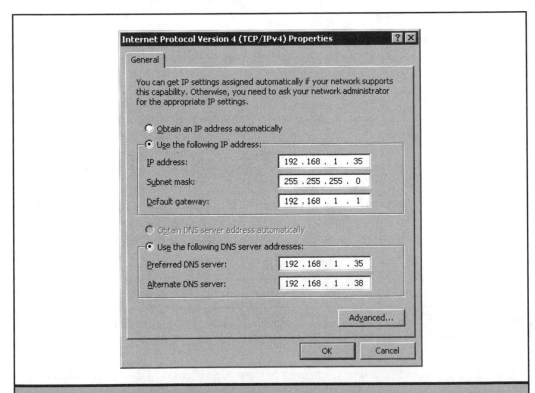

Figure 6-6.   Setting up a static IP address is needed before setting up DHCP and DNS.

Roles Summary does not show DHCP and DNS installed, use the remaining instructions to install DHCP.

8. Click Add Roles. The Add Roles Wizard opens. Before You Begin is displayed and suggests you have a strong Administrator password, static IP addresses, and the latest Windows Server 2008 Updates.

9. Click Next. Select Server Roles displays and you should see DHCP Server on the list, as shown in Figure 6-7.

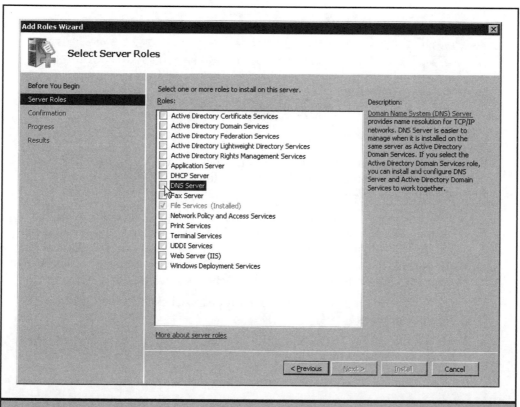

Figure 6-7.   Server Manager allows you to select the DHCP and DNS server roles.

10. If the DHCP Server check box is not checked, click it. If you don't have a static IP address entered for the server, you'll be reminded that you need to do that. Click Yes to confirm it. Go back and do Steps 3 through 6.

11. If DNS Server is not checked, click the check box, and then click Next. Click Next twice more in response to the DNS and DHCP information screens. If you haven't entered a preferred and alternate IP address for DNS, you are requested to do so. Click Next when you are ready.

Enable DHCP and DNS

Continuing in the Add Roles Wizard, the available static IP addresses are displayed for the use of a DHCP server.

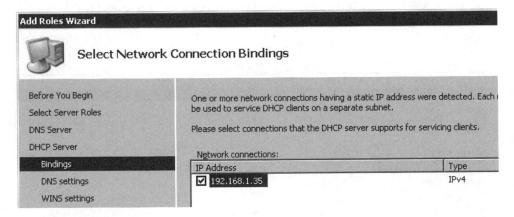

1. Click the IP address you want to use and click Next. If requested (and if you didn't just do it), enter the preferred and alternate DNS server IP addresses, and click Next. The Specify WINS Server Settings dialog box appears.

2. If you have Windows computers on your network prior to Windows 2000 (Windows 95/98/Me or NT), then you will need to set up WINS. In that case, select WINS Is Required For Applications On This Network, and enter the IP addresses for the preferred and alternate WINS servers. Otherwise, leave the default WINS Is Not Required On This Network selected.

3. Click Next. Add Or Edit DHCP Scopes appears. Click Add. The Add Scope dialog box appears.

4. Enter a name for the scope. Enter the starting and ending IP addresses for the range to be included in the scope. Enter the subnet mask for the IP addresses range and enter the default gateway, as shown here:

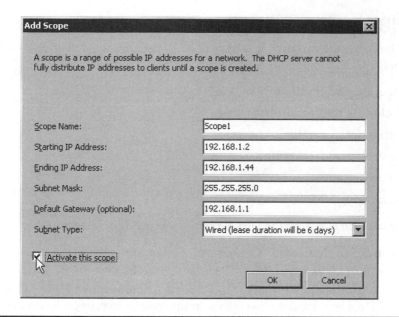

NOTE   A subnet mask divides an IP address into a subnet or network address and a host address. When you are working on a local network, only the host portion is needed, so it speeds up the process if only that portion of the address is searched. An IP address is 32 bits long, so if you say that half of it (16 bits) is a network address, the local network will only look at the 16-bit host address. The 16-bit subnet mask is 255.255.0.0.

5. Click Activate This Scope and click OK. The new scope appears in the list of scopes. Click Next. You are asked how you want to handle DHCPv6. The simplest approach is to leave the default of configuring the server for stateless operation that requires no further configuration from you.

6. Click Next. Enter the IPv6 addresses for the preferred and alternate DNS servers you entered earlier for IPv4 and click Next. A summary of your settings is shown. If they are not correct, click Previous and then Next as needed to correct them.

7. When you are ready, click Install. You'll see a progress bar showing the installation for the DHCP and DNS servers. When it is done, you'll get a message that the installations were successful. Click Close. In the Server Manager under Roles Summary, you should now see both DHCP Server and DNS Server.

Manage DHCP

Once you have installed DHCP, you may need to perform a number of DHCP management tasks for DHCP to operate the way you want, including:

▼ Creating additional scopes

■ Excluding ranges within a scope

■ Setting lease duration

■ Reserving addresses for particular clients

■ Changing scope properties

▲ Monitoring address leasing

You manage DHCP from the DHCP console, which is opened in either of two ways:

▼ **From Server Manager**   Click Start | Server Manager. In the console tree on the left, open Roles | DHCP Server | Server and click IPv4.

▲ **From Administrative Tools**   Click Start | Administrative Tools | DHCP. In the DHCP console window that opens, in the console tree, open Server and click IPv4.

The remaining steps in this section assume that you have IPv4 opened under the DHCP Server in either the Server Manager or the DHCP console, as shown in Figure 6-8.

Add DHCP Scopes

1. In either the Server Manager or the DHCP console with DHCP Server IPv4 selected, click Action | New Scope. The New Scope Wizard opens.

2. Click Next, enter a name and a description, and click Next again.

3. Enter a starting and ending IP address. The length and subnet mask are filled in automatically, but you can change them if needed. Click Next.

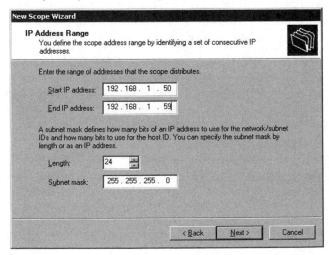

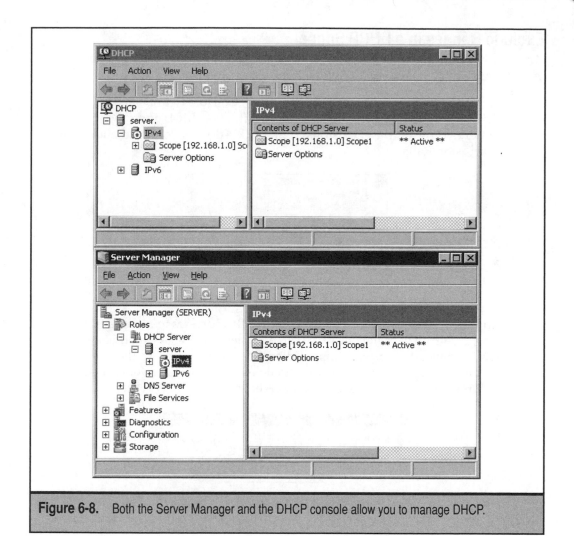

Figure 6-8.   Both the Server Manager and the DHCP console allow you to manage DHCP.

You can continue on in the New Scope Wizard and identify addresses to exclude from being distributed, specify the length of DHCP leases, reserve addresses for specific clients, and configure DHCP options. You can also do these functions for all DHCP scopes from the Server Manager or DHCP Console, as described in the following sections.

Exclude Ranges in a DHCP Scope

You may have certain addresses or a range of addresses within a DHCP scope that you do not want assigned. You can exclude those addresses so they are not used.

1. In either the Server Manager or the DHCP Console with DHCP Server IPv4 visible, in the console tree on the left, open IPv4; open the scope where you want the exclusions; right-click Address Pool; and click New Exclusion Range.

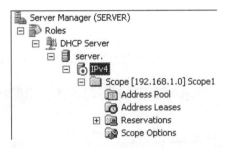

2. In the Add Exclusion dialog box, enter the IP addresses to exclude from the scope you are working on. These can be either a range, by entering a starting and ending address, or a single address, by entering it in just the Start IP Address box, as shown next. You should enter an exclusion for each static address that has been assigned to a server, workstation, or router.

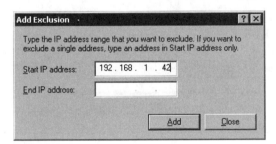

3. Click Add after entering each exclusion address or range. When you have entered all exclusions, click Close.

Set DHCP Lease Duration

DHCP address leases are for a fixed amount of time, which is set for a specific scope and is the days, hours, and minutes that a client can use an IP address assigned to it.

1. In either the Server Manager or the DHCP Console with DHCP Server IPv4 and the scope you want to set visible in the console tree, right-click the scope, and click Properties.

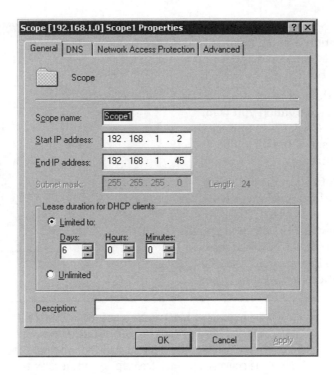

2. In the Scope Properties dialog box, under Lease Duration, enter or click the spinners for the days, hours, and minutes you want to allow a client use of an address.

    The default is 6 days, but the correct time for your operation could be anywhere from 1 hour for clients mainly jumping on and off a mail server, to 4 days for clients who are mainly traveling mobile-computer users, to Unlimited for clients in a stable desktop environment.

3. When you are ready, click OK to close the Scope Properties dialog box.

Reserve DHCP Addresses

If you want a client to have a particular and permanent IP address, you can configure that by creating a *reservation* that specifies an IP address to be assigned to the client. In this way, the IP address will not expire until the reservation is removed.

1. In the console tree under a DHCP scope, select Reservations, and click Add Reservations in the toolbar. The New Reservation dialog box opens.

2. Enter a name, an IP address, and the associated MAC physical address (you can get the MAC address from the Unique ID column shown on the list of Address Leases). Do not include the hyphens that are often used to display a MAC address (although they are not shown in the Unique ID column of the

list of Address Leases). Enter a Description if you want one, and leave the Supported Types as the default, Both.

3. Click Add and repeat the process for each reservation you want to make. Click Close to close the New Reservation dialog box when you're through.

4. Click Refresh in the toolbar. If Reservations is selected in the left pane of the DHCP window, your new reservation will appear on the right. Also, if you select Address Leases, you'll see the reservation in the list of leases.

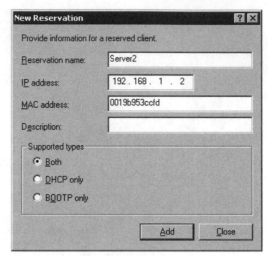

TIP Another way to get the physical or MAC address needed in Step 2 is to open the Command Prompt window (Start | Command Prompt) and type *ping* **ipaddress,** where ipaddress is either the numeric IP address or the computer name of the computer for which you need the MAC address, and press ENTER. Then, at the command prompt, type arp –a and press ENTER. The physical address will be displayed, as shown here:

```
Administrator: Command Prompt

C:\>ping server2

Pinging Server2 [fe80::658a:510f:235a:28bf%11] from fe80::
 with 32 bytes of data:
Reply from fe80::658a:510f:235a:28bf%11: time<1ms
Reply from fe80::658a:510f:235a:28bf%11: time<1ms
Reply from fe80::658a:510f:235a:28bf%11: time<1ms
Reply from fe80::658a:510f:235a:28bf%11: time<1ms

Ping statistics for fe80::658a:510f:235a:28bf%11:
    Packets: Sent = 4, Received = 4, Lost = 0 (0% loss),
Approximate round trip times in milli-seconds:
    Minimum = 0ms, Maximum = 0ms, Average = 0ms

C:\>arp -a

Interface: 192.168.1.35 --- 0xb
  Internet Address      Physical Address      Type
  192.168.1.1           00-a0-c5-42-b6-c8     dynamic
  192.168.1.33          00-01-03-21-99-ea     dynamic
  192.168.1.34          00-a0-d1-51-72-08     dynamic
  192.168.1.36          00-11-d8-0a-ce-9f     dynamic
  192.168.1.37          00-c0-a8-88-0a-6b     dynamic
  192.168.1.38          00-19-b9-53-cc-fd     dynamic
  192.168.1.39          00-0b-db-18-e1-ef     dynamic
```

Change DHCP Options

You can add to and change DHCP options at three levels:

▼ **Server level options**   Apply to all DHCP clients

■ **Scope level options**   Apply only to clients who lease an address from the scope

▲ **Client level options**   Apply to a client with a reservation

1. In the DHCP console tree, right-click Server Options and click Configure Options. The Server Options dialog box opens. Here you can make a number of settings that apply to all DHCP clients. For example, you can keep a list of DNS servers, as shown here:

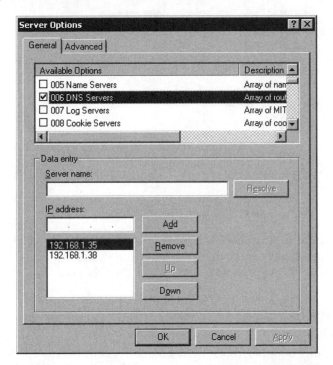

2. Click OK to close the Server Options dialog box, right-click Scope Options, and click Configure Options. You'll see a similar dialog box, called Scope Options, with a similar list of available options.

3. Click OK to close the Scope Options dialog box. If you previously created a reservation, open the Reservation object in the console tree, right-click a reservation in either the left or the right pane of the window, and click Configure Options, to get a third similar list of options.

4. Click OK to close the Reservation Options dialog box.

Monitor Address Leasing

You can monitor how the leasing operation is going to determine if DHCP is actually working and the usage of your scope.

1. In the DHCP console tree on the left in either the Server Manager or the DHCP Console, right-click the IPv4 server and click Display Statistics.

2. In the Server Statistics dialog box that opens, click Refresh to show the latest information. You can see how many requests there have been for IPv4 addresses, how many are in use, and what percentage of the scope that represents.

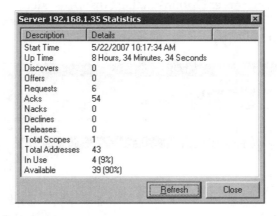

3. When you are ready, click Close.

Manage DNS

Managing DNS assumes that DNS has been installed on the server on which you want it to run. This should have been done earlier in this chapter, under "Install DNS and DHCP." As with DHCP, you manage DNS from the DNS console, which is opened in either of two ways:

▼ **From Server Manager**   Click Start | Server Manager. In the console tree on the left, open Roles | DNS Server | DNS | Server.

▲ **From Administrative Tools**   Click Start | Administrative Tools | DNS. In the DNS Manager window that opens, in the console tree, open Server.

The remaining steps in this section assume that you have Server opened under the DNS Server in either the Server Manager or the DNS Manager, as shown in Figure 6-9.

As was described earlier in "Understand the Domain Name System," the purpose of DNS is to be able to convert IP addresses and domain names, a part of which is a host name of a particular computer. To do this, DNS breaks the namespace into zones and provides for each zone a forward lookup table to resolve a domain/host name into an IP address and a reverse lookup table to resolve an IP address into a host/domain name. You can manually create and populate a DNS zone, or you can use Dynamic DNS to do that.

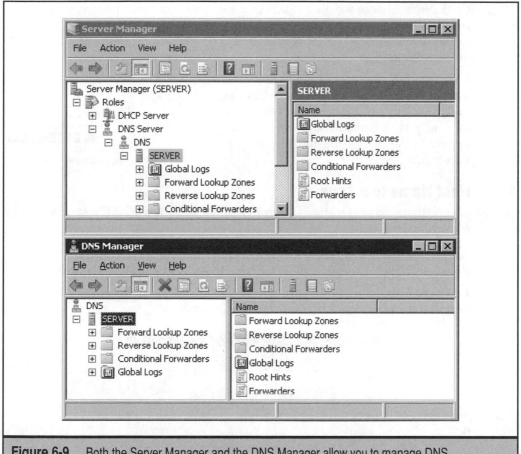

Figure 6-9.   Both the Server Manager and the DNS Manager allow you to manage DNS.

Create a New DNS Zone

Create a new DNS zone:

New Zone

1. Under the DNS Server, select Forward Lookup Zones, and click New Zone in the toolbar. The New Zone Wizard opens.

2. Click Next. Click the type of zone you want. Normally you want a primary zone on the computer you are working on.

3. Click Next. Enter a name for the zone. This may be contained in a domain, for example, *primary.mcgraw-hill.com*.

4. Click Next. Choose whether to create a new file or copy an existing one. Normally you want a new file.

5. Click Next. Choose whether to accept unsecured dynamic updates, or only more secure manual updates. Manual updating is the default, but shutting out dynamic updates takes away a good automation tool.

6. Click Next. A summary of your choices is displayed. If there are any errors, click Back and make any needed changes. When you are ready, click Finish. The new zone will appear in the console tree under Forward Lookup Zones.

Add a Host Name to a Zone

The initial zone that was just created is an empty database until you add hosts (computers on the network) to it.

1. Add a host name to a zone by right-clicking the zone in the console tree under Forward Lookup Zones and choosing New Host. The New Host dialog box opens.

2. Enter the host name and IP address, click Add Host, and then click OK when told that the host record was successfully created.

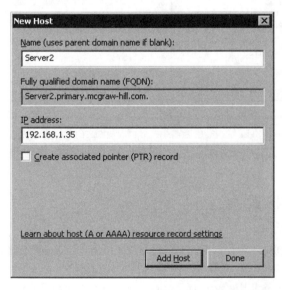

3. Repeat Step 2 for as many hosts as you want to enter. When you are finished adding hosts, click Done.

Set Up Reverse Lookup Zones

Reverse lookup zones, which allow the resolution of an IP number into a name, are only used in problem solving and by Internet Information Services (IIS) to add a name instead of an IP address in log files. To implement a reverse lookup capability, a special domain named In-addr.arpa is automatically created when DNS is set up. Within this domain, subdomains are defined for each *octet* or portion of an IP address between periods for the network portion of the address, and then *pointer* records are created for the final host portion of the address giving the host name and IP address. See how a reverse lookup zone is set up with these steps:

1. In the console tree on the left of either the Server Manager or the DNS Manager, right-click Reverse Lookup Zones and click New Zone. The New Zone Wizard appears. Click Next.

2. Accept the default of Primary Zone and click Next. Accept the default IPv4 Reverse Lookup Zone and click Next.

3. In the Network ID text box, enter the network portion of your IP address. For example, if your IP address range is 10.0.0.1 through 10.0.0.99 with a subnet mask of 255.255.255.0, then your network ID is 10.0.0.

4. Click Next. Accept Create A New File... and the inverted name, as shown next.

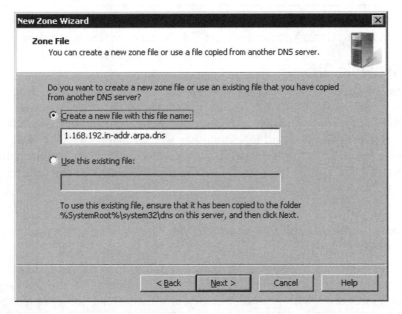

5. Click Next. Click Allow Both Nonsecure And Secure Dynamic Updates and click Next. Review the settings you've made. If you see something you want to change, click Back, make the change, return to the final screen, and click Finish.

6. Right-click the new Reverse Lookup Zone that was just created, and click New Pointer. The New Resource Record dialog box opens.

7. Enter the host portion (rightmost) of the IP address and the host name that corresponds with this.

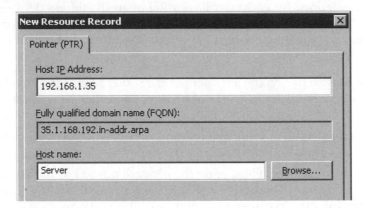

8. Click OK. Repeat Steps 6 and 7 as necessary to add additional pointers.

TIP You can automatically create pointer records every time you create a new Forward Lookup host record by clicking Create Associated Pointer (PTR) Record in the New Host dialog box.

Set Up Dynamic DNS

The process of adding hosts to a zone, while not terrible, is not something you want to do every time DHCP changes an address assignment. The purpose of dynamic DNS (DDNS) is to automatically update a zone host record every time DHCP makes a change. DDNS ties DHCP and DNS together so that when DHCP makes a change, it sends the information to the appropriate zone in DNS, which then reflects the change. Both DNS and DHCP must be correctly set for this to work. Use the following steps to do that:

1. In either the Server Manager or the DNS Manager under Forward Lookup Zones, right-click the zone to which you want to add DDNS, and click Properties.

2. In the General tab, opposite Dynamic Updates, open the drop-down list and click Nonsecure And Secure, if it isn't already selected. (If the DNS server has been integrated with Active Directory, you'll also have the option of Secure Only. Chapter 7 explains how you can click to allow only secure updates if you wish.)

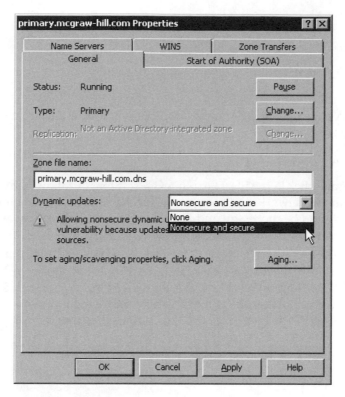

3. Click OK to close the zone's Properties dialog box.

4. In the Server Manager, in the console tree, under Roles open DHCP Server | Server | IPv4.

5. Right-click the scope that you want to tie to the DNS zone you have been working on and click Properties.

6. In the DNS tab, make sure Enable DNS Dynamic Updates... is checked and then click Always Dynamically Update DNS A And PTR Records.

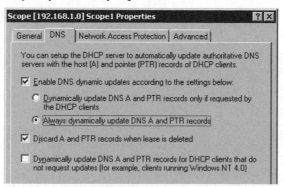

7. Click OK to close the Scope Properties dialog box. Close either the Server Manager or the DNS Manager, whichever you had open.

Test DNS

You can test to see whether DNS is working by doing the following:

▼ Trying to use it

■ Using a test facility in DNS

▲ Using Nslookup in the Command Prompt window, if you created a reverse lookup zone

Quickly try all three of these.

1. Click Start, click in the Start Search text box, type \\ followed by a computer name on the network, and press ENTER. If DNS and DHCP are working, the search should be successful and the computer found. Close the window that opened to show the network computer.

2. Open Server Manager | Roles | DNS Server | DNS, right-click the server within which you created a zone, and click Properties. Open the Monitoring tab, select both A Simple Query… and A Recursive Query…, and click Test Now. You should get test results at the bottom of the dialog box stating that both tests were passed. Close the Server Properties dialog box and the Server Manager.

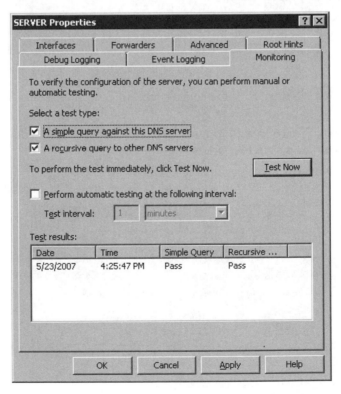

3. Click Start | Command Prompt, type **nslookup**, and press enter. If you created a reverse lookup zone that included the server, you get the name of the server and its IP address. Type a host name, press enter, and you get the full host name with its domain and its IP address. Type an IP address, and you get the full host name with its domain.

4. Type **Exit** and press enter to get out of Nslookup, and type **Exit** and press enter again to close the Command Prompt window.

NOTE Nslookup requires that you have a reverse lookup zone, which is one of the reasons for creating one.

Set Up Windows Internet Name Service

WINS has the same job as DNS: resolving or converting an easy-to-remember user-friendly name into an IP address, but is only needed if you have computers on your network with Windows versions prior to Windows 2000 (Windows 95, 98, Me, and NT). WINS utilizes the NetBIOS naming convention developed by IBM and Microsoft as part of an early networking scheme. NetBIOS, which operates at the Session (fifth) layer of the OSI networking model, normally interacts with NetBEUI at the Transport and Network layers of the OSI model (see Figure 6-10) and does so by converting a user-friendly name directly to

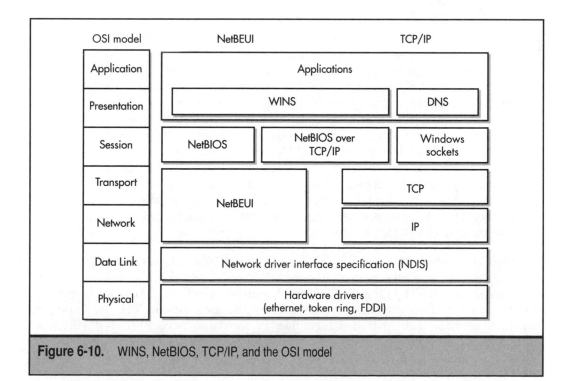

Figure 6-10.   WINS, NetBIOS, TCP/IP, and the OSI model

a physical (MAC) address. WINS, which like DNS is an application, maintains a database of NetBIOS names and their IP address equivalents. NetBIOS names using NetBIOS over TCP/IP, which calls on WINS, can then be used with TCP/IP in place of NetBEUI.

NOTE   Support for the NetBEUI protocol, which was used in communicating with earlier Microsoft networking systems, has been removed from Windows Server 2008.

WINS requires very little maintenance, initially building itself and maintaining itself as changes occur. You only need to turn it on and specify the server IP address in the clients. WINS, while still available in Windows Server 2008, has had its function largely usurped by DDNS, because DDNS is integrated into Active Directory, and because DNS offers security features that are not available in WINS. If your network has only Windows Server 2008 or Windows Server 2003 and Windows Vista and XP clients, you do not need WINS, because NetBIOS names are not used. If you have computers with earlier Windows operating systems (Windows 95, 98, Me, or NT) in your network, then WINS may be beneficial.

WINS can safely coexist with DNS, *if* you don't have security concerns about the WINS database being automatically created and updated, and if the integration with Active Directory is not important to you. In a shared environment, WINS handles the 16-character-maximum (the user can enter 15) single-part NetBIOS name used in all Microsoft operating systems up through Windows Me and NT 4, while DNS handles the multipart, 255-character-maximum domain name used in Windows Server 2008, Windows Vista, Windows Server 2003, and Windows XP.

NOTE   In smaller networks (having a practical maximum in the range of 35 to 50 computers, and an absolute maximum of about 70), you do not need to use either WINS or DNS. Each computer in the network periodically broadcasts to the other computers in the network for their NetBIOS names and their IP addresses and then stores this information in a working file on the computer making the initial request. This generates a lot of network traffic, and as the network grows, that traffic can be overpowering. You can reduce this traffic by manually creating and maintaining a static text file named Lmhosts (LM for LAN Manager, the original Microsoft networking system) that is checked before broadcasting on the network (search for Lmhosts.sam [it is probably in C:\Windows\ System32\ Drivers\Etc\], open it with Notepad, and follow the instructions at the beginning of the file to create it). Maintaining this file on a number of computers becomes a major chore and is the reason that WINS was developed. A similar static file, Hosts, can be used with DNS, but both of these text files are practical for only the smallest networks.

WINS, like DNS, resides on a server. To use it, a client queries the server with a NetBIOS name, and the server replies with an IP number for that name. When you set up a WINS server and start a client by giving it the server's address, the client automatically registers its name and IP address with the server. The server responds with the TTL, the amount of time it will maintain the registration. From then on, each time the client starts it will repeat this process, or if it is on for half of its TTL, it will automatically reregister its name.

Set Up WINS on a Server

Set up WINS on the server with these steps:

1. Click Start | Server Manager; in the tree on the left, right-click Features, and click Add Features. Scroll to the bottom of the list of features, click WINS Server, click Next, and click Install.

2. When you see Installation Successful, click Close.

3. In the Server Manager, open Features | WINS. Right-click Active Registrations, click Display Records, and then click Find Now at the bottom of the dialog box that opens. A list of NetBIOS names and IP addresses should be displayed, as shown here:

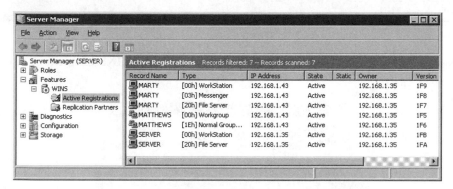

NOTE   It may take a while until the server finds the WINS clients, as much as half a day. The process proceeds much more quickly if you filter the clients you want by name or IP address in the Display Records dialog box.

4. If you have non-WINS clients, you can add static registrations for them by right-clicking Active Registrations and choosing New Static Mapping. The New Static Mapping dialog box opens.

5. Enter the computer name and the NetBIOS scope, if desired (the scope is an extension to the name used to group computers). Then click a type (see Table 6-1) and enter one or more IP addresses, as needed. When done, click OK to close the dialog box, and then close the WINS window.

Set Up WINS on Clients

Setting up a WINS client often is done on computers running something other than Windows Server 2008, Windows Vista, or Windows XP. The steps for doing that in Windows 98 are as follows:

1. Click Start | Control Panel, and double-click Network. The Network Properties dialog box opens.

2. Select TCP/IP for the network adapter and click Properties. The TCP/IP Properties dialog box opens.

Type	Explanation
Unique	A single computer with a single IP address
Group	A group name with only one IP address for the group
Domain Name	A domain name with up to 25 IP addresses for its members
Internet Group	A group name with up to 25 IP addresses for its members
Multihomed	A computer with up to 25 IP addresses for multiple NICs

Table 6-1. Types of Static WINS Registrations

3. Click the WINS Configuration tab and click Enable WINS Resolution. Enter the WINS server IP address and click Add.

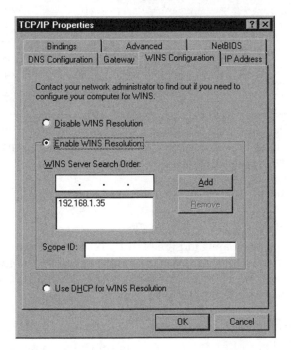

4. When you are done entering WINS servers, click OK twice to close all the open dialog boxes. Click Yes to restart your computer.

5. Repeat Steps 1–4 for each client on the network.

SET UP USER ACCOUNTS AND GROUP PERMISSIONS

To gain access to another computer or to other resources (such as a printer) on the network, a user must have been given permission to do so. Such permission begins with the user being a known entity by having a user account. You can have *local user* accounts, which provide access to one computer, and *domain user* accounts, which provide access to all the resources in the domain. Domain user accounts, as implemented by Active Directory, which can be very valuable and can provide the way to structure a network in many cases, are discussed in Chapters 7 and 15.

Instead of assigning permissions to individuals, you assign individuals to groups that have certain permissions. This section looks at setting up local user accounts, setting up groups, and assigning users to groups.

User accounts, groups, and permissions are an important part of network security, and the security aspects of these elements, such as password strategies, are discussed in Chapter 15. This section focuses on setting up the elements, not on how they should be used for security purposes.

NOTE If you are using or are going to use a domain, it is important to set up domain user accounts rather than local user accounts on computers within the domain. Local user accounts are not recognized by the domain, so a local user cannot use domain resources and a domain administrator cannot administer the local accounts.

Plan for Usernames and Passwords

Before setting up either domain or local user accounts, your organization should have a plan for the usernames and passwords that the company will use. The objectives are to be consistent and to use prudent practices. Here are some considerations:

▼ Are you going to use first name and last initial, first initial and last name, or full first and last names?

■ How, if at all, are you going to separate the first and last names? Many organizations don't use any separation, whereas others use either periods or the underscore.

■ How are you going to handle two people with the same first and last names? Adding a number after the name is a common answer; using the middle initial is another.

■ Do you need a special class of names, for example, for subcontractors in your organization? If so, how, if at all, do you want to differentiate them from other users? One method is to precede their names with one or more characters to indicate their position, such as "SC" for subcontractor.

■ Names must be unique, cannot be over 20 characters long (or 20 bytes long if a character takes over 1 byte), are not case-sensitive, cannot contain the @ character, and cannot consist solely of periods and/or spaces. Leading or trailing periods or spaces are ignored.

▲ Passwords must be unique; cannot be over 127 characters; can use both upper- and lowercase letters; should use a mixture of letters, numbers, and symbols; and should be at least 8 characters long.

TIP If your password is over 14 characters, you will not be able to log onto the network from a Windows 95/98/Me computer.

Set Up Local User Accounts

Windows Server 2008 and Windows Vista create several user accounts when installed, among which are two that initially are named Administrator and Guest. You can change the name and password for each of these accounts, but you cannot delete them. When you go through the installation of Windows Server 2008, as described in Chapters 2 and 3, you establish the initial password for the Administrator account, but all other account creation and maintenance is done outside Setup.

NOTE If your server is a domain controller (DC), you'll only be able to set up domain user accounts. Local user accounts can be created only on servers that are not DCs or on clients.

Follow these steps to see how local user accounts are set up (remember, if the server you are looking at is a domain controller, you will not be able to find the Local Users and Groups discussed in these steps):

1. Click Start | Server Manager, and, in the console tree, open Configuration | Local Users And Groups. Right-click Users and click New User. The New User dialog box opens.

2. Enter a User Name, Full Name, Description, and Password, as shown here. Select how you want to handle passwords, and click Create.

3. Repeat Step 2 for as many local users as you have. When you are done, click Close.

Set Up Groups and Their Members

Groups allow you to define what a particular type of user is allowed to do on the computer. Once you have done that, the users you have defined can be made members of these groups and will then have the same permissions as the groups to which they belong. Windows Server 2008 comes with a number of groups already defined, so the first step is to understand what those are. Then you can add one or more of your own groups.

1. In the Server Manager console tree, with Configuration and Local Users And Groups open, click Groups. The list of currently defined groups appears, as shown here:

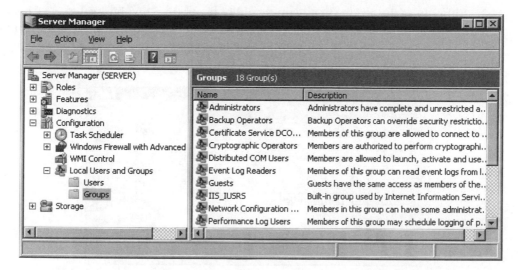

The standard set of groups provides a good spectrum of permissions, as you can see by reading the Description column in the Server Manager window.

2. Create a new group by right-clicking Groups in the left pane and choosing New Group. The New Group dialog box opens.

3. Enter the group name and a description, which should list the permissions the group has.

4. Click Add, and the Select Users dialog box opens. Either type the users you want to add in the lower text box, clicking Check Names after each entry, or click Advanced, click Find Now, select a name from the list, and click OK to transfer it to the list of names.

5. When you are done, click OK, click Create to create the new group, and click Close to close the New Group dialog box.

NOTE   Chapter 15 discusses in detail how to set permissions.

Add Users to Groups

Although you can add users to groups when you create the groups, you most often will add users to groups independently of creating groups, as follows (you should still have the Server Manager window open and Configuration | Local Users And Groups open in the console tree on the left):

1. Open Users by clicking it in the left pane, locate and right-click a user in the right pane whose group memberships you want to change, and click Properties. The user's Properties dialog box opens.

2. Click the Member Of tab, and click Add. The Select Groups dialog box opens.

3. Either type the groups you want to add in the bottom text box, selecting Check Names after each entry, or click Advanced, click Find Now, select a name from the list, and click OK to transfer it to the list of names, as shown next. When you have selected all the groups you want, click OK.

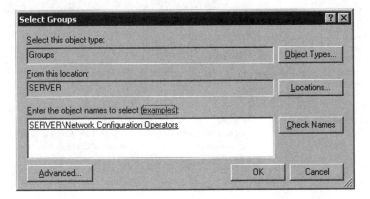

4. When you are done with the user account, click OK to close the Properties dialog box, and then click Close to close the Server Manager window.

The user's Properties dialog box contains several tabs not previously mentioned. These will be discussed in future chapters. Profile, for example, allows you to define a profile for a user so that when that user logs into a computer, the profile automatically sets up the desktop, menus, and other features for that user. It is discussed in Chapter 14. Another example is Dial-In, which sets up how a user will work with remote access and virtual private networking; it is the subject of Chapter 11.

Remember that local user accounts are limited to a single computer and cannot be centrally managed. The broader and more easily managed way to implement user accounts is with domains, which are discussed in Chapter 7.

CHAPTER 7

Using Active Directory and Domains

Probably the single biggest change in Windows 2000 over Windows NT was the addition of Active Directory (AD). In both Windows Server 2003 and Windows Server 2008, AD has been enhanced, making it an even more important part of the operating system. *Active Directory* provides a single reference, called a *directory service*, to all the objects in a network, including users, groups, computers, printers, policies, and permissions. For a user or an administrator, AD provides a single hierarchical view from which to access and manage all of the network's resources. AD utilizes Internet protocols and standards, including Kerberos, Secure Sockets Layer (SSL), and Transport Layer Security (TLS) authentication; the Lightweight Directory Access Protocol (LDAP); and the Domain Name Service (DNS). AD requires one or more domains in which to operate.

A *domain*, as used within Windows NT, 2000, and Windows Server 2003 and 2008, is a collection of computers that share a common set of policies, a name, and a database of their members. A domain must have one or more servers that serve as *domain controllers* and store the database, maintain the policies, and provide the authentication of domain logons. A *domain*, as used within the Internet, is the highest segment of an Internet domain name and identifies the type of organization; for example, *.gov* for government agencies, and *.net* for Internet service providers (ISPs). A *domain name* is the full Internet address used to reach one entity registered on the Internet. For example, www.mcgraw-hill.com or www.mit.edu.

THE ACTIVE DIRECTORY ENVIRONMENT

AD plays two basic functions within a network: that of a directory service containing a hierarchical listing of all the objects within the network, and that of an authentication and security service that controls and provides access to network resources. These two roles are different in nature and focus, but they combine together to provide increased user capabilities while decreasing administrative overhead. At its core, Windows Server 2008 AD is a directory service that is integrated with DNS, plus a user authentication service for the Windows Server 2008 operating system. This explanation, however, introduces a few new terms and involves a number of concepts.

While AD is both a directory and a directory service, the terms are not interchangeable. In Windows Server 2008 networking, a *directory* is a listing of the objects within a network. A hierarchical directory has a structure with a top-to-bottom configuration that allows for the logical grouping of objects, such that lower-level objects are logically grouped and contained in higher-level objects for as many levels as you want. This grouping can be based on a number of different criteria, but the criteria should be logical and consistent throughout the directory structure.

Two of the more common directory structures in use within networks are based on object function (such as printers, servers, and storage devices) and organizational responsibility (such as marketing, accounting, and manufacturing). The organizational model allows you to store objects in groups, or *containers*, based on where they are in an organization, which might have its own structure, such as departments within divisions.

A particular department would be the first organizational point within an organization. A container holding all the objects in a department is called an *organizational unit (OU)* and is itself grouped into higher-level OUs based on the logical structure.

After you create a group of OUs, you may find that the structure causes your directory to be cluttered and/or awkward to navigate. As a result, you may need to change your network to have more high-level OUs or more low-level OUs. At the top of all directories is the master OU that contains all the other OUs. This directory is referred to as the *root* and is normally designated by a single period. Such a hierarchical structure might look like this:

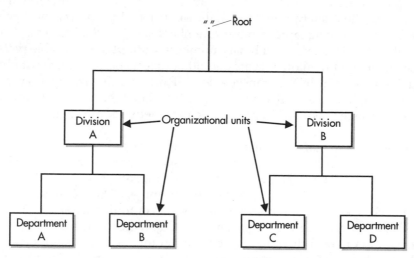

AD is just as basic as the organization just displayed. However, much of AD's core structure has already been mapped out by Microsoft and is consistent throughout all Windows Server 2008 implementations. For this reason, some of the containers, which are just OUs, have been assigned specific names and roles within AD. As this preconfigured directory structure is explained in the rest of the chapter, don't let the terms and names confuse you. Everything is still simply a collection of objects within OUs.

The "service" in "directory service" adds to a server features that are not otherwise available. Primarily, a directory service provides access to a directory of information, as well as to services that provide information about the location, access methods, and access rights for the objects within the directory service tree. This means that users can access a single directory and then be directly connected to a variety of other servers and services that appear to all be coming from the original directory. Much of this chapter discusses the different kinds of objects and methods of access that AD can provide to both users and administrators.

NOTE AD, Microsoft Exchange, and Novell Directory Services (NDS) are all based on the X.500 standard, which is an internationally recognized standard used to create a directory structure. Specifically, AD is based on the newer X.509 version of the X.500 family.

Integration with DNS

Much of AD's structure and services, as well as the namespace that it uses, are based on DNS (Domain Name System). (*Namespace* is the addressing scheme that is used to locate objects on the network. Both AD and the Internet use a hierarchical namespace separated by periods, as described earlier in this chapter.) How AD uses DNS will be discussed in a moment, but it is necessary to first look at the structure and workings of DNS and how it is used to build the AD foundation.

All servers and services on the Internet are given an Internet Protocol (IP) numerical address, and all Internet traffic uses this IP number to reach its destination. IP numbers change, and may host multiple services at the same time. In addition, most people have a hard time remembering large, arbitrary numbers such as IP addresses. IP addresses are decimal-based descriptions of binary numbers without a discernable pattern. DNS services were created to allow servers and other objects on the network to be given a user-friendly name, which DNS translates to an IP number. For example, a user-friendly name such as mail.mcgraw-hill.com might be translated, or *resolved*, in a DNS server to an IP address such as 168.143.56.34, which the network can then use to locate the desired resource.

DNS servers use hierarchical directory structures, just like the example described at the beginning of the chapter. At the core of DNS servers are root domains with a root directory, which is described by a single period. The first groups of OUs below the root are the various types of domains that can exist, for example, COM, NET, ORG, GOV, EDU, and so on. Over 250 of these top-level domains are controlled within the United States by InterNIC, an arm of the U.S. Department of Commerce, and run by a private, non-profit corporation named the Internet Corporation for Assigned Names and Numbers (ICANN), which controls a number of root servers that contain a listing of all the entries within each subdomain.

The next group of OUs following the ".COMs" consists of domain names, such as coke. com, microsoft.com, and mcgraw-hill.com. These domains are registered and administered by the organizations or individuals who own them. A number of companies have contracted with InterNIC/ICANN to register new domain names added to the Internet; you can see an alphabetical list of those companies at http://www.internic.com/alpha.html.

A domain name, such as mcgraw-hill.com, can contain both additional OUs, called *subdomains,* and actual server objects. In the example previously given, mail.mcgraw-hill.com, the mail server is an object in the mcgraw-hill.com domain. A server name such as mail.mcgraw-hill.com that contains all OUs between itself and the root is called a fully qualified domain name (FQDN). Figure 7-1 shows the name resolution process required when a client such as the one in the lower left of Figure 7-1 requests a DNS server to resolve an FQDN to an IP address by going up and back down the chain of DNS servers.

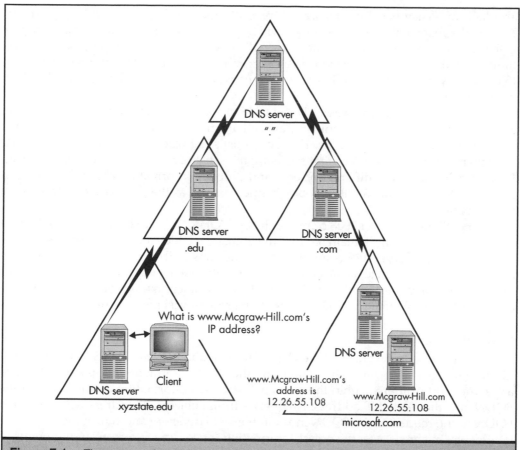

Figure 7-1.   The process of resolving a domain name to an IP address

Active Directory and Domains

AD and DNS share the same central OU, called a *domain*. For those familiar with Windows NT 4, Windows 2000, or Windows Server 2003, the domain concept should be a familiar one. A domain is a central authentication and directory service that contains all the information for a group of computers. NT 4 had a number of significant limitations in the utilization of domains. Primarily, domains were not actual directory servers, because they contained only users, groups, and computers in a nonhierarchical structure. Although all computers were able to use the central repository of information for authentication issues, the directory was not available for object location or resource management. In AD, the core features and look of legacy NT domains are still present, but they have been greatly extended. Among the many enhancements, which will be discussed over the course of this chapter, is the ability of AD domains to scale to virtually any size, as opposed to the 40,000-object limit placed on NT domain structures. Another enhancement is AD's ability to form transitive two-way trusts with other domains in the network (this will be discussed further, later in the chapter).

The close integration between AD and DNS can, at first, be a little confusing. Looking at AD and DNS, it is easy to think they are actually the same thing, because they use the same names and naming scheme. However, this is not true. In actuality, DNS and AD are separate directory services that are using the same names for different namespaces. Each directory contains different objects, and different information about the objects in its own database. However, those object names, as well as the directory structure, often are identical.

Every Windows Server 2008 computer has an FQDN. This is a combination of its own computer name and the domain name of the domain in which it currently resides. For example, Windows Server 2008 computers in the McGraw-Hill domain may very well have a computer name equal to *computername*.mcgraw-hill.com. However, that same computer may in fact be a member of the subdomain of editorial.mcgraw-hill.com. In this case, the computer's FQDN would actually be *computername*.editorial.mcgraw-hill.com.

DNS Directories

A DNS directory doesn't really store objects in its database. Rather, DNS stores domains, the access information for each domain, and the access information for the objects (such as servers and printers) within the domain. The access information is normally just the FQDN and the related IP address. All queries for an object's IP address will match the FQDN in the request to the FQDN index in the DNS directory and return (*resolve to*) the IP address. In some cases, the access information (or *resource reference*) simply points to another object (or *resource*) within the same or a different DNS domain.

A standard DNS domain is not capable of reversing this process by returning an FQDN when provided with an IP address. To make this kind of resolution possible, a reverse lookup zone is required, as discussed in Chapter 6. These domains are referenced as "in-addr-arpa" domains within the DNS hierarchy.

Among the other special functions of DNS that add features to a network is the Mail Exchanger reference that can be added to a DNS domain name. A Mail Exchanger reference (referred to as MX) enables mail servers to locate the mail servers of other domains to allow for the transferring of e-mail across the Internet.

Active Directory Services

AD services contain a lot more information than what is available in DNS directories, even though the names and structure are nearly identical. AD resolves all information requests for objects within its database using LDAP queries. The AD server is able to provide a varied amount of information about each object within its database. The information that AD can provide includes, but isn't limited to, the following:

▼   Username

■   Contact information, such as physical address, phone numbers, and e-mail address

■   Administrative contacts

■   Access permissions

■   Ownerships

▲   Object attributes, such as object name features; for example, Color Laser Jet Printer, 20 sheets per minute, duplex printing

Although DNS does not require AD, AD requires a DNS server to be in place and functioning correctly on the network before a user will be able to find the AD server. With Windows Server 2003 moving entirely to Internet standards for its network operating system (carried forward by Windows Server 2008), a method of locating network services had to be found other than using the NetBIOS broadcasts used in Windows NT. This was done through the use of a new DNS domain type known as *dynamic DNS (DDNS)* domains. A DDNS domain, which is integrated into AD, allows all domain controllers to use the same database, which is automatically updated as new Windows Server computers are added and removed from the network. The DDNS domain also allows DNS to function with networks based on DHCP (Dynamic Host Configuration Protocol), where the IP addresses of the network objects are constantly changing. Besides providing the name resolution for the network, the DDNS domains also contain a listing of all the domains and domain controllers throughout the network. This means that as new Windows Server systems are added to a network, they will query the DDNS servers to get the name and connection information, including IP address, of the domain controllers they are closest to.

NOTE   In Windows NT installations, Windows Internet Name Service (WINS) servers provided new workstations with the location of the domain controllers. To allow for compatibility with Windows 3.11, Windows 95, and Windows 98 workstations not running the AD client, WINS servers are still required on the network. Windows Server 2003 and 2008 and Windows 2000 servers as well as legacy NT servers have the ability to host WINS services and integrate them with DNS.

Active Directory and the Global DNS Namespace

AD domains are designed and intended to exist within the naming scheme of the global DNS domain operated through the Internet. This means that, by design, the DNS domain of your network would also match the AD domain-naming scheme. In some organizations, migration from a legacy NT local area network (LAN) is difficult, because independent LAN and Internet domains are already in place and entrenched. In this case, DDNS servers can be used for the LAN AD domain and hosted on internal DNS servers.

The external servers providing Internet web hosting services, such as the Simple Mail Transfer Protocol (SMTP) and the Hypertext Transfer Protocol (HTTP), would still use the Internet DNS structure and provide the necessary resource mapping in each domain to allow for coexistence, as shown here:

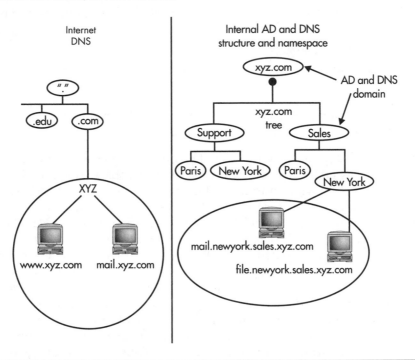

NOTE   The functions provided by a DDNS domain that are required for AD are the listing of the domain information and the location of the domain servers. These functions are provided by a resource object called a Service Location Resource (SRV). SRVs are not unique to Windows DDNS domains, and therefore some third-party DNS server products work with AD. However, configuring these third-party DNS servers to integrate with AD can be a significant undertaking.

INSTALL ACTIVE DIRECTORY

There are two ways to install AD: adding it to an existing domain, or forming a new domain. (For those a little more familiar with AD, some issues regarding forests and trees are affected here, as well, but those will be discussed later in the chapter.) Installing AD on a server turns the server into a *domain controller*, a server that hosts a central database of all users and groups within the domain and manages all domain-related functions, such as user logon authentication and trust relationships. This process can be done on existing NT servers or on Windows Server 2008, Windows Server 2003, or Windows 2000 AD servers. Windows 2000 was the first Windows platform that allowed for the promotion of member servers to domain controllers. If a domain contains multiple AD servers, then the AD services can be removed from a domain controller, and the server can be returned to a standard member server within the domain.

When installing AD into an existing legacy NT-based domain, the primary domain controller (PDC) of the domain has to be a Windows Server 2008, Windows Server 2003, or Windows 2000 server running AD. This is obviously only an issue in cases in which Windows Server 2008, Windows Server 2003, or Windows 2000 and legacy NT domain controllers exist in the domain (called a mixed-mode network). In cases where you are installing the first AD server in an existing legacy domain, the existing PDC will have to be upgraded to Windows Server 2008, Windows Server 2003, or Windows 2000, and then AD can be added. A Windows Server 2008, Windows Server 2003, or Windows 2000 server can exist without AD in an NT legacy domain, but before AD can be added, the PDC has to be upgraded to Windows Server 2008, Windows Server 2003, or Windows 2000.

TIP   In some cases, adding a new domain controller with no services other than the NT domain functions is advisable to make the upgrade as smooth as possible. This domain controller can then be upgraded to assume the role of PDC in the legacy domain. With this migration complete, the existing servers can be migrated in any manner, including reformatting and reloading the hard drive, that is advisable. Some companies, such as Hewlett-Packard, Dell, and IBM, have automated Windows Server 2003 and Windows 2000 (and probably Windows Server 2008 shortly) installation CDs for many of their servers, which will automatically load the correct drivers for their system's hardware. The extra domain controller can be removed from the network later or can be used to replace one of the existing domain controllers.

To install AD on Windows Server 2008, use the AD Domain Services Installation Wizard, which appears automatically if you are upgrading a domain controller, or it can be started after using Add Roles in the Server Manager (see "Install Server Roles" in Chapter 3) when you choose to make the server a domain controller and install AD. In the AD Installation wizard, you are asked if you want to create a new domain or add a domain controller to an existing domain, as shown in Figure 7-2.

CAUTION   Computers running Windows 95 or Windows NT 4 SP3 and earlier will no longer be able to log onto a Windows Server 2008 domain controller or to access domain resources unless you install the Active Directory client for those systems.

NOTE   Active Directory clients for Windows 95, Windows 98, and early versions on Windows NT 4 are available for download on the Microsoft web site on pages for the various operating systems.

When installing into an existing domain, your administrative rights on the domain will be checked. It is possible to have administrative rights on the server being upgraded but to not have sufficient rights on the domain and domain controllers to do the installation. After you install the AD service, you do the remaining configuration through the AD Users And Computers, AD Sites And Services, and AD Domains And Trusts, the first two of which are available in the console tree of the Server Manager, and all three can be opened, as shown in Figure 7-3, from Start | Administrative Tools.

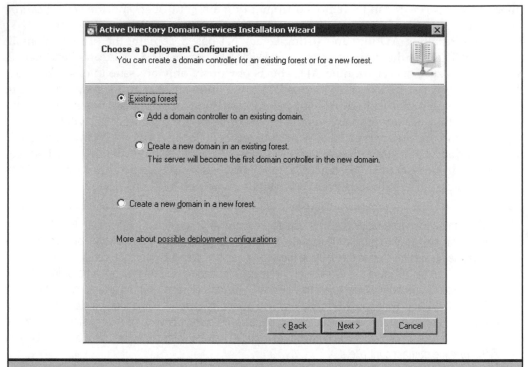

Figure 7-2.   Determine whether to create a new domain in a new forest, a new domain in an existing forest, or to add a domain controller to an existing domain

Replace Existing Domain Controllers

Windows Server 2008 servers functioning in native domains (domains that contain only Windows Server 2008 domain controllers) act as peers with all members containing the AD services database with equal read/write privileges. In legacy NT domains, only the PDC contains the master, read/write copy of the domain's directory store. All the other domain controllers in NT domains, referred to as *backup domain controllers (BDCs)*, contain read-only copies of the domain directory information store. BDCs are able to authenticate users and provide domain information, but all additions and modifications to the existing data have to be made to the PDC. When installed in mixed mode, an AD server will still respond to Remote Procedure Calls (RPCs) as if it were a PDC and then replicate directory changes to the legacy BDCs. This means that all remaining legacy domain controllers do not recognize that there have been any major modifications to the network. In Windows 2000 domains, all domain controllers act as peers, with all members containing the AD services database with equal read/write privileges similar

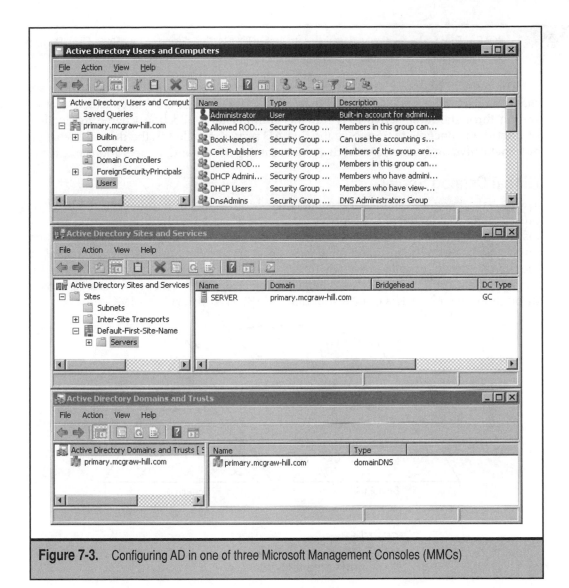

Figure 7-3.   Configuring AD in one of three Microsoft Management Consoles (MMCs)

to Windows Server 2003 and 2008. But if you mix Windows 2000 with Windows Server 2003 and 2008 domain controllers in the same forest, they will operate as if they are all Windows 2000 domain controllers, and several of the AD improvements in Windows Server 2003 and 2008 will not be available. When all Windows 2000 domain controllers have been upgraded to Windows Server 2003 or 2008, the functionality level can be advanced to the newer version, providing access to all the new features.

NOTE There are read-only domain controllers (RODCs) by design. See "Read-Only Domain Controllers" later in the chapter for more information.

The method of operation used by AD is that of *multimaster replication,* which means that changes can be made to any AD server and those changes will be replicated to other servers throughout the network. Within this multimaster replication scheme are a couple of important concepts that involve the first AD server installed in the domain, which is automatically configured to be both a global catalog server and an operations master.

Global Catalog Server

The global catalog is a database type that is at the core of the directory services. The *global catalog* contains a listing of the services that can be accessed within the network, and not just the local domain. The global catalog can be kept on multiple domain controllers, but it always has to be installed on at least once, and by default it is always created on the first AD server installed in a new forest. (The forest concept is explained later in the chapter.) The configuration of the global catalog and its placement on various servers throughout the network is done through the AD Sites And Services MMC.

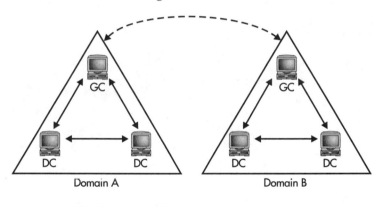

DC = Domain controller
GC = Global catalog
—— = Domain directory replication
– – = Global catalog replication

TIP When operating in mixed mode, all domain controllers can perform user logins independently. However, when operating in native mode, a query to a global catalog server is required (because it determines a user's global group memberships). Therefore, the rules for installing multiple global catalogs within a network are very similar to those for installing additional BDCs to an NT 4 domain. When installing multiple distant sites, having a global catalog server in each site will decrease the network load on WAN links otherwise used to provide user authentication. Additionally, having multiple global catalog servers to distribute the network load of authentication traffic evenly across multiple servers, instead of stacking this load onto a single server to handle, is much more efficient. Of course, the need for additional global catalog servers increases the network bandwidth consumed for directory synchronization.

In general, the global catalog servers within a network provide two main features: logon and querying. When operating a domain in native mode, universal groups are allowed to exist within the forest. Because universal groups can contain users and groups from multiple domains, the universal group cannot exist within an individual domain. Therefore, the global catalog maintains the universal groups within the network as well as each group's memberships. In Windows 2000 domains, this means that whenever operating a network in native mode, the AD server logging a user into the network has to query a global catalog server to determine the universal group memberships that the user may be a part of. In cases in which a user logs in and a global catalog server is not available, the user will be granted access only to the local computer. This avoids any potential security issues in which a global group based in the domain granted a user access to a resource that the universal group excluded the user from gaining access to. In case of an emergency, however, any user account that is a member of the local domain's Domain Admin group will be allowed to log into the network. In Windows Server 2008, domain controllers can cache universal group memberships that they have looked up on a global catalog server during user logon, so the next time a universal group member logs in through a particular domain controller, the membership can be confirmed locally. This both reduces network traffic and provides confirmation when the global catalog server is down.

The second major feature provided by the global catalog, querying, is a little more obvious. A large network may have numerous domains that all exist together. In this case, the global catalog provides a single place for all of the network's users to reference whenever searching for specific resources. The alternative to the global catalog in this instance would be the requirement for each user either to know the exact location of the resources the user wants to use, or to search each domain independently. The querying feature of AD provides another main reason to have multiple global catalog servers throughout a network.

Operations Master

The second main service added to the first AD server within a network is the operations master. Within Windows Server 2008 domains, there is a need to centralize some changes to the directory services. Even though AD is based on the multimaster replication model, and all domain controllers are peers within Windows Server 2008, there are still some changes that can cause too many issues if configured from multiple locations. For this reason, only one Windows Server 2008 domain controller within any forest and within any domain is assigned to become the operations master for that domain or forest. For domain operations, three roles are assigned to the domain's operations master:

- ▼ **PDC emulator**   Looks like a PDC to legacy network members in a mixed-mode network

- ■ **Relative ID master**   Assigns blocks of security IDs to the other domain controllers in a network

- ▲ **Infrastructure master**   Updates the other domain controllers for changes in usernames and group-to-user references

A forest has only two roles that are assigned to the forest's operations master:

▼ **Domain naming master**   Adds and removes domains in a forest

▲ **Schema master**   Updates the directory schema and replicates that to the other domain controllers in a forest

UNDERSTAND ACTIVE DIRECTORY STRUCTURE AND CONFIGURATION

An AD network contains a number of objects in a fairly complex structure and can be configured in several ways. This section focuses on some of the main objects in Active Directory, as well as some of the basic configuration involved with each of these objects as follows:

▼ AD objects and what they do

■ Domains, trees, forests, and the other OUs within AD

▲ Sites and site-based replication

Active Directory Objects

An *object* within AD is a set of attributes (name, address, and ID) that represents something concrete, such as a user, printer, or application. Like DNS, AD groups and lists these objects in OUs, which are then grouped into other OUs until you reach the root. Also, like DNS, AD then provides access to and information about each of these different objects. As a directory service, AD maintains a list of all objects within the domain and provides access to these objects either directly or through redirection. The focus of this section is the foundation and structure of the objects in AD. By recalling the differences between AD and DNS and the objects that they contain, you can appreciate the wide variety of objects allowed in directory services. In the case of AD and the other X.500-based directory services, the creation and use of this variety of objects is governed by the schema used in the directory.

Schema

The *schema* defines the information stored and subsequently provided by AD for each of its objects. Whenever an object is created in AD, the object is assigned a globally unique identifier, or GUID, which is a hexadecimal number unique to the object. A GUID allows an object's name to be changed without affecting the security and permissions assigned to the object, because the GUID is still the same. Once the object is created, AD uses the schema to create the fields defined for the object, such as phone number, owner, address, description, and so forth. The information for each of these fields is supplied by the administrator or a third-party application pulling the information from a database or preexisting directory structure, such as Microsoft Exchange.

NOTE   For reverse-compatibility reasons, support for security identifiers (SIDs), NT 4's version of GUIDs, is also maintained within AD.

Add to the Base Schema

Because the schema provides the rules for all objects within AD, you'll eventually need to extend the default object classes that come standard within AD. One of the first times this will happen is when a mail server is added to the network, which will require that mail-specific attributes be added to the AD schema. This addition may also require that new object classes be created. The process of adding classes and attributes is done by modifying or adding to the AD schema. The modification of the schema takes place using an automated installation function that affects the schema for the entire network. Schema updates cannot be reversed, so always exercise caution when updating the schema.

TIP   It is possible to modify the schema through the Active Directory Service Interface (ADSI) and by using the LDAP Data Interchange Format utility. It is also possible to modify the schema directly by using the AD Schema tool. These programs should be used only by AD experts and should always be tested in a lab environment before being implemented on production servers.

Publish Items to the Directory

On the surface, Windows Server 2008 functions very much like legacy NT-based products, especially in its sharing and security functions. When an item is shared or a new resource is added to Windows Server 2008, such as a printer, the object is shared and secured using nearly the same process as with legacy NT servers. Additionally, not all Windows NT-based servers may become AD servers. With these two facts in mind, some method is needed to distribute information about objects hosted on Windows Server 2008 servers throughout the network into AD. This process is called *publishing*. When an object is published in AD, information about the resource is added to AD, and users are then able to access that resource through AD. The main benefit provided by publishing is that it allows large networks with resources hosted by servers throughout their various sites to all share their information from a central point on the network. Users within the network can access the AD servers and search for, locate, and access the resources they need through the single entry point of AD.

Some objects are added to AD automatically, such as user, group, and server objects. However, some objects have to be published in AD by an administrator. The two most common items that most administrators will find themselves adding to AD are directories and printers.

Directory Publishing   To add a directory to AD, the directory or folder must first be created in Windows Explorer or Computer and secured using the Sharing and Security tabs in the directory's Properties dialog box, as shown next. This security has to include both share-level security and the NTFS permissions associated with the directory and all of the files and subdirectories within that share.

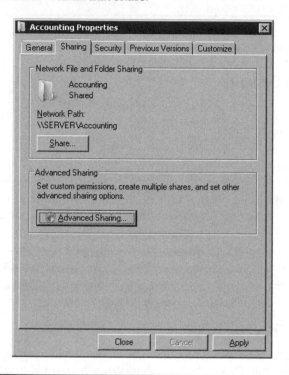

TIP With the advent of AD, new methods of organizing and providing access to network resources have been added to the network administrator's tools. However, the methods for administering network security that were used with Windows NT are still very much in effect.

Printer Publishing   Publishing a printer in AD is a simple process that provides several new features that were not available prior to Windows 2000. Primarily, when a number of printers exist within an AD network, users within that network can search for printers according to specific features, such as color, resolution, or duplexing.

To publish a printer in AD, the printer must first be installed and configured to function on the print server in question. (The print server in this case can be any Windows Server 2008, Windows Server 2003, or Windows 2000 Server or any Windows Vista, XP, or 2000 Professional computer to which a printer is attached.) After a printer is configured, is shared, and has the proper security set (see Chapter 13 for details on how to do this), it is ready to be published in AD. In fact, the default action taken by a Windows Server 2008/2003/2000/Vista/XP print server is to publish any printer automatically after it has been installed and shared. Once published, the printer can then be managed and accessed through all AD servers within the domain, and it is automatically included in the global catalog for the other domains within the forest.

In some cases, especially domains still running in mixed mode, non-Windows Server 2008/2003/2000/Vista/XP print servers may be hosting printers that are of significant importance to the domain. In this case, an object can be added to the AD domain by using the URL of the printer share. This can be accomplished using the AD Users And Computers MMC, selecting the domain, and choosing Action | New | Printer (shown next).

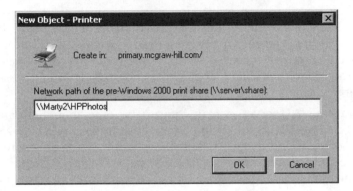

 NOTE Resources shared on the network should not always be published in AD. Only objects used by a large part of the network or that need to be available for possible searches should be published. Publishing objects in AD increases the domain's replication traffic that is necessary to ensure all AD servers have the most recent information. In large networks with multiple domains, the replication traffic to synchronize the global catalog servers for each domain can be overwhelming if poorly planned.

The Structure of Active Directory

There are various OUs within AD that have very specific roles within the network. These roles are established via the schema. To administer and configure an AD network, you need to understand what each of these OUs is and the role that each plays within the network.

Active Directories are made up of one or more domains. When the first AD server is installed, the initial domain is created. All AD domains map themselves to DNS domains, and DNS servers play a crucial role within any AD domain.

Domains

Domains are at the core of all Windows NT/2000/Windows Server 2003/2008-based network operating systems. This section looks at the structure of domains within AD, as well as the various factors involved in creating multiple domains within a network.

Domains in AD delineate a partition within the AD network. The primary reason for creating multiple domains is the need to partition network information. Smaller networks have very little need for more than one domain, even with a network spread across multiple physical sites, since domains can span multiple Windows Server 2008 sites.

(The site concept is covered in more detail later in this chapter.) However, there are still reasons to use multiple domains within a network:

▼ **Provide network structure** Unlike in legacy NT domains, there is no real limit to the number of objects that can be added to an AD domain running in native mode. For this reason, most networks do not need to establish separate domains for each business unit. However, in some very large networks, various political factors may necessitate multiple domains. For example, one company may own several subsidiary companies that are completely autonomous from the parent company. A central AD shared between the companies provides numerous benefits; a shared domain may not make as much sense. In this case, a separate domain can be set up for each company.

■ **Replication** AD servers contain information only about their own domain. Global catalog servers are required to publish information between domains for user access. This means that all objects within a domain are replicated to all the other domain controllers, but external resources are replicated only between global catalog servers. In large networks spread across multiple WAN links, each physical site should be its own domain, to ensure that unnecessary replication traffic does not consume the limited bandwidth of the WAN links.

■ **Security and administration** Although AD provides the appearance of a central network infrastructure to the users of the network, administrative abilities and user permissions will not cross domain partitions. This limitation is overcome through the use of global and universal groups and trust relationships, but domains are truly separate administrative groups that may or may not be linked together.

▲ **Delegation of administration** Although the delegation of administrative authority throughout the network makes multiple domains easy to handle, and Windows Server 2008 provides a number of administrative tools, there still may be benefits for some networks in splitting domains along the lines of administrative authority and responsibility.

Forests

Besides domains, AD is composed of forests, trees, and other custom OUs. Each of these OUs exists on a specific level of AD's hierarchy, beginning with the uppermost container, forests. A *forest* is the highest OU within the network and can contain any number of trees and domains. All domains within a forest share the same schema and global catalog. In essence, forests are similar to DNS's root container. Most organizations implementing AD will have only one forest; in fact, smaller organizations that have only one domain may not even realize the existence of the forest, because all functions appear to exist on the domain level only. In effect, the forest is used as the main directory for the entire network. The forest encompasses all the trees, domains, and other OUs, as well as all the published information for all the objects in the forest, as you can see next:

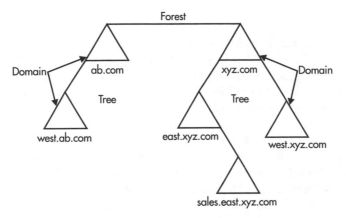

Domains within a forest are automatically configured with two-way transitive trusts. A *trust relationship* allows two domains to share user and group resources so that users authenticated by a "trusted" domain can access resources on the "trusting" domain. *Transitive trusts,* shown in Figure 7-4, allow user accounts within a domain to use a second domain's trust relationships to access resources in a third domain. Legacy NT domains did not support transitive trust relationships. In Figure 7-4, a user account from Domain A is able to access resources in Domain C because both Domains A and C have established transitive trust relationships with Domain B. If Figure 7-4 were illustrating a legacy NT domain, a trust relationship would have to be directly established between Domains A and C before the resources could be accessed.

Creating additional forests in a network should be undertaken with great care. The additional forests can cause a tremendous amount of administrative overhead, especially when adding AD-aware messaging platforms, such as Exchange. Other than the obvious political issues, there are very few reasons for any one network to have multiple forests.

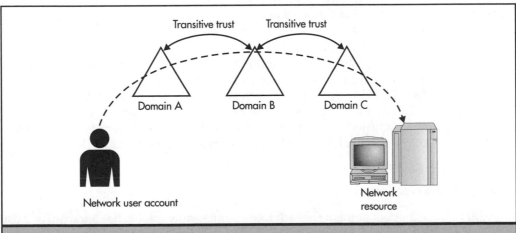

Figure 7-4. Transitive trust relationships allow Domain A to access resources in Domain C

Trees

Within AD, trees are used more for administrative grouping and namespace issues than anything else. Basically, a *tree* is a collection of domains that share a contiguous namespace and form a hierarchical environment. For example, it is possible for an organization such as Microsoft to split its DNS structure so that the Microsoft.com domain name is not the primary name used in e-mails and resource references. For instance, assume that Microsoft is split geographically first, so that there is a West Coast OU and an East Coast OU within the Microsoft domain, and that these OUs (or child domains) each contain a tree of further divisions, such as Sales and Tech Support, which could be further split into Operating Systems and Applications. In this example, so far, Microsoft would have two trees within its DNS structure, West Coast and East Coast. Both of these domains are then split further still, creating a potential FQDN of a server within the technical support department as follows:

```
ServerName.OperatingSystems.TechSupport.WestCoast.Microsoft.Com
```

The entire discussion of trees within AD so far has focused entirely on DNS, since AD has to match the DNS domain structure in the network, although the directory services contained by the two services are independent. In cases in which an organization has decided to implement multiple domains, and those multiple domains exist within a contiguous DNS naming scheme, as previously outlined, the network will have formed a tree connecting the multiple domains. Because the DNS requirements to host such a domain are very large, most organizations implementing trees host the DNS services for the tree internal to the network only and maintain a separate DNS substructure for Internet hosting services.

All domains within a tree are linked by two-way transitive trust relationships, although the domains are independent. Domains within a tree, just like domains within a forest, share a trust relationship and a namespace (in the case of a tree, it's a contiguous namespace), but the independence and the integrity of each domain remain unchanged. Administration of each domain, as well as directory replication of each domain, is conducted independently, and all information shared between the domains is done through the trust relationships and the global catalog.

When there are multiple trees within a forest, it is possible for each tree to maintain its own independent naming scheme. Looking at the Microsoft example, if you move up the DNS hierarchy, the Microsoft forest may very well include both MSN.com and Microsoft.com. In this case, there is no clear upper layer to the AD domain structure.

The first domain created in the forest is called the *forest root domain*. Two default groups exist within the entire forest, and they exist within the forest root domain:

▼ Enterprise Administrators

▲ Schema Administrators

Additionally, the root domain for each tree automatically establishes a transitive trust relationship with the forest root domain. This relationship is highlighted in Figure 7-5, which

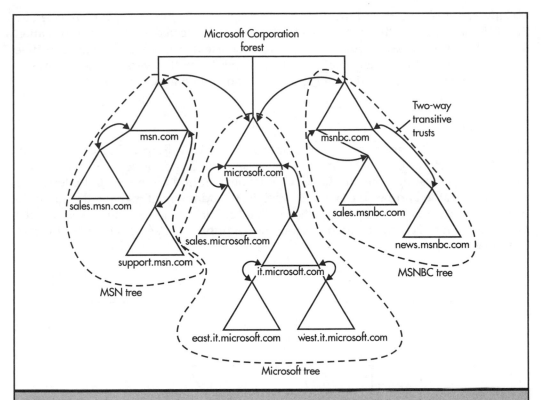

Figure 7-5.   Transitive trust relationships among trees in a hypothetical Microsoft forest

is based on the hypothetical Microsoft AD structure. In this example, a third domain is added, MSNBC.com, to further highlight the transitive trusts that are formed throughout the network. Microsoft.com is the forest root domain in this example.

> **TIP**   Domains cannot be moved between forests and cannot be removed if they contain child domains. Therefore, it is best to plan the entire AD network from top to bottom, before the first AD is installed. A little time spent planning can save a lot of time improvising.

Shortcut Trusts

The transitive trust relationships that exist between domains in AD forests can be a very tricky subject. Specifically, the overhead and time involved using the transitive trust relationships to pass all authentication requests throughout a network can sometimes be tremendous. Looking back to the Microsoft example and Figure 7-5, assume that the users who exist in the Microsoft IT group are always logging into the News.MSNBC .com domain to fix some problems. This means that all login traffic is first passed up the

MSNBC.com tree, and then down the Microsoft.com tree, before being authenticated by the IT domain. In cases like these, a *shortcut trust* can be created to pass the information directly between the two domains in question. Shortcut trusts are one-way transitive trusts that are used for authentication in large networks with diverse tree structures. A modified version of the forest from Figure 7-5 is shown in Figure 7-6, with the necessary shortcut trust added.

Other OUs

OUs are simply containers in which multiple objects and additional OUs can be stored. Within AD, some of these OUs are predefined and serve specific roles within the network, such as creating domains. Other OUs revolve around the needs and interests of the administrator, and not those of AD. Within AD, administrators have the ability to create their own AD structure below the OUs that are predefined or that serve a specific role. These other OUs can be used to group users, printers, or servers together for ease of administration.

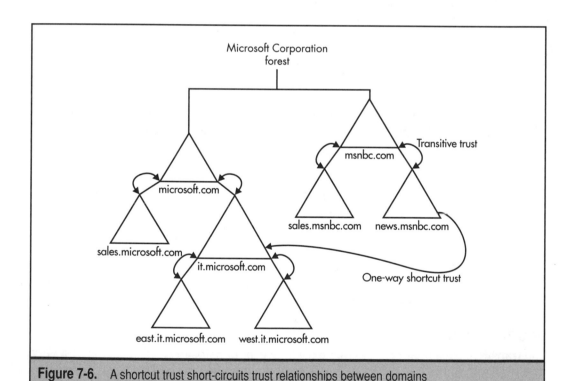

Figure 7-6.   A shortcut trust short-circuits trust relationships between domains

There aren't a lot of rules on the creation of OUs within AD, so instead you must rely on general guidelines and practical uses. Initially, recall that users have the ability to search AD for the resources they need to use. This searching function allows users to indicate the specific resource or type of resource they want to locate, so this should be considered the primary means by which most users will operate with AD. Therefore, administrative needs rather than user needs can determine the creation of OUs. Group policies can be set in OUs that allow the administrator to customize the desktop and permissions of the users and resources within that container. Likewise, giving permission to an entire OU allows an administrator to easily delegate to others administrative rights to specific objects within the domain without compromising the security of the overall network.

Sites

Domains are at the root of the directory services in Windows Server 2008. Everything within AD is simply a collection of one or more domains. Even with the fundamental role of domains defined, many issues still need to be addressed. For example, how is inter-domain synchronization handled within small and large domains? How does a large domain span multiple physical networks? How is inter-domain replication traffic controlled? For the answers to all of these questions, a new concept needs to be introduced. Windows Server 2008 domains can be divided into units called *sites*. Sites can be used to regulate replication traffic across slower WAN links and can use various connection methods and replication schedules to ensure a minimal network overhead bandwidth. In general, sites provide a number of basic services for Windows Server 2008 networks, including:

▼ Minimizing the bandwidth used for inter-site replication

■ Directing clients to domain controllers in the same site, where possible

■ Minimizing replication latency for intra-site replication

▲ Allowing the scheduling of inter-site replication

In general, sites are not related to domains, even though they provide a solution to many of the issues faced by domains previously listed. Sites map to the physical layout of the network, such as offices, floors, and buildings, whereas a domain's layout can be affected by everything from the physical structure to the political structure to the administrative needs of a network. Organizations should split a domain into multiple sites whenever the network will span a connection that is less than LAN speed, which has been 100 Mbps, but increasingly is 1,000 Mbps. Because most WAN connections will be routed, a separate IP subnet should exist on both sides of the WAN connection. For this reason, Microsoft has mapped most site discrimination to IP subnets. Officially, a site is a collection of "well-connected" (meaning LAN speed or better) Windows Server 2008 systems on the same IP subnet. Sites are managed and created using the AD Sites And Services console.

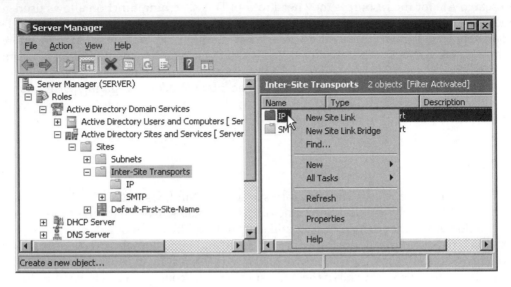

REPLICATE ACTIVE DIRECTORY AMONG SITES

In AD, *replication* means the copying of directory information among domain controllers so that they all have the same information and any of the domain controllers can be queried with the same results. Within an AD domain, four main categories of information require replication: configuration, schema, domain, and global catalog information. Each of these categories is stored in separate directory partitions. These partitions are what each AD server replicates and are used by different servers throughout the forest depending on their role within the network. The following three partitions are held by all the AD servers in a forest:

▼ **Configuration data partition** Holds information stored and used by AD-aware applications and is replicated across all domains in the forest.

■ **Schema data partition** Holds the definitions of the different types of objects, as well as their allowable attributes, and is replicated across all domains in the forest.

▲ **Domain data partition** Holds information unique to the domain in which the server resides. It contains all the objects in the directory for the domain and is replicated only within the domain. The data in this partition is not replicated between domains and will differ greatly from domain to domain.

The fourth type of partition is used by global catalog servers to allow directory information to be shared between domains:

▼   **Global domain data partition**   Holds information about all the objects in the global catalog but includes details on only a few of the objects' attributes, to allow quick searches for and access to resources in external domains, and to reduce the bandwidth used in replications. This information is replicated to all the other global catalog servers within the network. When a client in a foreign domain actually needs access to the resources or the nonreplicated attributes of a resource, the client is directed to that resource's native domain.

NOTE   Most replication among domain controllers is done over the network. This can be a problem if it is a low-bandwidth network or if a number of domain controllers are added rapidly. For that reason, Windows Server 2008 allows the Active Directory database files to be backed up to tape, CD, DVD, or a removable hard disk and used as the source of an initial replication on a new domain controller or global catalog server.

Internal Site Replication

There will always be at least one site within every AD implementation. When the first Windows Server 2008 domain controller is installed, it creates a site called the Default-First-Site-Name. The new domain controller then adds itself to that site. Whenever new domain controllers are added to the network, they are automatically added to this new site first; they can be moved later. There is, however, an exception to this statement. When a new site is created, one or more IP subnets are assigned to that site. After there are two or more sites, all new domain controllers added to the forest will have their IP addresses checked and will be added to the site with a matching IP address.

Directory information within a site is replicated automatically to ensure all domain controllers within the site have the same information. Additionally, all inter-site replication occurs in an uncompressed format, which consumes more network traffic but less system resources. For these reasons, a site should always be a LAN network of high-speed connections (10MB or higher). When multiple domains exist within a single site, replication occurs only among domain controllers in a given domain. However, replication traffic between global catalog servers occurs across the site on an as-needed/uncompressed basis as well. Figure 7-7 shows the single-site replication traffic between two domains.

Site-to-Site Replication

When deciding to split a network into multiple sites, a number of new issues arise. These issues, and the configuration needed to make multiple sites work, are the subject of the remainder of this section.

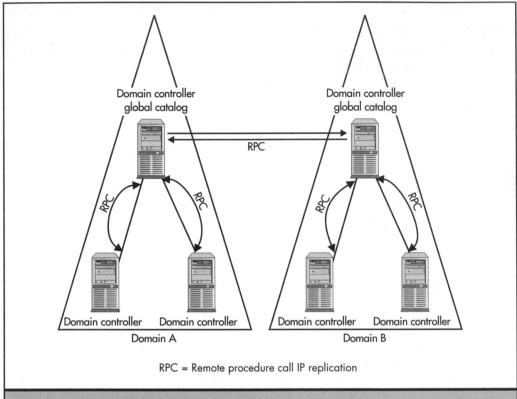

Figure 7-7. Replication traffic between two domains within the same site

Two main rules should be adhered to whenever planning a multisite design, to minimize the potential problems:

▼ Sites always should be split by geographic regions. When two or more LANs are connected by WAN links, each LAN should represent its own site.

▲ Whenever possible, each site should have its own AD and global catalog server. In some smaller networks, this server may be the only server in the site, in which case it should also serve as the DNS and DHCP server. This will increase fault tolerance as well as client performance, while decreasing WAN bandwidth utilization.

Site Connectivity

Sites are connected using *site links,* which are domain controllers configured to serve as a connection to a particular site. Site links have to be manually configured using the AD Sites And Services console. When creating a site link, the administrator has a number of configuration options.

The first of these configuration options is the replication schedule. An administrator can determine when replication should occur across a particular site link. When setting the replication schedule, an administrator will set the replication cost, replication availability, and replication frequency associated with the site link. When the site link is created and configured, AD automatically creates a connection object, which will use the information provided by the site link to actually transfer the information between the domains.

By default and design, all site links are transitive, which allows sites to be used in the same manner transitive trusts are used. This means that a site can replicate its changes to another site, via a site connector to a third site, as long as the third site has a valid connection to both sites. In some organizations in which multiple field offices all connect to central corporate offices, this kind of replication allows for the greatest efficiency. All sites replicate their information to the central office site, which in turn replicates the information back out to the other field offices.

Protocols

There are two protocol options within any network for connecting sites together. Both options, though, are protocols within the TCP/IP protocol stack. There is no way to connect two sites using anything other than IP.

▼ **RPC (IP replication)**   Remote Procedure Call (RPC) is an IP-based, connection-oriented protocol that is at the base of legacy Exchange installations. RPC is fast and reliable when used on connection-friendly networks (networks that allow packets to travel the same path and arrive in sequence at the destination). However, RPC is less than reliable in large mesh networks, such as the Internet. RPC communication is still the default replication method for servers within the same site as well as for intra-site communication for other Microsoft services such as Exchange.

▲ **SMTP**   A feature that was introduced with Windows 2000 and Exchange 2000 is the ability to connect sites using SMTP connectors. SMTP cannot be used for replication between servers in the same site (although it is the default for Exchange Server). SMTP is not capable of replicating the domain partition, and therefore it is suitable only for linking two sites that are also separate domains. SMTP can pass the schema, configuration, and global catalog partitions very efficiently.

NOTE   SMTP is, by nature, very insecure. All SMTP messages are sent in formats that can be easily interpreted by the most basic of sniffing tools. For this reason, using the SMTP protocol to connect two sites requires that an enterprise certification authority be installed and configured on the network. This allows for all SMTP traffic generated by AD to be encrypted using at least 56-bit encryption.

Collision Detecting and Resolution

What happens when the same object is modified from two different spots in the network at the same time, or when two objects with the same name are created at the same time within the network? Even in the most basic networks, if two domain controllers exist, the two directories that exist on each domain controller will not be exactly the same at all times, because replication takes time. Legacy versions of NT dealt with this issue by allowing only one read/write copy of the directory to exist on the network at any one time. This meant that all changes could be made only by one server, and those changes were then propagated to the read-only copies of the directories that the remaining domain controllers maintained.

When a change to an object occurs before a previous change to that object has been completely replicated, a replication *collision* occurs. AD can track the versions of objects by looking at each object's version number. When an object is changed, its version number is increased, so that when a server receives an update, it can compare the version number of the incoming object with the version number of the existing object. When the existing object's version number is less than the version number coming in, the replication continues and all is considered well. A collision occurs when the version number of the existing item is equal to or greater than the version number of the incoming item. In this case, AD compares the timestamp of the incoming object to the timestamp of the existing object to determine which one it's going to keep. This is the only instance in which time is used in replication. If the timestamps don't settle the issue, the item with the highest GUID is kept. In situations in which the incoming version number is actually lower than the existing version number, the replication object is considered to be stale and is discarded.

Read-Only Domain Controllers

In Windows Server 2008, when creating a new domain, you have the option to create a *read-only domain controller (RODC)*. A RODC provides all the benefits of a local DC, such as faster logons and searches with a local index, but depends on the replication traffic from other DCs for its information. No information may be entered into a RODC and it does not replicate its information to other DCs. This is particularly useful in remote offices that may not have an administrator or in other instances where the physical security of the RODC is questionable.

Windows Server 2008 provides for a "staged" installation of RODC where a CD or DVD can be prepared with all the setup information for a RODC and used by someone other than an administrator to install the RODC (see Chapter 4 "Remote Installation Services").

ACTIVE DIRECTORY SUMMARY

Active Directory is one of most important features of Windows Server 2008. AD is a directory service based on the X.500 directory scheme that contains a variety of predefined and preconfigured objects and OUs. A large part of any Windows Server 2008 administrator's job will be the administration and configuration of the special objects and OUs within the AD forest. Additionally, the namespace of AD has to match that of a DNS domain, and in cases in which the AD domain and the Internet DNS domain for the company don't match, separate DNS domains have to be maintained, because AD requires DNS to allow for client connectivity.

If used correctly, AD can add tremendous value and reliability to a network, as well as decrease the administrative overhead involved in the network's daily maintenance. However, if configured incorrectly or if ill-planned, AD can drastically increase the administrator's workload, and decrease the network customer's satisfaction. When dealing with AD, a little bit of forethought and planning can save a lot of work and pain.

PART IV

Communications and the Internet

CHAPTER 8

Communications and Internet Services

Networking today definitely extends beyond the local area network (LAN) to include the Internet itself, as well as using the Internet and other forms of communication to access your LAN or other computers. This part of the book covers the ways that you and your organization can reach out from your LAN to connect to others, or allow others to connect to you. Chapter 8 provides an overview of communications and how to set up the various Windows Server 2008 communications features. It then discusses establishing a dial-up connection and using it with the Remote Access Service (RAS). This chapter concludes by explaining how to set up and use an Internet connection with Internet Explorer for accessing the Web. Chapter 9 looks at Internet Information Services (IIS), how it's set up, and how it's managed. Chapter 10 describes virtual private networking (VPN), using the Internet to connect to a remote LAN with a high degree of security, and Chapter 11 discusses terminal and application services, which is the current equivalent of the decades-old method of accessing a time-sharing mainframe with a dumb terminal.

Communication may include a modem or other device to connect a single computer to a method of transmission, or it may use a router or other device to connect a network to the method of transmission. Communications can be over copper wires, fiber-optic cable, microwave, ground or cell wireless, or satellite transmission.

Windows Server 2008 includes a number of programs that control or utilize communications, among which are Internet Explorer, for web browsing; the New Connection Wizard, for the Internet and other connections; and the Phone And Modem Options dialog box, to establish and maintain connections. In addition, Windows Server 2008 includes programs to set up and manage RAS networking over communications lines.

Communications can be broken into:

▼ Telephony connections between computers other than the Internet

▲ Connections to and through the Internet

SET UP AND USE TELEPHONY CONNECTIONS

Telephony (telephone lines, their switches, and their terminations) has been used to connect computers for some time. The original approach was to use a *modem* (short for "modulator-demodulator") to convert a digital signal (patterns of ones and zeros) in a computer to an analog signal (current fluctuations) in a phone line and then use a second modem on the other end to convert the analog signal back to digital for use in the connecting computer. Modems can be internal (inside the computer), in which case the phone line connects to the computer, or external, where the phone line plugs into the modem and the modem plugs into a serial port in the computer. Fast modems receive data at up to 56 Kbps (thousand bits per second) and send data at up to 33.6 Kbps.

For approaching ten years, telephone companies have been offering several forms of full digital signals over phone lines, so that a modem (as just described) isn't necessary—all you need is a connection between the digital line and the computer. Two forms of digital telephone service are ISDN (Integrated Services Digital Network) and DSL (digital sub-scriber line). ISDN was the first digital service and is both expensive and relatively slow (a maximum speed of up to 128 Kbps) when compared with DSL. There are several forms of DSL, the most common of which is ADSL (asymmetric digital subscriber line), over which data is received at over 5 Mbps and sent at over 1 Mbps. Most often, an ISDN or DSL line is terminated in a router that directly connects to your network and not to a computer. Later in this chapter, though, you'll see how a computer with Windows Server 2008 can act as a router for lines terminated in it through an ISDN or DSL adapter.

NOTE   Sometimes an ISDN or DSL adapter is called a "modem," but it is not an analog-to-digital converter, which is the major point in the acronym "modem." Therefore in this book they are not included in discussions on modems.

Install a Modem

There are several ways to install modem support within Windows Server 2008. During installation of the operating system or the first time you attempt to connect to the Internet, support for a modem will be installed for you if you have a Plug and Play modem. If you set up a dial-up connection and you don't have modem support installed, it will be installed for you, again with a Plug and Play modem. Here, though, we'll look at installing a modem by itself, which you will need to do if it has not been automatically installed. Later, we'll also look at installing it with an Internet connection.

To install a modem, of course, you must have one built in, plugged in, or attached to your computer. A *built-in* modem is built right on the main or "mother" board inside your computer. A *plugged-in* modem is a card that plugs into an expansion slot on the mother board. Both built-in and plugged-in modems are considered *internal* modems. An *external* modem is a small box that plugs into a serial or communications (COM) port on the outside of your computer. Both external and internal modems may have switches or jumpers that need to be set, or they may be *Plug and Play,* which means that they do not have switches or jumpers—software sets them up automatically. Whichever kind of modem you have, the instructions that came with it should tell you whether it is internal or external, how to plug it in, and how to set it up.

With a modem physically attached to your computer (and, if external, turned on), use the following instructions to install it in Windows Server 2008:

1. In Windows Server 2008, click Start | Control Panel, and double-click Phone And Modem Options. The first time you do this, the Location Information dialog box will open. If you see the Phone And Modem Options dialog box, skip to Step 3.

2. Click the down arrow and click the country you are now in. Type the area or city code, and if needed, type the carrier code and the number to access an outside line. If your phone requires pulse dialing, click that. Finally, click OK. The Phone And Modem Options dialog box will open.

3. Click the Modems tab. If it shows Unknown Modem, select that and click Remove. If it shows a likely modem, such as what is shown next, you already have a modem installed and you can skip to the next section.

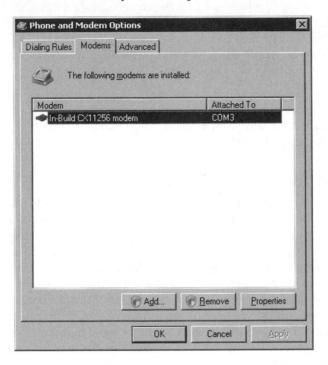

4. Click Add. You are told that Windows will try to detect your modem and are reminded to attach and turn on the modem, and to quit any programs that may be using it. Click Next. If it did not find a modem, click Next for a list of possible modems. If only the correct modem is displayed, skip the next step. If several modems are shown and one is correct and the rest are not, uncheck the incorrect ones and skip the next step. If an incorrect modem or Unknown Modem is shown, select it and click Change.

5. From the list of modems, select the correct manufacturer from the list on the left and the correct model from the list on the right and click Next. If your modem is not on the list but you have a disk, click Have Disk, insert the disk, select the drive, click OK, select the manufacturer and model, and click OK.

6. Select the COM port to which the modem is connected and click Next. Windows starts to install your modem. If you are using an older modem, you may be told that the driver does not have a digital signature. If so, click Yes to continue. Finally, you are told that your modem has been installed successfully. Click Finish.

7. Back in the Phone And Modem Options dialog box, select your newly installed modem, and click Properties. In the Properties dialog box, click the Diagnostics tab, and then click Query Modem. You will be told that the query process will take several seconds. If your modem is properly installed, you'll see a set of

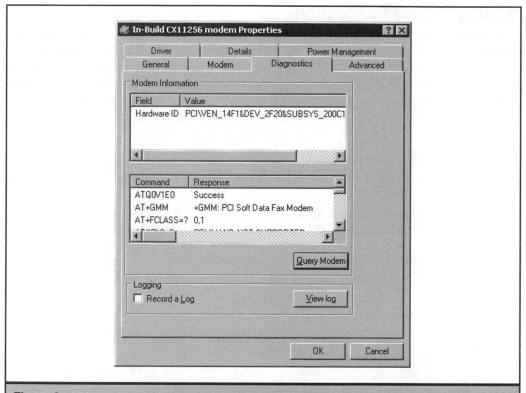

Figure 8-1. Commands and responses resulting from running modem diagnostics

commands and responses, as shown in Figure 8-1. Not all of the responses have to be positive. The point is that Windows Server 2008 is talking to the modem.

If you do not get the set of commands and responses, you will probably get some sort of error message, such as Modem Not Found, which has three possible causes: the modem is not operating correctly, the wrong driver is installed, or the wrong COM port is being used. You generally can tell whether the COM port is correct by looking at what Windows detected. It may not detect the type of modem correctly, but it generally detects the port that has a modem attached to it. To find the correct manufacturer and model for the driver, you may need to look at the actual modem by physically opening the computer. To get a driver that is not in the Windows driver database, use another computer to connect to the Internet, browse to the modem manufacturer's web site, and download the correct driver. Put that driver on a disk and take it to the computer you are installing on. If you are certain that both the port and driver are correct, then the modem may be malfunctioning.

8. Click OK to close the Properties dialog box, and then click OK to close the Phone And Modem Options dialog box.

Establish a Dial-up Connection

Establishing a dial-up connection on Windows Server 2008 identifies a particular destination to which you want to dial—a phone number that is dialed and a connection that is made to your modem. The following steps, which assume that a modem has already been set up (as done in the preceding section), show how to establish a dial-up connection (if you are working on a domain controller, you may either create a dial-up connection in this section and/or create a remote access service in the next section, "Set Up Remote Access Service"):

1. Click Start | Control Panel, double-click Network And Sharing Center, and click Set Up A Connection Or Network. The Set Up A Connection Or Network dialog box will open.

2. Click Set Up A Dial-up Connection and click Next. As shown in Figure 8-2, enter the phone number that will be the destination of the connection. Enter your username and password. If you want to display the password characters, click Show Characters, and if you want the computer to remember the password so you don't have to enter it, click Remember This Password.

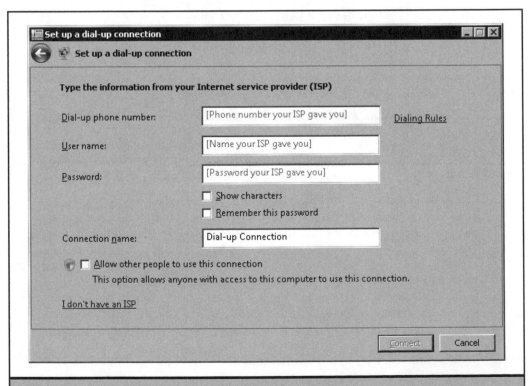

Figure 8-2.   You need a phone number, username, and password for a dial-up connection.

3. Enter a name for the dial-up connection, and if you want to create this connection for anyone's use, click Allow Other People To Use This Connection.

4. Click Connect. You'll see a dialog box that shows you the progress of the connection. Upon completion, given a correct phone number, username, and password, you should be connected to the computer you dialed.

NOTE   After the initial setup of the dial-up connection, you can connect using it again by clicking Start | Control Panel, double-clicking Network And Sharing Center | Connect To A Network, and double-clicking this connection. If you go into the Start menu properties, you can put Connect To on the Start menu and save a couple of clicks.

A dial-up connection can be used with RAS, discussed next.

SET UP REMOTE ACCESS SERVICE

Remote Access Service provides access to a LAN from a dial-up line, a leased line, or another connection. RAS acts as a host or server to a dial-up or other connection guest or client. RAS commonly is used by travelers whose laptops have a dial-up connection that can be used from a remote location to connect through RAS to the home office LAN. To set up RAS requires three separate tasks: add a RAS server role, enable and configure RAS, and set up the port and policies to support RAS.

Add a Routing and Remote Access Service Server Role

The first task is to add a Routing and Remote Access Service role to the server.

1. Click Start | Server Manager. Under Roles Summary, click Add Roles. The Add Roles Wizard will open. Click Next.

2. Click Network Policy And Access Services and then click Next. Read the introduction message and click Next again.

3. Click Routing And Remote Access Services, as shown in Figure 8-3, click Next, and click Install. The process may take several minutes. When it is done you will be told the installation succeeded. Click Close.

Back in the Server Manager you'll see, under "Roles," Network Policy And Access Services, but it will have an "X" in a red circle indicating that it hasn't been enabled and turned on.

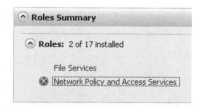

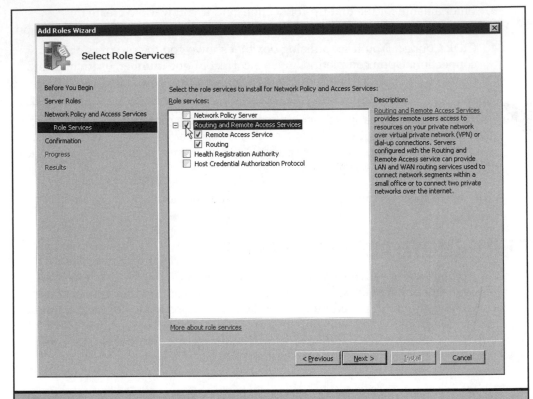

Figure 8-3. Selecting Routing And Remote Access Services as a Server Role

Enable and Configure RAS

The second task is to enable and configure RAS, which is done with the Routing And Remote Access Server Setup Wizard.

1. Click Start | Administrative Tools | Routing And Remote Access. In the left pane, click SERVER (Local).

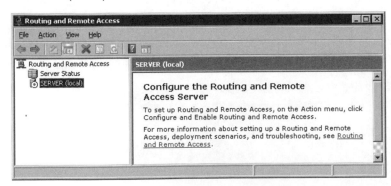

2. Click the Action menu and click Configure And Enable Routing And Remote Access. The Routing And Remote Access Server Setup Wizard will open.

3. Click Next and make sure that Remote Access (Dial-up or VPN) is selected, as shown in Figure 8-4.

4. Click Next. You are asked if you want RAS to use VPN and/or Dial-up; click Dial-up and then click Next. If you have more than one network connection, select the one that you want RAS clients assigned to and click Next.

5. You are asked how you want addresses assigned; leave the default Automatically and click Next.

6. When asked if you want to Use Routing And Remote Access To Authenticate Connection Requests or use a RADIUS Server, leave the default of No, Use Routing And Remote Access To Authenticate Connection Requests and click Next.

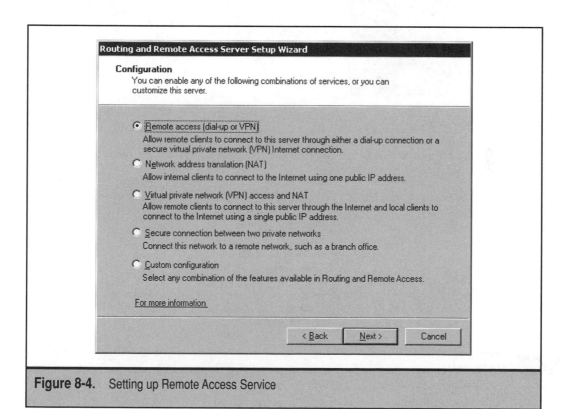

Figure 8-4. Setting up Remote Access Service

7. Finally, you are shown the summary of your settings, like the one shown next. Choose whether you want to see the Help pages on managing a remote access server, and then click Finish.

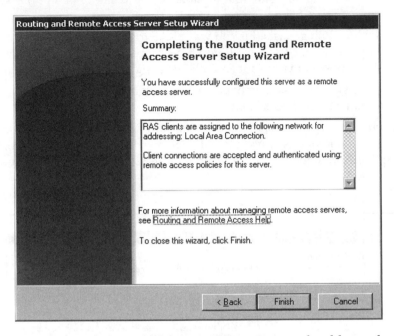

In the left pane, the Routing And Remote Access server should now have a green up-arrow, indicating it is now enabled.

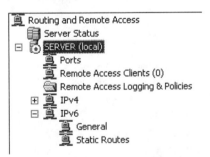

NOTE   If you are setting up RAS on a server in Active Directory that is not the primary domain controller and you are not a domain administrator, a domain administrator must add the server on which you are working to the RAS and IAS Servers group in the Computers folder of the Active Directory Users And Computers window and to the list of servers in Routing And Remote Access on the primary domain controller. To support the relaying of DHCP messages from remote access clients, the domain administrator must configure the properties of the DHCP Relay Agent with the IP address of your DHCP server.

Set Up the Port and Policies

The final task is to set up the port and networking policies on the server to support RAS.

1. In the right pane, under the Routing And Remote Access server, right-click Ports, and click Properties. The Ports Properties dialog box will open.

2. Click your modem, which is your dial-in port, and click Configure. The Configure Device dialog box will open.

3. Click Remote Access Connections (Inbound Only), enter the phone number for this device, as shown next, click OK, and then click OK again.

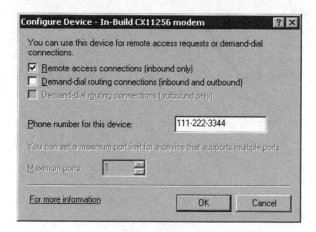

4. Back in the Routing And Remote Access window, right-click Remote Access Logging and Policies, and click Launch NPS. The Network Policy Server will open.

5. Click Network Policies. In the right pane, right-click Connections To Microsoft Routing And Remote Access Server and click Properties. The Connections To Microsoft Routing And Remote Access Server Properties dialog box will open.

6. Policy Enabled should already be checked. If not, click it. Click Grant Access. To make life simpler, but less secure, you can click Ignore User Account Dial-in Properties. Under Type Of Network Access Server, click the down arrow and click Remote Access Server (VPN-Dial up). Your dialog box should look similar to Figure 8-5.

7. Click OK and close the Network Policy Server, Routing And Remote Access, and Server Manager windows that are open.

NOTE   You must also have the client that is coming into the RAS server set up with a user account on the server. See Chapter 6.

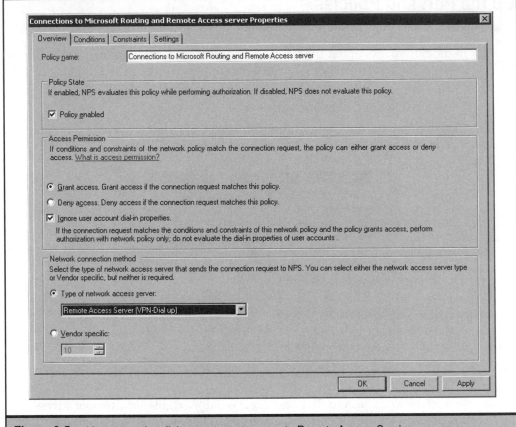

Figure 8-5. Your network policies must grant access to Remote Access Service.

Use Remote Access Service

With a dial-up connection set up on the guest or client computer (see "Establish a Dial-up Connection" earlier in this chapter for this example, a laptop in a remote city running Windows Vista) and a remote access server set up and enabled on the host computer (see preceding several sections, for this example, a server in the home office running Windows Server 2008), you can use RAS with these steps:

1. Log onto the dial-up client (here the laptop with Vista) with a username and password that can be authenticated by the RAS. Then, on the client, click Start | Control Panel, double-click Network And Sharing Center, click Connect To A Network, and double-click the dial-up connection you want to use. The Connect Dial-up Connection dialog box opens.

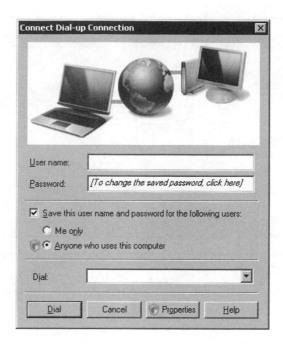

2.   Enter the appropriate username and password and click the Dial button. You will see messages stating that the number you entered is being dialed, that the username and password are being checked, that the computer is being registered on the network, and then that the connection is complete. Click OK. The connection icon will appear on the right of the taskbar.

3.   Utilize the connection by opening Windows Explorer | My Network Places | Entire Network | Microsoft Windows Network, and finally the domains or workgroups, computers, and shares that you want to access.

4.   Transfer information across the dial-up connection in the same way as you transfer any information in Windows Explorer, by locating the destination folder in the left pane, selecting the files or folders to be transferred in the right pane, and then dragging the information from the right pane to the folder in the left pane.

5.   When you are done using the RAS connection, you can terminate it by double-clicking the connection icon in the taskbar or clicking the connection icon in the Connect To A Network window (opened from the Network And Sharing Center), and then clicking Disconnect.

While a dial-up connection is operational, you can see the connection in the Routing And Remote Access window on the server and see who it is by opening the server and clicking Remote Access Clients in the right pane, as shown in Figure 8-6. If you right-click the user in the right pane and click Status, you can see how much information has been transferred, and disconnect the user, if desired.

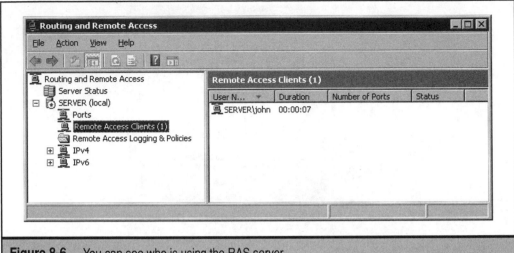

Figure 8-6. You can see who is using the RAS server.

SET UP AND MAINTAIN THE WINDOWS SERVER 2008 ROUTER

Routers are network devices that are used to join two separate, independent networks, such as a LAN and the Internet. Routers operate at the Network (third) layer of the OSI (Open Systems Interconnection) networking model and therefore use the full IP address, consisting of both network and host components (see Chapter 5 sections "The OSI Model" and "Routers"). A router looks at all the traffic on both networks but transfers only those packets that are specifically addressed to the other network. Routers also provide a network address translation (NAT) function. NAT allows your LAN to use a set of non-Internet-usable IP addresses, such as 10.0.0.9, but when the LAN users access the Internet, they are assigned an Internet-usable IP address, with the router translating between the two. Finally, a router can be used to connect two networks that use two different protocols, such as TCP/IP (Transmission Control Protocol/ Internet Protocol) and IPX (Internetwork Packet Exchange).

Normally, a router is a stand-alone electronic device (or "box") separate from a computer, to which two networks are connected. One of the network connections may be a phone connection (DSL, ISDN, or T1 line), and the other may be a standard 10/100BaseT Ethernet connection, or both may be Ethernet connections, or some other combination. Windows Server 2008 can provide some of a router's capabilities, the most important of which are the functions of connecting a LAN to the Internet or WAN (Wide Area Network), NAT, and connecting two networks with dissimilar protocols. To function, the Windows Server 2008 must be connected to both networks, for example, the Internet and the LAN. The LAN connection is just the standard network interface card (NIC), while the Internet or WAN connection is some sort of telephone line termination in or directly connected to the computer, such as a modem, an ISDN adapter, or a DSL termination.

Set Up the Windows Server 2008 Router

If you want to set up a server connection to the Internet that can be used by the entire network, then the server that you want to be the router must have both LAN and communications connections. Also, you must be an administrator or have Administrator privileges. You can then set up this router function through the Routing And Remote Access window and the following steps:

TIP   If you are not using DHCP, you need to set up Internet connection sharing from Network Connections. See the following section "Maintain a Windows Server 2008 Router."

1. If the Routing And Remote Access window isn't already open, click Start | Administrative Tools | Routing And Remote Access.

   If you have set up RAS earlier in this chapter and it is currently running, you must disable it to install the Internet Connection Server by clicking Disable Routing And Remote Access, and click Yes when asked if you want to continue.

   If you did not set up RAS earlier in this chapter, you need to enable the Routing And Remote Access Service server role, as described in "Add a Routing and Remote Access Service Server Role" earlier in this chapter.

2. Right-click the Routing And Remote Access Server, and, in any case, click Configure And Enable Routing And Remote Access. The Routing And Remote Access Server Setup Wizard will open. Click Next.

3. Click Network Address Translation and click Next. If you want to use an existing Internet connection, click Use This Public Interface To Connect To The Internet (if your Internet connection has its own routing, as is the case with DSL, this option will be grayed).

   If you want to create a new dial-up Internet connection, such as might be used with a modem, click Create A New Demand-Dial Interface To The Internet, and in any case, click Next. To create a demand-dial interface, click Next again to open the Demand-Dial Interface Wizard, where you need to click Next.

4. Accept the default name of Remote Router or enter the name you want to use for the interface, and click Next. Click Connect Using A Modem, ISDN Adapter, Or Other Device and click Next. Choose the specific modem or adapter to use, and click Next. Enter the phone number and click Next.

5. Select the options that you want to use. In most cases, the default Route IP Packets On This Interface is all you need. After selecting the needed options,

click Next. Enter the username, domain name, and password; confirm the password; and click Next. Click Finish twice.

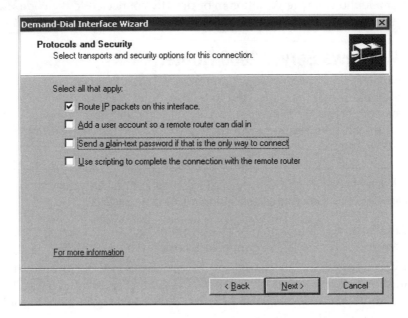

Maintain a Windows Server 2008 Router

You can see, test, and maintain the router you have just installed in the Routing And Remote Access window. In the next set of steps, you locate the new router, connect it to its destination, and see how to set up IP filters and the hours the router can be used:

1. If the Routing And Remote Access window isn't open already, click Start | Administrative Tools | Routing And Remote Access.

2. Click Network Interfaces. In the right pane, you should see your demand-dial interface, similar to mine (Remote Router) shown here:

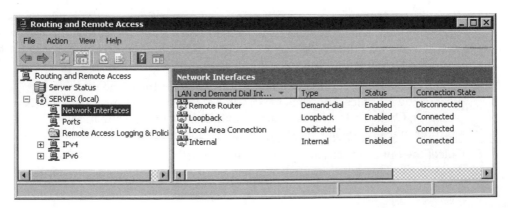

3. Right-click your demand-dial entry and click Set Credentials. Here, you can change the username, domain, and password that are used to connect to the ISP. When you open this dialog box, the password is cleared and must be reentered. Also, you may not need to enter a domain. Click OK after you have completed the entry.

4. Right-click the demand-dial entry and click Connect. You may hear the modem dialing and see a message with the status of "Connecting." When the actual connection is made, the Connection State in the Routing And Remote Access dialog box will change to Connected.

5. Right-click the demand-dial interface and click Set IP Demand-Dial Filters. This enables you to specify either IP addresses that will be the only ones allowed into the network or, conversely, IP addresses that are not allowed into the network. Click New to add the IP addresses, which can be within the LAN or in the remote network. After you have set the filters you want, click OK.

6. Right-click the demand-dial interface and click Dial-out Hours. Here, you can specify the hours that the demand-dial connection will not be available by selecting a particular hour and clicking Denied. For example, if you want from 11:00 P.M. Saturday through 3:00 A.M. Sunday to be blocked out, the dialog box will look like the next image after you have selected times. After you have set the times you want, click OK.

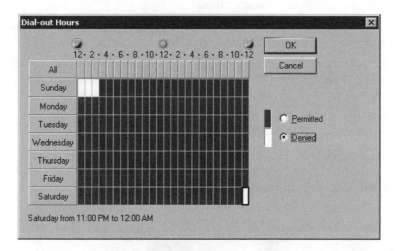

7. Right-click the demand-dial interface and click Properties. This allows you to set the properties of the connection, including the phone number, the type of connection, several security options, and network properties. When you are done, click OK and then close the Routing And Remote Access window.

To use the router, you need to install an Internet connection in the client that connects through a LAN. See "Set Up and Use an Internet Connection" after the next section.

Set Up Internet Connection Sharing

Internet connection sharing is a small system alternative to server routing. Internet connection sharing allows a small network of computers to all connect to the Internet through one computer, running Windows Server 2008, that is physically connected to the Internet using phone lines, a cable modem, or some other means. You first set up the connection to the Internet as explained earlier in this chapter, then use the following steps to share that connection.

NOTE Internet connection sharing is an alternative to using the Windows Server 2008 router with Network Address Translation (NAT), as described in "Set Up the Windows Server 2008 Router" earlier, and the two cannot be enabled on the same computer at the same time.

TIP You must have at least two networking or communications connections, one through which the computer is connected to the Internet and another through which the computer is connected to the other computers.

1. Click Start | Control Panel, double-click Network And Sharing Center, and click Manage Network Connections.

2. Right-click the connection that you want to share and click Properties. In the Properties dialog box that opens, click the Sharing tab.

3. Under Internet Connection Sharing, click Allow Other Network Users To Connect Through This Computer's Internet Connection, as shown in Figure 8-7.

4. If desired, click Establish A Dial-up Connection Whenever A Computer On My Network Attempts To Access The Internet.

5. Click OK to close the Properties dialog box. In the Network Connections dialog box, you should see "Shared" in the connection you are sharing. Click Close to close the Network Connections dialog box.

Dial-up (1)

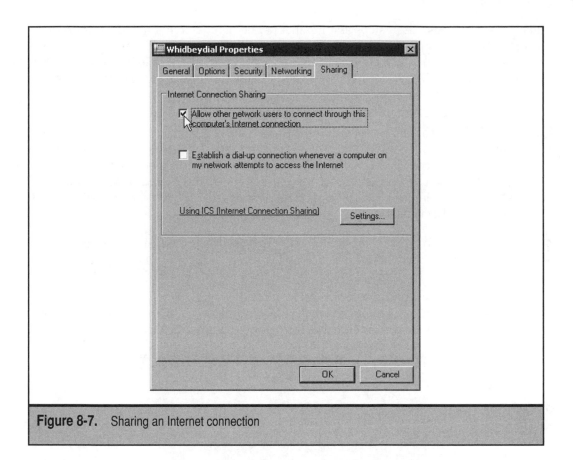

Figure 8-7.   Sharing an Internet connection

SET UP AND USE AN INTERNET CONNECTION

An Internet connection is one of the major reasons (and sometimes the only reason) to own a computer. In businesses, more and more work is being done through business-to-business transactions over the Internet. Making the most of the Internet connection is therefore of significant importance.

Connecting to the Internet

If a computer can connect to the Internet over the LAN, Windows Server 2008 Setup will automatically connect that computer to the Internet and no further work needs to be done to accomplish it. The problem is that it is not obvious whether you are connected. The only way to tell is to try to use the Internet and see what happens. Try that now with the next set of steps. These steps assume that neither a modem nor a dial-up connection has been previously set up, although they do assume that a physical connection between the computer and the Internet has been made. This could be a phone line and a modem, a phone line and a DSL router, a TV cable and a cable modem, or some other device that allows the connection.

NOTE To connect to the Internet, you need to have an existing account with an Internet service provider (ISP); if you are using a modem, you need to know the phone number for your modem to dial (the ISP's modem phone number); and, in all cases, you need the username and password for your account. If you want to use Internet mail, you need to know your e-mail address, the type of mail server (POP3, IMAP, or HTTP), the names of the incoming and outgoing mail servers, and the name and password for the mail account.

1. Open Internet Explorer by double-clicking its icon if on the desktop, by clicking the Start menu and clicking its icon if there, or by clicking Start | All Programs | Internet Explorer. Internet Explorer will open.

   If this is the first time Internet Explorer has opened, you will be told about Internet Explorer Enhanced Security. Read this and click the link to learn more. In essence you must identify each site you visit as a trusted site.

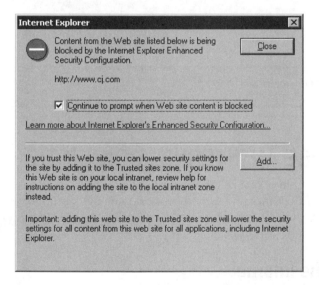

TIP If you don't want to have to identify each site and subsite you visit as a trusted site, you can turn off Internet Explorer Enhanced Security by clicking Start | Server Manager. In the Server Summary under Security Information, click Configure IE ESC. In the Internet Explorer Enhanced Security Configuration dialog box, you can turn off Enhanced Security for Administrators and/or Users groups.

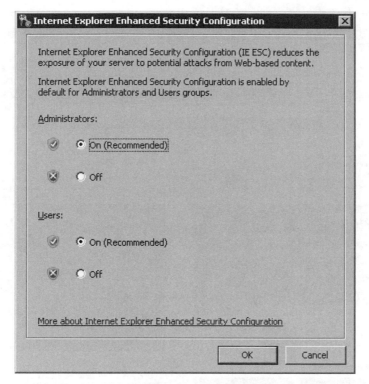

2. In the Address bar, type **http://www.msn.com** and press ENTER. If you haven't turned off IE Enhanced Security, you'll be asked if you want to add the site to your Trusted Sites Zone. Click Add if so, click Add again, and click Close. These steps are needed with each new site you visit, but won't be repeated here.

    If Internet Explorer opens with the MSN initial page, an example of which is shown in Figure 8-8, you know you already have an Internet connection and you can skip the remainder of the steps in this section.

3. If you do not have an Internet connection or it is not operating, you will see one of several dialog boxes: a message asking if you want to work offline, a message in Internet Explorer itself that says Internet Explorer cannot display the web page, or the Set Up A Connection Or Network dialog box will open. In all cases you either need to create a new Internet connection, or repair an existing one.

    If Internet Explorer did not find the Internet and the Set Up A Connection Or Network dialog box did not open, start it by clicking Start | Control Panel, double-clicking Network And Sharing Center, and clicking Set Up A Connection Or Network.

4. Click the type of connection you want to use and click Next. You are asked how you want to connect to the Internet. You'll see choices that match the means you have for a connection from among dial-up, broadband, wireless, or possibly others. Click the one that is correct for you.

Figure 8-8. Connecting to the Internet and MSN home page

5. Depending on what you choose, you will be asked for the logon information needed for that choice, such as phone number, username, and password for a dial-up choice. Enter that information, and, if needed, click Connect; otherwise click Close.

6. Once more open Internet Explorer and, if asked, click Connect. If you still do not connect to the Internet, you may have a hardware problem and, for example, need to reinstall your modem, in which case you should go to "Install a Modem" earlier in this chapter and then return here; otherwise, go to the next step.

TIP   If you think you have a modem set up and you are not getting connected when you open Internet Explorer, look at the Internet Options in Internet Explorer by clicking the Tools button on the command bar, choosing Internet Options, and clicking the Connections tab. See if you have a connection specified and whether it dials the connection. If not, make the necessary corrections.

7. When you have successfully installed your Internet connection, you will be shown an information screen on security. In the Address bar, type **http://www.msn.com** and press enter. You will be connected to MSN's home page, similar to the one shown in Figure 8-8.

Find Information on the Internet

Once you are connected to the Internet with Internet Explorer open, you most probably will want to go to pages other than the MSN home page. There are a number of ways to do that, including the following:

▼   Navigating within a web site

■   Going directly to a web site

■   Searching for a web site

▲   Setting up a different default home page

Navigate Within a Web Site

A good web site gives you many ways to navigate within it. As you look at the MSN home page in Figure 8-8, you see a number of terms or phrases that become underlined when you move the mouse pointer over them. These are *links* that, when clicked, take you to another part of the web site. The home page is almost all links of several kinds including headings, terms by themselves, and article lists. Also, there is normally a Search capability, similar to the one at the top of the MSN home page. Here, you can select where you want to search (Web, Images, and so on), enter a term or a phrase to search for, and click Search.

Report: Feds hope ref helps probe
- Bonds to resume homer chase at home
- Doping official takes shot at PGA Tour
- Red Sox pitcher back after cancer bout

TIP   Often, if you enter a phrase in a text search, the search will be done on each word, not on the complete phrase. To fix that, in many text searches, you can enclose the phrase in quotation marks and the search will be done on the entire phrase.

Internet Explorer also provides tools to navigate within a site: the Back and Forward arrows on the toolbar take you to the preceding and next pages, respectively. Also, the down arrows on the right of the Back and Forward arrows will list the last several pages you have viewed in each direction.

Go Directly to a Web Site

To go directly to a site, you must know the address, or URL (Uniform Resource Locator), for that site. With increasing frequency in publications, letterheads, and advertising, you will find an organization's URL. When you have a site's URL, you can enter it into the Address bar at the top of Internet Explorer, as shown next, and then press ENTER or click the green right-pointing arrow, which takes you directly to the site. URLs that you frequently use can be stored in the Favorites folder, on the desktop, and in the Links bar of Internet Explorer. If you select one of these addresses and you are not already connected to the Internet, you will be connected automatically (or you might have to click Dial in a connection dialog box), Internet Explorer will open, and the addressed site will be displayed.

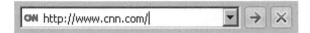

Place a URL in Favorites   You can store a URL in the Favorites folder by entering it or otherwise displaying it in the Address bar of Internet Explorer, clicking the Add To Favorites button, and clicking Add To Favorites. The Add A Favorite dialog box will open, show you the name the site will have in the Favorites folder, and allow you to place the URL in a subfolder with the Create In option.

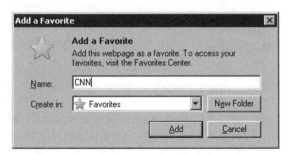

TIP   The Favorites folder is in each user's area of the hard disk. By default, this is C:\Users\ username\Favorites. This should be backed up from time to time.

Place a URL on the Desktop   You can place a URL on the desktop or on the Quick Launch toolbar by dragging the icon on the left of the Address bar of Internet Explorer to the desktop or Quick Launch toolbar. This creates a shortcut that, when double-clicked or clicked, connects to the Internet, opens Internet Explorer, and displays the site.

Place a URL in the Links Folder   The Links folder is a subfolder of Favorites and can be in the upper part of the Internet Explorer window. Right-click the toolbars area and click Lock The Toolbars to unlock the Links bar. Again right-click the toolbars area and click Links. The Links bar will appear above the tabs. You can add a URL to the Links folder and bar by dragging the icon in the Address bar to the Links bar. You can place it within the Links bar in the location you want. You can remove any unwanted links by right-clicking them and choosing Delete.

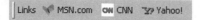

Search for a Web Site

If you don't know a web site's URL, you can search for it in either of two ways. If it is a web site that you have been to recently, you likely can find it in your web site history. If you have not been to the site recently, you can do a full search of the Internet to find it.

Check History   To check the history of your web site visits, click the Favorites Center and click History in the Favorites Center toolbar. Your history will appear left of Internet Explorer and, by default, will show you the sites you have visited by day for the current week, and then by week for the last several weeks. By opening a day or week, you can see and select a URL that you have previously visited and have it quickly displayed.

You can determine how many days to keep History and clear History by clicking the Tools button on the command bar and choosing Internet Options. In the General tab of the dialog box that opens, under Browsing History, click Settings; you can set the Days To Keep Pages In History. Also in the Internet Options dialog box General tab, under Browsing History, you can click Delete, and then click Delete History.

NOTE   You can sort the History list by clicking the down arrow next to the History button in the Favorites Center toolbar.

Search the Internet   You can search for a web site on the Internet at three levels:

▼ Type in the Address bar what you believe is part of the URL, and Internet Explorer will search for a site that has in its URL the text you entered. For example, entering "3com" (the company) or "united" (for United Airlines), you will be taken to Microsoft's Live Search site displaying a list of possible URLs, as you can see in Figure 8-9, from which you can usually find the site you want.

TIP   You can change how Internet Explorer responds to Address bar search (typing less than a full URL) by clicking the Tools button on the command bar, clicking Internet Options, clicking the Advanced tab, and scrolling down to Search From The Address Bar.

■ Click in the Live Search box in the top bar of Internet Explorer, enter a word or phrase, and click Search (the magnifying glass icon). A list of web sites containing that word or phrase will be displayed. You can then click a site in the list and it will be displayed. As described in the earlier tip, if you want to search for a complete phrase, you need to place the phrase within quotation marks.

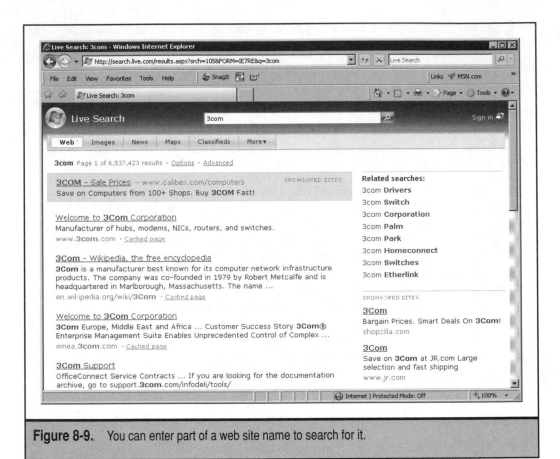

Figure 8-9.   You can enter part of a web site name to search for it.

▲   Use another search site such as Google, Yahoo, Ask, or AltaVista by typing the name in the Address bar (see Figure 8-10 for AltaVista's home page). Internet Explorer 7.0 (IE7) in Windows Server 2008 depends entirely on the MSN search engine and does not give you direct links to other search engines that are available. These other search sites provide different results for the same searches, and so it is often worthwhile to check several sites. You can do this not only when searching for web pages, but also when searching for a person's mailing address or e-mail address, finding a business, locating a map, looking up a word, finding a picture, finding a reference in a newsgroup, and searching your previous searches.

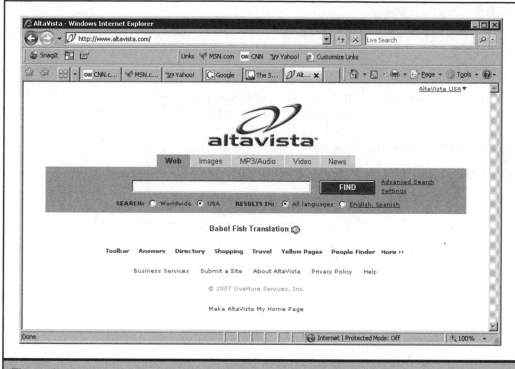

Figure 8-10.   There are a number of alternative sites for searching the Web.

Set Up a Different Default Home Page

The page that opens when you first start Internet Explorer or click the house icon in Internet Explorer's command bar is called Home, your home page. If you want to set, say, the CNN home page as your home page, you can do so with these steps:

1. Open Internet Explorer and display the page that you want to be your home page, which is the CNN home page in this example.

2. Click the down arrow next to the Home icon and click Add Or Change Home Page.

3. Click Use This Webpage As Your Only Home Page, and click Yes.

Use Tabs

Internet Explorer 7 (IE7), which comes with Windows Server 2008, has added the ability to have several web pages open at one time and easily switch between them by clicking the tab associated with the page. The tabs reside on the *tab row*, immediately below the Address bar, along with the Favorites Center and Add To Favorites, as shown in Figure 8-11. Under normal circumstances, only one page is open at a time, as in earlier versions of Internet Explorer. If you open a second page, it replaces the first page. IE7, however, gives you the ability to open multiple pages as separate tabs that you can switch among by clicking their tabs.

Open Pages in a New Tab

To open a page in a new tab:

1. Open your first web page in any of the ways described earlier in this chapter.

2. Click New Tab on the right end of the tab row, or press CTRL-T, and open a second web page in any of the ways described earlier in this chapter.

   –Or–

   Type a Web address in the Address bar, and press ALT-ENTER.

   –Or–

   Type a search request in the search box, and press ALT-ENTER.

   –Or–

   Hold down CTRL while clicking a link in an open page.

   –Or–

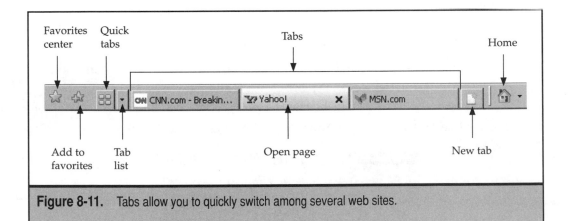

Figure 8-11.   Tabs allow you to quickly switch among several web sites.

Hold down CTRL while clicking the arrow on the right of a site in your Favorites Center.

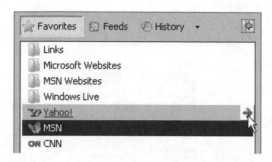

3. Repeat any of the alternatives in Step 2 as needed to open further pages.

Switch among Tabs

To switch among open tabs:

▼   Click the tab of the page you want to open.

–Or–

■   Click Quick Tabs in the tab row, or press CTRL-Q, and click the thumbnail of the page you want to open (see Figure 8-12).

–Or–

■   Click Tab List in the tab row, and click the page you want to open.

–Or–

■   Press CTRL-TAB to switch to the next tab to the right, or press CTRL-SHIFT-TAB to switch to the next tab to the left.

–Or–

▲   Press CTRL-N, where N is a number from 1 to 8 to switch to one of the first eight tabs numbered from the left in the order they were opened. You can also press CTRL-9 to switch to the last tab that was opened, shown on the right of the tab row.

NOTE   To use CTRL-N to switch among Internet Explorer's tabs, you need to use a number key on the main keyboard, not on the numeric keypad.

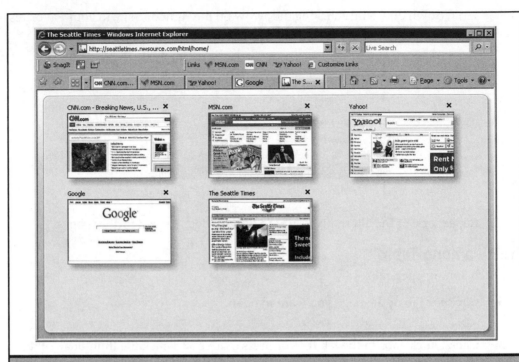

Figure 8-12. Through the Quick Tabs button, you can see thumbnails of all your open pages side-by-side.

Close Tabs

To close one or more tabs:

▼ Right-click the tab for the page you want to close, and click Close on the context menu, or click Close Other Tabs to close all of the pages except the one you clicked.

–Or–

■ Press CTRL-W or click its close "X" to close the current page.

–Or–

■ Click the middle mouse button (if your mouse has one) on the page you want to close.

–Or–

▲ Press ALT-F4 to close all tabs (confirm by clicking Close Tabs in the dialog box that appears), or click CTRL-ALT-F4 to close all tabs except the currently selected one.

TIP Press just the *ALT* key to view Internet Explorer's menus as an alternative to using the options on the IE7 command bar.

CHAPTER 9

Internet Information Services Version 7

This chapter introduces you to Internet Information Services version 7 (IIS 7) and the role that IIS plays within Windows Server 2008. The chapter describes how to install, migrate to, customize, maintain, and manage IIS to meet various business and networking goals.

EXPLORE THE IIS 7 ENVIRONMENT

IIS is a collection of services, protocols, and applications integrated into Windows Server 2008 that handles the server's interaction with "the Web," the Internet, an intranet (within an organization), or an extranet that combines the Internet with one or more intranets. IIS is primarily a web server, which hosts web pages and applications that respond to requests from other computers running web browsers. IIS does this by sending text, images, audio, and video, and by performing other web services to or with the requesting computer.

NOTE   Windows Vista includes a limited version of IIS 7. The version in Windows Vista is designed for people developing web sites and for small businesses to bring up a very limited intranet site within the business. The limitations in Vista depend on the version of Vista used. In the best case with Windows Vista Ultimate, Business, or Enterprise, IIS can service only ten client connections at a time and some of the IIS features are not available. In Windows Server 2008, IIS 7 can handle an unlimited number of clients and all features are available. This book will discuss only the server version of IIS 7.

Whenever you use a web browser to connect to a web site, such as www.microsoft.com, you connect to a web server; download the text, media, and images found there; and then look at this information on your local computer. Obviously, the quality and complexity of each web site varies tremendously, as does the quality and stability of web servers. This chapter will discuss the unique features and functions offered by IIS 7 that support both high quality web sites and improved server stability.

While it is easy to think of IIS as just a web server, IIS actually supports a variety of other services. The following are some of the areas that represent the diversity of functions offered by IIS:

▼ **ASP.NET**   Active Server Pages using the Microsoft .Net framework is a method of creating dynamic elements on web pages. ASP.NET allows a web page to respond to a user's action, (such as loading the page or clicking on an object on the page) as well as the handling and authentication of web-based forms.

■ **WebDAV**   Web-based Distributed Authoring and Versioning is a protocol used to build web applications that allows collaboration in the creation, searching for, moving, copying, and deleting of web-based information.

■ **SharePoint Services**   Provides for the creating, updating, organizing, and retention of information within a team of individuals sharing the information. SharePoint Services uses a prebuilt web site structure within which both custom and ready-made web pages can be added. Multiple people can easily add new information to and update information on these pages, with the information organized and stored in a SQL database.

■ **FTP**   File Transfer Protocol is an industry-standard file-exchange protocol that allows different types of computers, including mainframes, mid-sized computers, and laptops running a variety of operating systems (OSs) to exchange files across the Internet or an intranet in a quick and efficient manner. With FTP, data that's input and processed within a mainframe environment can be FTP'd to a Windows-based computer and automatically input into a SQL database with no user interaction, through the use of scripts running on each end.

▲ **SMTP**   Simple Mail Transfer Protocol allows for the formation and transfer of text messages between systems. In short, SMTP is e-mail. If you've ever used e-mail over the Internet, you've used SMTP. Within Windows Server 2008, SMTP is a part of Active Directory and can be used to link Active Directory sites together across the Internet. With SMTP, Windows Server 2008 organizations can be integrated through the Internet using nothing but standard Internet technologies.

NOTE   Windows Server 2008 uses the IIS certificate server to keep the information exchanged between the two Active Directory sites encrypted and secure.

IIS 7 Features

While IIS 7 builds on a significant line of previous versions, it has a number of new or enhanced features. Version 7 is more modularized, allowing the tailoring of an installation to the particular tasks needed by being able to select just the modules desired. Also, IIS 7 now provides a unified server platform for web hosting, ASP.NET, SharePoint Services, and Windows Communication Foundation (allowing the communication among several computers on a network). Additionally, there are enhancements in the areas of security, reliability, administration, and scalability.

Security

Microsoft has a continuing effort to improve the security of IIS, including many changes to reduce suspected vulnerable areas. In addition, IIS 7 includes a number of features to enhance security, such as advanced digest authentication, selectable Cryptographic Service Provider, configuring worker process identity, and disabling unknown extensions.

▼ **Advanced digest authentication**   Enhances digest authentication by storing and transmitting security credentials, such as passwords, in a particularly difficult-to-break encryption technique called MD5 hash.

■ **Selectable Cryptographic Service Provider (CSP)**   Allows an administrator to switch between using basic computer hardware (CPU, RAM, and hard disk) and software (Windows and the Registry) to perform the functions of calculating and storing private and public keys used in encryption, and handling some or all of those functions on a smart card or a cryptographic accelerator card.

■ **Configuring worker process identity**   Allows the configuration of application pools, where server-based web processes are run, to have a particularly limited set of privileges in order to block hackers.

▲ **Disabling unknown extensions**   Allows configuring IIS so that it will pass on only known file extensions and block unknown ones with an "access denied" error message.

Reliability

Reliability can be broken into two main areas: preventing applications from crashing (undesired termination), and containing such a crash so that it doesn't bring down IIS or the OS. Preventing third-party applications from crashing is a finger-pointing contest between Microsoft and the application developers, so the focus in improving IIS reliability is to better contain applications so that they cannot affect the rest of the system. Microsoft has made a number of changes in IIS to accomplish this, including establishing a dedicated operation mode, isolating applications through worker processes and application pools, limiting queued requests for an application, establishing a separate Web Administration Service (WAS), and monitoring the health of worker processes.

▼ **Dedicated operation mode**   Allows applications to run in an isolated environment in contrast to standard application mode used in earlier versions of IIS where applications run as a part of the web service. Many of the other reliability enhancements depend on using dedicated operation mode.

■ **Application pools and worker processes**   Provide for the isolation of applications by assigning them to particular application pools that are run with specific worker processes. Application pools can be configured with a set of time and space limits and to use a given set of resources, including a particular processor in a multiprocessor server. Application pools and worker resources require dedicated application mode.

■ **Limiting queued requests**   Allows the setting of limits with dedicated application mode on the number of requests that can be queued for a particular application pool. This limits the amount of system resources that any one application pool can utilize.

■ **Web Administration Service (WAS)**   Provides a web management space that is separate from application processes to keep management functions isolated from any problems in web applications. WAS is used to configure application pools, to determine their health (whether or not they are running), and to restart them.

▲ **Health monitoring**   Allows in dedicated application mode the determination of how an application pool is running and, under prescribed circumstances, terminating and optionally restarting it. If the application pool has crashed, it can be terminated and immediately restarted; if the application pool is idle, it can be terminated and restarted on demand; if it has repeatedly failed, it can be disabled and not allowed to restart; and if a detectable part of a pool has failed, it can be separated from the process and restarted as another process.

Administration

IIS 7 administration is handled either with a task-based interface in the Internet Information Services (IIS) Manager or with a command-line facility. IIS 7 allows you to see the diagnostic and health information about the server, including what is currently being executed. Also, IIS 7 now allows the configuration of user and role permissions for both sites and applications. In IIS 7, you can still use all of the IIS 6 management tools, which are required for management of FTP.

▼   **Metabase enhancements**   Allows the direct reading and editing of the IIS configuration and schema information even while IIS is running, the easy rollback to a previous version of the configuration and schema information if it gets corrupted, and the backing up and restoring of the information with a password.

■   **Import/export web site configurations**   Provides the means to export from one node to an entire tree of a web site's configuration information to a readable file that can be imported into another server.

■   **Command-line scripts**   Allows the direct or indirect administration of web sites, FTP sites, virtual directories, web applications, and configuration information using command-line scripts.

▲   **IIS provider in WMI**   Allows the management and configuration of IIS programmatically using the Windows Management Instrumentation (WMI) program interfaces to query and configure the metabase.

Scalability

As a web site or web hosting service grows, it needs to do so with as little disruption to the customer as possible. IIS 7 has added a number of features to improve this ability to smoothly grow, called scalability, including a 64-bit version of IIS, use of full Windows clustering, multiple worker processes, caching of ASP templates, using tracing for capacity planning, and better bandwidth management.

▼   **A 64-bit version of IIS**   Allows running IIS and its web applications on the Intel and AMD 64-bit processors with the capability to handle large loads.

■   **Use of Windows clustering**   Allows using the operating system's built-in capability for clustering, the connecting of multiple computers with potentially shared resources, and the capability to balance the load among the computers. Upon failure of one computer in a cluster, the load is automatically switched to another computer. IIS 7 makes full use of Windows Server 2008's clustering capability.

■   **Multiple worker processes**   Allows running multiple web applications simultaneously, each in its own protected environment. In multiple processor computers, a given worker process can be run on a dedicated processor. IIS 7 provides for multiple worker processes, each running one or more applications.

■ **ASP template caching**   Provides for caching (holding in active memory, which can be either RAM or hard disk) common pieces of ASP script, called "templates," so that when those templates are reused, they are made usable very rapidly, because they are immediately available and do not need to be recompiled.

■ **Tracing for capacity planning**   Allows the analysis of how various workloads are handled with different hardware configurations to plan the hardware needed as the workload grows.

▲ **Bandwidth management**   Provides for the control of the level and quality of user service through bandwidth throttling, application pool queue limits, process accounting, and connection limits and timeouts.

Internet Services in IIS 7

IIS 7 publishes information using standard Internet services and protocols, including the World Wide Web (WWW), FTP, SMTP, and Network News Transfer Protocol (NNTP).

▼ **WWW services**   Uses Hypertext Transfer Protocol (HTTP) to allow users to publish content to the Web using Hypertext Markup Language (HTML), Extensible Markup Language (XML), and ASP. Files are placed in folders or subdirectories connected to a web site. These documents can be viewed by using an Internet browser, such as Internet Explorer. Because of the graphical nature of HTML, businesses can use this format to display and explain products and services, as well as to create e-commerce applications to purchase these products and services.

■ **FTP services**   Used to transmit files over the Internet. This is an older protocol that provides a reliable and speedy transfer of files. FTP can be used with a web browser via web-FTP, to speed up downloading large files from normal web sites, as well as with an independent legacy FTP client connected to the FTP server, which can provide access to files that are independent of HTTP protocols. While some web browsers can be used to access FTP servers, separate FTP clients are often used. Although all Microsoft clients contain an FTP client as part of the TCP/IP stack, this client is DOS and command-line driven (type **ftp** at the command prompt). Several third-party 32-bit FTP clients are available that can run within Windows and that provide additional features not provided by the built-in FTP client. Examples are WS_FTP, available from http://www.ipswitch.com/; SmartFTP, available from http://www.smartftp.com/; and Core FTP, available from http://www.coreftp.com.

■ **SMTP services**   Used for Internet e-mail, SMTP is dependent on TCP/IP protocols and uses the Domain Name System (DNS) servers on the Internet to translate an e-mail name such as billg@microsoft.com to an IP address like 207.46.230.219.

▲   **NNTP services**   Allows a web site to host newsgroups, which provide for the exchange of threaded messages connected to a single topic. Messages are sent to the news server, which posts them to the appropriate newsgroup. A *newsgroup* is a community of people interested in a specific subject. The people in this community log onto the newsgroup to read and reply to messages on the subject of the newsgroup.

WWW services are installed with IIS by default in all cases. By utilizing the WWW services, graphical HTTP sites can be hosted. FTP, SMTP, and NNTP services augment IIS and can be optionally installed with it. These services allow multiple communication options. Using FTP services, files can be distributed quickly across the Internet. Both WWW and FTP services allow multiple sites to be set up on one IIS server, such that the one web server can appear to be multiple WWW and/or FTP sites to a user on the Internet.

SETTING UP A WEB SERVER

When setting up IIS for web-hosting purposes, you need to create one or more dedicated web servers. In some larger organizations, the potential load on the web servers can be dramatic. In smaller organizations, however, a single-server installation is often adequate. The design of any two networks is rarely going to be exactly the same, because different demands affect even the most basic of network installations.

When designing and eventually installing a web server based on IIS 7 and Windows Server 2008, you need to consider a variety of factors, primarily what services the web site will host and what connection security the site will implement. For web sites hosting information that is free and available for everyone to see, anonymous access can be used, where all users connecting to the web server will automatically be granted access to the server based on the Guest account and will not be prompted for a username or password. This situation then allows the user to pass secure information to the server (such as credit card data to place an order) via technology such as SSL (discussed in Chapter 15). When data is being hosted on the server that needs to be secure from unauthorized access, some form of authentication is required, such as Windows Authentication or Kerberos.

Install IIS 7

Windows Server 2008 Setup does not by default install IIS, although you can get a specialized Web Server edition where it is installed. In the cases where IIS is not installed by default, it can be installed by selecting the appropriate role in the Server Manager, as explained later in this chapter. Using the default installation of IIS from Server Manager, only some of the many IIS features are installed. A comparison of the default and optional services (a number of which are beyond the scope of this book) that are installed is shown in Table 9-1.

Category	Service	Default	Description
Common HTTP Features	Static Content	Yes	HTML text pages and images downloaded to each client.
	Default Document	Yes	Specifies a page automatically loaded when the site opens.
	Directory Browsing	Yes	Allows the client to see the directory for the web site.
	HTTP Errors	Yes	Allows customization of error message for the client.
	HTTP Redirection		Redirects client requests to a different location.
Application Development	ASP.NET		Provides object-oriented programming for a web site.
	.NET Extensibility		Lets code developers add and change server functionality.
	ASP & CGI		Active Server Pages and Common Gateway Interface programmability for automating web pages.
	ISAPI Extensions		Internet Server Application Programming Interface allows programming of compiled dynamic web content.
	ISAPI Filters		Allows the inclusion in programs of a review of all requests made to the web server.
	Server-Side Includes		SSI is a real-time scripting facility that dynamically generates HTML pages.
Health and Diagnostics	HTTP Logging	Yes	Logs activity on a web site.
	Logging Tools		Allows the management of web server logs.
	Request Monitor	Yes	Captures HTTP requests to monitor application activity.

Table 9-1.   Services Installed by Default with IIS 7 in Windows Server 2008

Category	Service	Default	Description
	Tracing		Traces failed requests to troubleshoot web performance.
	Custom Logging		Allows the creation of your own logging module.
	ODBC Logging		Allows the logging of activity to an ODBC database.
Security	Basic Authentication		Provides browser-compatible authentication for small intranets. Not recommended for the Internet.
	Windows Authentication		Low-cost authentication for intranets without firewalls.
	Digest Authentication		Higher-level authentication that works with firewalls and proxy servers.
	Client Certificate Mapping Authentication		Uses client certificates (digital IDs) through Active Directory to authenticate web site users.
	IIS Client Certificate Mapping Authentication		Uses client certificates (digital IDs) through IIS to authenticate web site users.
	URL Authorization		Allows attaching rules to a web site to limit who uses it.
	Request Filtering	Yes	Screens server requests to limit attacks on it.
	IP & Domain Restrictions		Limit web site access to specific IPs and domains.
Performance	Static Content Compression	Yes	Provides compression of static content to speed its transmission. Such content can be cached to reduce real-time load.

Table 9-1.   Services Installed by Default with IIS 7 in Windows Server 2008 (*Continued*)

Category	Service	Default	Description
	Dynamic Content Compression		Provides compression of dynamic content to speed its transmission. This cannot be cached, thus increasing real-time load.
Management Tools	IIS Management Console	Yes	IIS 7's primary management interface for both local and remote web servers (not used for FTP or SMTP).
	IIS Management Scripts & Tools		Used for managing web server programmability from a command prompt.
	Management Service		Used to configure the IIS 7 user interface, the IIS Manager, and remote management of IIS 7.
	IIS 6 Management Compatibility		Used to see and manage IIS 6 scripts and applications.
	IIS 6 Metabase Compatibility		Used to configure and query the metabase used by scripts and applications from earlier versions of IIS.
	IIS 6 WMI Compatibility		Allows the use of the Windows Management Instrumentation (WMI) scripting interface in IIS 7.
	IIS 6 Scripting Tools		Allows the use of IIS 6 scripting tools in IIS 7.
	IIS 6 Management Console		Allows the use of IIS 6 management console and the management of FTP and SMTP.
FTP Publishing Service	FTP Server		Allows the creation of an FTP server.
	FTP Management Console		Provides the management of an FTP server.

Table 9-1.   Services Installed by Default with IIS 7 in Windows Server 2008 (*Continued*)

When you do a new installation of Windows Server 2008 and until you tell it otherwise, Initial Configuration Tasks automatically opens at the completion of Setup and when you start up Windows Server. When you close the Initial Configuration Tasks window, Server Manager automatically opens. At any time, you can also open Server Manager and install IIS 7 using these steps:

1. If Server Manager is not automatically open on your desktop, click Start | Server Manager. The Server Manager window will open.

2. In the Roles Summary, click Add Roles, click Next after reading Before You Begin, and a list of server roles will appear in Select Server Roles of the Add Roles Wizard.

3. Click Web Server (IIS). You are asked if you want to add the features required for Web Server (IIS). Click Add Required Features and click Next. Read the Introduction To Web Server (IIS) and any additional information you want. When you are ready, click Next.

4. From the list of role services, see Figure 9-1, select those that you want to be installed based on what you want to do with the web server (see Table 9-1).

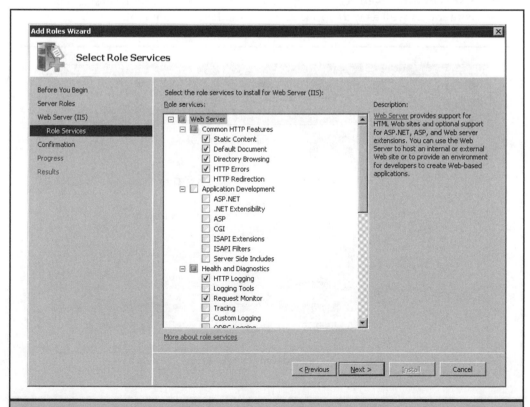

Figure 9-1. IIS 7 has many features or modules that you can optionally install.

5. When you are comfortable with your selections, click Next. You are shown the roles and services you have chosen. If you change your mind, click Previous, make the necessary change, and click Next again. When ready, click Install. IIS will be installed with your choices of optional services, and configured by the Add Roles Wizard.

6. When installation is complete (it may take several minutes), you are told the installation was successful. Click Close to complete the installation.

Migrate to IIS 7

The migration or upgrading process is dependent on the type of web server being upgraded:

▼ **Current users of IIS**   Will be upgraded to version 7 by Windows Server 2008 Setup. Once installation is complete, you can see that IIS is installed in the Server Manager window, as shown in Figure 9-2. Setup and configuration are for the most part automatic, and current users of IIS will have few problems making the transition to IIS 7.

■ **Users of other web servers**   Need to transfer configuration settings and content, as well as web applications, to the IIS environment.

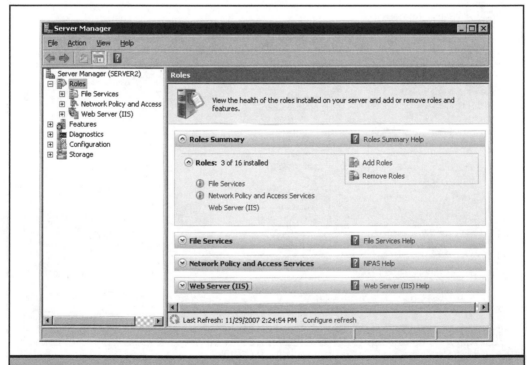

Figure 9-2.   If you are upgrading from a server running IIS, IIS 7 will automatically install.

▲ **Sites with FrontPage Server Extensions**   Will be upgraded to version 7 by Windows Server 2008 Setup, but the FrontPage Server Extensions will not be updated and the IIS WWW Publishing Service will be disabled so the FrontPage metadata is not destroyed. You can download the FrontPage Server Extensions for IIS 7 from http://www.iis.net/downloads/.

TIP   If you are upgrading from a Windows web server and you have removed IIS before doing the upgrade using Add Or Remove Programs, Windows Server 2008 Setup will still install IIS 7.

Plan the Migration

When an organization has a current Internet and/or intranet site or sites, planning is an essential part of any migration, to maintain that site's presence. In choosing a migration path, the primary considerations are as follows:

▼ Risk to the current system and total downtime acceptable

■ Existing hardware role in the new installation

■ Content changes expected to web data (are new web pages expected with the new servers?)

■ Potential network load and available network resources

▲ Additional services that the organization is planning on adding

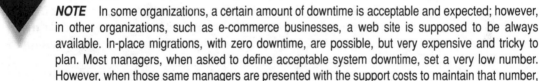

NOTE   In some organizations, a certain amount of downtime is acceptable and expected; however, in other organizations, such as e-commerce businesses, a web site is supposed to be always available. In-place migrations, with zero downtime, are possible, but very expensive and tricky to plan. Most managers, when asked to define acceptable system downtime, set a very low number. However, when those same managers are presented with the support costs to maintain that number, they normally set a more realistic goal. In general, you can expect to find an inverse exponential relationship between downtime allowed and planning/resources (the less the downtime, the more planning) needed for the migration to take place.

Migration Methods

There are at least three ways to carry out a migration to IIS 7, as described in the next several sections.

NOTE   When upgrading existing Windows web servers, the installation options are automatically chosen for Windows Server 2008 and match those of the system being upgraded. This means that IIS itself will install only if it is currently on an existing Windows web server or if you removed it with Add Or Remove Programs.

Migrate to a Clean Windows Server 2008 Installation   Perform a clean installation of Windows Server 2008 and then use Server Manager to install IIS 7 on a computer other than the production web server, called a "staging" server. Migrate settings, content, and applications from the production web server to the new IIS 7 server. Test and debug the new server before it is deployed. Although this is the ideal solution, in many cases it may not be practical, due to software, hardware, and cost factors.

Hardware Needed	Pros	Cons
A second computer is required, in addition to the existing production web server.	Minimum downtime. You can put new, updated hardware in place at the same time you perform the migration. You also avoid taking your production web server offline until the new server is tested and deployed. Following deployment, if problems arise with the new server that didn't appear during testing, you can use the original server as a backup.	High cost. You might need new hardware. However, the cost will be offset at least partly by the time saved conducting the migration as well as troubleshooting any problems that occur during the migration. If you are running an e-commerce site, the added revenue of leaving the site up may cover some or all of the cost of new equipment.

Migrate to a Mirror of the Existing Web Server   If you are migrating from a computer running Microsoft Windows, you can use this approach. On a second computer that is a hardware duplicate of the one you want to migrate, copy the hard disk that exists on the production web server using a product such as Symantec's Ghost, and then use the Windows Server 2008 Setup to upgrade to Windows Server 2008 and IIS 7. The web configuration settings, content, and applications would be on the new web server as a part of creating the mirror. Test and debug the new server before deploying it. This option allows for the testing of third-party applications to be installed on the new, mirrored server, to test for compatibility with Windows Server 2008 and IIS 7.

Hardware Needed	Pros	Cons
A second computer is required that is a duplicate of the existing production web server. You also need a program such as Symantec's Ghost.	Minimum downtime. You can put new, updated hardware in place at the same time you perform the migration. You also avoid taking your production web server offline until the new server is tested and deployed. Following deployment, if problems arise with the new server that didn't appear during testing, you can use the original server as a backup.	High cost. You might need new hardware. However, the cost will be offset at least partly by the time saved conducting the migration as well as by troubleshooting any problems that occur during the migration. If you are running an e-commerce site, the added revenue of leaving the site up may cover some or all of the cost of new equipment.

Upgrade the Production Web Server   If your circumstances allow, you can take your production web server currently running Windows and IIS 5 or 6 offline long enough to upgrade it and get Windows Server 2008 and IIS 7 installed. The majority of your web configuration settings, content, and applications should fully migrate to IIS 7 "in place" on the production web server. Nevertheless, you'll need to thoroughly test and debug the server before deploying it.

Hardware Needed	Pros	Cons
No new hardware is required unless it is needed to run Windows Server 2008, such as memory.	There is no hardware cost.	Downtime. If the server installation does not go as planned, this could be one of those really long weekends that all administrators dread. However, in most IT shops where cost is a factor, this may be the only option where you do not need a second server.

Implement Security

IIS 7 starts "locked down." You need to install certain IIS processes in order to run potentially harmful applications. The elements of this locked-down stance include:

▼   Not installing IIS by default on all Windows Server 2008 editions except the Web Server Edition.

■   Not installing by default any dynamic web content or web automation services including ASP, ASP.NET, Server-Side Includes, and WebDAV and allowing only static pages to be delivered by IIS. See Table 9-1 for the full list. (The Web Edition of Windows Server 2008 by default has ASP and ASP.NET enabled.)

■   Not allowing any applications to run that have not been mapped or registered in IIS.

▲   Not allowing direct editing of the IIS metabase configuration file.

Nevertheless, IIS 7 does by default in all editions enable anonymous access to all but administrative web sites. This means that once the web server is running, security should be addressed. All sites need some level of security. Securing the site is important regardless of the size of the company or who will be using the site, and it is important to consider both internal and external users. Statistically, the users most likely to require security policies are those in your own organization. Laxity about internal security is where the majority of problems pop up. In setting up security, you should develop and implement policies for handling the following issues:

▼ **Installing IIS**   On what servers do you want IIS running?

■ **Dynamic web content**   What types of dynamic web content do you want enabled?

■ **Running applications**   What application extensions do you want mapped in IIS?

■ **Setting NTFS and IIS permissions**   What are the assignments to various groups?

▲ **Security certificates**   How are they going to be used and managed?

Installing IIS is discussed earlier in this chapter, and setting permissions and using certificates are discussed a bit in later sections of this chapter and in Chapter 15. Enabling dynamic web content and enabling applications are discussed in the next two sections.

Enable Dynamic Web Content

Since the dynamic web content services, such as ASP and ASP.NET, that provide for running scripts and applications on the web server are not installed by default, to enable them simply requires their installation. Within Windows Server 2008, this means adding their role services in the Server Manager (you must be a member of the Web Server Administrator role on the local server):

1. Click Start and click Server Manager. In the Server Manager tree on the left, open Roles and click Web Server.

2. In the content pane on the right, scroll down until you see Role Services as shown in Figure 9-3.

3. Click Add Role Services. Click the role services you want. If the Add Role Services dialog box appears, click Add Required Role Services. When you are ready, click Next.

4. Review the list of role services that will be installed. If you want to change anything, click Previous. Otherwise, click Install.

5. When the process is complete, you will be told the role services were installed successfully. Click Close and close the Server Manager.

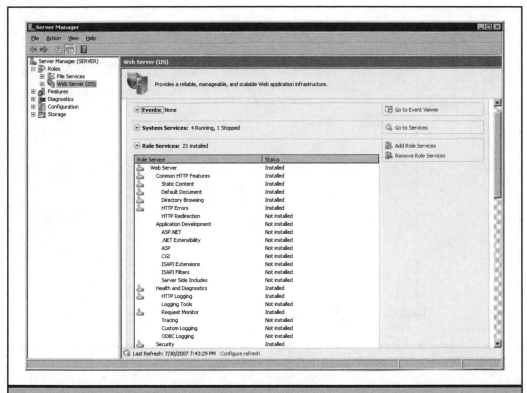

Figure 9-3.   Enable dynamic content by adding the specific role services you want in Server Manager.

CUSTOMIZE AND MAINTAIN IIS 7

After you have completed installing IIS, it is managed with the IIS Manager. The IIS Manager allows the administration of the IIS server components and services, as well as the web sites being hosted. It can be opened through the Server Manager, the Administrative Tools menu, or from the command line. The IIS Manager is the same in all cases. The Server Manager view is shown in Figure 9-4.

Figure 9-4. The IIS Manager opened in the Server Manager

The three alternatives for opening the IIS Manager (the Server Manager, the Administrative Tools menu, or the command line) are performed as follows:

▼ Click the Server Manager icon in the Quick Launch toolbar. In the Server Manager tree on the left, open Roles, open Web Server, and click Internet Information Services (IIS) Manager. Depending on the role services you have installed, your Server Manager window should look similar to Figure 9-4.

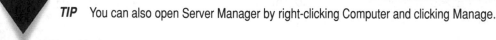

TIP You can also open Server Manager by right-clicking Computer and clicking Manage.

■ Click Start and click Administrative Tools | Internet Information Services (IIS) Manager. The IIS Manager will open by itself, as you can see in Figure 9-5.

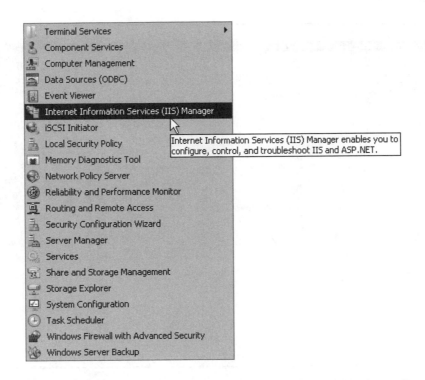

TIP To easily open the IIS Manager in the future, right-drag (pressing and holding the right mouse button while dragging) the IIS Manager option from the Administrative Tools menu to the desktop or Quick Launch toolbar and click Copy Here.

▲ Click Start, click Run, type **inetmgr**, and press ENTER. The IIS Manager will again open by itself.

IIS Manager

In all cases the IIS Manager window is the same. This gives you access to the IIS components and services, which vary depending on the role services that you installed, as well as the ability to manage web sites.

Use the IIS Manager

The IIS Manager shown in Figures 9-4 and 9-5 has a number of controls that allow you to customize how the web server operates, maintain a high level of operation, and manage web sites and applications. There are four elements in the IIS Manager windows: the Navigation toolbar, the Connections pane, the Workspace, and the Actions pane. There is a fifth element to the window, although it is not in the Server Manager, the menus (File, View, Help).

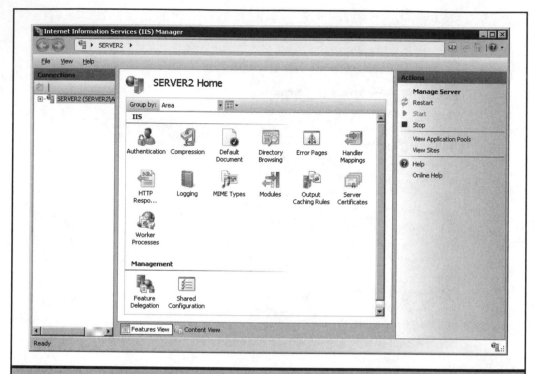

Figure 9-5. The IIS Manager can be opened on its own from Administrative Tools and from the command line.

Navigation Toolbar

The Navigation toolbar at the top of the IIS Manager window is very similar to the Address toolbar in Windows Explorer with the following controls:

- ▼ **Back** and **Forward** buttons move one page in either direction.
- ■ **Server Connections** allows the selection of the server to manage and its connections.
- ■ **Refresh Page** updates the currently displayed page.
- ■ **Stop** halts the current action.
- ■ **Home** opens the home page for the selected web server or web site.
- ▲ **Help** opens IIS Help.

Connections Pane

The Connections pane on the left of the IIS Manager window provides means to navigate within a server, among the web sites and applications on a server, within a web site, and within an application pool. The navigation tree operates similarly to the folder tree in Windows Explorer with the ability to open and close nodes. At the top of the Connections pane is the Connections toolbar with up to four buttons, depending on your installation and permissions:

▼ **Create New Connection** allows you to connect to an additional web server, web site, or application using the Connection Wizard.

■ **Save Current Connection** saves the current set of connections displayed in the Connections pane.

■ **Up** takes you up one level in the Connections pane.

▲ **Delete Connection** deletes the currently selected node in the Connections tree.

Workspace

The Workspace in the center of the IIS Manager window has both a Features View and a Content View, with the Features View the default shown in Figures 9-4 and 9-5. With the minimum default installation of IIS, there are 15 features that you can use to manage IIS:

▼ **Authentication** is used to determine how users gain access to the web server, or, if within a web site, gain access to it. Anonymous authentication is enabled by default and must be disabled if you want to use other types of authentication, which require the installation of the role services for those types. See "Install IIS 7" and Table 9-1 earlier in this chapter.

■ **Compression** reduces the file size for files that are being sent to browsers that can handle compression and, as a result, speeds transmission. Compression of static files is enabled by default, but not of dynamic files (see Table 9-1) because of the CPU resources used in compressing dynamic files at the time they are transmitted.

■ **Default Document** specifies the filenames that can be used in a hosted web site and opened automatically when the web site user does not specify a name.

■ **Directory Browsing** enables a web site user to see and browse web site folders and files. Here you not only can enable a directory, which is disabled by default, but also you can specify what information is made available.

■ **Error Pages** creates and manages the custom error messages or web pages that are returned to web site users when a particular status code is encountered. Figure 9-6 shows the list of default pages that are used. These are HTML files that you can directly edit, or you can replace the default page with another page or a URL.

■ **Handler Mappings** determines how a web server responds to requests of specific types of files and folders. For example, for a static file, the file itself is returned.

■ **HTTP Response Headers** defines specific information ("header") about a web page and specifies the value(s) that are associated with that header. For example, a header named "author" would have the author(s) of the page.

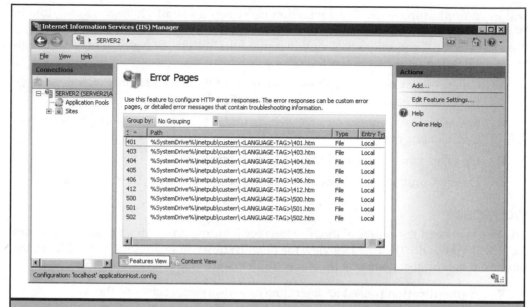

Figure 9-6. IIS starts out with a set of error pages that you can change or replace.

- **Logging** determines how and when IIS logs information about the web server, web site, or application. You can determine when new logs are started and what information is collected.

- **MIME Types** manages the list of MIME (Multipurpose Internet Mail Extensions) page types that can be returned by the web server.

- **Modules** manages the list of code modules that can be used by the web server to process requests.

- **Output Caching Rules** determines what types of files are cached and how that is done.

- **Server Certificates** requests and manages certificates issued to hosted web sites for their secure operations.

- **Worker Processes** lists and manages the applications ("worker processes") that are running on the web server, showing the CPU percentage and the amount of memory being used.

- **Feature Delegation** determines whether each of the preceding features configurations can be read only or can be both read and written, as shown in Figure 9-7.

- ▲ **Shared Configuration** determines whether the web server's configuration and encryption keys can be shared with another IIS web server.

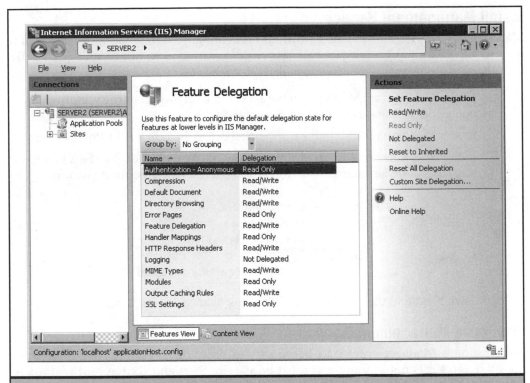

Figure 9-7. When you delegate at the web *server* level, you do so to the web *site* level. When you delegate at the web *site* level, you do so to the web *application* level.

Actions Pane

The Actions pane on the right of the IIS Manager window displays the actions that are available for the feature that is selected in the Workspace, as you can see in Figures 9-6 and 9-7.

Administer Web Servers Remotely

Because it may not always be convenient to perform administration tasks on the computer running the IIS web server, IIS 7 provides a remote administration capability. To facilitate this, you must first enable Management Service.

TIP You can also remotely administer a web server by opening the desktop of any computer for which you have permission using Windows Server 2008 Terminal Services, as explained in Chapter 11, and from that desktop you can open the IIS Manager for the remote server.

Install Management Service

Management Service allows you to turn on and configure remote administration of a web server as well as to delegate web server administration to nonadministrators. By default, Management Service is not installed. To install it:

1. Click Start | Server Manager. In the server tree on the left of the window that opens, open Roles and click Web Server (IIS).

2. Under Web Server (IIS) on the right, scroll down and click Add Role Services.

3. In the Add Role Services Wizard that opens, scroll the list of Role Services until you can click Management Service. If asked, click Add Required Features.

4. Click Next and then click Install. When installation is complete, click Close.

Configure Management Service

Once installed, Management Service becomes a feature of IIS and can be configured from IIS. By default it is not running and must be started. Start and configure it with these steps:

1. Open the IIS Manager either by double-clicking its icon on the desktop if you put it there as suggested earlier, or by clicking Start | Administrative Tools | Internet Information Services (IIS) Manager. The IIS Manager will open with a new Start Page as shown in Figure 9-8.

2. In the right pane of the Start Page, click Connect To Localhost under Connection Tasks.

3. Scroll down the center Workspace pane until you see the Management section, and double-click Management Service.

Management

Feature   IIS Manager   IIS Manager   Management   Shared
Delegation   Permissions   Users   Service   Configuration

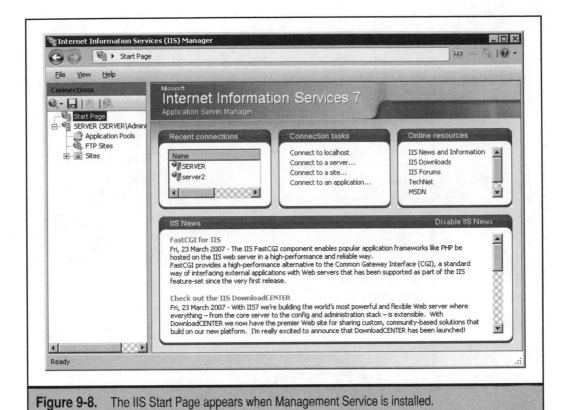

Figure 9-8.   The IIS Start Page appears when Management Service is installed.

4. In the Management Service workspace, click Enable Remote Connections and make any other configuration changes that are correct for your situation. My settings are shown in Figure 9-9.

5. In the Actions pane, click Start. You are asked if you want to save the service settings. Click Yes. The service is started and its settings are frozen.

Use Remote IIS Management

With Management services operating, you can open and manage any IIS server on the local area network with the appropriate permissions. Here's how:

1. Open the IIS Manager either by double-clicking its icon on the desktop or by clicking Start | Administrative Tools | Internet Information Services (IIS) Manager.

2. In the Start page, click Connect To A Server. The Connect To Server Wizard will open.

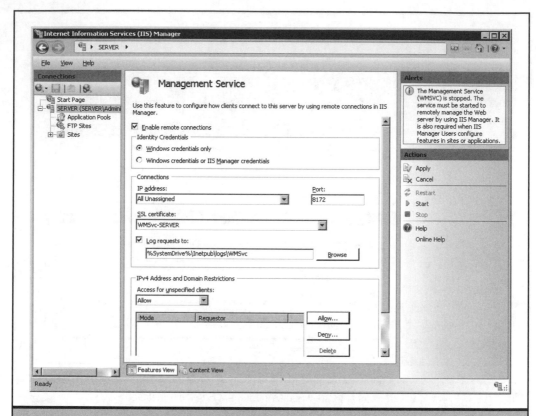

Figure 9-9. Management Service must be started in order to remotely manage a web server.

3. Enter the computer name (this is the name of a computer on the network, such as "Server2," or it can be the IP address, such as 192.168.57.62), click Next, enter a username and password, click Next, if asked about a certificate, click Connect, and, when told that the new connection was created successfully, click Finish. The new server will appear in the server tree on the left of the IIS Manager.

NOTE The default administrative port on the server is 8172, as you might have noticed in configuring Management Service. If you leave that port, you do not need to specify the port when entering the server name. If you use some other port, you will need to enter it. For example, "Server2:8081" or "192.168.57.62:8081."

4. Open the new server and then the folders beneath it as shown in Figure 9-10. When you are done looking at the remote server, close the IIS Manager.

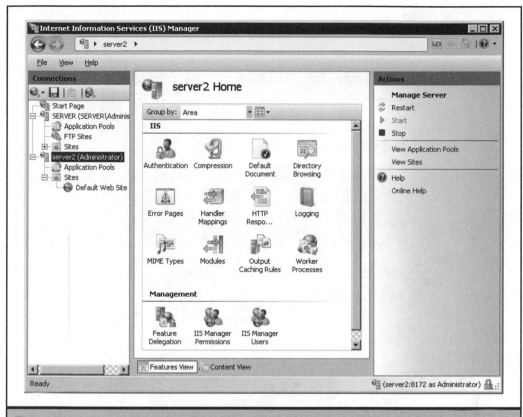

Figure 9-10.   Remotely administrating an IIS web server

Create Web Sites

Once the server and its management are set up, web sites can be hosted and managed by IIS 7, which can handle one site or many sites. Each site can appear as a separate location to Internet web surfers. When you install IIS 7, a default web site is set up for you. You can publish your content in the default web site immediately. Most organizations, though, start with a new site, so that the site can be customized to the needs of the organization. You can add new sites to a computer by launching the Web Site Creation Wizard with the following instructions:

1. In the IIS Manager (opened through Start | Administrative Tools | Internet Information Services (IIS) Manager), open the server you want as the host, and click the Sites folder.

2. In the Actions pane, click Add Web Site. The Add Web Site dialog box will open. Enter a name for the site, and enter or browse to the physical location of the web site's files.

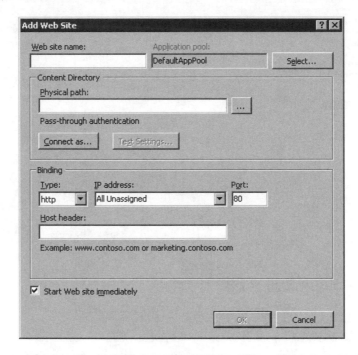

3. Under Binding, enter address elements you want bound to the site (see the related Note). For example, enter the IP address to use for the site, or open the drop-down box and click the IP address for the server. Accept the default port address of 80 and leave the Host Header blank.

NOTE Each site must have at least one of the three address components (IP address, TCP port, or host header) unique; otherwise, the site will not be started and you will get an error message telling you about the problem when you try to start it. See "Host Multiple Sites," next in this chapter.

4. When you are ready, click OK. The new site will appear on the IIS Manager, as shown in Figure 9-11.

5. Click Browse Web Site to actually open the web site in your default browser.

Host Multiple Sites

Multiple web sites can be hosted simultaneously on a single computer running IIS. This gives the appearance of separate and distinct sites to the web surfer. Each IIS server has the capability to host one or more domain names. For this reason, sites are sometimes referred to as *virtual servers*.

Figure 9-11.   The Default Web Site is bound to a TCP port, while the second site is bound to an IP address.

A web site has three identifiers it uses to identify itself on the Internet or an intranet. When queried, it must be able to respond with each of these settings:

▼   A port number

■   An IP address

▲   A host header name

By changing one of these three identifiers, you can host multiple sites on a single computer:

▼   **Port numbers**   By using appended port numbers, your site needs only one IP address to host many sites. To reach your site, clients would need to attach a port number (unless using the default port number, 80) at the end of the static IP address. Using this method of hosting multiple sites requires clients to type the actual numerical IP address followed by a port number, for example, 192.168.57.62:81. Host names or "friendly names" cannot be used.

■   **Multiple IP addresses**   To use multiple IP addresses, you must add the host name and its corresponding IP address to your name resolution system, which is DNS in Windows Server 2008. Then clients need only type the text name in a browser to reach your web site. Multiple IP addresses can be hosted on the same network card.

NOTE If you are using the multiple IP addresses method of hosting multiple sites on the Internet, you will also need to register the text names with an InterNIC accredited registrar. You can find a list of InterNIC accredited registrars at http://www.internic.net/.

▲ **Host header names** Sites can also use host header names with a single static IP address to host multiple sites. As with the preceding method, you would still add the host name to your name resolution system. The difference is that once a request reaches the computer, IIS uses the host name passed in the HTTP header to determine which site a client is requesting. If you are using this method of hosting multiple sites on the Internet, you will also need to register the host header names with InterNIC.

NOTE Be aware that older browsers do not support host header names. Only IE 3.x and later, or Netscape Navigator 3.x and later will work.

The majority of multiple web site hosting is done with multiple host headers.

Web Site Management

Whether your site is on an intranet or the Internet, the principles of publishing information are the same. Here are the steps:

1. Web files are placed in directories on the server.
2. The directories are identified to IIS as belonging to a web site.
3. When a user establishes an HTTP connection to that site, IIS sends requested files to the user's browser.

While the process to store the files is simple, part of the web site manager's job must be to determine how the site is deployed, and how it and the storage will evolve. Most successful web administrators are kept busy accommodating ever-changing web content. Step back a minute from the content and look at the basics of managing a web site's infrastructure, from redirecting requests to dynamically altering web pages.

Define Home Directories

Each web site must have a home directory, which is where the root site information is stored. As a user logs into a specific site, IIS knows the home directory and the default first document that all users see when connecting, and it provides that document to the requesting user's browser for translation and display. For example, if your site's Internet domain name is www.mycompany.com, your home directory is C:\website\mysite\, and the default document is Default.htm, then browsers use the URL http://www.my-company.com, which causes IIS to access your home directory C:\website\mysite\ and transmit the file Default.htm.

On an intranet, if your server name is Marketing, then browsers use the URL http://marketing to access files in your home directory. A default home directory is created when IIS is installed or when a new web site is created. The web site properties determine the location of the files.

Change the Home Directory

When setting up a web site and an FTP site on the same computer, a different home directory is specified for each service (WWW and FTP). The default home directory for the WWW service is C:\inetpub\wwwroot\. The default home directory for the FTP service is C:\inetpub\ftproot\. The home directory can be changed to any location on the network and can be listed as a URL or a path statement. Here is how to change the home directory:

1. In the IIS Manager, open the local server and the Sites folder, click Default Web Site to select it, and click Basic Settings in the Actions pane.

2. Drag over the Physical Path, and type in the path name, share name, or URL (WWW only) of your directory, as shown next for the default web site. You can select:

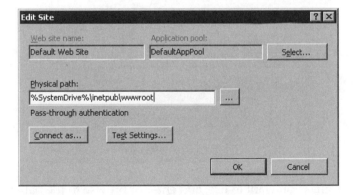

▼   A directory located on a hard disk on your computer

■   A shared directory located on another computer

▲   A redirection to a URL (not available with FTP)

Virtual Directories

Virtual directories allow access to files located on a directory not within the home directory. This is a big advantage when trying to access information to be published on an intranet that is located in multiple locations across the network. Using virtual directories is one way to link that information more easily. For the browser, everything seems to be in one location. For the administrator who has to collect everything, it can be easier to store each person's data in a separate virtual directory.

A virtual directory has an alias that the web browser uses to access that directory. As added benefits, using an alias often is more convenient than typing a long path and filename, and the URL for a site does not have to change when the directory changes; only the mapping between the alias and the physical location needs to change.

Create Virtual Directories   Create virtual directories to include those files in your web site located in directories other than the home directory. To use a directory on another computer, specify the directory's Universal Naming Convention (UNC) name in the form *servername\drive\path\filename*, and provide a username and password to use for access permission. Use the following steps to create a virtual directory:

1. In the IIS Manager Connections pane, click the web site to which you want to add a virtual directory.

2. In the Actions pane (or right-click the site and then in the context menu), click Add Virtual Directory. The Add Virtual Directory dialog box will open.

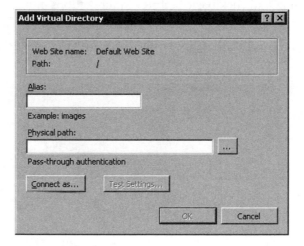

3. Enter the alias you want to use, and enter or browse to the path that contains the actual files.

4. Click OK. The virtual directory will appear in the IIS Manager, as shown in Figure 9-12.

Delete Virtual Directories   To delete a virtual directory, use the following steps:

1. In the IIS Manager Connections pane, click the web site with the virtual directory you want to delete.

2. In the Actions pane, click View Virtual Directories, click the directory, and click Remove in the Actions pane. Click Yes if you are sure you want to delete the item.

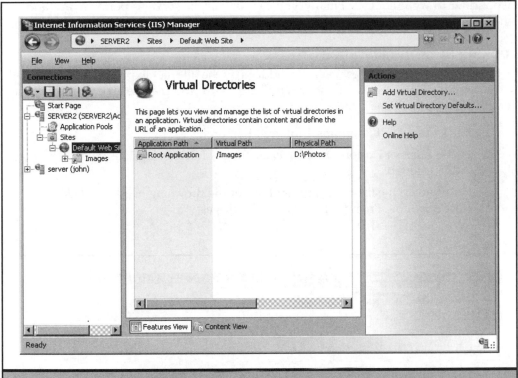

Figure 9-12.   Virtual directories allow you to refer to files outside of the site's home directory.

NOTE   Deleting a virtual directory does not delete the corresponding physical directory or files.

Troubleshoot IIS

A lot of issues affect the performance of IIS and the web sites being hosted. Problems have four main causes: hardware issues, software issues, incorrect settings, and site activity issues. The trick is to determine which of these is the culprit and then implement a fix. IIS 7 and the hardware that runs it are very complex with a large number of areas that can use alternative configurations. Also, making changes in one area can have unforeseen consequences in another. To attack this complex tangled ball of yarn, IIS 7 has provided a number of new and improved tools for diagnosing problems as well as a number of features that facilitate problem solving. One very obvious benefit of IIS 7 is its modularity, which allows you to not install role services or features you are not using and thereby eliminate that area from being a problem.

Troubleshooting web server problems begins by learning all you can about what is happening, and that starts with looking at the error messages you receive. You then can look at the logs that IIS is keeping of web activity and try to trace how the site is responding to web requests. Finally, you can look at the server's performance and see where the bottlenecks are.

Looking at Error Messages

By default the error messages that are produced by the Internet Explorer (IE) are "friendly" and not very informative, as shown in Figure 9-13. You may be able to improve that by turning off the "friendly" feature:

1. Click Start | All Programs | Internet Explorer.
2. In the Internet Explorer toolbar, click Tools | Internet Options, and click the Advanced tab.
3. Scroll down the list of settings and under the Browsing heading, click to uncheck Show Friendly HTTP Error Messages.

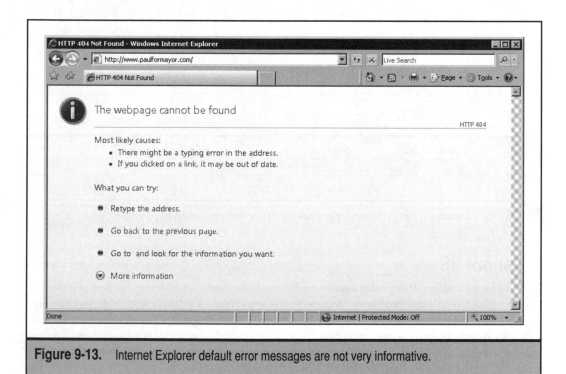

Figure 9-13. Internet Explorer default error messages are not very informative.

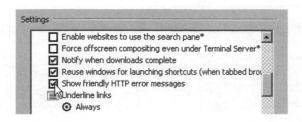

4.   Retry opening the page that gave the error. If you are still getting the same or an even less informative error message, try looking at the error message in IE on the server computer. Here, by default, you should see detailed error messages as shown in Figure 9-14.

5.   If you get "friendly" error messages when you open IE directly on the server, open the IIS Manager, click the web site in the Connections tree on the left, double-click Error Pages in the center Workspace pane, and in the Actions pane, click Edit Feature Settings.

6.   In the Edit Error Pages Settings dialog box, click Detail Errors For Local Requests…, and click OK. Now when you open the site in error you will get the detailed message shown in Figure 9-14.

Figure 9-14. On detailed error pages you will get suggestions on causes and possible fixes.

Review Logs

IIS 7 keeps extensive logs of what is happening on a web server and the hosted sites. You can tailor these logs to your needs and easily review them.

1. Click Start | Administrative Tools | Internet Information Services (IIS) Manager. In the Connections tree on the left, click the server whose logs you want to configure; if needed, scroll down the Workspace pane, and double-click Logging.

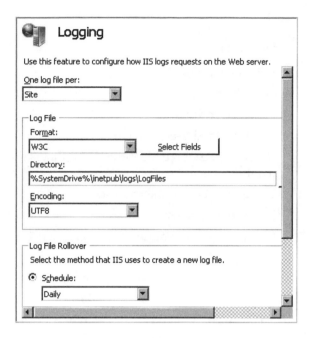

2. Make any desired changes to Logging, note the directory where the logs are kept, and, in the Actions pane, click Apply. Try to open the web site.

3. Click Start | Computer and navigate to the directory noted in the last step (%SystemDrive% is normally the C: drive). Display folders in the left pane if they aren't already, open the Logs and LogFiles folders, and double-click a log file for the day you want to look at. Notepad will open and display the log file.

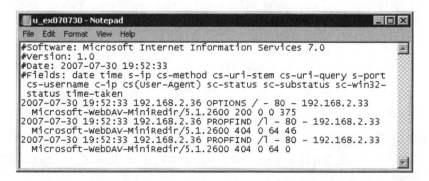

The log file #Fields: line shows the fields that are being displayed. (You can control the fields displayed by clicking Select Fields in the Logging feature.) The meaning of the default fields is shown in Table 9-2.

Field Name	Description
date	Date the request occurred.
time	Time the request occurred.
s-ip	Server IP address.
cs-method	HTTP method used in the request.
cs-uri-stem	Universal Resource Identifier (URI) that is the target of the request.
cs-uri-query	URI query used in the request.
s-port	Server port address.
cs-username	Name of the authenticated user. Hyphen is anonymous user.
c-ip	User IP address.
cs (user-agent)	The browser used to generate the request.
sc-status	HTTP status code (error code, like 404).
sc-substatus	HTTP substatus code (error decimal code, like 1 in 404.1).
sc-win32-status	Windows status code.
time-taken	Time the request took in milliseconds.

Table 9-2.   Default Fields Used in IIS Log Files

The HTTP status and substatus codes are described in several places on the Internet, but probably best on Microsoft's TechNet at:

```
http://technet2.microsoft.com/windowsserver/en/library/852e7f92-58c3-
47f3-8b37-8a630839a90d1033.mspx?mfr=true.
```

The HTTP methods are described at: http://www.w3.org/Protocols/rfc2616/rfc2616-sec9.html.

Implement Tracing

Tracing, which is an IIS 7 role service that is not installed by default, traces failed requests to troubleshoot web performance. When it's installed, you can establish a set of rules that will generate log entries when the rules are met. The rules can specify status codes, methods, and other end products. Use the following steps to install the role service, set up the rules, and implement tracing:

1. Click Start | Server Manager. In the Server Manager tree on the left, open Roles and click Web Server (IIS). Scroll down the right pane and click Add Role Services.

2. Scroll Role Services, click Tracing, click Next, click Install, and click Close. Close Server Manager.

3. Click Start | Administrative Tools | Internet Information Services (IIS) Manager, and in the Connections tree on the left, click the web site you want to trace.

4. In the Actions pane under Configure, click Failed Request Tracing, click Enable, make any desired changes to the directory and/or the maximum number of trace files, and click OK.

5. Scroll the Workspace in the center, and double-click Failed Request Tracing Rules.

6. In the Actions pane, click Add, select the content to trace, and click Next. Select the conditions and enter the specifics that will generate a trace log entry. Select the trace providers, and click Finish. The rule will be added to the tracing rules.

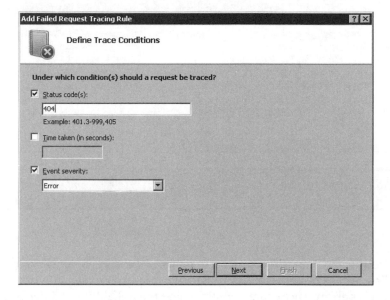

7. Click Start | Computer and navigate to the directory C:\inetpub\logs\ FailedReqLogFiles and open the folder that you see. Finally, double-click the XML file. Internet Explorer will open and display the summary.

8. Click the Compact View tab to see the trace steps and the detail for each step, as shown in Figure 9-15.

Look at Server Performance

As your web server traffic builds and you start hearing complaints about slow sites, you are going to want to look at your server performance. "Server," of course, covers a lot, including memory use, CPU load, disk speed, and network traffic. The Reliability and Performance Monitor, shown in Figure 9-16, can give you substantial insight into your hardware performance.

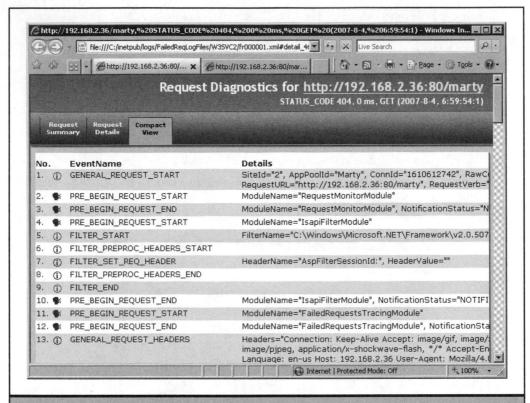

Figure 9-15.   Tracing can give you a lot of insight into what is causing your problem.

When troubleshooting IIS, you need to collect a baseline against which to compare problems. To collect a baseline for your IIS server, apply a typical network load to it, and log the server's performance characteristics using the Reliability and Performance Monitor ("Perfmon"). This provides a picture of how the server looks with respect to CPU, disk, network, and memory. Then, when performance is questionable, you can compare the baseline to the current situation and determine where a possible bottleneck is occurring. Open the Reliability and Performance Monitor, and then consider and choose the performance measures you want to use to establish a baseline for your web server.

1. Click Start | Administrative Tools | Reliability and Performance Monitor, or alternatively, click Start, click Start Search, type **Perfmon**, and press ENTER. The Reliability and Performance Monitor will open as shown in Figure 9-16.

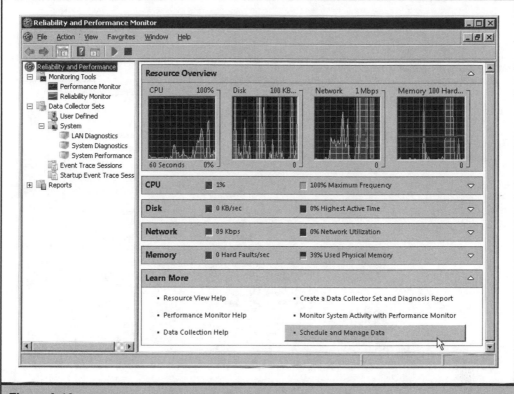

Figure 9-16.   The Reliability and Performance Monitor tracks resource usage.

2. Click the down arrows on the right of each of the four resource areas (CPU, Disk, Network, and Memory) and consider how the information can be useful to you.

3. In the left pane, open Monitoring Tools and click Performance Monitor. Initially you only see the processor time. Click Add (the green cross in the toolbar). In the Add Counters dialog box that opens, scroll down the list of available counters and double-click several you are interested in.

4. Click the counters you want to track and click Add. When you have added all the counters you want, click OK. The Performance Monitor will now display tracking for all the counters you added, as is shown for my choices in Figure 9-17 (probably tracking more than are readable).

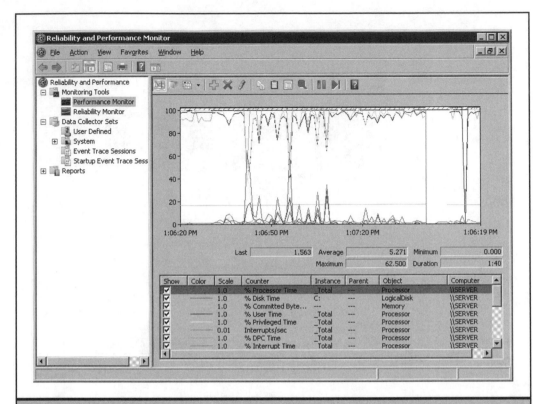

Figure 9-17. The Reliability and Performance Monitor lets you track a large number of performance measures.

The number of performance measures or *counters* and their diversity can be daunting. In the Add Counters dialog box, you can get more information about each counter by selecting the counter and clicking Show Description. The explanation of the counter and how it is used will appear at the bottom of the dialog box, as you can see in Figure 9-18.

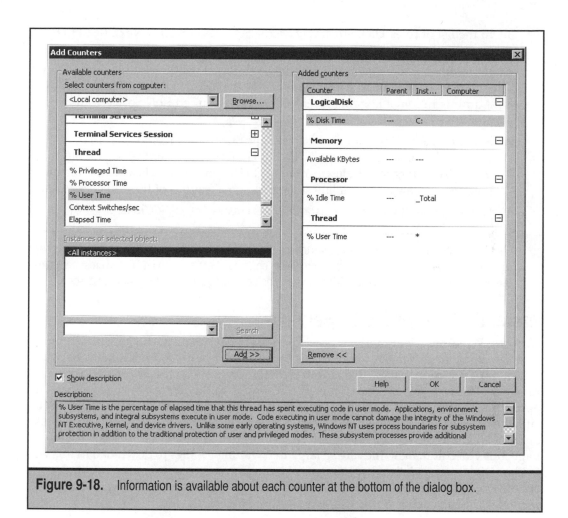

Figure 9-18. Information is available about each counter at the bottom of the dialog box.

UNDERSTAND AND MANAGE WINDOWS MEDIA SERVICES

Windows Media Services enables streaming of multimedia content over all types of networks. These networks can range from low-bandwidth, dial-up Internet connections to high-bandwidth local area networks. Windows Media Services (called "Streaming Media Services") is a server role installed from the Server Manager:

1. Click Start | Server Manager. In the server tree on the left, click Roles.
2. Under Roles Summary in the right pane, click Add Roles and click Next.

3. In the list of roles, click Streaming Media Services and click Next. Read the Introduction To Streaming Media Services and click Next.

4. If you think you will want them, click Web-Based Administration and Logging Agent. If you are asked if you want to add the features required for Web-Based Administration or Logging Agent, click Add Required Role Services and click Next.

5. You are asked if you want to use Real Time Streaming Protocol (RTSP) or Hypertext Transfer Protocol (HTTP), but HTTP is grayed out since port 80 is being used for normal (nonstreaming) HTTP connections. Click Next three times (because you are also installing some additional features of IIS) and click Install.

6. When you are told that the installation is successful, click Close.

NOTE   Streaming audio and video allows the media to be played on the receiving computer as it is being downloaded, instead of waiting for it to completely download before playing it. The Microsoft Windows Media Player, included in Windows XP and Vista, can be used to play streaming audio and video.

Understand Windows Media Services

Utilizing Windows Media Services, a media server can stream audio and video content over the Web. To understand why this is significant, it helps to understand the way a typical HTTP session works. First, a web browser sends out a request for a URL over the network. The web server hosting the URL responds to the request and downloads the appropriate information to the browser. Once the web pages are downloaded from the site, the browser displays them. When the user clicks another link, the browser requests another URL and the server responds. This works great for small file sizes, such as a web page, but video and audio files are so large that waiting for files to download in this way is like waiting for paint to dry. Windows Media Services uses streaming technology to enable you to load and play the audio or video while it is still downloading. This greatly increases the satisfaction of the user who is downloading the file.

Stream Methods

There are two ways to stream audio and video. One uses a web server alone; the other separates the web tasks from the streaming media tasks. The second method utilizes a streaming media server to stream audio or video, in conjunction with a web server used to download the rest of the web information.

Stream with a Web Server   The server sends the audio and video files in the same fashion as it would send any type of file. The streaming client stores, or *buffers*, a small amount of the audio or video stream and then starts playing it while continuing the download. Buffering theoretically allows the media to continue playing uninterruptedly during periods of network congestion. In fact, it is normal for it to get interrupted on a dial-up or other lower-speed connection. The client retrieves data as fast as the web server, network, and client connection allow.

Stream with a Media Server   With a media server, the first step is to compress the media file and copy it to a specialized streaming media server (such as Microsoft's Windows Media Services). Next, a reference is made on the web page so that IIS knows when and where to retrieve the streaming data for the page. Then data is sent to the client such that the content is delivered at the same rate as the compressed audio and video streams. The server and the client stay in close touch during the delivery process, and the streaming media server can respond to any feedback from the client.

Stream with Windows Media Services   Designed specifically for the task of delivering live or on-demand streaming media rather than many small HTML and image files, a Windows Media Services server offers many advantages over standard web servers:

▼   More efficient network throughput

■   Better audio and video quality to the user

■   Support for advanced features

■   Cost-effective scalability to a large number of users

■   Protection of content copyright

▲   Multiple delivery options

Windows Media Services, diagrammatically shown in Figure 9-19, automatically switches to the appropriate protocol, so no client-side configuration is necessary.

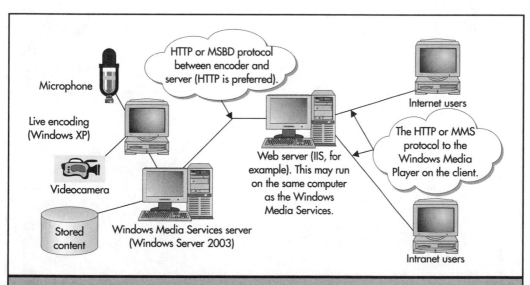

Figure 9-19.   Windows Media Services interacts with a web server to provide streaming content to a client's browser.

Manage Windows Media Services

Once Windows Media Services is installed, you can configure and manage it on an on-going basis directly through the Windows Media Services window or through the web administration. Look at the Windows Media administration window:

Click Start | Administrative Tools | Windows Media Services.

The Windows Media Services window will open. Open the local server and click the Getting Started tab to display the windows shown in Figure 9-20. The links open Help files explaining how to accomplish various functions, while the buttons perform specific functions. Start by testing the Windows Media Services server. This not only tests your streaming server, but also sets up streaming on demand and describes some key Windows media concepts. When you are done, close the Windows Media Services window.

TIP In addition to using the Windows Media Services window, you can manage Windows Media Services with the Web Administrator if you have installed it. Click Start | Administrative Tools | Windows Media Services (Web).

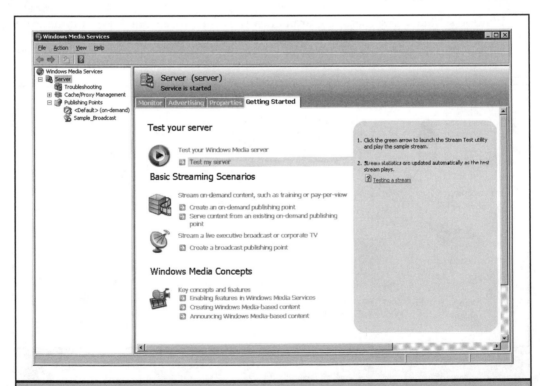

Figure 9-20. Windows Media Services provides streaming media in several formats.

CHAPTER 10

Virtual Private Networking

*V*irtual private networking (VPN) uses an insecure public network to handle secure private networking. Most commonly today, that means connecting to or extending a LAN using the Internet, which replaces leased lines and/or dedicated value added networks (VANs) at considerable savings. VPN allows a traveling worker to connect to and utilize an organization's LAN by first connecting to and utilizing the Internet. The key ingredient in VPN is security. VPN allows you to use a public network with a high degree of certainty that the data sent across it will be secure. You can think of VPN as a secure pipe through the Internet connecting computers on either end, as you can see in Figure 10-1. Information is able to travel through the pipe securely and without regard to the fact that it is part of the Internet. This concept of a pipe though the Internet is called *tunneling*. The secure "tunnel" is achieved by first encrypting the data, including all its addressing and sequencing information (where the individual piece of data, called a "datagram," fits in a longer message), and then encapsulating or wrapping that encrypted data in a new Internet Protocol (IP) header with routing and addressing information, as shown next. The outer package can then weave its way through the servers and routers of the Internet without the inner datagram ever being exposed, and should it ever be, it is still encrypted.

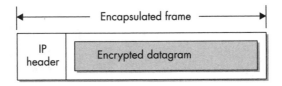

VPN replaces both leased lines between facilities and the need for long-distance dial-up connections. For example, before VPN a company needed a leased line between the headquarters and a branch office in another city. With VPN, each office just needs a local, probably high-speed, connection to the Internet, which is then used with VPN to securely transmit information between the offices. In another example, before VPN a traveling worker would make a long-distance call into a remote access server to connect to the company's LAN, incurring a long-distance charge. With VPN, the worker uses a hotel Internet connection or places a local call to an Internet service provider (ISP) to connect to the Internet, which is then used with VPN to connect to the company's LAN. In both cases, significant cost savings are achieved.

VPN establishes a secure pathway across the Internet from a client connected to the Internet on one end to a server connected to the Internet on the other. This is called a *point-to-point* connection. Once the connection is made between the two points, it conveys information as though a private line were being used, without regard to the many servers and routers in the path and with a high degree of security. This is done in Windows Server 2008 and Windows Vista with one of three protocols:

▼   Point-to-Point Tunneling Protocol (PPTP)

■   Layer Two Tunneling Protocol (L2TP)

▲   Secure Socket Tunneling Protocol (SSTP)

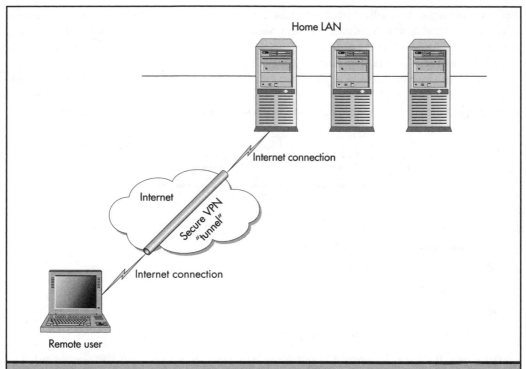

Figure 10-1.   Virtual private networking can be thought of as a secure pipe through the Internet.

Point-to-Point Tunneling Protocol

Point-to-Point Tunneling Protocol (PPTP) was originally developed by Microsoft to do VPN with Windows NT 4 and Windows 9x/Me. PPTP, which incorporates and extends the Point-to-Point Protocol (PPP) and the Microsoft Point-to-Point Encryption (MPPE), is the simplest to install of the VPN protocols and is an industry standard (RFC 2637). See Chapter 5, under "Networking Protocols," for a discussion of networking standards documents called Requests for Comments (or RFCs).

NOTE   If you want to use VPN with Windows NT 4 or Windows 9x/Me, you have to use PPTP.

The Point-to-Point Protocol

Point-to-Point Protocol (PPP), the foundation protocol for all three tunneling protocols (PPTP, L2TP, and SSTP), which is used in many areas of the Internet, including many e-mail connections, is an industry standard defined in several RFCs, but primarily 1661. PPP operates at the second or Data Link layer of the Open Systems Interconnection (OSI) model (see Chapter 5, under "The OSI Model") and provides the functions of compressing and encapsulating the information, as well as authenticating the client and the server.

PPP is built upon two other protocols, the Link Control Protocol (LCP) for handling the connections and authentication, and the Network Control Protocol (NCP) for handling the compression and encapsulation. The TCP/IP networking protocol determines the properties of NCP and how it does its job.

PPP defines the building of a *frame* that takes the datagram built at the third or Networking layer of the OSI model (see Chapter 5, "IP" under "Networking Protocols"), compresses and encapsulates it, and adds address and control information, so it looks like this:

Starting delimiter 1 byte	Address 1 byte	Frame control 1 byte	Network protocol 1 byte	Data variable	FCS 2 bytes	Ending delimiter 1 byte

The PPP frame

▼ **Starting and ending delimiters** mark the start and end of the frame.

■ **Address** is the destination address.

■ **Frame control** is a sequence number to maintain the proper order.

■ **Network protocol** is the protocol (IP) being used.

■ **Data** is the actual datagram being transferred.

▲ **FCS** is the frame check sequence used for error checking.

In PPP, LCP establishes the connection between the server and the client and then negotiates between the two computers to determine the type of authentication to be used, as well as several of the link parameters, such as the maximum frame length. NCP is used to determine the networking protocol to be used and then, based on that, how the datagram will be compressed and encapsulated.

Although PPP has a prominent role in authentication, it doesn't actually carry out the authentication; that function is performed by one of several authentication protocols. VPN and Windows Server 2008 have several authentication protocol options, each with several variants. The two recommended are:

▼ Microsoft Challenge Handshake Authentication Protocol version 2 (MS-CHAP v2)

▲ Extensible Authentication Protocol-Transport Level Security (EAP-TLS)

Challenge Handshake Authentication Protocol   *CHAP,* the most common and widely supported of the primary authentication methods, depends on using a password known to both the client and the server in the authentication. (CHAP is defined in several RFCs, primarily 1994.) Unlike in earlier authentication methods, though, the password is not transmitted during authentication. Instead, the server sends out a unique string of characters called the "challenge string." The client uses its password and the challenge string to compute a Message Digest hash and send it back to the server. The server also computes the hash according to its knowledge of the password and the string it sent and compares that hash to the one sent by the client. If the two hashes are the same, the client is authenticated. A *hash* is an algorithm or function that is very easy to calculate if you know the originating data, but it is very difficult if not impossible to compute the data from the hash.

Microsoft has developed two variants of CHAP: MS-CHAP and MS-CHAP v2, which are designed to work with Windows 9*x* through Vista, as well as with Windows Server 2003 and 2008, and are what is used with VPN. MS-CHAP primarily differs from CHAP by using a different Message Digest hash algorithm, by encrypting the challenge and the response, and by not requiring that the password be stored in a reversibly encrypted form. MS-CHAP v2 primarily differs from MS-CHAP by being more secure with stronger encryption keys, by authenticating both the client to the server (as in CHAP and MS-CHAP) and the server to the client, and by providing separate encryption keys for sending and receiving information.

Extensible Authentication Protocol If in place of a password, a smart card or other device is used for identification, then EAP is used for authentication. EAP, which is a networking standard defined in RFC 2284, is a general framework that allows an arbitrary authentication method to be negotiated and used. With Windows Server 2008, VPN, and smart cards, EAP-TLS (Transport Layer Security) is the protocol of choice. EAP-TLS causes certificates stored both on the server and on a smart card at the client to be exchanged, and, if the certificates are accepted, to authenticate both the client and the server. In the process, shared encryption keys can be exchanged, as well as other information. EAP-TLS provides a very high level of mutual authentication.

Microsoft Point-to-Point Encryption

Once a PPTP connection has been made, the end points authenticated, and the details of the transmission negotiated—all the functions of PPP—the data to be transmitted must be encrypted so that it is secure on the Internet. That is the function of MPPE. MPPE can provide three levels of encryption using a 40-bit, 56-bit, or 128-bit private key (see Chapter 15 for a description of private and public keys and how they are used in encryption). The keys are generated as part of the authentication process in MS-CHAP, MS-CHAP v2, or EAP-TLS, so one of these authentication methods must be used.

Layer Two Tunneling Protocol

While Microsoft was developing PPTP, Cisco was developing a protocol called Layer Two Forwarding (L2F) to do VPN. This has been combined with PPTP to come up with the second protocol supported by Microsoft in Windows 2000 through Server 2008: L2TP. L2TP has become a recent industry standard, primarily defined in RFC 2661, and although it is the more secure and robust of the first two VPN protocols, it has many similarities with PPTP, primarily that it makes full use of and extends PPP for authentication, compression, and encapsulation. Unlike PPTP, though, L2TP as it has been implemented in the latest versions of Windows uses Internet Protocol Security (IPSec) to handle encryption in place of MPPE (see RFC 2888). This is what makes L2TP more robust and secure.

NOTE In Windows Server 2008, L2TP is designed to run over IP networks such as the Internet and does not directly support running over X.25, Frame Relay, or ATM networks.

Internet Protocol Security

IPSec is actually a set of authentication and security protocols that can operate without interference and in addition to other protocols being used. Thus, L2TP can use the authentication services in PPP and then additionally use the authentication that is part of IPSec. As a result of this, IPSec can provide unbroken security over several segments of a network that, for example, begins on a private network, goes out over a public network, and then returns to a private network, so long as all the networks are using IP. IPSec accomplishes this by doing its authentication and encryption at the third or Network layer of the OSI model, ahead of PPP, which operates at the second or Data Link layer, as shown in Figure 10-2. IPSec can use either a 56-bit Data Encryption Standard (DES) key or Triple DES (3DES), which uses three 56-bit DES keys for the very highest security.

Secure Socket Tunneling Protocol

SSTP is the newest of the tunneling protocols and was developed to better handle firewalls and web proxies. SSTP can be used only with Windows Vista Service Pack 1 or later and Windows Server 2008. SSTP uses the Secure Socket Layer (SSL) with Hypertext Transfer Protocol Secure (HTTPS) to encrypt and encapsulate PPP frames and transfer them over TCP port 443 to get through firewalls and web proxies. As with the other two tunneling protocols, SSTP's use of PPP provides for EAP-TLS and MS-CHAP v2 authentication, while the use of SSL employs a widely used security facility at the transport level to do the encryption, key negotiation, and integrity checking.

Table 10-1 shows a comparison of the three tunneling protocols.

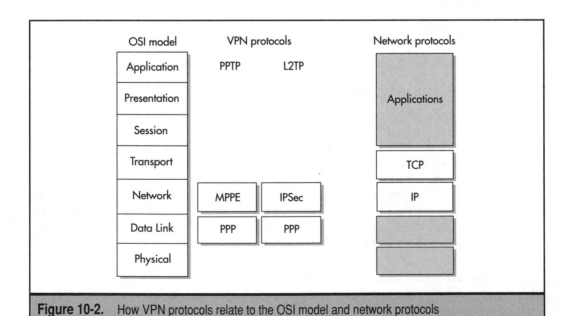

Figure 10-2.   How VPN protocols relate to the OSI model and network protocols

Area	PPTP	L2TP	SSTP
Use with Windows 98/Me & NT4	Yes	No	No
Use with Windows 2000, XP, Vista, Server 2003	Yes	Yes	No
Use with Windows Vista SP1 & Server 2008	Yes	Yes	Yes
Ease of installation	Easiest	Hardest	Harder
Ease of use	Easiest	Hardest	Harder
Degree of security (data can't be read)	Good	Better	Better
Degree of integrity (data can't be modified)	None	Good	Good
Degree of authentication (verified source of data)	None	Best	Better

Table 10-1. Comparison of the Three Tunneling Protocols

PREPARE FOR VPN

To set up VPN, you need to have both networking and Remote Access Service (RAS) set up and running. With that done, setting up VPN is just an enabling and configuration task. Setting up networking is described in Chapter 6, and Chapter 8 discusses setting up RAS. Here, these topics will be briefly reviewed, but you should refer to the primary chapters if you have questions about these topics.

NOTE   It is very important that you know RAS is operating correctly before setting up VPN. Too often, a problem in RAS is the cause for VPN to not operate correctly.

Check Networking and RAS Hardware

Networking and RAS hardware includes at a minimum a network adapter and probably also a communications interface device, such as a modem; an ISDN (Integrated Services Digital Network) or DSL (digital subscriber line) adapter; or a router on the network with a connection to a DSL, T-1, or frame-relay communications line. Assuming that this hardware has been installed in accordance with the manufacturer's instructions, then it was most likely automatically set up in Windows Server 2008 either when the operating system (OS) was installed or when the hardware was installed and detected by the OS. Here, you should only need to make sure that the correct driver has been installed and that the device is operating properly. You can do both of these through the Device Manager and these instructions:

1. Click Start | Control Panel and double-click Device Manager.
2. Open the local computer and Network Adapters, and double-click the network adapter that you want to check. The Properties dialog box for that device will open as shown in Figure 10-3.

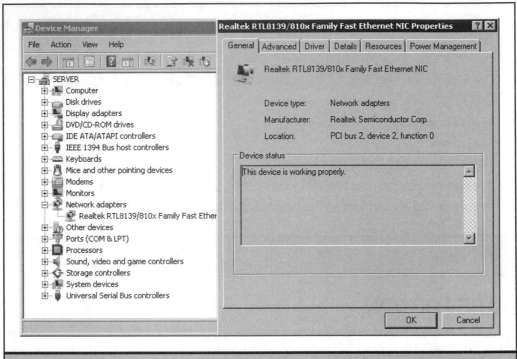

Figure 10-3.   You can check if a device is working through the Device Manager.

3. If the device is operating properly, you should see a statement to that effect, as you can see in Figure 10-3, in which case, click OK to close the Properties dialog box.

4. If the NIC is not operating properly, you may be given some indication as to what is the problem. If you are told there is a driver problem, click the Driver tab and click Update Driver. If there is a resource-sharing problem, click the Resources tab and see if it indicates where the problem is; if so, click Change Setting and make the necessary change. If there is some other problem or if you were not able to cure a driver or resource problem, go back to Chapter 6, which has more detail on setting up a network adapter.

5. When you have the network adapter properly installed, close its Properties dialog box and, if present, open the Properties dialog box for the communications device in the computer. Again you should see a summary device status. If the device is a modem, click the Diagnostics tab and click Query Modem. After waiting a few moments, you should see a list of commands and responses. It does not matter if you get "Command Not Supported" so long as you get other normal-looking responses, such as you see here (Chapter 8 has more detail on setting up a modem):

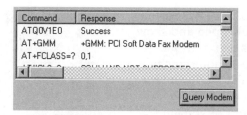

6. If the device is operating properly, click OK to close the Properties dialog box. Otherwise, use a procedure similar to Step 4 to isolate and correct the problem(s). When you are done, close the Properties dialog box and the Device Manager window.

Although you may think that hardware is not a problem, it is wise to check it out and eliminate it as a possible reason VPN is not working.

Configure Networking

When Plug and Play networking hardware is installed or when Windows Server 2008 is installed and detects Plug and Play networking hardware, the networking components of Windows Server 2008 are automatically installed. Since you have already determined that your hardware is installed and operating, it is highly likely that networking is as well. Check that here:

1. Click Start | Control Panel, double-click Network and Sharing Center, and observe if you are connected to a network and possibly the Internet. If so, networking has been set up on the server you are looking at.

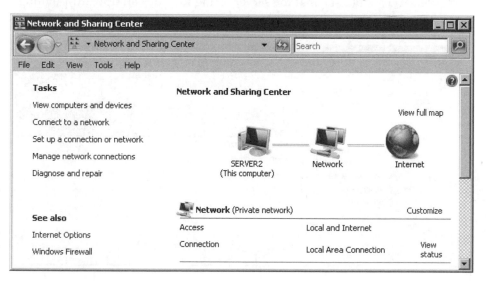

2. Click View Status. The Local Area Connection Status dialog box will open and show a significant activity of bytes sent and received.

3. Click Properties. The Properties dialog box should open and show the components set up for the connection. These should include, at a minimum, File And Printer Sharing For Microsoft Networks and Internet Protocol Version 4 (TCP/IPv4), and probably Client For Microsoft Networks, like this:

4. Double-click Internet Protocol Version 4 (TCP/IPv4) to open its Properties dialog box. What you see here will depend on the role of this computer in the network. At least one server must have a fixed or static IP address (with Use The Following IP Address selected) and be the DHCP (Dynamic Host Configuration Protocol) and DNS (Domain Name System) server.

5. Close Internet Protocol (TCP/IP) Properties, Local Area Connection Properties, Local Area Connection Status, and the Network and Sharing Center.

6. If you found in Step 4 that this server did have a fixed IP address, then check DHCP by clicking Start | Administrative Tools | DHCP, and opening the local server. You should see that the server listing includes an upward-pointing green arrow (saying the service is enabled) and at least one scope.

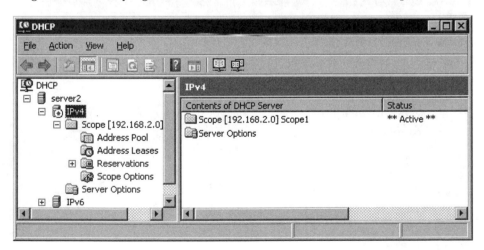

7. Close the DHCP window. If any of the preceding steps did not produce the expected results or some problem was observed, go back to Chapter 6 and review setting up a network.

8. If you are using Active Directory, click Start | Administrative Tools | Active Directory Users And Computers, open the local domain, and then click Users. Double-click the user you want to allow to dial in (or create a new user if needed—see Chapter 6), click the Dial-In tab, click Allow Access, and click OK. Close the Active Directory Users And Computers window.

TIP   For RAS and especially for VPN, you need to have a static IP address assigned by an Internet authority. In other words, you need an IP address that is acceptable across the Internet, not one, such as 10.0.0.2, that you assigned yourself.

Set Up Remote Access Service

RAS is enabled in Windows Server 2008 by establishing a server role for it as a part of the Network Policy And Access Services, as described in Chapter 8. Once Network Policy And Access Services is set up, RAS is enabled and configured through Administrative Tools. To do this, you must have administrative privileges and use these steps:

1. Click Start | Administrative Tools | Routing And Remote Access to open the Routing And Remote Access window. The local server should have a downward-pointing red arrow if it is not enabled, or an upward-pointing green arrow if it is.

2. If RAS is not enabled, select the local server (the computer you are working on), click the Action menu, and click Configure And Enable Routing And Remote Access. The Routing And Remote Access Server Setup Wizard will open. Click Next.

3. Click Remote Access (Dial-Up Or VPN) and click Next. Click Dial-Up (make sure it works before choosing VPN) and click Next.

4. If you have multiple network connections, click the one you want your RAS clients to use and click Next. Click Automatically assign IP addresses, since you do have a DHCP server.

5. Click Next. Choose whether to use Remote Authentication Dial-In User Service (RADIUS) authentication for several RASs. It provides another level of authentication that you may or may not need. Click Next.

6. Review the summary of your selection, click Back to make any changes, and then click Finish. You are told that to support the relaying of client DHCP messages, the DHCP Relay Agent must be configured. Click OK. If your DHCP server is on the same subnet as the RAS server, which is normally the case, you do not need a DHCP Relay Agent.

When RAS has been enabled and configured as is done with the preceding steps, your RAS window should look like this:

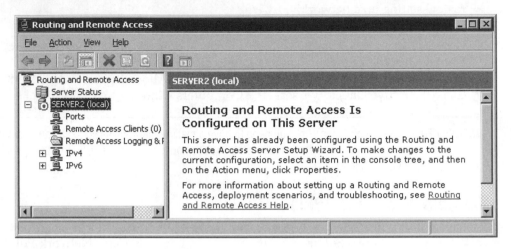

Test RAS

It is very tempting at this point to jump ahead and set up VPN; after all, that is the objective here. But it is prudent to make sure RAS is working properly before going ahead. To test RAS, you must have a dial-up connection on a client. It is assumed that the client is running Windows XP or Vista, that the server is Windows Server 2008, and that both have a communications connection that is already installed and running possibly using the modem (Chapter 8 has instructions for installing a modem).

Set Up a Dial-Up Connection

If you haven't already set up a dial-up connection on the client, do so with these steps:

NOTE   Your client's user interface may be different if it uses an OS other than Windows Vista.

1. On a Windows Vista client computer, click Start. If you have an existing network or Internet connection, click Connect To. If you have a dial-up connection, then you can go on to the next section.

2. If you do have a network connection, but not a dial-up connection, click Set Up A Connection Or Network.

3. If you don't have an existing network connection, click Start | Control Panel and double-click Network and Sharing Center. In the Network and Sharing Center dialog box that opens, click Set Up A Connection Or Network in the Tasks pane on the left.

4. In either case, click Set Up A Dial-Up Connection and click Next. Enter the phone number of the server including, if necessary, "1" and the area code. Enter the username and password that were provided to you by the server administrator.

5. Enter a name for the connection. If you have multiple profiles on the client, determine if you want the connection for anyone's use and click Connect. You should be able to connect to the server. Make sure of that before going forward.

Use RAS

With a dial-up connection set up on the client and a remote access server set up and enabled on the server, you can use RAS with these steps:

1. Log onto the dial-up client as you normally do. Then, on the client, Click Start | Connect To, click the dial-up connection you want to use, and click Connect.

2. As needed, enter the appropriate username, the password, and possibly the domain, and click Dial. You will see messages stating that the number you entered is being dialed, that the username and password are being checked, that the computer is being registered on the network, and then that the connection is complete. Click Close. The connection icon will appear on the right of the taskbar.

3. Test the connection in the client by clicking Start | Network and the domains or workgroups, computers, drives, and folders that you want to access. If you can see folders and files, the remote access connection is working.

4. Test the connection in the server by clicking Start | Administrative Tools | Routing And Remote Access. In the Routing And Remote Access window, open the local server and click Remote Access Clients. You should see that at least one client is connected, like this:

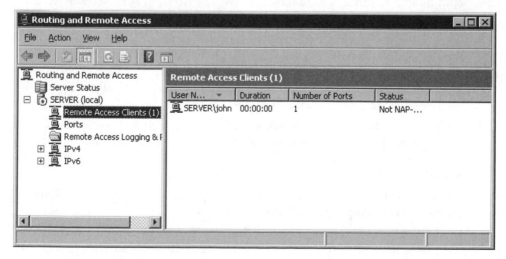

5. When you are done testing the RAS connection, you can terminate it by double-clicking the connection icon in the taskbar of the client and then clicking Disconnect in the dialog box that opens.

With RAS fully accessible from a remote dial-up client, you know that all but the unique VPN components are fully operational on the two computers that you tested. If your dial-up RAS connection did not work, look back at Chapter 8, which discusses this in more detail.

SET UP A VPN SERVER

VPN, like RAS, has both client and server components. The most common setup, and the one described here, is for the client (assumed to be running Windows Vista) to have a connection to the Internet, and for traffic to travel across the Internet to the server (assumed to be running Windows Server 2008), where a VPN termination is active and allows access to the LAN. See how this is done, first in terms of configuring the server and then the setup that is needed on the client.

Reconfigure RAS

VPN requires that you have RAS configured for VPN, so the following instructions assume that you have gone through the steps in the previous sections and must reconfigure RAS:

1. Click Start | Administrative Tools | Routing And Remote Access. Right-click the local server and click Disable Routing And Remote Access. Answer Yes, you really want to delete the RAS service.

2. With the local server still selected, click the Action menu and click Configure And Enable Routing And Remote Access. The Routing And Remote Access Server Setup Wizard will open. Click Next.

3. If you have two network adapters in your server (one for VPN and one for the LAN), click Remote Access (Dial-Up Or VPN), as shown in Figure 10-4; otherwise, click Custom Configuration. Then click Next. Click VPN Access and click Next. If it appears, accept the default of automatically assigning IP addresses using your DHCP server. Then click Next.

4. If offered the choice, decide if you want to use Remote Authentication Dial-In User Service (RADIUS) to manage the authentication of several RAS servers. If you have only one RAS server, the answer is obvious; if you have several, then RADIUS would be worthwhile. Click Next.

5. You are told that you have successfully completed the Routing And Remote Access Server Setup Wizard. Click Finish.

6. Click Start Service. You may be told that to support the relaying of client DHCP messages, the DHCP Relay Agent must be configured. If so, click OK. If your DHCP server is on the same subnet as your VPN server, you do not need a DHCP Relay Agent. RAS will be configured for VPN.

7. In the Routing And Remote Access window, open the local server and click Ports. Here there are initially 128 PPTP, 128 L2TP, and 128 SSTP ports set up for VPN, some of which are shown in Figure 10-5.

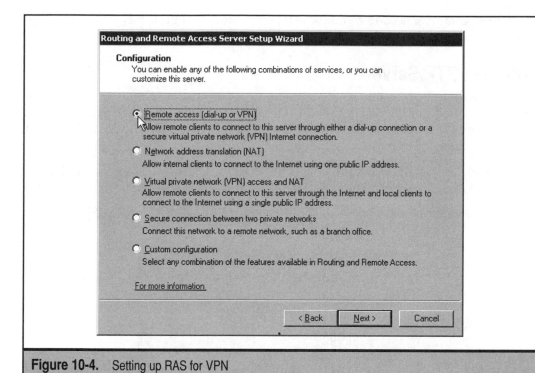

Figure 10-4.   Setting up RAS for VPN

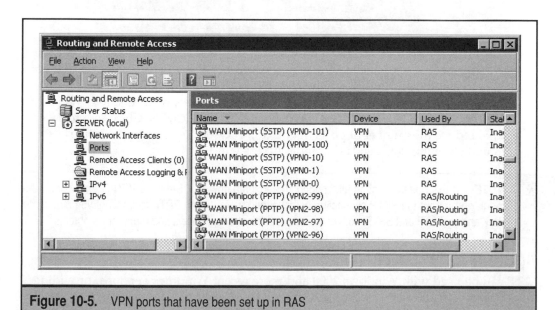

Figure 10-5.   VPN ports that have been set up in RAS

At this point, you need to choose which of the three VPN protocols you want to use and then configure that protocol.

Configure a PPTP Server

PPTP is the easiest of the three VPN protocols to set up and can be used with a wide range of clients, from Windows 95 (with upgrade 1.3 to Dial-Up Networking) to Windows Server 2008, but it provides a lower level of security. You can configure PPTP and adjust the number of its ports with these steps:

1. Right-click Ports in the left pane of the Routing And Remote Access window and click Properties. The Ports Properties dialog box will open.

2. Click WAN Miniport (PPTP) and then click Configure. The Configure Device— WAN Miniport (PPTP) dialog box opens, like this:

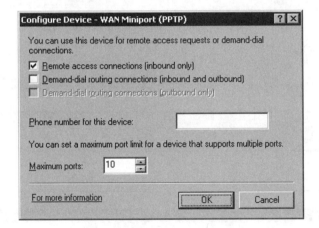

3. Given that you are using VPN over the Internet and you don't want the client to dial and come in through the server's modem, uncheck the Demand-Dial Routing Connections (Inbound And Outbound) check box. Set a reasonable number of PPTP ports that you will be using and click OK. Click Yes, you want to reduce the number of ports (if you do); click OK to close Ports Properties; and close the Routing And Remote Access window.

NOTE At this point, it is generally a good idea to jump down to "Set Up a VPN Client," set up the client, and try out the PPTP connection as described there. When PPTP is working, you can come back and try L2TP and SSTP, both of which cause most people (including me) more problems.

Configure a L2TP Server

L2TP can be used with Windows 2000 and more recent Windows versions, providing a higher degree of data integrity, data authentication, and data confidentiality. It also is more difficult to set up because of the need to configure the additional security and authentication infrastructure. Because L2TP uses IPSec and the most common form of IPSec uses computer certificates for authentication, you must have a certification authority active on the network and have it set up to automatically issue certificates to VPN computers. The first steps, then, are to install or confirm the presence of a certificate authority and to assure that it is properly set up. Then the filters that are an integral part of IPSec can be configured, and finally L2TP over IPSec can be selected and its ports set up.

Install and Configure a Certificate Authority

If you are not sure if a certificate authority is installed on your LAN or if you know it is not, follow these instructions to check out or install and configure it (you must be logged on as an administrator or domain administrator):

> **TIP**   If you do not have Active Directory installed, you are going to need it, so you should install it before installing Active Directory Certificate Services. See Chapter 7.

1. Click Start | Server Manager; in the tree on the left, click Roles; in the right pane under Roles, click Add Roles; and click Next.

2. Click Active Directory Certificate Services if it isn't already checked (if it is, Certificate Services is already installed on this computer and you can jump to the next section). Click Next, read the caution that if you install Certificate Services, you will not be able to rename the computer, and click Next again.

3. Click each of the certification authority options to determine those that you need. For L2TP only, the first option, Certification Authority (CA), is needed. Click Next when ready.

4. If you are not using Active Directory, leave the default Standalone; otherwise click Enterprise, and in either case click Next.

5. If you are installing the first certification authority, click Root CA; otherwise click Subordinate CA and click Next.

6. If you don't have a private key or want to create a new one, click Create A New Private Key; otherwise click Use Existing Private Key. In either case, click Next. If you are creating a new key, you can select the cryptographic service provider (CSP), the key length, and the hash algorithm. In most cases, except if you are using smart cards, you want to leave the defaults shown in Figure 10-6. If you are using smart cards, you may need to select a CSP that is used by the smart card.

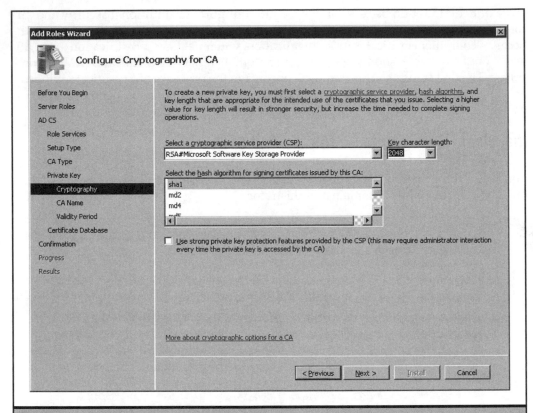

Figure 10-6. You can configure the cryptographic settings for your private key, but in most cases, the defaults are adequate.

7. Click Next, enter the name for the CA, and click Next again. Select the validity period or leave the default of 5 Years and once more click Next.

8. You are shown where the certificate database and log will be stored. Change that if you wish and then click Next. The summary of your settings is displayed. If you want to change anything, click Previous. When you are ready, click Install.

9. Click Close when you are told that you have successfully completed installation. Close Server Manager.

Administer a Certificate Authority

Once a CA is installed, it can be administered through the Certification Authority window. Here's how:

1. Click Start | Administrative Tools | Certification Authority (if you just installed it, Certification Authority may be out of alphabetical sequence in the menu).

2. In the left pane, open the local server and click Issued Certificates. You should see at least the certificate issued to the server, like this (if you don't see the certificate, restart the server and the certificate should appear):

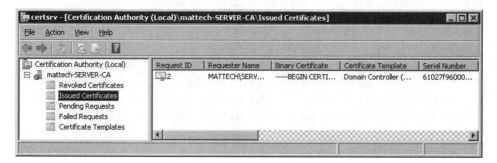

3. Right-click the certificate in the right pane and click Open. Here, you can see who issued it, the dates it is valid, and the type of public key it uses. Click OK to close the certificate.

4. Right-click the local server in the left pane and select All Tasks. In the submenu, you can stop the issuing of certificates and back up and restore the CA.

5. Back in the context menu with All Tasks, click Properties. In the Properties dialog box that opens, click the Policy Module tab and again click Properties. In the Request Handling tab, you can choose manual or automatic issuing of certificates, as you can see here:

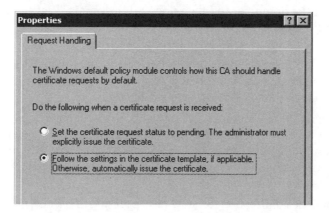

6. Close both Properties dialog boxes. Back in the Certification Authority window, you'll see a Pending Requests folder. If you selected manual certificate issuing, then all certificate requests will go into this folder. When you are done looking at the Certification Authority window, close it.

Start and Configure IPSec

IPSec is controlled by group policies, which can be set at various levels, the primary of which is the domain. This means that you must have Active Directory (AD) set up and the server that hosts VPN must be a domain controller. See Chapter 7 for setting up AD and domain controllers. Assuming you are on an AD domain controller, start and configure IPSec at the domain level by first setting up group policy management:

1. Click Start | Server Manager and click your server in the tree on the left. Open Roles and click Network Policy And Access Services.

2. In the right pane, click Add Role Services. Click Network Policy Server, Routing And Remote Access Services, and Host Credential Authorization. As you click each, read its description on the right. Click Host Credential Authorization Protocol. Click Add Required Role Services.

3. Click Next. Accept the default of choosing an existing certificate for SSL encryption, click your new certificate server, and click Next. Click Next again on the Web Server (IIS) page. On the Web Server Role Services list, you'll see that several services have been checked.

4. Click Next and review the roles and services that are about to be installed. If you want to change anything, click Previous. When you are ready, click Install. When you are told that installation was successful, click Close.

5. While still in the Server Manager, in the tree on the left, click Features, and in the right pane, click Add Features. In the list of features, click Group Policy Management (if it isn't already installed), click Next, and click Install. When installation is complete, click Close, and close the Server Manager.

6. Click Start | Administrative Tools | Group Policy Management. Open the forest and the domains, and then open your domain. Right-click the Default Domain Policy and click Edit.

7. In the left pane, double-click Computer Configuration, double-click Windows Settings, double-click Security Settings, and double-click IP Security Policies On Active Directory. Click the Action menu and click Create IP Security Policy. The IP Security Policy Wizard opens. Click Next.

8. Enter the name and a description of the policy and click Next. If you are using only Windows Vista computers as VPN clients, do not accept the automatic activation of the default response rule, which automatically responds to remote computers that request security. Click Next, make sure Edit Properties is checked, and click Finish.

9. The Properties dialog box for your new policy will open with a single IP filter. Click Add. The Security Rule Wizard will open. Click Next.

10. Click The Tunnel Endpoint Is Specified By The Following IP Address, enter the IP address of the computer to which the server will be connecting, and click Next. Click Remote Access and click Next.

11. Click All IP Traffic for the IP filter to use and click Next. Click Permit, again click Next, and then click Finish. Close your policy's Properties dialog box.

12. In the Group Policy Management Editor window, right-click your new IPSec policy in the right pane and click Assign, as shown in Figure 10-7. Leave IP Security Policies under Security Settings in the Group Policy Management Editor window open.

Start to Issue Certificates

Certificates like IPSec are controlled by group policies at various levels. Start issuing domain-level certificates by connecting the computers that need them to the LAN and use these steps:

1. In the left pane of the Group Policy Management Editor window, under Security Settings, click Public Key Policies. In the right pane, right-click Automatic Certificate Request Settings and click New | Automatic Certificate Request. The Automatic Certificate Request Setup Wizard will open.

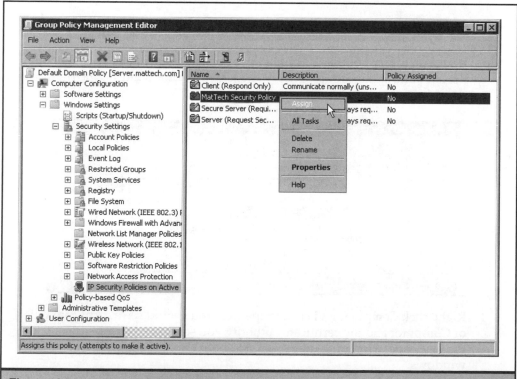

Figure 10-7. Setting up IPSec is a major part of setting up L2TP.

2. Click Next. Click Computer as the certificate template to use, click Next, and click Finish.

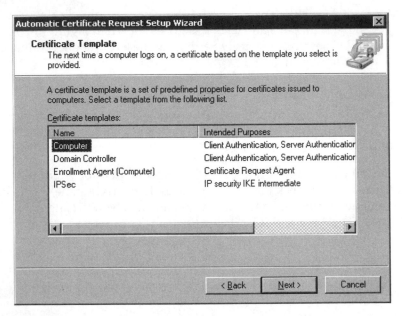

3. With Public Key Policies | Automatic Certificate Request Settings open in the left pane of the Group Policy Management Editor window, the right pane should show Computer and its icon, like this:

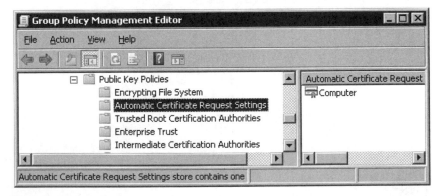

4. Right-click Computer and click Properties. You should see a certificate type of Computer and the certificate authority you set up and chose earlier. Close the Computer Properties dialog box and both Group Policy Management windows.

Select and Configure L2TP over IPSec

The final step in setting up L2TP for use with VPN is to select L2TP over IPSec and con-figure the L2TP ports.

1. Click Start | Administrative Tools | Routing And Remote Access. In the left pane, open both the local server and IPv4, and click General. In the right pane, note the IP Address of the LAN, and then right-click Local Area Connection and click Properties.

2. Click Inbound Filters and click New. In the Add IP Filter dialog box, click Destination Network and enter the IP address for the LAN and a subnet mask of 255.255.255.255. For the Protocol, click UDP and then in both the Source Port and Destination Port, enter **500** (given that this is your first IPSec input filter), as you can see in Figure 10-8, and then click OK.

3. You are returned to the Inbound Filters dialog box, where you should select Drop All Packets Except Those That Meet The Criteria Below. Click OK.

4. Back in the Local Area Connection Properties dialog box, click Outbound Filters and click New. In the Add IP Filter dialog box, click Source Network and enter the IP address for the LAN and a subnet mask of 255.255.255.255. For the Protocol, click UDP and then in both the Source Port and the Destination Port, enter **500** (given that this is your first IPSec output filter) and then click OK.

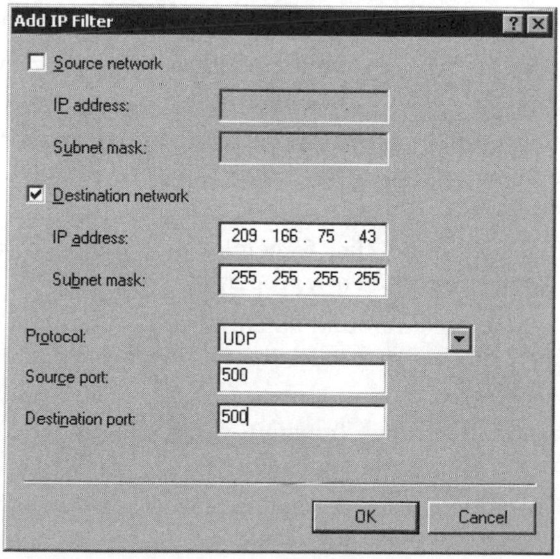

Figure 10-8.   L2TP depends heavily on IP filters.

5. In the Outbound Filters dialog box, click Drop All Packets Except Those That Meet The Criteria Below. Click OK. Click OK again to close the Local Area Connection Properties dialog box and return to the Routing And Remote Access window.

6. Right-click Ports in the left pane of the Routing And Remote Access window and click Properties. The Ports Properties dialog box will open.

7. Click WAN Miniport (L2TP) and then click Configure. The Configure Device— WAN Miniport (L2TP) dialog box opens similarly to what you saw under "Configure a PPTP Server."

8. Uncheck the Demand-Dial Routing Connections (Inbound And Outbound) check box. Set a reasonable number of L2TP ports that you will be using and click OK. Click Yes, you want to reduce the number of ports; click OK to close Ports Properties; and close the Routing And Remote Access window.

Configure an SSTP Server

NOTE   SSTP only works with Windows Vista SP1 and later, and Windows Server 2008.

If you have set up L2TP, SSTP is easy, because in the process of setting up L2TP you also got SSL (Secure Sockets Layer) established, which is used with SSTP. So if you haven't set up L2TP, go through those steps and then continue here:

1. Click Start | Administrative Tools | Routing And Remote Access. Open the local server, right-click Ports in the left pane of the Routing And Remote Access window, and click Properties. The Ports Properties dialog box will open.

2. Click WAN Miniport (SSTP) and then click Configure. The Configure Device— WAN Miniport (SSTP) dialog box opens.

3. Set a reasonable number of SSTP ports that you will be using and click OK. Click Yes, you want to reduce the number of ports (if you do) and click OK to close Ports Properties.

4. Open IPv4 in the left pane, click General, and in the right pane, right-click Local Area Connection, and click Properties.

5. In the General tab, click Inbound Filters, click Receive All Packets Except Those That Meet The Criteria Below, click the filter you established for L2TP, click Delete, and click OK.

6. Click Outbound Filters, click Transmit All Packets Except Those That Meet The Criteria Below, click the filter you established for L2TP, click Delete, and click OK.

7. Click OK to close the Local Area Connection Properties dialog box, and close the Routing And Remote Access window.

8. Click Start | Administrative Tools | Windows Firewall With Advanced Security. In the left pane of the Windows Firewall window, click Inbound Rules; in the

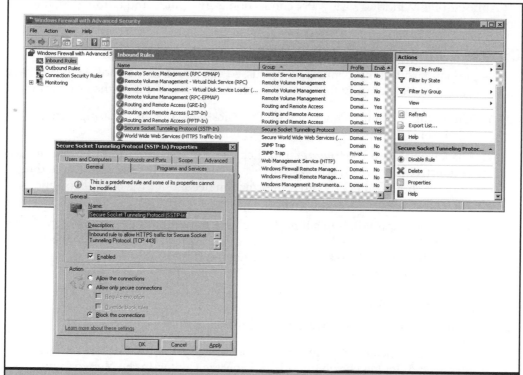

Figure 10-9. The firewall is automatically configured with exceptions for PPTP and L2TP, but SSTP must be enabled.

center pane, scroll down and click Secure Socket Tunneling Protocol (SSTP-In); and in the right pane, click Properties. The SSTP-In Properties dialog box will open as you see in Figure 10-9.

9. Make sure under General that Enabled is checked and then click Allow The Connections. Click OK to close the Properties dialog box, and then close the Windows Firewall window.

SET UP A VPN CLIENT

Setting up a VPN client is a relatively simple task. You need to set up a connection for the client to connect to the Internet and then a connection between the client and the VPN server. In Windows 2000, XP, and Vista, and in Server 2003 and 2008, there is an integrated and automated approach to these two tasks, whereas in earlier versions of Windows, you have to separately set up the dial-up connection to the Internet and then without the help of a wizard create the VPN connection.

Although the Windows Vista VPN connection is integrated and automated, it is still done in two steps, connecting to the Internet and connecting to the VPN server.

Choose a Windows Vista Internet Connection

This is the standard Internet connection discussed elsewhere in the book, so if you have an Internet connection already that you know works, you can skip to the next section.

1. Click Start | Control Panel, and double-click Network and Sharing Center. Click Set Up A Connection Or Network.

2. Click Connect To The Internet and click Next. If you have multiple ways to connect, choose which you want to use to connect and click Next. Depending on your choice, enter any other information needed for the connection and click Next as needed, and then click Finish.

3. If you are using a dial-up connection, click Connect and/or Dial as needed to try out the connection. If all your settings are correct, you should connect. If not, go back over the preceding three steps and make the necessary corrections. Leave this connection active for the next set of steps.

Connect to a VPN Server

The VPN connection is just another network connection.

1. If the Network and Sharing Center is not already open, click Start | Control Panel, and double-click Network and Sharing Center. In the Network and Sharing Center window, click Set Up A Connection Or Network.

2. Click Connect To A Workplace and click Next. Click No, Create A New Connection and click Next.

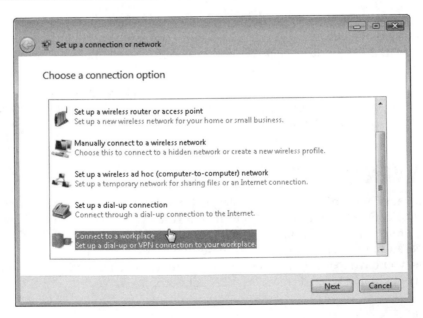

3. Click Use My Internet Connection (VPN), enter a registered host name (such as osborne.com) or an IP address like 123.10.78.100, and your destination name, as shown in Figure 10-10.

4. If you have multiple profiles on the client, determine if you want to allow other people to use this connection, and click Next.

5. Enter the username and password required by the VPN server, choose whether to save the username and password for yourself or for anyone using this computer, and click Connect. You will see several brief messages saying that you are connecting and then that you are connected. Click Close.

6. Click the type of network (Home, Work, Public) that the VPN connection represents, and then click Close. You should be connected to the VPN server and see your connection in the Network and Sharing Center window.

7. Click Manage Network Connections. The Network Connections window should open and look something like Figure 10-11. You should be able to browse the portions of the network for which you have permission.

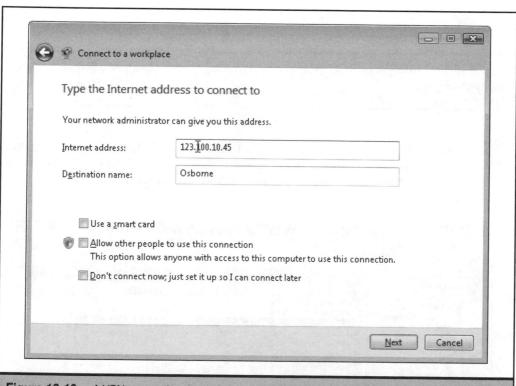

Figure 10-10. A VPN connection depends on having a host name or IP address.

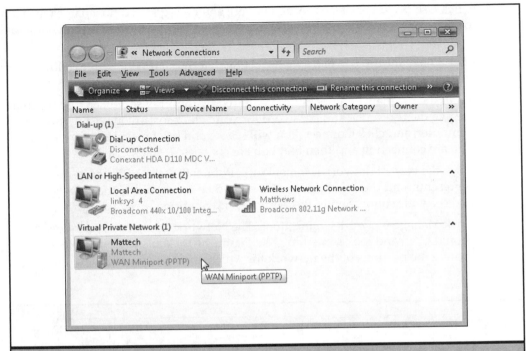

Figure 10-11. In the Network Connections window, you should see both a network connection and a VPN connection.

8. In the VPN server, you should be able to see the connection in the Routing And Remote Access window by opening the local server and Remote Access Clients. Also, click Ports and scroll down the list. You should see one port that is active, like this:

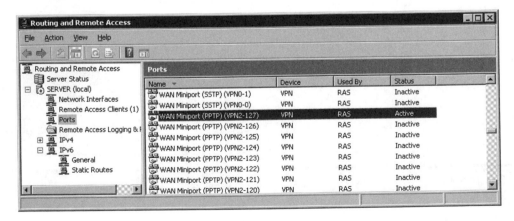

9. If you opened the Routing And Remote Access window, close it. In the client,
    in the Network Connections window, right-click the VPN connection and click
    Disconnect.

If you did not connect, take heart, I didn't either, the first time. There are a number
of reasons that connection may not happen. If RAS worked, that eliminates many of the
potential reasons. First try connecting with PPTP. If you set up both PPTP and L2TP before trying the connection, go back to "Reconfigure RAS," use the instructions there and
in the sections following "Reconfigure RAS" to disable RAS, reestablish it just for PPTP,
and then try the connection. If it still doesn't work, carefully go over all the steps to set
up the service you want to use and look for what you did differently.

Connect Using L2TP and SSTP

Once you have PPTP working, and only then (because if you have PPTP working, you
have eliminated a lot of possible areas for problems), try L2TP and SSTP (if your hardware allows) with these steps:

1. If the Network and Sharing Center is not already open, click Start | Control
    Panel, and double-click Network and Sharing Center. In the Network and
    Sharing Center window, click Manage Network Connections.

2. Right-click your working VPN connection and click Properties. Click the
    Networking tab, click the down arrow under Type Of VPN, and click the type
    you want to use. Click OK to close the VPN Properties dialog box.

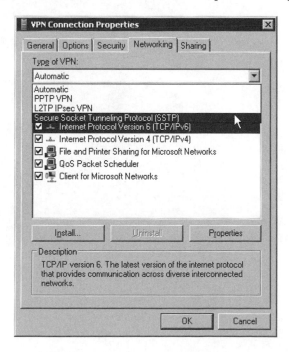

3. Double-click your updated VPN connection, enter your name and password, and click Connect.

4. Jump up to Step 5 in "Connect to a VPN Server" immediately preceding, and continue to the end of that section.

As I've already said several times, L2TP and to a slightly lesser degree SSTP are extremely complex with a lot of elements that you need to get correctly set up. If you can do it, your security is greatly enhanced.

VPN is a very handy tool for mobile workers and is really worth all the trouble it takes to set it up (well, maybe all the trouble PPTP takes—I'm not so sure L2TP is worth its extra trouble!).

CHAPTER 11

Terminal Services and Remote Desktop

*T*erminal Services (TS) for Windows Server 2008 allows a minimal computer called a *thin client* or a *terminal* to connect to a Windows server, display a Windows desktop, and use Windows remotely, with Windows and its applications running on the server. The thin client (called simply "client" in much of this chapter) can run Windows XP, Server 2003, Vista, or Server 2008, or, with third-party software, a number of other operating systems (OSs). It can even access the server over the Internet. Only the user interface runs on the client, which returns keystrokes and mouse clicks to the server. The client computer can have a slower processor, a modest amount of memory, and a small hard disk or even no hard disk. To the application running on the server, the user appears to be on that machine, and to clients, the application appears to be running on their machines, given a reasonable network speed. Multiple terminal sessions can be running on the server, but each client sees only its own session. A good use of thin clients with TS is one where the client is used for a single purpose, such as order entry, ticketing, or inventory tracking, where it is beneficial for the application and its related database to be on a server.

UNDERSTAND TERMINAL SERVICES

Terminal Services in Windows Server 2008 represents a significant enhancement over previous versions of TS that makes it significantly easier to both use and manage. Among the more important enhancements are TS RemoteApp, TS Web Access, TS Gateway, TS Session Broker, and Remote Desktop Connection 6.0. All of these and others will be described in the remainder of this chapter.

Why Use Terminal Services

There are a number of reasons to use TS, among which are:

▼ To allow multiple people to use the same application, possibly with a common database, especially "line of business" applications and applications that are frequently updated or seldom used (applications heavy with graphics and multimedia are not good candidates for TS)

■ To centralize the focus of application deployment, administration, and maintenance on a centralized server(s)

■ To control applications that are available to users and how they are configured

■ To use legacy hardware with older OSs when the latest Windows can't be used

■ To access a computer remotely, say, one at work from one at home, or from one on the road

▲ To manage several to many servers remotely with remote administration

Terminal Services Modes and Components

TS has two distinct modes that it handles:

▼ **Applications Server Mode**, which allows a client computer to display a Windows desktop and run applications remotely from a server

▲ **Remote Administration Mode**, which provides the means to remotely administer a computer running Windows Server 2008 including Internet Information Services (IIS)

TS is an integral part of Windows Server 2008, as it was in Windows Server 2003, and provides a powerful, full-capability set of terminal services. Third-party companies, though, such as Citrix, provide advanced applications in the TS arena that run on Windows 2003 and 2008 servers. You can reach Citrix at http://www.citrix.com.

TS works with the Transmission Control Protocol/Internet Protocol (TCP/IP), common to Windows Server 2008 networking and the Internet, and uses the Remote Desktop Protocol (RDP). RDP is a broad protocol facilitating the simultaneous transmission of a wide range of data, including user, application, licensing, and encryption information. RDP also has the capability to transmit audio and video information.

The two modes are accomplished in Windows Server 2008 using nine separate components of TS, as shown in Figure 11-1:

▼ **TS Manager**, which provides the administrative functions for TS and Terminal Server including viewing and controlling user sessions and processes.

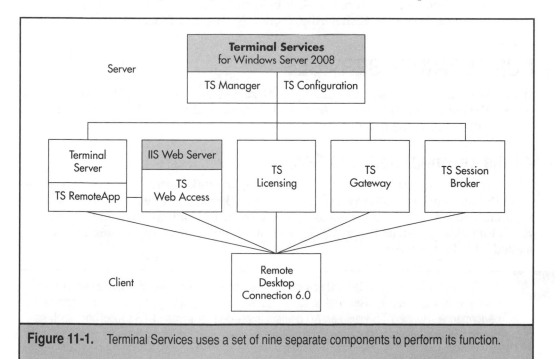

Figure 11-1. Terminal Services uses a set of nine separate components to perform its function.

- ■ **TS Configuration**, which allows you to determine the TS connections that are on the computer and their properties, as well as the server settings.

- ■ **Terminal Server**, which is a TS role service that provides the central core of TS that allows multitasking on a server.

- ■ **TS RemoteApp**, which is an element of Terminal Server that provides remote access to standard Windows programs.

- ■ **TS Web Access**, which is installed as a TS role service, but is really an Internet Information Services (IIS) web application that provides access to TS RemoteApp by use of a web browser.

- ■ **TS Licensing**, which is a TS role service that provides for client licensing of Windows TS.

- ■ **TS Gateway**, which is a TS role service that provides secure, encrypted access to resources on a LAN connected to the Terminal Server by remote users.

- ■ **TS Session Broker**, which is a TS role service that provides load balancing among several terminal servers (a "farm") and reconnects a TS client to an existing session in that farm.

- ▲ **Remote Desktop Connection 6.0**, which is separate client software that is preinstalled on Windows Server 2008 and Windows Vista Business and Ultimate, and can be downloaded for Windows Server 2003 SP1 or SP2 and Windows XP Professional SP2, that allows the client to connect to and use TS. Remote Desktop Connection 6.0 is required to use Windows Server 2008 Terminal Services, Terminal Server, TS RemoteApp, TS Web Access, and TS Gateway.

SET UP TERMINAL SERVICES

In this section, we'll talk about setting up, configuring, and managing TS, Terminal Server, and the other TS role services except TS Licensing and Remote Desktop Connection, which will be discussed in later sections.

Install the Terminal Services Roles

TS is a role that is installed from the Server Manager, while Terminal Server, TS Web Access, TS Licensing, TS Gateway, and TS Session Broker are all role services that you can separately select while you are installing the TS role. TS Configuration and TS Manager are automatically installed with TS Services, while TS RemoteApp is automatically installed with Terminal Server.

NOTE   It is not recommended that you install TS on an Active Directory domain controller because it increases your security risks and, since TS uses a lot of computer resources, it degrades AD's performance. Running TS within an AD domain is needed for some of TS's functions, such as TS Session Broker, and provides added capabilities to others, such as TS Licensing.

NOTE   To install the TS role and the role services discussed here, if you have not already done so, you will be told to also install Network Policy And Access Services, Web Server (IIS), and Windows Process Activation Service. The Add Roles Wizard will automatically lead you through those additional installations.

1. If the Server Manager is not already open, click Start | Server Manager. In any case, click Roles in the left pane of the Server Manager window and click Add Roles in the right pane.

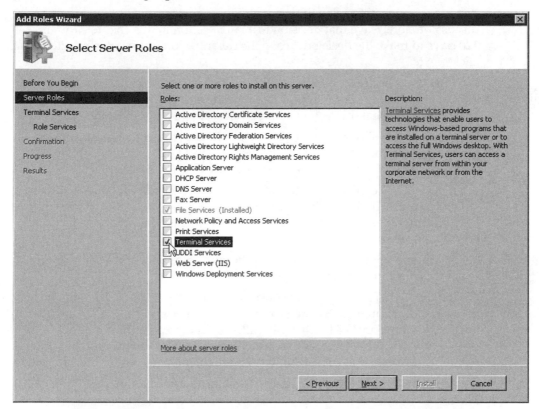

2. Click the role services that you want to install. For the sake of following the discussion here, click Terminal Server, TS Session Broker (you must be in a domain), TS Gateway (click Add Required Features), and TS Web Access (click Add Required Role Services), and click Next.

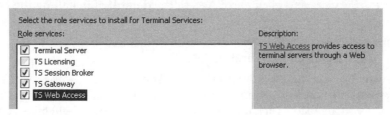

3. Read the note about the need to install any application you want to run with TS *after* installing TS and click Next.

4. Read about Network Level Authentication and decide if you want to use it. A major factor is that it is available only with Remote Desktop Protocol (RDP) 6.0, which is in Windows Vista and Windows Server 2008 and can be downloaded for Windows XP SP2 and Windows Server 2003 SP1 or SP2, but it significantly enhances security. Click your choice and click Next.

5. You are asked to determine the type of TS licensing you want to use. For the discussion here, leave that decision to a later section in this chapter. You have 120 days to make the decision. Leave the default, Configure Later, selected and click Next.

6. Add the users or user groups that will use TS by clicking Add, clicking Advanced, clicking Find Now, double-clicking a user or group in the list, and clicking OK. Repeat this as you need. When you are ready, click Next.

7. You are told that TS Gateway requires a certificate to use the Secure Sockets Layer (SSL) protocol to encrypt transmissions and you have three options for a certificate (see Figure 11-2), two of which are discussed here:

   a. If you have a certificate on the server already, click the first option; if the certificate is in the Windows certificate store, it will be listed. Otherwise, click Import and follow the steps of the Certificate Import Wizard, clicking Next as needed.

   b. If you don't have a certificate, click the second option, and a self-signed certificate will be created for you.

8. Click Next. A TS connection authorization policy (TS CAP), which allows users to pass through a TS Gateway and access a network, and a TS resource authorization policy (TS RAP), which allows users to pass through a TS Gateway and utilize particular computers running Terminal Server and other resources, are explained. Click Now to create the policies now and click Next.

9. Add the user groups that will use TS Gateway as described in Step 7 and click Next.

10. Enter the name for your TS CAP, accept the default of using a password, and click Next. Enter the name for your TS RAP, choose whether to use specific computer groups you select or all computers on the network, and click Next.

11. If it is not already installed, read the introduction to Network Policy And Access Services and click Next. Accept the default of installing the Network Policy Server role service and click Next.

12. Read the introduction to Web Server IIS and click Next. Accept the default role services that are checked and click Next.

13. Review the roles and role services that will be installed to implement TS and its services. If you want to change anything, click Previous and make the change. When you are ready, click Install. The installation process will take a few minutes.

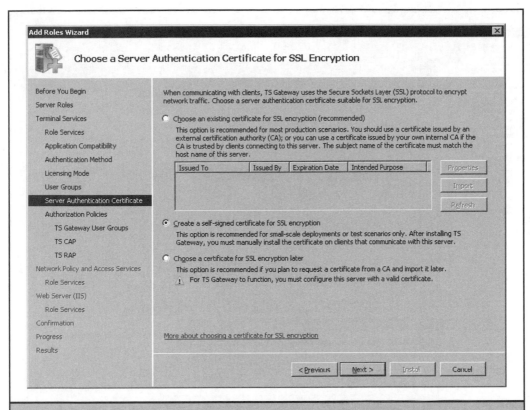

Figure 11-2.   You must have or create a security certificate in order to use TS Gateway.

14. Click Close, and click Yes to restart your computer. After restarting your roles, role services will be configured and you will be given a warning message that TS Licensing is not installed and that you have 119 days to do that (the day you install it counts as the first day). When it is done, you will be told it was successful. Click Close.

NOTE   The warning message that TS Licensing is not installed and that you have so many days to do that will reappear every time you restart your computer. This is called "nagware" and it is unfortunate that Microsoft is using it.

15. Open Roles in the left column of the Server Manager and click Terminal Services. In the right pane, you should see three informational events that tell you that your TS RAP, TS CAP, and certificate have been created; the system services that are running; and the role services that are installed, as shown in Figure 11-3.

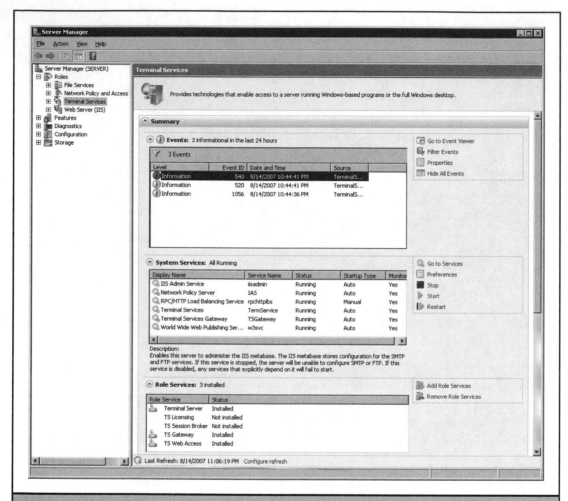

Figure 11-3. The results of your TS roles installation are shown in the Server Manager.

TIP Since there's no obvious way to tell which of the three informational events is which, you can select each and click Properties to find out.

NOTE Remote Desktop Connection, although not installed by default on Windows Server 2008, is automatically installed when you install TS. See "Use Applications Server Mode" later in this chapter.

Terminal Services Configuration

Once you have installed the TS role and the Terminal Server role service, you can configure TS using TS Configuration. TS Configuration allows you to determine the TS connections that are on the computer and their properties, as well as the server settings. There can be only one connection for each network interface card (NIC) or network adapter in the computer, and all connections use RDP with TCP/IP. Therefore, if you have only one NIC or network adapter, the default connection is all that you need. There are, though, some important settings in the connection's Properties dialog box. Look at both the connection's settings and the server settings that are available in TS Configuration with these steps:

1. Open TS Configuration by clicking Start | Administrative Tools | Terminal Services | Terminal Services Configuration.

   Or, in the Server Manager window, open Roles and Terminal Services, and click Terminal Services Configuration.

   In either case, Terminal Services Configuration will open, either within the Server Manager, as you see in Figure 11-4, or within its own window.

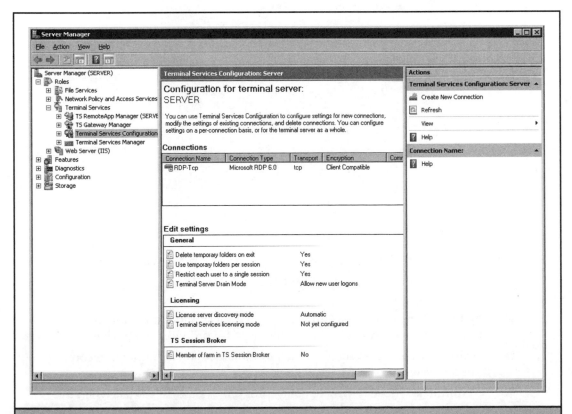

Figure 11-4. TS Configuration is where you add and configure connections and other settings.

2. Add additional connections if you have more than one NIC or network adapter, by clicking Create New Connection in the Actions pane on the right. The Terminal Services Connection Wizard will open. Click Next, enter the connection name and comments, and click Next. Select the network adapter to use and the number of connections. Click Next, review your settings, and click Finish.

3. To change the properties of an existing connection, right-click the connection, such as the default RDP-TCP connection, and click Properties. The RDP-TCP Properties dialog box will open.

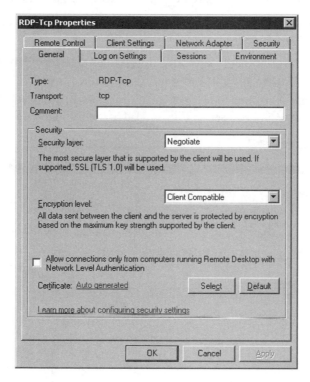

4. Go through each of the tabs. The settings you can change are as follows:

    ▼ **General** Add a comment to the connection's description and switch to High encryption.

    ■ **Log On Settings** Provide automatic logon by specifying the logon information to always use and whether a password will be requested.

    ■ **Sessions** Determine when to end a terminal session and how to reconnect if disconnected.

    ■ **Environment** Specify which, if any, program should be started when the user logs on, and what folder it should point to.

- **Remote Control**   Determine whether to allow the remote control or observation of a user's terminal session and set the conditions under which it is allowed.

- **Client Settings**   Specify which of the client devices and capabilities will be available during a terminal session.

- **Network Adapter**   Specify the NIC or network adapter that will be used for this connection and the maximum number of connections to be allowed.

▲ **Security**   Determine the permissions to be allowed for a particular group or user and add groups and users as desired.

5. When you have completed any changes you want to make, click OK to close the connection's Properties dialog box and return to Terminal Services Configuration.

6. Click Server Settings. The settings will appear on the right of the windows. These settings are self-explanatory. The settings are changed by right-clicking one of them, clicking Properties, and choosing the desired settings as shown next.

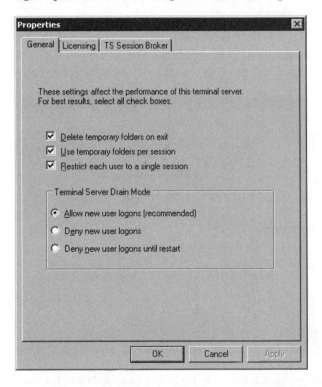

7. When you have completed making your changes, click OK to close the Properties dialog box.

Terminal Services Manager

TS Manager allows you to look at and manage the terminal servers within your trusted domains, including the users, processes, and sessions that are currently active on each server. As with TS Configuration, you can open TS Manager from Start and from the Server Manager.

NOTE   When you open TS Manager, you get a message that certain features, such as Remote Control And Connect, work only in a client session and are disabled in a console or server session. In other words, you must access the server and run TS Manager from a client in order to use Remote Control And Connect.

1. Open TS Manager by clicking Start | Administrative Tools | Terminal Services | Terminal Services Manager and click OK to close the message about Remote Control And Connect.

    Or, in the Server Manager, open Roles and Terminal Services, and click Terminal Services Manager.

    In either case, the TS Manager for the local server will open.

2. Click the Sessions tab in the middle pane, and the Server Manager window will look something like this if you have only the administrator as a user:

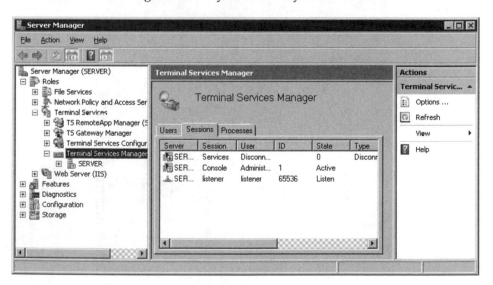

3. If you right-click a client session in the middle pane, for example, the Administrator, and open its context menu, you can disconnect it, reconnect if disconnected, send a message to the client, take control of the client if the client allows you, reset the client, and display the status of the session, which shows the incoming and outgoing bytes, frames, and errors.

NOTE   Many of the context menu options just described are also available in the Actions pane on the right.

4.   Clicking the Processes tab shows the programs that are currently running in the remote session.

5.   When you are done looking at the TS Manager, close it.

USE APPLICATIONS SERVER MODE

TS Applications Server Mode is a true multiuser environment similar to the mainframe timesharing systems that were popular in the 1970s prior to the advent of the PC. Each applications server user has an independent slice of the server and its resources. That means that the server can get overloaded. Applications servers with any significant number of simultaneous users (over five) require a powerful computer (probably 64-bit) with a substantial amount of memory (4 gigabytes [GB] or more—which you can only do with a 64-bit processor). The client, on the other hand, as described earlier, does not require much power to display the user interface, collect keystrokes and mouse events, and transmit the information to the server. Most of the processing is at the server.

Applications Server Mode uses the Terminal Server with TS RemoteApp to provide access to specific applications on the server from a remote client using Remote Desktop Connection (RDC). The previous section, "Set Up Terminal Services," described how to install and set up the overall service. In this section, we'll look at how to set up one of two ways to use that service, the running of programs or applications on the server from a separate, remote computer. To do that we'll review a couple of preparatory steps that need to be taken, then how to set up and manage TS RemoteApp, and finally, how to set up and use RDC.

Prepare for Terminal Services

You need to take several steps after installing TS and before going ahead with TS RemoteApp and RDC:

▼   **Install Programs**   After you install TS, you need to install the programs that will be used by the TS remote clients. If you already had programs installed on the server prior to installing TS, it is a good idea to uninstall and reinstall them. If you are installing several programs with shared files, such as Microsoft Office, it is a good idea to install all the programs on the same server. On the other hand, if you have several programs that will be heavily used or that may not be compatible, it is a good idea to install them on separate TS servers.

■ **Verify Settings** Although when TS was installed, remote connections were enabled, it is recommended that you verify that is the case on your server.

1. Click Start | Control Panel and double-click System. Under Tasks on the left, click Remote Settings.

2. In the System Properties dialog box Remote tab under Remote Desktop, you should see the middle option selected as shown next.

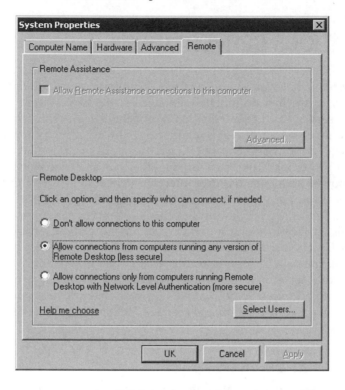

3. If your users are using RDC 6.0 (in Windows Vista and Server 2008 by default and downloadable for Windows XP and Server 2003), you can choose the bottom option to use the more secure Network Level Authentication.

4. Leave the System Properties dialog box open for the final preparatory step.

▲ **Add Users** The clients or users of TS must be set up as users on the terminal server. They can be members of either Remote Desktop Users or local Administrators. To best apply group policies (see Chapter 15), it is recommended that all remote users be members of the Remote Desktop Users group even if they are also members of other groups.

1. In the System Properties dialog box Remote tab, which should already be open from the last set of steps, click Select Users.

2. Click Add. In the Select Users dialog box, type the names already set up on the network, or click Advanced, click Find Now to search for names, click a name (or names by holding CTRL) from the Search Results, and click OK.

3. When you have added the names you want to add, click OK. The name(s) should be listed in the Remote Desktop Users group.

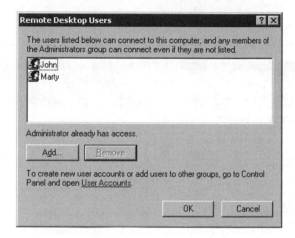

4. If the users are listed as you want, click OK to close the Remote Desktop Users dialog box, then click OK again to close the System Properties dialog box, and finally, close the System window.

Manage TS RemoteApp

Prior to Windows Server 2008, a remote connection to a terminal server displayed the desktop of the server, and the client could start the applications that the user wished to use. With Windows Server 2008 TS RemoteApp, specific applications are made available to the remote clients and when they are run, given reasonable network speed, it appears to the user that the application is on his or her computer. TS RemoteApp provides both the means to select the applications the remote client can use and the means to package and deliver the program to the user, as well as the primary way of managing remote clients and their access to the terminal server. These functions are performed with the TS RemoteApp Manager, which can be opened either from Start or the Server Manager.

1. Open the TS RemoteApp Manager by clicking Start menu | Administrative Tools | Terminal Services | TS RemoteApp Manager.

   Or, in the Server Manager, open Roles and Terminal Services, and click TS RemoteApp Manager.

   In either case, the TS RemoteApp Manager will open for the local server, as you can see in Figure 11-5.

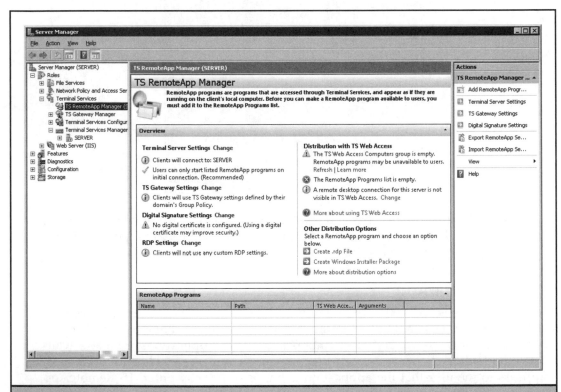

Figure 11-5. TS RemoteApp Manager determines what remote clients can do.

2. In the Actions pane on the right, click Add RemoteApp Programs. The RemoteApp Wizard will open.

3. Select the programs that you want the remote clients to run. For each of the programs, click Properties. Consider any changes you want to make to the name, the location of the startup file, the alias, whether it is available through TS Web Access, and whether the user can use command-line arguments.

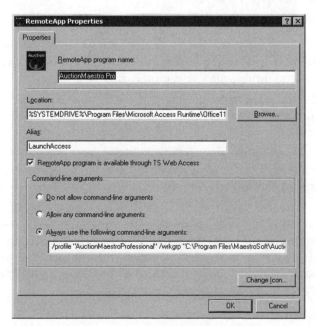

4. Click OK when you are finished with a program's properties dialog box. When you have selected all the programs you want to make available, click Next. You are shown the list of programs and their properties that you want to make available. If you see something you want to change, click Back; otherwise click Finish. The programs will appear in the list at the bottom of TS RemoteApp Manager.

RemoteApp Programs			▲
Name	Path	TS Web Acce...	Arguments
AuctionMaestro Pro	C:\Program Files\Microsoft A...	Yes	/profile "Aucti...
SnagIt 8	C:\Program Files\TechSmith\...	Yes	Unrestricted

5. In the body of TS RemoteApp Manager, you can click the word "Change" in a number of areas, or click any of the three Actions pane options beneath Add RemoteApp Programs, and in all cases, open the RemoteApp Deployment Settings dialog box.

6. The default RemoteApp Deployment Settings are generally what you want to use, but it is good to review them to see what they are so you can change them in the future if the need arises. For example, if you want to use a digital signature, then the tab by that name is where you would add it. Click OK to close the RemoteApp Deployment Settings dialog box.

Distribute a RemoteApp Program

Once you have identified a RemoteApp, the RemoteApp Manager provides two ways to package and deliver the program to a remote user:

▼ Create a Remote Desktop Protocol (.rdp) file that the user can place on her or his desktop and double-click to remotely run the program.

▲ Create a Windows Installer package (.msi) that the user can put in his or her Start menu or on her or his desktop and click or double-click to remotely run the program.

TIP   There is a third way to access a RemoteApp program through TS Web Access that will be discussed later in this chapter.

NOTE   For a remote client to use a RemoteApp program, the client must be running Remote Desktop Connection (RDC) 6.0, which is included in Windows Vista and Windows Server 2008. RDC 6.0 is also available for download from Microsoft Windows XP SP2 and Windows Server 2003 SP1 or SP2. Go to http://support.microsoft.com/default.aspx/kb/925876.

Create an .rdp File

A Remote Desktop Protocol file is a small program that, when double-clicked, will contact the terminal server and start the program it belongs to on the remote client's desktop, although the program will actually be running in the server.

1. In TS RemoteApp Manager (see "Manage TS RemoteApp" earlier for opening), click the program, or hold CTRL and click several programs. (If you select several programs, a separate .rdp file is created, but the settings will be the same for all programs selected at the same time.) Click Create .rdp Files in the Actions pane.

2. In the RemoteApp Wizard, click Next. Accept the default location in which to save the file, or browse to a different folder. Make any other changes to the setting that you want (these settings are the same as those that were set in the TS RemoteApp Manager) and click Next.

3. Review the settings that will be used to create the .rdp file. If you want to change anything, click Back. When you are ready, click Finish. The Windows Explorer will open and show you the program in the folder you choose (see Figure 11-6).

4. Close the Windows Explorer.

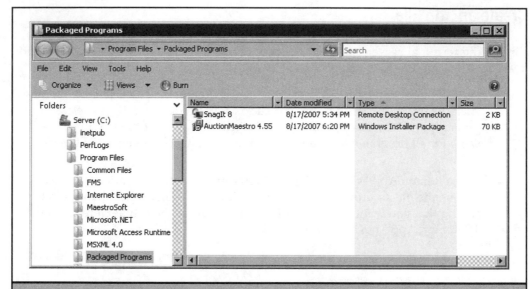

Figure 11-6.   By default, both .rdp and .msi program files are stored in C:\Program Files\Packaged Programs.

Create an .msi Package

A Microsoft Windows Installer package will install itself on the client's computer such that when it is clicked in the Start menu or double-clicked on the desktop, it will contact the terminal server and start the program it belongs to on the remote client's desktop, although the program will actually be running in the server.

1. In TS RemoteApp Manager (see "Manage TS RemoteApp" earlier for opening), click the program, or hold CTRL and click several programs. (If you select several programs, a separate .msi package is created, but the settings will be the same for all programs selected at the same time.) Click Create Windows Installer Packages in the Actions pane.

2. In the RemoteApp Wizard that opens, click Next. Accept the default location in which to save the file, or browse to a different folder. Make any other changes to the setting that you want (these settings are the same as those that were set in the TS RemoteApp Manager) and click Next.

3. In Configure Distribution Package, determine where the .msi shortcut appears on the client machine, Desktop, or Start menu, and click Next.

4. Review the settings that will be used to create the .msi package. If you want to change anything, click Back. When you are ready, click Finish. The Windows Explorer will open and show you the program in the folder you choose (see Figure 11-6).

5. Close the Windows Explorer.

Distribute a RemoteApp Program

After creating either an .msi package or an .rdp file, you can distribute them by doing any of the following:

▼ Put the files in a shared folder on the server and have the client copy them to his or her computer.

■ Put the files on a CD and have the CD automatically start the .msi package or have the client copy them from the CD to her or his computer.

■ Use an existing software distribution process such as Microsoft System Management Server.

▲ For the .msi package you can also use Active Directory Group Policy (see Chapter 15).

You can export and import RemoteApp programs and settings both to another terminal server and to a file using the Export RemoteApp Settings and Import RemoteApp Settings in the Actions pane of the TS RemoteApp Manager. Also, you can change the properties and remove a RemoteApp program by right-clicking it in the RemoteApp Programs list and clicking either Properties or Remove.

Using Remote Desktop Connection with RemoteApp Programs

To use RemoteApp programs requires that RDC 6.0 be installed on the client computer. This is automatically done with Windows Vista Business and Ultimate and Windows Server 2008. In Vista it is also automatically enabled and ready for use. In Server 2008 it must be enabled, which is automatically done when you install TS, and can be manually done in the Initial Configuration Tasks window or in the Server Manager, Server Summary section. An earlier Note explained how to get RDC 6.0 for Windows XP and Windows Server 2003.

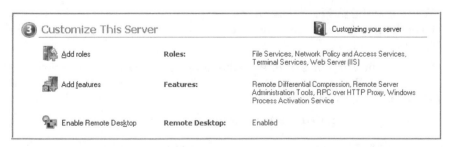

With RemoteApp programs, RDC is only tangentially used; you'll see it on startup of the RemoteApp program, but then it is gone.

Using an .rdp File

An .rdp file is in a sense a shortcut to a remote program on a terminal server. Its use is very simple. When it is made available to the client in any of the ways mentioned in "Distribute a RemoteApp Program," the client should:

1. Drag the .rdp file to his or her desktop if it isn't already there.

2. Start the program by double-clicking it. Enter a username and enter a password that has been registered on the server. Click OK.

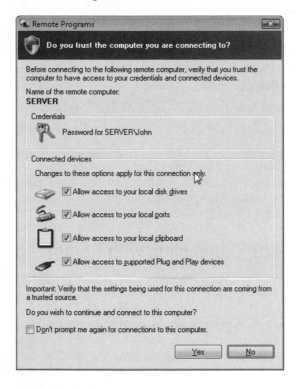

3. Verify that the server is trusted, make any desired changes to the list of the local devices that are available, and click Yes. The Remote Desktop Connection window will open.

4. Log onto the terminal server with the same username and password entered earlier. The RDC window will close and the remote program window will open. The client can use the program as if it were running on her or his computer.

5. Close the program to disconnect or log off from the terminal server.

Figure 11-7 shows two instances of the SnagIt screen-capture program (used to take the figures and illustrations in this book) running under Windows Vista. The program on

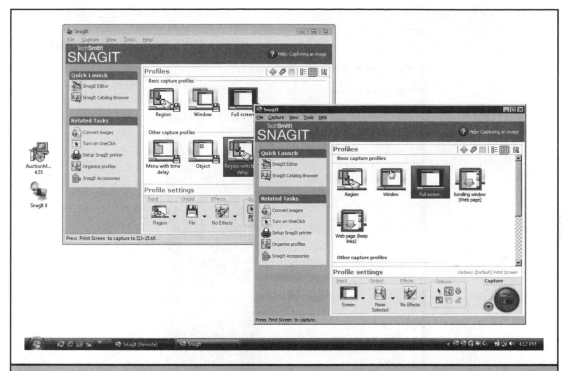

Figure 11-7. Two instances of the same program can run on the client both in native mode and as a RemoteApp program.

the left is running in native mode on the client, as you can see by the Vista title and menu bars. The program on the right is running remotely from the terminal server and has a Server 2008 title and menu bars and the taskbar icon says "(Remote)."

NOTE   In Figure 11-7, both an .rdp file and an .msi package are shown as desktop icons on the left. The .rdp file is the SnagIt 8 icon on the bottom.

Using an .msi Package

An .msi file is an installer package that will install the link to the RemoteApp program on the client computer. Once the link is installed, there is an option on the Start menu to the remote program on a terminal server. When the .msi package is made available to the client in any of the ways mentioned in "Distribute a RemoteApp Program," the client should:

1. Drag the .msi package to his or her desktop if it isn't already there.
2. Double-click the .msi package to begin the installation. Several dialog boxes will appear giving you the status of the installation and you will be asked if you will allow the installation to take place. Click Allow.

3. Start the program by clicking Start | All Programs. Scroll down to and click Remote Programs, and then click the remote program to be run. Select a username and enter a password that has been registered on the server. Click OK.

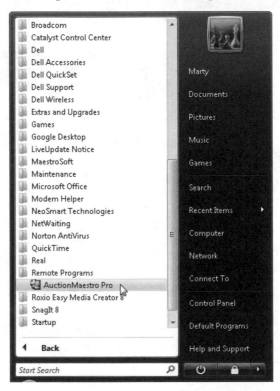

4. Verify that the server is trusted, make any desired changes to the list of the local devices that are available, and click Yes. The RDC window will open.

5. Log onto the terminal server with the same username and password entered earlier. You will be asked if you will allow the installation to take place.

6. Click Allow. The RDC window will close and the remote program window will open. The client can use the program as if it were running on her or his computer.

7. Close the program to disconnect or log off from the terminal server.

TIP   You can place a shortcut to the program installed with the .msi package on the desktop by opening the Windows Explorer, opening C:\Program Files\Remote Packages\, right-clicking the program, and clicking Send To | Desktop (Create Shortcut).

Set Up and Use TS Web Access

TS Web Access is a web-based terminal server connection that allows a client to use a browser to run TS RemoteApp programs over the Internet or an intranet. This requires that Internet Information Services (IIS) be already installed on the terminal server as described in "Install the Terminal Services Roles" earlier in this chapter. TS Web Access is a Terminal Services role service that must be separately installed from TS. This was suggested in "Install the Terminal Services Roles," and if you have not done that, go back to that section and do it now. With the role service installed, configure and use TS Web Access.

NOTE You need to have RDC 6.0 installed on the client for TS Web Access to operate. RDC 6.0 is on Windows Vista and Windows Server 2008 and can be downloaded for Windows XP SP2 and Windows Server 2003 SP1 or SP2.

Configure TS Web Access

If the TS Web Access server with IIS 7 and the TS RemoteApp terminal server are on the same computer and you have followed all the previous steps to set up and deploy TS RemoteApp programs, then you should not need further configuration of TS Web Access. If the two servers are on different computers, then continue here. TS Web Access is a web application that runs on the IIS web server. It can be configured either from the Start menu or from its web page in a browser.

1. Click Start | Administrative Tools | Terminal Services | TS Web Access Administration.

    Or, on the terminal server, click Start | Internet to open the Internet Explorer. In the address field, type **http://localhost/ts**.

    In either case, if needed, enter a local administrator username and password, and click OK. TS Web Access will open in the Internet Explorer and, if there is a terminal server with TS RemoteApp programs on the web server, TS Web Access will display the TS RemoteApp programs that have been set up, as shown in Figure 11-8.

2. Click Configuration. The Editor Zone appears on the right of the browser window. Under Terminal Server Name, type the name of the server on which the TS RemoteApp programs have been set up that you want to make available through TS Web Access.

3. Click Apply and then click RemoteApp Programs. You should see the TS RemoteApp programs you want to make available.

Use TS Web Access

Given that you have done all the preceding setup and configuration, the client use of TS Web Access is very simple.

Figure 11-8.   TS Web Access can be used to configure itself.

1. On the client computer, click Start | Internet to open the Internet Explorer. In the address field, type **http://*server name*/ts** where *server name* is a host name on the LAN, an IP address, or a fully qualified domain name (FQDN).

2. Enter a username and password, and click OK. If the message "ActiveX Control Not Enabled" appears, click the warning message in the Information bar, and click Add-On Disabled | Run ActiveX Control. Finally, click Run in the security warning.

   TS Web Access will open in the browser displaying the TS RemoteApp programs that have been set up, similar to what was shown in Figure 11-8, but without the Configuration option.

3. Click the program to be run. A Trust Warning message will appear. Click Yes to proceed. A security warning may appear. If so, click Allow.

TIP   If when you click the program nothing happens, you need to add the TS Web Access server to the Trusted Sites zone in Internet Explorer. In Internet Explorer, click Tools on the toolbar and click Internet Options. Click the Security tab, click Trusted Sites in the list of zones, and click Sites. In the Add This Website To The Zone text box, if it is not already entered, type the web site address entered in Step 1, uncheck Require Server Verification..., click Add, click Close, and click OK to close the Internet Options dialog box.

4. Enter your username and password and click OK. You are told the remote computer you will be connecting to and the resources you will have available. Make any changes you want to the resource list and click Connect.

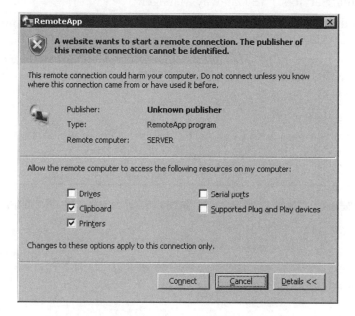

5. The program will open on the client and can be used as it would be normally.
6. When use of the TS RemoteApp program is completed, close the program and close the web browser.

Set Up TS Gateway

TS Gateway provides secure access to an organization's internal network where, with the proper credentials, the user can access the resources on the network, including computers, drives, and printers. TS Gateway provides all of the security, and possibly more than is available in L2TP VPN, yet it is easier to set up and easier to use. Most importantly, TS Gateway works well with firewalls, so that you can have pretty tight firewall settings and still remotely access the network on the other side of a firewall and across a network address translator (NAT).

TS Gateway is a role service within the TS role. In the "Install the Terminal Services Roles" section earlier in this chapter, it was recommended that TS Gateway be installed at the same time TS was installed. If you haven't installed the TS Gateway role service, return to the "Install the Terminal Services Roles" section and do that now, including identifying or creating a security certificate and TS CAP and TS RAP policies.

TS Gateway is controlled by TS Gateway Manager, where you can control, among other items, who connects, what resources they use, whether redirection is allowed, and the specific security features in use. The TS Gateway Manager can be opened from either the Start menu or from the Server Manager.

1. Open the TS Gateway Manager by clicking Start | Administrative Tools | Terminal Services | TS Gateway Manager.

   Or, in the Server Manager, open Roles and Terminal Services, and click TS Gateway Manager.

   In either case, the TS Gateway Manager will open. Double-click your server name in the middle pane to open the TS Gateway server, as you can see in Figure 11-9.

2. In the middle pane:

   a. Click Monitor Active Connections to see a list of connections, to change the connection limit, and to edit and disconnect a connection.

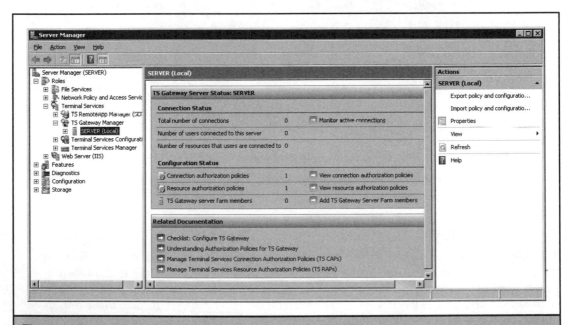

Figure 11-9. TS Gateway Manager determines what remote clients can do.

b. Click View Or Modify Certificate Properties to see a list of certificates and their properties or to create a new one.

c. Click View Connection Authorization Policies (CAP) or View Resource Authorization Policies (RAP) to create a new policy and to change, disable, or delete the current policy.

3. In the Actions pane, click Properties to open the server Properties dialog box. Here, you can limit the number of connections, select an existing certificate to use or create a new one, and manage several other features of TS Gateway. Close the server Properties dialog box when you are ready.

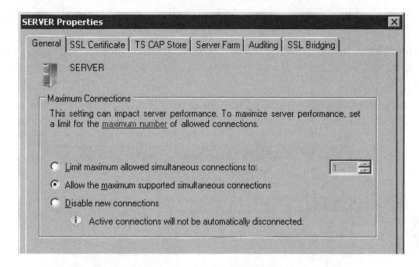

In the Actions pane, you can also export and import the TS Gateway server policies and configuration settings to and from a file that you can use with other servers.

TS Gateway should be considered as an excellent alternative to VPN that is arguably more secure, or at least as secure as L2TP or SSTP, and that is definitely easier to set up.

Enable TS Session Broker

TS Session Broker works with a "farm" of two to five terminal servers, all members of which provide the same programs and services to the remote clients. TS Session Broker will spread out and balance the TS load among the several servers and will reconnect a client to an existing session within the load-balanced farm. When a client initially seeks terminal services, TS Session Broker will look at the various servers and assign the client to the least-loaded server. If the client should end the session or, for some reason, become disconnected and then return, TS Session Broker will reconnect the client to the server and session to which it was originally connected. If one server is down, TS Session Broker will automatically pass over that server in favor of one of the others. Finally, each of the servers can be given a relative weight in terms of their ability to handle a TS load, so more powerful and capable servers can be given a larger load.

To use TS Session Broker, all servers in the farm must be running Windows Server 2008 with the Terminal Services role and with both the Terminal Server and TS Session Broker role services installed as described in "Install the Terminal Services Roles" earlier in this chapter. To create the farm, one IP address is assigned to it and all servers are given a DNS registration to that IP address. This registration, the enabling of TS Session Broker, and the assigning of the relative weight is done on *each server in the farm* through TS Configuration.

1. Open TS Configuration by clicking Start | Administrative Tools | Terminal Services | Terminal Services Configuration.

   Or, in the Server Manager window, open Roles and Terminal Services, and click Terminal Services Configuration.

   In either case, Terminal Services Configuration will open, either within the Server Manager or within its own window, as shown earlier in the chapter in Figure 11-4.

2. At the bottom of the middle pane (in Server Manager) under TS Session Broker, right-click Member Of Farm In TS Session Broker and click Properties.

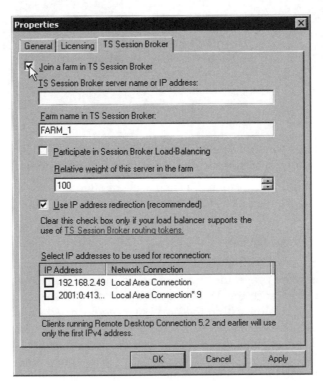

3. Click Join A Farm In TS Session Broker and enter a registered server name or IP address for the first, or lead, server in the farm (this becomes the farm's address) and a farm name.

4. Click Participate In Session Broker Load-Balancing, enter the relative weight of each of the servers, click Use IP Address Redirection (otherwise load balancing can't take place), click the IP address to use for the particular server you are entering when reconnecting a client, and click OK.

With a moderate number of terminal servers, TS Session Broker provides an excellent way to balance and manage the TS load among them.

IMPLEMENT TS LICENSING

A client accessing terminal services is able to use the latest version of Microsoft Windows and the applications running on it without having as recent a version of Windows and the applications installed. As a result, Microsoft collects license fees for this service using a license server to manage this function. The license server is any server on which the TS Licensing role is installed.

The way TS Licensing works is that when a client contacts a terminal server wishing to log on, the terminal server contacts the license server to determine if the client has a Terminal Services client access license (TS CAL). If not, the terminal server will request one. Given that enough TS CALs have been purchased and installed, the license server will issue the TS CAL and enter the fact in its database. For the first 120 days, you do not need a license server and if you install one, it will issue temporary free licenses for the balance of the 120-day period. After the 120 days expire, you must purchase TS CALs from Microsoft and install them on the server. With the purchased TS CALs, the license server will issue longer-term or permanent licenses to devices (computers) and users.

Terminal Server Licenses

To use terminal server licensing, the TS Licensing role must be installed and activated on the network and TS CALs must be installed. The license server can be any server on the network running Windows Server 2008, and because of the traffic it will generate, you may *not* want the license server to also be a terminal server. The license server doesn't have to be a very powerful computer and can work with terminal servers running Windows 2000 and Windows Server 2003, as well as Windows Server 2008. The license server stores all of the TS CALs that have been installed for a network, and all of the terminal servers on the network must be able to quickly access the license server before clients are allowed to connect to the terminal server.

NOTE   You do not need to have licenses or a license server to use Remote Desktop or Remote Desktop for Administration.

During the installation of the Terminal Server role service, you were asked the type of TS CALs that you want to use:

▼ **Per Device**, which requires a TS CAL for each computer connected to the terminal server. Per Device TS CALs can be used by any user.

▲ **Per User**, which requires a TS CAL for each user connected to the terminal server and is only usable with Active Directory. Per User TS CALs can be used on any computer.

The <u>Terminal Services licensing mode</u> determines the type of Terminal Services client access licenses (TS CALs) that a license server will issue to clients that connect to this terminal server.

Specify the Terminal Services licensing mode that you want this terminal server to use.

◉ Configure later

   Remind me to use the Terminal Services Configuration tool or Group Policy to configure the licensing mode within the next 120 days.

○ Per Device

   A TS Per Device CAL must be available for each device that connects to this terminal server.

○ Per User

   A TS Per User CAL must be available for each user that connects to this terminal server.

ⓘ The licensing mode that you specify must match the TS CALs that are available from your Terminal Services license server.

TIP   To decide the type of licensing you need, determine if you have relatively fewer users using a larger number of computers all accessing TS; then you might want to consider Per User TS CALs. In most other cases, you probably want Per Device TS CALs, which is the default.

You could have also chosen, as recommended, to put off the decision for some of the 120-day grace period. We'll address this in a moment in the discussion of configuring TS Licensing.

NOTE   Per Device TS CALs are issued for a finite period and will be renewed if the TS CAL is used. If the TS CAL has not been used in its allotted time, it will be reclaimed and added back to the pool of available TS CALs to be assigned to the next device attempting to access the terminal server. Per Device TS CALs can also be revoked by an administrator.

Install the TS Licensing Role Service

Installing the TS Licensing role service is similar to installing others (assuming that Terminal Services is already installed):

1. If the Server Manager is not already open, click Start | Server Manager. In any case, in the left pane of the Server Manager window, open Roles, click Terminal Services, and scroll the right pane until you see Role Services.

2. Click Add Role Services, click TS Licensing, and click Next.

3. Select the scope over which the license server will provide licenses (see Figure 11-10): the workgroup of which the license server is a part, the domain of which the license server is a part, or the forest of domains that include the license server.

4. Enter or select the folder path in which the licensing database will be stored. Click Next, click Install, and, when you are told the installation is complete, click Close.

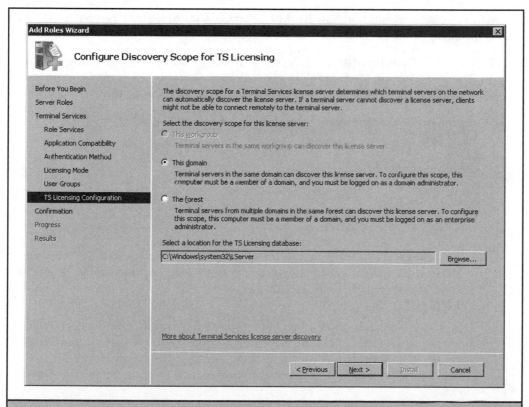

Figure 11-10.   Installing TS Licensing requires determining the scope for the license server.

Activate a TS Licensing Server and Install Licenses

To issue licenses, a TS Licensing server must be activated and have a set of licenses installed. This is accomplished through the TS Licensing Manager's Activate Server Wizard using one of three means:

▼ **Automatic Connection** by the licensing server directly connecting to the Microsoft Clearinghouse over the Internet, meaning that the licensing server must have an Internet connection.

■ **Web Browser** by an administrator manually entering the needed information into a browser on any computer connecting over the Internet to the Microsoft TS web site using a URL provided by the Activate Server Wizard.

▲ **Telephone** by an administrator calling the local Microsoft Customer Support Center using a phone number provided by the Activate Server Wizard.

With a decision in mind on how the Microsoft Clearinghouse will be contacted, open the TS Licensing Manager and start the Activate Server Wizard:

1. Click Start | Administrative Tools | Terminal Services | TS Licensing Manager. The TS Licensing Manager window will open showing the server you installed in the preceding series of steps with a Not Activated status, like this:

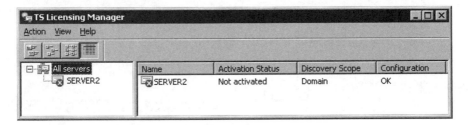

2. Click All Servers so that you can see your new server in the left pane console tree, right-click the new server in either the left or right pane, and click Activate Server. The Terminal Server License Server Activate Server Wizard will open. Click Next.

3. Select the connection method you want to use (Automatic Connection, Web Browser, or Telephone) and click Next. Assuming the Automatic Connection method, enter your name, company, and country or region and click Next. Enter your e-mail address, organizational unit, and street address and click Next.

4. You are told your license server has been successfully activated. Leave the check box checked and click Next to install client licenses (assumed here). Alternatively, uncheck the check box and click Finish to delay installing client licenses. Assuming you clicked Next, the Install Licenses Wizard will open, as shown in Figure 11-11.

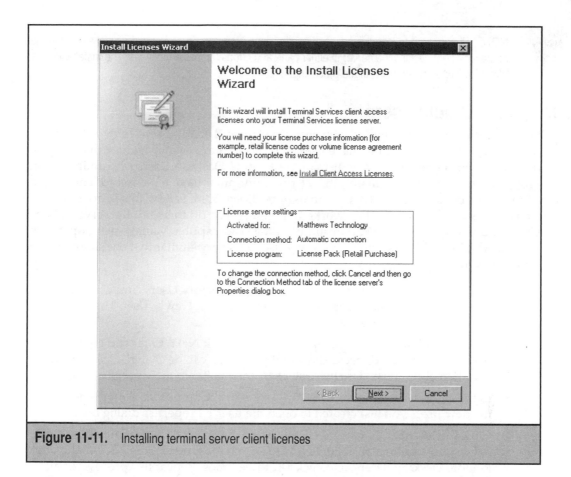

Figure 11-11.   Installing terminal server client licenses

5. Click Next. Select the type of license program that you or your organization has purchased. After you select a program, the dialog box will display information about that program and display a sample license code. If the information and sample code match what you have, click Next.

6. Enter the license code(s), click Add for each, and when you are done, click Next. Click Finish when you are told the licenses were successfully installed.

NOTE If you want to install licenses at another time, you can do so in the TS Licensing Manager window by right-clicking the server in either pane and choosing Install Licenses. The Install Licenses Wizard will open as you saw in the preceding steps.

Set Up and Enable Users

Once licensing has been handled, you need to set up and enable users. For you to do that, the server or the domain must have user accounts that are established for that purpose (meaning that the users are members of the Remote Desktop Users or Administrators groups on the server or domain), the user account must have a password, and the accounts must be enabled for TS or remote connections. Here is how this is done with an Active Directory domain (with a workgroup you would do this with the server's Local Users and Groups—Start | Administrative Tools | Computer Management, open System Tools and Local Users And Groups, and use steps very similar to those shown below for a domain):

1. Click Start | Administrative Tools | Active Directory Users And Computers. Open the local domain, right-click Users, and click New | User. The New Object–User dialog box will open.

2. Enter the full name and the logon name and click Next. Enter and confirm the password to be used, decide how that password can be changed, click Next, and then click Finish. Use these steps to enter as many new users as desired.

3. In the right pane of Active Directory Users And Computers, double-click one of the new users you just created to open the user's Properties dialog box.

4. Click the Member Of tab and click Add. In the Select Groups dialog box, click Advanced and then click Find Now to search for groups. Scroll down and click Remote Desktop–Users, and click OK three times. Repeat this process for all the users who will use TS or Remote Desktop.

5. Close Active Directory Users And Computers, click Start | Control Panel, and double-click System. Click Remote Settings. In the Remote Desktop portion of the dialog box, click Allow Connections From Computers Running Any Version Of Remote Desktop, as shown earlier in this chapter under "Prepare for Terminal Services," and then click OK and close the System window.

USE REMOTE ADMINISTRATION MODE

Remote Administration Mode uses the TS environment much as Applications Server Mode does, but it is limited to a maximum of two users, who must be members of the administrator group, so it does not demand much from the server, does not require licensing, and can be easily used to manage a server without a significant impact on the other processes going on in the server. To do that, it does not include the multiuser and process scheduling components that are present in full TS, but it does use RDC.

Enable Remote Desktop Connection

Remote Desktop Connection uses the same RDC 6.0 that was discussed earlier in the chapter. As you saw earlier, Windows Server 2008 has RDC 6.0 installed by default so that nothing further needs to be done to have the programs available to use. *But*, Windows Server 2008 by default has RDC disabled, and to use it, you must enable it. You can do that very simply with these steps:

1. Click Start | Control Panel | System, and click Remote Settings to open the System Properties dialog box tab dealing with Remote Assistance and Remote Desktop shown earlier in this chapter under "Prepare for Terminal Services."

2. In the Remote Desktop section in the lower part of the tab, click Allow Connections From Computers Running Any Version Of Remote Desktop.

3. Click OK when you are told that the Remote Desktop Firewall exception will be enabled, and then click OK to close the dialog box.

Managing Through Remote Desktop Connection

Using RDC, you can perform virtually any administrative function you can do sitting in front of the computer, and you can do it over a LAN, over a remote access (RAS) connection (see Chapter 8), or over the Internet using VPN (see Chapter 10). You can use the full Control Panel and Administrative Tools including Active Directory, Computer Management, DHCP, DNS, Server Manager, Remote Desktops, and Task Scheduler.

Since the person sitting remotely has all but complete control of the server, it is mandatory that security for this person be kept very tight. Some of the security elements to consider include:

▼ Implementing a firewall in front of the server

■ Using VPN or TS Gateway for access across the Internet

■ Using strong passwords for all administrators

■ Carefully limiting the individuals or groups that have remote administrative access

▲ Carefully reviewing the policies that affect remote administration

Use Remote Desktop Connection

RDC does not require a server for one end of the connection. For example, you can have Windows Vista Business on one computer running at your office and Windows XP Professional SP2 with RDC 6.0 downloaded and installed at home, and from the home computer with the appropriate permissions, you can access the office computer using RDC through either RAS or VPN and do almost anything on the office computer you could do if you were sitting in front of it. Since the office computer is not truly a server, it is called a "host." The home computer is the client. The host must be Windows Vista Business or

Ultimate, or Windows Server 2008, but the client can be any computer that can run Remote Desktop Connection 6.0 (see "Using Remote Desktop Connection with RemoteApp Programs" earlier in the chapter). In Windows Vista, the client is installed and enabled by default, but Windows Server 2008 must be enabled as described in "Enable Remote Desktop Connection."

The user of RDC must be at least a member of the Remote Desktop Users group on the host computer and needs to be an administrator if he or she wants to perform functions limited to administrators. With RDC, only one user can be using the host at any one time, although several user sessions can be active. When the remote client logs onto the host, the host is "locked" so that another user cannot access it, although programs that are running can continue to run, and you can apply user switching to move to another user session. User switching can also be used on the client to switch from the person who is using RDC on the host, to another user, and then to switch back.

Put Remote Desktop Connection to Work

Once you are connected to either an RDC host or a TS server, you can do almost everything that you could do if you were sitting in front of the host. You can run programs, access data, and perform most management and other functions you could otherwise perform. In addition, the RDC toolbar, or "connection bar," allows you to close the RDC window without logging out, so your programs will keep running; to minimize the window, so you can see the actual machine you are sitting at; and to maximize the window. Also, there is a push-pin icon that determines whether the connection bar is always on the desktop or is there only when you move the mouse to the top center of the screen.

Set Up Remote Desktop Connection

RDC gives you the capability of transferring information between the host computer and the local client computer you are using. This means that you can print to a local printer connected to the client (the default), work with files on both the remote host and the local client in the same window (not the default), and cut and paste between both computers and documents on either one (also not the default). The local client resources that are available in an RDC session are controlled by the Remote Desktop Connection dialog box options. Use the following steps to explore what you can do with these settings:

1. On any Windows computer running RTC 6.0 that will be the client, click Start | All Programs | Accessories | Remote Desktop Connection. The Remote Desktop Connection dialog box opens. Click Options and the box expands to give you a number of controls for Remote Desktop in six tabs, as shown in Figure 11-12.

2. Click the Display tab. The default for a LAN is to use Full Screen and up to Highest Quality (32 bit) if your computer can handle it, and to display the connection bar. If your LAN has particularly heavy traffic and is slow, you might want to lower the screen size and colors.

Figure 11-12.   Expanded Remote Desktop Connection provides controls.

3. Click the Local Resources tab. As you can see in Figure 11-13, here you can determine if you want sound brought to the client and the ability to use shortcut keys. Again, if you have a slow network, you might not want to do either of these. If you want to transfer a small amount of information between the two computers with cut and paste, leave the default Clipboard selection; if you want to print on the printer attached to the local client, leave the default Printers selection; and if you want to transfer a sizable amount of information between the computers, click More and click Drives.

4. If you want to start a program when you open RDC, click the Programs tab, click the check box, and enter the path and filename of the program and the starting folder to use.

5. Click the Experience tab and select the connection speed you are using. This will determine which of the items below the drop-down list box are checked. You can change the individual items if you want.

Figure 11-13. Controlling the resources that are available with RDC

6. Click the Advanced tab and under Authentication Options open the drop-down list. The default, Warn Me If Authentication Fails, is a good middle ground. If you are connecting to a Windows Server 2008 TS server with TS Gateway installed, click Settings. The default Automatically Detect TS Gateway Server Settings is recommended. Click OK if you went into the Gateway Server Settings dialog box.

7. Click the General tab and enter the name of the host computer. If you will use several settings, save the ones you just made by clicking Save As, entering a name, and clicking Save.

8. Finally, click Connect, enter your password, and click OK. If you have said that you want the local disk drives available, you will get a message saying that you should proceed only if you trust the computer you are connecting to. Click Yes or No.

9. Depending on the security on the host, you may have to enter your username and password again as you are logging onto the host. The host desktop will open on the client's desktop, maybe filling the screen if that was the choice.

10. Move the mouse pointer to the center top of the window and the RDC connection bar will appear. If you want to keep the connection bar on the screen, click the push-pin on the left.

11. At this point you can do anything on the host that you have permission to do. When you are done using RDC, leave it by:

   ▼ Clicking the Close button in the connection bar. This leaves you logged on, and any programs you have running will remain that way. If you restart Remote Desktop Connection with the host computer and no one else has logged on locally, you will return to the same session you left.

   ▲ Clicking Start | Log Off. This terminates your Remote Desktop session, and all programs are stopped. If you restart Remote Desktop Connection with the host computer, you will begin a new session.

Use Remote Desktop

Most of what you can do in the Remote Desktop or Terminal Server window is obvious; it is the same as directly using Windows. There are two functions, though, that are unique to this environment. An example will show how they work.

Saving to a Local Disk   With the default settings, all files and folders referenced during an RDC or TS session are on the host or server computer. If you reference a folder on disk C:, it is by default disk C: on the host or server. If you specified that you wanted the local disk drives available in the Remote Desktop Connection dialog box, then you can use either the disks on the host/server or those on the local computer. For example, if after turning on the local disk drives when you connected, you are working in a program on the host/server and click Save As, the disk drives you save to are both the host and the client.

You do have to be careful about the terminology. You should know the names that have been given to the client and host computers and their various drives. Normally the host or server disks are listed first and, if unnamed, will be called "Local Disk (C:)," meaning "local" to the desktop you have open, the host or server. The disks on the client will be called "C on *client*," where *client* is the name of the client computer. You can see how easy it is to use either drive.

Printing to a Local Printer   Using the default settings, all printing is directed to the default printer on the client. For example, if you open the Print dialog box from a program running on the host, you will get the client default printer.

If you want to use a different printer, you have three alternatives:

▼ Install another printer in Windows during the RDC or TS session by clicking, if in Windows Vista, Start | Control Panel and double-clicking Printers.

■ Select a different printer as the default printer in the client computer before starting the RDC or TS session.

▲ Turn off the use of the local printer in the Remote Desktop Connection dialog box as you are logging on. This will then allow you to use the default printer on the host/server.

PART V

Administering
Windows Server 2008

CHAPTER 12

Managing Storage and File Systems

The foundation task of a server is to store, retrieve, and manage files. If that is not done easily and efficiently, there is little reason for the server. This chapter looks at how Windows Server 2008 handles this function. In the process, the chapter discusses the structure and systems used for file storage, and the management features that Windows Server 2008 makes available in this area.

UNDERSTAND STORAGE AND FILE SYSTEMS

Windows Server 2008 is meant to work in a wide range of computing environments and with several other operating systems. As a result, the structure of its file storage has to be flexible. This is manifest in the types of storage that are available and in the file systems that Windows Server 2008 can utilize.

Types of Storage

Prior to Windows 2000, there was only one type of storage, called *basic storage*, which allowed a drive to be divided into partitions. Windows Server 2000 added *dynamic storage*, which allows the dynamic creation of volumes. On a disk-by-disk basis, you must choose which type of storage you want to use, because you can use only one type on a drive. You can have both types in a computer that has two or more drives.

Basic Storage

Basic storage, which provides for the partitioning of a hard disk, is the default type of storage in Windows Server 2008 and is the type of storage used in versions of Windows prior to Windows 2000, including Windows NT and MS-DOS. Partitioning uses software to divide a single disk drive into *partitions* that act as if they were separate disk drives. There are primary partitions and extended partitions. (Partitions are the same as simple volumes, which are discussed throughout this chapter.)

NOTE   Windows Server 2008 has made the distinction between partitions and volumes fuzzy. It used to be that the divisions of basic disks were partitions, while the divisions of dynamic disks were volumes. In Windows Server 2008, basic disks have "primary partitions" and "extended partitions" listed under a heading "Volume." Also, if you right-click a storage object, you get "Extend Volume," "Shrink Volume," and "Delete Volume" in the context menu. As a rule of thumb, you can think of volumes and partitions as being synonymous. The only true difference is that volumes can span two or more drives, while partitions are limited to a single drive. Because of the menu options, we will generally call storage objects "volumes," but we will also use "primary partition" and "extended partition," because Windows Server 2008 does that.

Primary partitions are given a drive letter, are separately formatted, and are used to boot or start the computer. There can be up to four primary partitions on a single drive. One partition at a time is made the *active* partition that is used to start the computer. You can put different operating systems in different partitions and start them independently (called "dual"-booting, although you can now have three or more of them). Since each partition is formatted separately, another use of partitions is to put data on one partition and the programs and operating system on another partition, allowing you to reformat the applications/OS partition without disturbing the data, or vice versa.

> **NOTE**   There are some limitations and/or downsides to dual-booting. See "Decide Whether to Dual-Boot" in Chapter 2.

One partition on a disk drive can be an *extended partition* in place of a primary partition, so there can be only three primary partitions if there is an extended partition. An extended partition does not have a drive letter and is not formatted; rather, you divide an extended partition into *logical drives,* each of which is given a drive letter and separately formatted. An extended partition with logical drives allows you to divide a disk into more than four segments. You do not need to have a primary partition to create an extended partition.

Partitions or volumes are usually created and changed while you are doing a clean install of an OS. In Windows Server 2008, though, you can use Disk Management (see "Disk Management," later in this chapter) to create a new volume if there is enough unpartitioned pace, or you can delete or shrink a volume to create more unpartitioned space. If you delete a volume, you lose all of its contents and must reformat any new partition that is created. You can only shrink a volume if there is unused space.

Dynamic Storage

Dynamic storage uses a single partition spanning an entire disk that has been upgraded from basic storage. This single partition can be divided into volumes. Volumes, which in their simplest form are the same as partitions, may also have additional features. The following are the five different types of volumes:

▼ **Simple volumes**   Identify disk space on a single drive and are the same as partitions.

■ **Spanned volumes**   Identify disk space on 2 to 32 disk drives. The space is used sequentially, as it is on a single drive. When the first drive is filled, the second drive is used, and so on. If any disk in a spanned volume fails, the entire volume fails.

■ **Mirrored volumes**   Consist of a pair of simple volumes on two separate disk drives on which the exact same information is written simultaneously. If one disk fails, the other can be used.

■ **Striped volumes**   Identify disk space from 2 to 32 disk drives, where a portion of the data is written on each drive at the same time. This makes for very fast reading and writing, but if any disk fails, the entire volume fails.

▲ **RAID-5 volumes**   Consist of striped volumes on at least three disks where error-correction information has been added such that if any disk fails, the information can be reconstructed. (RAID stands for *redundant array of independent disks* or, alternatively, *redundant array of inexpensive disks.*)

TIP   Mirroring and striping are actually two of the three RAID levels that Windows Server 2008 supports, RAID-5 being the third. Mirroring is Level 1, and striping is Level 0. Special hardware disk controllers may be needed for mirrored, striped, and RAID-5 volumes.

Dynamic storage can be changed in real time without rebooting the computer. Using Dynamic Volume Management (discussed later in the chapter), you can upgrade basic storage to dynamic storage and add, delete, and change the size of volumes, all without rebooting (although you must reboot after the initial conversion to dynamic storage). You cannot upgrade to dynamic storage either in portable computers or on removable storage.

File Systems

File systems determine the way data is stored on a disk and are the data structure or format of the data. When you format a disk, you must specify the file system that will be used. In Windows Server 2008, you have a choice of FAT (file allocation table), FAT32, and NTFS (new technology file system).

FAT and FAT32 File Systems

FAT was the original file system used in MS-DOS and early versions of Windows through Windows 3.*x* and Windows for Workgroups. The initial releases of Windows 95 used VFAT (virtual FAT), and Windows 95 OSR2 (original equipment manufacturers, or OEMs, service release 2) and Windows 98 used FAT32. FAT is a 16-bit file system with a maximum disk partition size of 512MB; it uses a maximum eight-character filename with a three-character extension. VFAT is also a 16-bit file system, but it supports disk partitions up to 2GB and allows long filenames of up to 255 characters. FAT32 is a 32-bit file system, allows disk partitions of over 2TB (terabytes or trillion bytes), and allows long filenames. In Windows NT, 2000, Server 2003, and 2008, FAT partitions can go up to 4GB.

FAT, VFAT, and FAT32 store information using a fixed-sized increment of the disk, called a *cluster*. Clusters range in size from 512 bytes to 64KB, depending on the size of the disk partition, as shown in Table 12-1. Therefore, as the size of the partition increases, the minimum cluster size increases. A large cluster size can be very inefficient if you are storing a lot of small files. FAT32 made a big improvement in the minimum cluster size and is therefore a major benefit with today's large disks.

Since most files are substantially larger than the cluster size, a number of clusters are necessary to store a single file. The FAT has an entry for each file, containing the filename, the creation date, the total size, and the address on the disk of the first cluster used by the file. Each cluster has the address of the cluster after it, as well as the address of the preceding cluster. One cluster getting corrupted can break cluster chains, often making the file unreadable. Some utilities occasionally can restore the file by several techniques, including reading backward down the cluster chain. The common end-result is orphaned clusters, which can only be deleted.

Clusters can be written anywhere on a disk. If there is room, they are written sequentially, but if there isn't room, they can be spread all over the disk. This is called *fragmentation*, which can cause the load time for a file to be quite lengthy. Utilities are available,

Disk Partition	FAT and VFAT Cluster	FAT32 Cluster
0–31MB	512 bytes	512 bytes
32–63MB	1KB	512 bytes
64–127MB	2KB	512 bytes
128–255MB	4KB	512 bytes
256–511MB	8KB	4KB
512–1023MB	16KB	4KB
1024–2047MB	32KB	4KB
2–4GB	64KB	4KB
4–8GB		4KB
8–16GB		8KB
16–32GB		16KB
33GB and above		32KB

Table 12-1.   Cluster Sizes Resulting from Various Partition Sizes

including one in Windows Server 2008, to defragment a partition by rearranging the clusters so that all the clusters for a file are contiguous (see "Drive Defragmentation," later in this chapter).

NTFS File System

NTFS was developed for Windows NT and contains features making it much more secure and less susceptible to disk errors than FAT or FAT32. NTFS is a 32-bit file system that can utilize very large (in excess of 2TB) volumes and can use filenames of up to 255 characters, including spaces and the preservation of upper- and lowercase. Most importantly, NTFS is the only file system that fully utilizes all the features of Windows Server 2008, such as domains and Active Directory.

NOTE   NTFS can also be used in Windows 2000, Windows XP, Windows Server 2003, and Windows Vista.

One of the most important features of NTFS is that it provides file- and folder-level security, whereas FAT and FAT32 do not. This means that with FAT or FAT32, if someone gets access to a disk, every file and folder is immediately available. With NTFS, each file and folder has an *access control list (ACL)*, which contains the *security identifiers (SIDs)* of the users and groups that are permitted to access the file.

Other features that are available under NTFS and not under FAT or FAT32 are the following:

▼ File encryption

■ File compression

■ Remote storage management (in Windows 2000 Server and Windows Server 2003 and 2008 only)

■ Disk quotas

▲ Improved performance with large drives

The first four items are discussed further later in this chapter. The improved performance with large drives occurs because NTFS does not have the problem of increasing cluster size as the disk size increases.

The sum of all this is that NTFS is strongly recommended. The only situation in which you would not want to use NTFS would be if you wanted to dual-boot with another operating system that could not read NTFS, and even in this case the best solution would be to use an older computer to run the legacy software and to use NTFS with Windows Server 2008.

Convert a FAT or FAT32 Drive to NTFS

Normally, you would convert a drive from FAT or FAT32 to NTFS while you are installing Windows Server 2008. Chapter 3 has instructions to do that. You can also convert a FAT or FAT32 volume or drive at any other time in either of two ways:

▼ By formatting the volume or drive

▲ By running the program Convert.exe

"Disk Management," upcoming in this chapter, discusses formatting, which deletes everything on the volume or drive. Using Convert.exe preserves the volume or drive. Use the following instructions to use Convert.exe:

NOTE   Many of the steps in this chapter require that you be logged on either as the Administrator or as someone with Administrator permissions.

1. Click Start | Command Prompt. The Command Prompt window opens.

2. At the command prompt, type **convert** *drive***: /fs:ntfs** and press ENTER, where *drive* is the drive letter of the volume or physical drive that you want converted. If you would like to see a list of the files that are being converted, you can add /v after /fs:ntfs and a space. The volume or drive will be converted.

3. When you see "Conversion Complete," at the command prompt, type **Exit** and press ENTER.

Convert.exe has five switches:

▼ **/fs:ntfs**   Specifies a file system conversion to NTFS.

■ **/v**   Specifies verbose mode, which displays all the files being converted.

■ **/cvtarea:*filename***   Uses a file named *filename* that is created outside of Convert (you can use Fsutil File Createnew *filename filesize* at the command prompt to create the file) and is in the root directory of the drive to be converted. Convert will use this file to store NTFS metadata files such as the Master File Table (MFT) that will increase the efficiency of Convert and reduce the amount of fragmentation of the resulting NTFS volume.

■ **/nosecurity**   Specifies that the security settings of the converted files and folders will be set such that anybody has access.

▲ **/x**   Specifies that the volume will be dismounted, so any open connection with the volume will be disconnected.

The only way to return a volume or drive to FAT or FAT32 after converting it to NTFS is to reformat it.

File System Management

The Windows Server 2008 file system extends well beyond a single drive, or even all the drives in a single machine, to all the drives in a network. It even includes volumes stored offline on tape or disk. The management of this system is significant, and Windows Server 2008 has a very significant set of tools to handle it. Among these are the following:

▼ File Services role

■ Share and Storage Management

■ Disk Management

■ Dynamic Volume Management

■ Distributed File System

▲ Windows Server Backup

FILE SERVICES AND DISK MANAGEMENT

In Windows Server 2008, the File Services role encompasses all of the functions needed for storage and disk management, including:

▼ Providing stand-alone file server services

■ Managing the sharing of storage system resources

▲ Configuring and managing storage system devices and options

The File Services role is not installed by default, but as soon as you go into the Network and Sharing Center and turn on File Sharing, the File Services role is installed automatically. If for some reason the Files Services role is not installed, use the following steps. In all cases, open File Services as described in Step 4.

1. Click Start | Server Manager. Under Roles Summary, click Add Roles. The Add Roles Wizard will open. Click Next.

2. Click File Services and then click Next. Read the introduction message and click Next again.

3. Click File Services, click Next, and click Install. The process may take a minute. When it is done, you will be told the installation succeeded. Click Close.

4. In the left pane, open Roles and then click File Services to open File Services in the right pane, as shown in Figure 12-1.

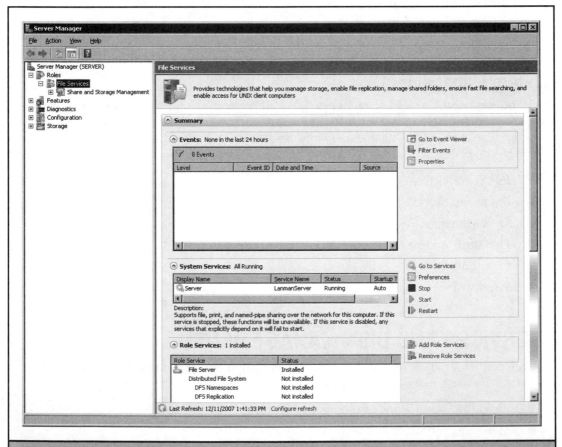

Figure 12-1. File Services is the umbrella for all storage and disk management in Windows Server 2008.

With the enabling of the File Services role, File Server and Share and Storage Management role services are also installed. The complete set of role services available with File Services is described next.

▼ **File Server** provides a network resource for storing information (files or programs) that can be used by other members of the network with appropriate permission. File Server also facilitates backing up of network storage resources.

■ **Share and Storage Management** allows the sharing of folders, drives, and other storage objects in a single management console instead of separate dialog boxes for each device. Share and Storage Management is also used with a Storage Area Network (SAN) to provide logical unit numbers (LUNs) to allocate storage space.

■ **Distributed File System (DFS)** provides flexible and fault-tolerant file sharing and replication using:

    ▼ **DFS Namespaces**, which enables the grouping of shared folders on multiple servers into a single structured namespace, as if it were a single folder with subfolders on a single server.

    ▲ **DFS Replication**, which synchronizes the contents of common folders on multiple servers within a network. Using the Remote Differential Compression (RDC) protocol, portions of files that have changed on one server are replicated across the network.

■ **File Server Resource Manager (FSRM)** provides the reports, filters, and controls to manage the content, type, and quantity of information stored on servers using quotas and defined file screening.

■ **Services for Network File System (NFS)** provides for the sharing and transfer of files between servers running Windows Server 2008 and UNIX using the NFS protocol.

■ **Windows Search Service** allows network clients to quickly search for files on the server on which it is enabled. Windows Search Service and Indexing Service (see next) cannot run at the same time.

▲ **Windows Server 2003 File Services** provides compatibility with older systems through two services:

    ▼ **File Replication Service (FRS)**, which synchronizes the contents of common folders on multiple servers like DFS Replication and allows the inclusion of Windows 2000 and Windows Server 2003 servers.

    ▲ **Indexing Service**, which is a legacy alternative to Windows Search Service that focuses on cataloging of information prior to searching for it, and then using that catalog or index to quickly find information.

Share and Storage Management

Share and Storage Management, which is new to Windows Server 2008, provides a single location to create, manage, and share storage within a network. Share and Storage Management manages the logical storage units in a network in contrast to Disk Management, discussed next, which manages the physical storage units on a network. Share and Storage Management uses its own pane within Server Manager and two wizards to provide its functions:

▼   **Provision Storage Wizard** provides for creating and configuring storage partitions or volumes by dividing storage systems into logical units with logical unit numbers (LUNs) and then configuring those units including assigning a share name, storage type, and size, as well as identifying the servers that will use them.

▲   **Provision a Shared Folder Wizard** provides for the creating, sharing, and management of folders including the assigning of the folder's share name and its permissions, location, and file-sharing protocols.

You can open Share and Storage Management from either Server Manager or Administrative Tools:

1. If Server Manager is not already open, click Start | Server Manager. Then open Roles and open File Services, and click Share and Storage Management.

   Or, click Start | Administrative Tools | Share and Storage Management.

   In either case, the Share and Storage Management window (shown in Figure 12-2) or panes within Server Manager will open.

   The middle pane has two tabs, Shares and Volumes. As shown in Figure 12-2, the Shares tab lists the shared folders, or *shares*, on the local server in two separate entries, one for the public share, and one for the private administrative share with the $ as the last character in its name, which prevents it from being displayed to users.

2. Click the Volumes tab, which lists the physical partitions, or *volumes*, that have been created on the storage devices connected to the local server. As you can see in Figure 12-3, there is often a high correlation between shared folders or shares and physical volumes, but there is no requirement that you can't share individual folders within a partition, and most systems have a Public folder that is shared.

3. Return to the Shares tab, right-click a share, and click Properties. The Properties dialog box opens. You can enter a description and then click Advanced to open that dialog box. Here you can set a user limit, enable filters that determine who can display the folders, and, in the Caching tab, choose how the share contents

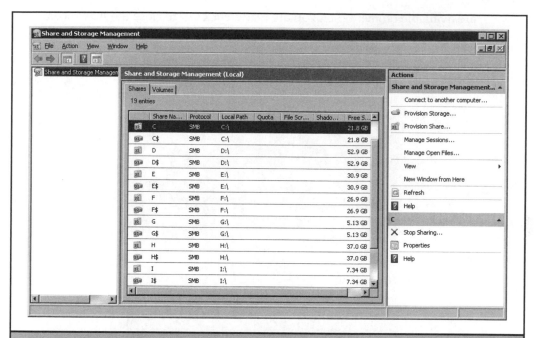

Figure 12-2. Share and Storage Management provides for the management of shared storage.

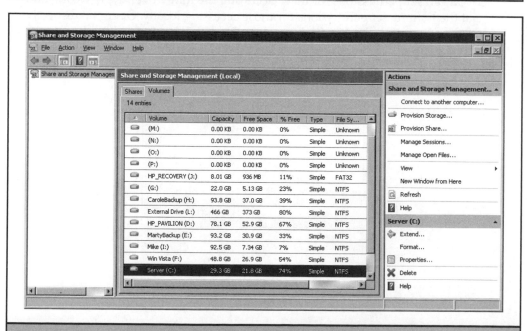

Figure 12-3. Share and Storage Management also provides for the management of physical volumes.

are available offline. When you are ready, click OK to close the Advanced dialog box.

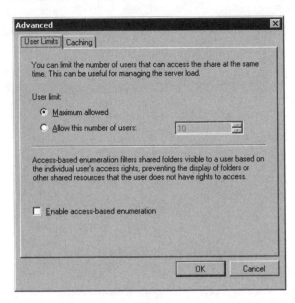

4. Back in the Properties dialog box, click the Permissions tab. Here, at the top, you can set permissions for those accessing the folder over the network, and at the bottom, set permissions for those accessing locally. Open the respective dialog boxes, set the permissions, close the dialog boxes as needed, and when ready, close the Properties dialog box.

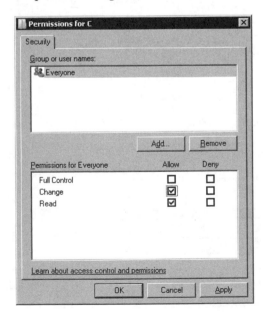

5. Click the Volumes tab and right-click a volume. The context menu allows you to extend the size of the partition, format or delete it, and set its properties. Click Properties.

6. The Properties dialog box that opens is very similar to the drive dialog box that has been in Windows for several versions. Here you can change the volume name; choose to compress or index it; error check, defragment, and back it up; review hardware and security properties; and create shadow copies. Close the Properties dialog box when you are ready.

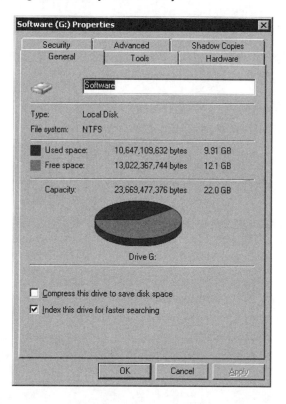

NOTE The options on the context menu that opens when you right-click either a share or a volume are available at the bottom of the Actions pane after a share or volume is selected.

Use the Provision Storage Wizard

The Provision Storage Wizard allows you to create, configure, and manage volumes.

1. In Share and Storage Management's Actions pane, click Provision Storage Wizard. The Provision Storage Wizard opens and asks from where you want to create a new volume—an existing disk or an attached storage device. Make your choice and click Next.

2. Select the specific disk, LUN, or subsystem and click Next. Enter the size of the volume and once more click Next. Specify the drive letter or mounting point and click Next.

3. Choose whether to format the drive, enter the volume label and allocation unit size, decide if you want a quick format, and click Next.

4. Review your settings, click Previous to make any needed changes, and then click Create. When the process is complete, you will get a confirmation similar to Figure 12-4. Click Close.

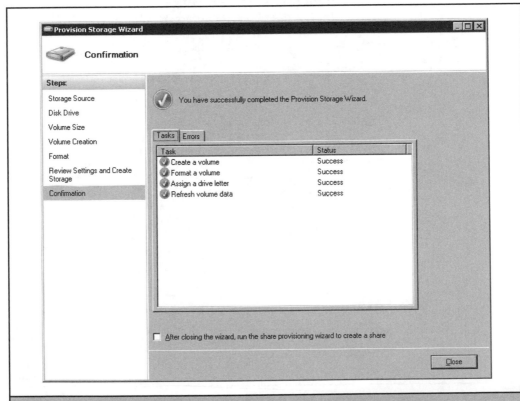

Figure 12-4.   Provision Storage Wizard can create a volume that is shared by Provision a Shared Folder Wizard.

Use the Provision a Shared Folder Wizard

The Provision a Shared Folder Wizard allows you to create, configure, and manage shares.

1. In Share and Storage Management's Actions pane, click Provision a Shared Folder Wizard. The Provision a Shared Folder Wizard opens and asks you to identify the existing or new folder you want to share, as shown in Figure 12-5.

2. Click Browse, select a folder, or click Make New Folder and enter a name, and click OK. Click Next. If you want to change NTFS permissions, click Yes, Change NTFS Permissions; click Edit Permissions; make the needed changes; and click OK.

TIP If you did not run the Provision Storage Wizard and want to create a volume to share with Provision a Shared Folder Wizard, you can do this from within the Provision a Shared Folder Wizard by clicking Provision Storage in the wizard's first screen.

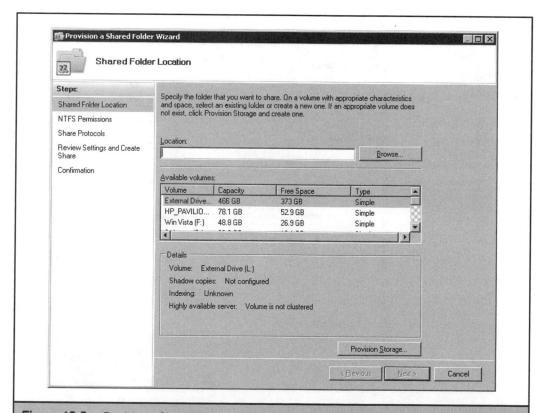

Figure 12-5.   Provision a Shared Folder Wizard lets you create shares within the volumes on a server.

3. Click Next. Choose the file-sharing protocol between Server Message Block (SMB) protocol, which is the primary Windows file-sharing protocol, and Network File System (NFS) protocol, which is required if UNIX servers are on the network. Click Next.

4. Enter any comments about how the share is to be used, and, if any of the advanced settings need to be changed, click Advanced, make the needed changes, click OK, and click Next.

5. Select the type of permissions that will be used with this share and click Next. Choose whether to publish the new share to a Distributed File System (DFS) namespace, which groups shared folders on multiple servers to increase and simplify availability (you must have separately created the DFS namespace), and click Next.

6. Review the settings that you have made, an example of which is shown in Figure 12-6, and, if needed, click Previous to make any changes, and then click Create. Click Close when you are told that the share has been successfully created.

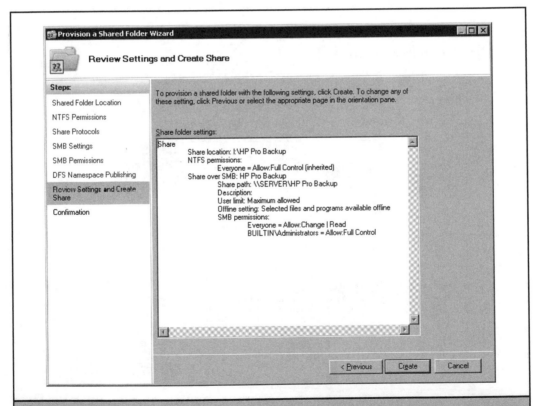

Figure 12-6.   The process of provisioning a share lets you set all of the characteristics of the share.

Disk Management

Disk Management provides a means for managing physical storage devices, both local and remotely across the network. Disk Management includes partitioning, compression, defragmentation, and quotas, as well as storage security. As was said previously, Disk Management works with physical storage devices, while Share and Storage Management works with logical storage objects. A number of storage functions can be carried out in either environment. Disk Management can be opened from either Computer Management or the Server Manager:

Click Start | Administrative Tools | Computer Management. In the Computer Management window, click Storage in the left pane and click Disk Management. Or, click Start | Server Manager. In the Server Manager's left pane, open Storage and click Disk Management.

In either case, the Disk Management pane appears, as shown in Figure 12-7.

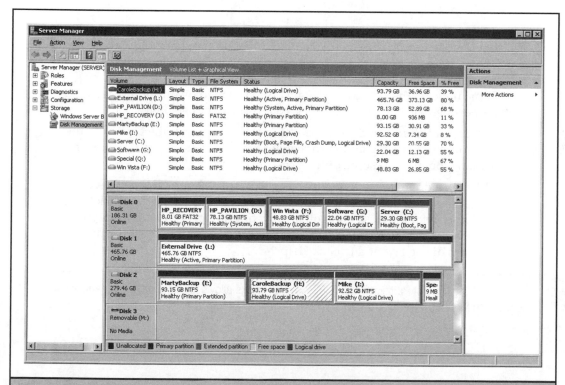

Figure 11-7.   Disk Management provides a physical view from which to manage storage.

Disk Management Pane

The Disk Management pane has two main sections: a character-based listing of partitions or volumes and drives at the top, and a graphic display of the same objects at the bottom. Explore the Disk Management pane:

1. Right-click an object in the Volume column of the character-based listing to open its context menu.

From this menu, you can open or explore (they do the same thing) the volume to see its contents in Windows Explorer; select the volume to be the active (bootable) volume; change the drive letter and path; format or delete the volume if it isn't the active or system volume; extend or shrink the size of the volume; open the volume's Properties dialog box; and get help.

2. Right-click a volume on the right of the graphic display at the bottom of the pane. You'll see a menu similar to that in Step 1 (depending on the type of partition, you may see some differences).

3. Right-click a drive on the left of the graphic display. You will see a drive context menu that allows you to convert to a dynamic disk if you click a basic disk that is not removable and you are in a desktop computer, not a laptop. This menu also allows you to convert to a GPT disk, and to open the drive's Properties dialog box and to click Help.

NOTE   Using a GUID Partition Table (GPT) vs. MBR disks allows for more than four partitions and is required for disks larger than 2TB.

4. Click the Action menu or More Actions in the Actions pane. Here you can quickly refresh the current status of storage objects; rescan all drives, which is usually done only when the computer is restarted and is used to display a drive that has been added or removed without restarting the computer (*hot swapping*); display the menu for the volume or drive that is currently selected (All Tasks); and access Help.

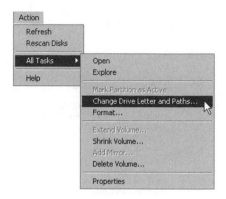

Customize the Disk Management Pane

The Disk Management pane can be customized through both the toolbar and the View menu. You will probably use Disk Management a lot, so it may be worthwhile to take the time to customize it:

1. Click the View menu. The first two options let you determine what is in the top and bottom sections of the pane. The default is a list of volumes at the top and the graphical view at the bottom. The third alternative for either the top or bottom view is a list of disk drives, which is the same information that is presented in the graphical view.

2. Try several changes to see if any suit you more than the default. Figure 12-8 shows a compact alternative with the Disk List on top and the Volume List on the bottom. Keep the layout you like best.

3. Either click the Settings button on the right of the toolbar or reopen the View menu and click Settings. The Settings dialog box opens. In the Appearance tab, you can choose the colors and patterns used to represent the various types of partitions and volumes.

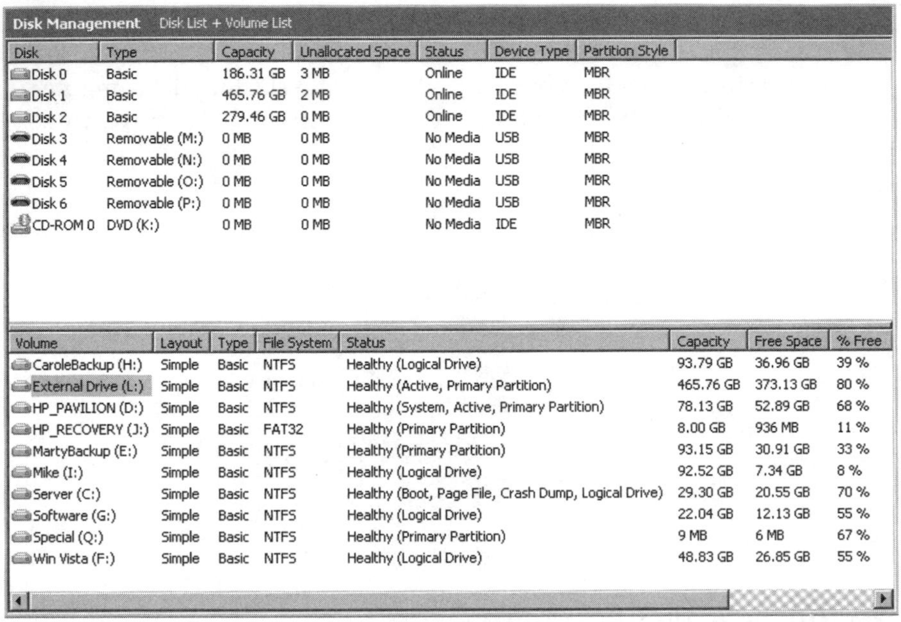

Disk Management Disk List + Volume List

Disk	Type	Capacity	Unallocated Space	Status	Device Type	Partition Style
Disk 0	Basic	186.31 GB	3 MB	Online	IDE	MBR
Disk 1	Basic	465.76 GB	2 MB	Online	IDE	MBR
Disk 2	Basic	279.46 GB	0 MB	Online	IDE	MBR
Disk 3	Removable (M:)	0 MB	0 MB	No Media	USB	MBR
Disk 4	Removable (N:)	0 MB	0 MB	No Media	USB	MBR
Disk 5	Removable (O:)	0 MB	0 MB	No Media	USB	MBR
Disk 6	Removable (P:)	0 MB	0 MB	No Media	USB	MBR
CD-ROM 0	DVD (K:)	0 MB	0 MB	No Media	IDE	MBR

Volume	Layout	Type	File System	Status	Capacity	Free Space	% Free
CaroleBackup (H:)	Simple	Basic	NTFS	Healthy (Logical Drive)	93.79 GB	36.96 GB	39 %
External Drive (L:)	Simple	Basic	NTFS	Healthy (Active, Primary Partition)	465.76 GB	373.13 GB	80 %
HP_PAVILION (D:)	Simple	Basic	NTFS	Healthy (System, Active, Primary Partition)	78.13 GB	52.89 GB	68 %
HP_RECOVERY (J:)	Simple	Basic	FAT32	Healthy (Primary Partition)	8.00 GB	936 MB	11 %
MartyBackup (E:)	Simple	Basic	NTFS	Healthy (Primary Partition)	93.15 GB	30.91 GB	33 %
Mike (I:)	Simple	Basic	NTFS	Healthy (Logical Drive)	92.52 GB	7.34 GB	8 %
Server (C:)	Simple	Basic	NTFS	Healthy (Boot, Page File, Crash Dump, Logical Drive)	29.30 GB	20.55 GB	70 %
Software (G:)	Simple	Basic	NTFS	Healthy (Logical Drive)	22.04 GB	12.13 GB	55 %
Special (Q:)	Simple	Basic	NTFS	Healthy (Primary Partition)	9 MB	6 MB	67 %
Win Vista (F:)	Simple	Basic	NTFS	Healthy (Logical Drive)	48.83 GB	26.85 GB	55 %

Figure 12-8. An alternative layout for the Disk Management pane

4. Select the colors you want to use and click the Scaling tab. Here you can choose the way that disks and disk regions (volumes) are graphically displayed relative to each other. To show capacity logarithmically is probably the best choice if you have drives and regions of substantially different sizes.
5. Make the choices that are correct for you and click OK. Reopen the View menu and click Customize. The Customize View dialog box opens. Here you can customize the parent (Computer Management or Server Manager) window (called "MMC" in the dialog box, for Microsoft Management Console), as well as the Disk Management pane (called a "Snap-In").
6. Try several changes to see if you like them, and configure the window the way that is best for you. When you are finished, click OK to close the Customize View dialog box.

Drive and Volume Properties

There are separate Properties dialog boxes for drives and for volumes. What you may have thought of as the drive properties are really volume properties. See this for yourself next:

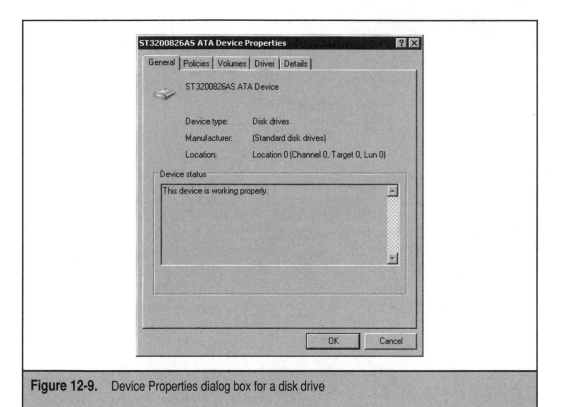

Figure 12-9.   Device Properties dialog box for a disk drive

1. Right-click a drive on the left side of the graphic view and click Properties. The Device Properties dialog box, similar to Figure 12-9, opens. This is primarily an information dialog box, although you can troubleshoot the drive, set write-caching policies, open the Properties dialog box for each of the drive's volumes, update or change the driver for the drive, and view the nomenclature for the drive.

2. Click the Volumes tab, click a volume in the lower part of the Device Properties dialog box, and click Properties. The Properties dialog box for the volume opens, as you can see in Figure 12-10 (very similar to the dialog box we saw in "Share and Storage Management," but with additional tabs). This dialog box also provides some information, but unlike the Device Properties dialog box, it is primarily a place to perform tasks on volumes. Many of these functions are discussed elsewhere in this chapter, although sharing and security are discussed in Chapter 15.

3. Click each of the tabs of the Properties dialog box to see the many features and tools that are available. Two features that are not discussed elsewhere are Error-Checking in the Tools tab and the Hardware tab.

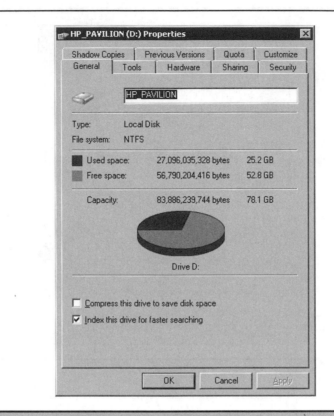

Figure 12-10.   Properties dialog box for a partition or volume

4. Click the Tools tab and click Check Now in the Error-Checking section. The Check Disk dialog box opens and explains that you can, at your option, automatically fix file system errors, such as lost clusters, and look for and attempt to recover data that is in a bad sector on the disk.

5. Select what disk checking you want to do and click Start. If the drive you are checking is on an active server, you are told that exclusive access is not available and thus disk checking could not be done; you are asked whether you want to do the checking the next time you restart the computer. Choose what you want to do, by clicking Schedule Disk Check or Cancel.

6. Click the Hardware tab. Here you see a list of the drives in the computer. If you select a drive and click Properties, you'll see yet another device Properties dialog box (the same Properties dialog box you opened in Step 1 and that is shown in Figure 12-9).

7. Click the Customize tab (not in the Properties dialog box for the volume on which you have Windows Server 2008 installed). This tab allows you to choose the template for the folder contents and the image to use on the folder icon. All other tabs are discussed elsewhere.

8. When you are done looking at the Properties dialog box for the volume, click OK to close it.

NOTE The Properties dialog box for a volume can be opened by right-clicking a volume and choosing Properties.

Add and Remove a Disk Drive

If you have hardware that allows hot swapping (adding and removing standard, normally not removable disk drives while the computer is running), or you have a removable disk drive that is meant to be removed while the computer is running, Windows Server 2008 has several tools to support this that don't require restarting the computer. Normally, a computer scans its disk drives to determine what is available only when it is started or restarted. Windows Server 2008 makes this scan available while the computer is running, through the Rescan Disks option in the Action menu or in the More Actions menu in the Actions pane. Also, if you just remove a disk drive, either hot-swappable or removable, without preparing for it, problems can result, such as losing data or causing your computer to crash. To accommodate this, the Windows Server 2008 Hardware Wizard has an Unplug/Eject option, and you can even put an Unplug/Eject icon on the taskbar for this purpose.

CAUTION Don't add or remove a disk drive while the computer is running unless you know for sure that the hardware supports such action. Significant damage can occur to both the drive and the computer or to either one of them.

Add a Disk

You can add a removable or hot-swappable disk by simply placing it in its slot and pushing it all the way in. After physically adding the disk, Windows Server 2008 will often recognize it and display an AutoPlay message giving you one or more options of what you can do with the disk. If Windows doesn't recognize it, click the Disk Management pane and click Rescan Disks from the Action menu. After rescanning, the drive should appear in Disk Management, and you can work with it, including partitioning and formatting it as you wish (see the upcoming section "Partition and Format Drives").

If you bring in a disk that has been used on, and contains data from, another computer, use Rescan Disks as just described. After rescanning, the new disk may be marked "Foreign" if Windows Server 2008 detects that the disk is a dynamic disk from another Windows Server 2008 computer (which stores its own configuration data). Right-click the foreign drive, click Import Foreign Disks, and follow the directions that you see.

Remove a Drive

If you want to remove a drive that is either hot-swappable or removable, it is important to prepare the drive for that event by telling Windows Server 2008 that you are going to remove it, before you actually do so. Knowing this, Windows will prevent further writing to the drive and perform any hardware-specific tasks, such as spinning down the drive and/or ejecting the platter. Depending on your drive and how it has been implemented in Windows Server 2008, you'll have various ways to tell the operating system that you want to remove the drive.

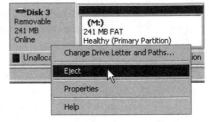

On some devices, such as removable drives, you can right-click the drive on the left of the graphical part of the Disk Management pane and click Eject. The disk will be prepared and ejected. Other devices have similar commands.

With removable disks you may have a Safely Remove Hardware icon in the tray on the right of the taskbar. If you double-click this icon, a dialog box will open in which you can click Stop, select the device, and click OK to prepare the disk to be removed. You will be told the disk can now be removed. Click OK and close the dialog box.

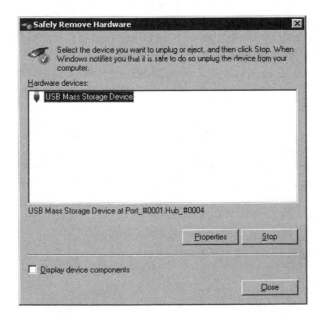

Partition and Format Drives

The first step in preparing a disk for use is to partition it and then format it. Partitioning can be done only when there is unallocated space on the drive—space that is not currently used for an existing partition or volume. If you have no unallocated space, then the only way to create a new volume is to either delete or reduce (shrink) the size of an existing one. Therefore, start out looking at deleting and shrinking volumes, then adding and extending volumes, formatting them, adding logical drives, and changing drive letters.

TIP   Free space is the amount of space available to create logical drives from extended partitions. Unallocated space is space that is not allocated to anything.

CAUTION   Deleting a volume and then formatting it eliminates all information in the volume. Be very sure you want to do this before you execute the commands.

Delete Volumes

To delete a volume, as with the rest of the partitioning and formatting functions, you should have the Disk Management pane open. Right-click the volume to be deleted and click Delete Volume. You are warned that all data will be lost. Click Yes if you are sure you want to do that. The volume is deleted and the space it used is unallocated.

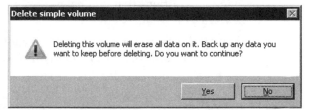

Shrink Volumes

The ability to directly shrink and expand volumes is new to Windows Server 2008. Right-click the volume to be shrunk and click Shrink Volume. Enter the amount of space to shrink the volume, and click Shrink. It may take a few minutes to do the shrinking. When it is completed, the space will be shown as unallocated.

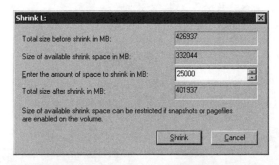

Add Simple Volumes

Adding a simple volume is a little more complex and has its own wizard. To add a volume:

1. Right-click an unallocated area of a disk and click New Simple Volume. The New Simple Volume Wizard opens.

2. Click Next. Select the size of the partition. The maximum is the size of the unallocated space; the minimum is 8MB, as you can see in Figure 12-11. When you have selected the size, click Next.

3. Assign a drive letter. The drop-down list shows you the options available, which is the alphabet less the other drives already in the computer. There are two other options: you can make this new volume a folder on any other drive that supports drive paths (most do), and you can leave the drive letter unassigned. Make your choice and click Next.

4. Choose how you want the volume formatted (if at all), the label to use, and whether you want to use file and folder compression, as shown in Figure 12-12. Then click Next.

5. Review the options that you have chosen and use Back to correct any that are not what you want.

6. When all the choices are the way you want them, click Finish. The volume will be created and formatted as you instructed.

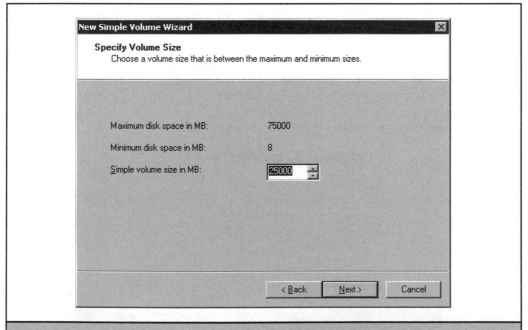

Figure 12-11. You can select the size of the volume you are creating.

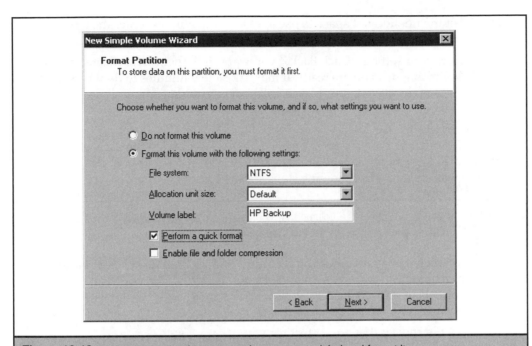

Figure 12-12.   As you are creating a new volume, you can label and format it.

TIP   One good reason to attach a new volume to an existing drive and folder is to increase the space available in an existing, but empty, shared folder ("a share") on a server, so the users can continue to use an existing path for storing or accessing files.

NOTE   The first three volumes that you create are automatically primary partitions. If you create a fourth volume with unallocated space left, the fourth partition and unallocated space become an extended partition with one new volume and free space. You can have only four volumes in a primary partition. An extended partition, though, can be divided into 23 logical drives.

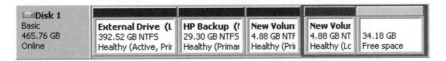

Extend Volumes

The ability to directly extend and shrink volumes is new to Windows Server 2008. To be able to extend volumes, you must have unallocated space on the disk.

1. Right-click the volume to be extended and click Extend Volume. The Extend Volume Wizard will open. Click Next.

2. Select the unallocated space to use to extend the volume, enter the amount of space to use, and click Next.

3. Review your settings. Click Back if you want to change any of them, and then click Finish when you are ready. It may take a few minutes to do the expanding. When it is completed, the volume will show the added space.

Format Volumes

Often, you'll format a volume when you create it, as described in the earlier section, but you can also separately format the volume, independent of whether it was done when the volume was created. The following steps show you how:

NOTE If you try to format the volume that contains the copy of Windows Server 2008 you are currently running, you'll get a message box that says you can't.

1. Right-click the volume that you want to format, and click Format. A small Format dialog box opens, asking for the label, the file system, and the allocation unit size.

2. Make the choices that are correct for you and click OK. You will be warned that all data on the volume will be erased. Click OK. The drive will be formatted.

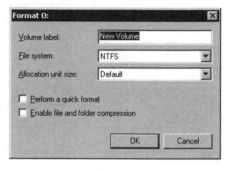

Add Logical Drives

Adding logical drives to an extended partition is the exact same process as creating a new volume as described in the previous section "Add Simple Volumes":

1. Right-click an unallocated area of a disk and click New Simple Volume. The New Simple Volume Wizard opens. Click Next.

2. Specify the volume size and click Next. If desired, select the drive letter or identify a folder path in which to mount the volume and click Next.

3. Choose the way you want the logical drive formatted, click Next, review the choices you have made, and click Finish. The logical drive will be created as you specified it.

4. Repeat Steps 1–3 for as many logical drives (up to 23) as you want.

Change Drive Letters

Changing a drive letter is similar to the previous functions:

1. Right-click the volume or logical drive whose drive letter you want to change, and click Change Drive Letter And Paths. The Change Drive Letter And Paths dialog box opens.

2. You can add additional drive letters and paths on existing drives, edit existing drive letters to change them, and remove (delete) existing drives and/or paths.

3. Click Add, Change, or Remove; fill in the necessary information; click OK (you are reminded that changing drive letters might cause a program that depends on that drive not to run); and click Close.

Data Compression

Data compression allows you to store more information in a given amount of disk space. Different types of files compress differently. For example, some graphics file formats, like .tif, can be compressed to under 20 percent of their original size, whereas other graphics file formats, like .jpg, may not get under 90 percent because they are naturally compressed. Compressed files, folders, and volumes can be used in the same manner as you use uncompressed data. They are uncompressed as they are read and are recompressed when they are saved again. The negative side of compression is that all file-related actions (reading, writing, copying, and so on) take longer.

Data compression in Windows Server 2008 is a lot different from the early compression schemes, in which your only choice was to compress an entire volume. In Windows Server 2008, you can compress a volume, a folder, or a file. You can also automatically compress files that have not been used for a given period, as a way to archive them.

NOTE Data compression in Windows Server 2008 can be done only with NTFS-formatted volumes, and the cluster size must be no larger than 4KB.

Compress Volumes

To use compression on a volume, open the Disk Management pane and follow these steps:

1. Right-click the volume to be compressed and click Properties. The drive's Properties dialog box opens, as previously shown in Figure 12-10.

2. Click the check box for Compress This Drive To Save Disk Space and then click OK. You are asked whether you want to compress just the root folder (for example, D:/) or all the subfolders and files in the root folder.

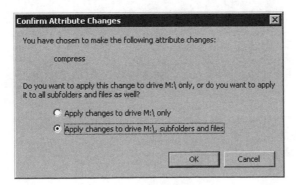

NOTE   A folder can be compressed without its subfolders being compressed, and the subfolders can be compressed without the containing folder being compressed.

3. Make the choice that is correct for you and click OK. You see a message box showing that the compression is taking place. When the message box goes away, the compression is complete.

NOTE   To uncompress data, reverse the steps used to compress it. For a volume, remove the check mark in the Properties dialog box and confirm that you want to uncompress.

Compress Files and Folders

You can compress individual files and folders. This is done from Windows Explorer or My Computer, as follows:

1. Open Windows Explorer or Computer, right-click the file or folder, and click Properties. The file's or folder's Properties dialog box opens.

2. Click Advanced. The Advanced Attributes dialog box opens, as you can see in Figure 12-13.

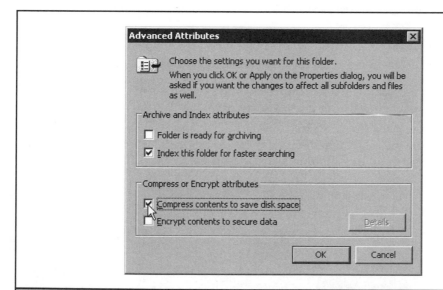

Figure 12-13.   You can compress volumes, folders, and files.

3. Click Compress Contents To Save Disk Space and then click OK twice to close both the Advanced Attributes and the Properties dialog boxes. A Confirm Attributes Changes dialog box opens, giving you a choice between applying the changes to the current folder only or to include the subfolders and files it contains.

4. Make the choice that is correct for you and then click OK. The compression will be done. If the file or folder is large enough for the compression to take a minute or more, you'll see a message telling you the compression is taking place.

If you reopen the Properties dialog box for the file or folder, you will be shown both the actual size and the size on disk, as shown in Figure 12-14.

NOTE   All files and folders have a Size On Disk value, but for uncompressed files and folders it is usually larger than the actual size due to minimum cluster size taking more space than what is needed for a file or folder.

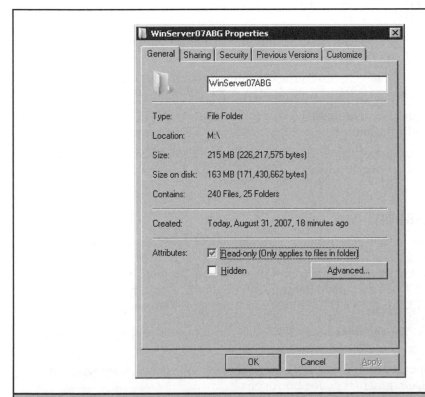

Figure 12-14.   Compressing a folder can save a good amount of space.

Use NTFS-Compressed Files

If you compress just some of your files and folders, you'll want to know which are compressed and which aren't, and to understand how the files behave when they are copied and moved. To know which files and folders are compressed and which aren't, Windows Server 2008 by default changes the color in which encrypted and compressed files and folders (actually their labels) are displayed. If you don't want that, or that feature in your system has been turned off, click Windows Explorer's Tools menu, click Folder Options, and in the View tab of the Folder Options dialog box that opens, scroll the list to the bottom and click Show Encrypted Or Compressed NTFS Files In Color.

☑ Show encrypted or compressed NTFS files in color

When you are copying and moving compressed files and folders, they are a little slower to process and don't always end up the way they started out. Here are the rules for copying and moving:

▼ When you copy a compressed file or folder within its original volume or between NTFS volumes, the file or folder inherits the compression of the folder to which it is copied.

■ When you copy a compressed file or folder to a FAT volume or a floppy disk, the file or folder decompresses.

■ When you move a compressed file or folder within its original volume, the file or folder retains its original compression.

■ When you move a compressed file or folder between NTFS volumes, the file or folder inherits the compression of the folder to which it is moved.

▲ When you move a compressed file or folder to a FAT volume or a floppy disk, the file or folder decompresses.

Drive Defragmentation

As explained earlier under "File Systems," files are made up of smaller segments called clusters, and these clusters may not always be stored together in one contiguous region of a disk. The result is the fragmentation of files, causing an increased file-access time. Windows Server 2008 has a utility to defragment the files in a volume, which can be formatted as FAT, FAT32, or NTFS. Defragment a volume with these steps:

1. In the Disk Management pane, right-click the volume to defragment, and click Properties.

2. In the Properties dialog box, click the Tools tab, and click Defragment Now. The Disk Defragmenter dialog box opens.

3. Windows Server 2008 will analyze your drives and let you know if your performance could be improved by defragmentation. If so, click Defragment Now.

 Your file system performance can be improved
It is recommended that you defragment now.

Defragment now...

4. Select the disks or volumes to defragment, and click OK. Depending on the amount of information in the volume, this will take some time.

5. When the defragmentation is complete, click Close in the Disk Defragmenter and then click OK in the volume Properties dialog box.

 NOTE   The Disk Defragmenter can take a lot of processor resources and significantly slow down disk access. It is therefore important to do the defragmentation when use of the computer is light.

TIP   You can schedule a defragmentation to be repeated on a periodic interval.

Drive Quotas

With NTFS, you can monitor and set policies and limits on the disk space used in a volume, and make sure that one user does not take up more of the disk than is desired. This is particularly important on Internet and intranet file servers. See how to set quotas next:

1. In the Disk Management pane, right-click the volume in which the quotas are to be set, and click Properties.

2. In the Properties dialog box, click the Quota tab, and then click Enable Quota Management. Set the limits, warnings, and logging that you want to use. Figure 12-15 shows one possible group of settings.

3. When you have the settings that you want, click OK. After you have used the volume for a while, return to the Quota tab in the volume's Properties dialog box and click Quota Entries to open the Quota Entries window. This shows who is using the volume and how that usage relates to the quotas that have been set.

4. Close the Quota Entries window and click OK to close the Properties dialog box.

 NOTE   Disk quotas are reported by user logon name within a volume. Compression is ignored when calculating quota usage, and the free space reported to a user is the space remaining within their quota.

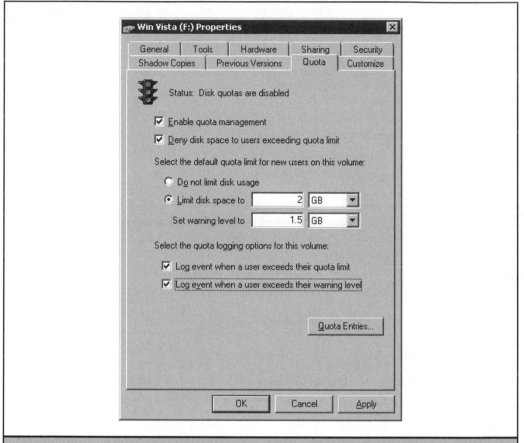

Figure 12-15.   Setting disk quotas prevents one user from using a disproportionate share of a volume.

File and Folder Encryption

Windows Server 2008 NTFS allows the encryption of individual files and folders. With an encrypted file, if someone gets access to the computer, that person still cannot access the file. The person who is logged on when the file is encrypted must be logged on to read the file. Any other person will find the file unreadable, although to all indications, the file is the same. (Chapter 15 discusses file and folder encryption further.) Here's how to encrypt a file or a folder:

1. In the Windows Explorer or Computer, right-click the file or folder to be encrypted and click Properties. The Properties dialog box opens.

2. Click Advanced. The Advanced Attributes dialog box opens, as shown earlier in Figure 12-13.

3. Click Encrypt Contents To Secure Data and click OK twice. If you chose a file in Step 1, you are warned that you have chosen to encrypt a file without encrypting the folder and as a result the file could become decrypted when it is modified. You are given a choice of encrypting both the file and the folder (recommended) or encrypting only the file. Make your choice and click OK.

NOTE   If you try to encrypt a folder, you get a Warning that asks if you want to apply the changes (encrypting) to the folder only, or apply it to subfolders and files as well.

If you sign off the computer and someone else signs on, or if someone tries to access the file over the network, they will find the file unreadable. Also, if you look at the file in the Windows Explorer, it will, by default, have a colored entry alerting you to the fact that it is encrypted.

NOTE   You cannot both encrypt and compress a file or folder. If you select one of these attributes, you cannot select the other.

IMPLEMENT DYNAMIC VOLUME MANAGEMENT

Dynamic Volume Management enables you to create, change, or mirror volumes without rebooting, by using dynamic storage and disks. A dynamic disk has a single partition within which you can create volumes. Simple volumes are the same as dynamic volumes except that dynamic volumes are dynamic (can be changed on the fly), can span disks, and include additional types for advanced hardware (striped, mirrored, and RAID-5).

NOTE   Windows Server 2008 has negated a major benefit of dynamic disks: the ability to extend and shrink volumes, which you can now do with basic disks.

Convert to Dynamic Storage

Most basic disks can be converted to dynamic disks very easily. The exceptions are disks on portable computers and removable disks. Also, the disk must have 1MB of unallocated space, and Windows Server 2008 can be installed in a dynamic volume only if that volume has been converted from a basic root or boot volume. Here's how to convert:

CAUTION   The only way to change a dynamic disk back to a basic disk is to delete all volumes, and therefore all files in those volumes, and then right-click the drive and click Convert To Basic Disk.

1. In the Disk Management pane, right-click a disk on the left of the graphical display and click Convert To Dynamic Disk from the context menu.

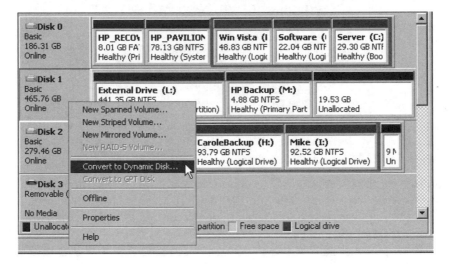

2. Confirm the disk that you want to convert and click OK. The Disks To Convert dialog box opens showing the disk(s) to be converted. If you click Details, you are shown the volumes that will be automatically created within the disk.

3. Click OK if you opened the Convert Details and then click Convert. You are warned that you will not be able to boot an operating system from the disk, except the current boot volume, if any. You are asked if you really want to continue.

4. If you, in fact, want to convert, click Yes. If you do click Yes, then click OK. Conversion will proceed. When it is complete, if you have converted a boot volume, you will be told that the computer will be restarted. Click OK; otherwise you will see that the primary partitions and logical drives have all changed to simple volumes, like in the next illustration.

Create Volumes

You can create a new volume within the unallocated space of a dynamic drive. Do that with these steps:

1. Right-click the unallocated space of a dynamic drive and click New Simple Volume. The New Simple Volume Wizard appears.

2. Select or enter the size of the new volume and click Next. Assign a drive letter or choose to mount the volumes in an empty NTFS folder and click Next. Choose how you want the drive formatted and again click Next.

3. Confirm the steps you want taken, going back and fixing those that are not correct if necessary, and then click Finish. The volume will be created and formatted.

NOTE   Extending and shrinking dynamic volumes uses the same process as extending and shrinking simple volumes described earlier in this chapter under "Partition and Format Drives."

Create a Spanned Volume

A spanned volume can include disk space on 2 to 32 disks, and to the user it looks like a single volume. This is a way to get a large volume, but it is also risky, because every disk that is added to the volume increases the chance the entire volume will fail if one of the disks does. Create a spanned volume with the following steps:

TIP   In Windows Server 2008 you can create spanned, striped, and mirrored volumes starting with either or both basic and dynamic drives, but the basic drives will be converted to dynamic in the process with the penalty that any operating systems on them, other than the current one, will no longer be bootable. Also, a spanned, striped, or mirrored drive cannot use space on the current booting disk.

1. In Disk Management, right-click an area of unallocated space on one of the disks to be included in the volume and click New Spanned Volume. The New Spanned Volume wizard opens. Click Next.

2. Select the disks that you want to include in the spanned volume and the amount of space to use on each disk, as shown in Figure 12-16.

3. Click Next. Assign a drive letter or a folder at which to mount the volume and again click Next.

4. Specify how you want the folder formatted or choose to mount the new volume in an empty NTFS folder and click Next. Choose if and how to format the new volume and again click Next.

5. Confirm the tasks you want performed and click Finish. The volume will be created and formatted, with the final result displayed in both disks.

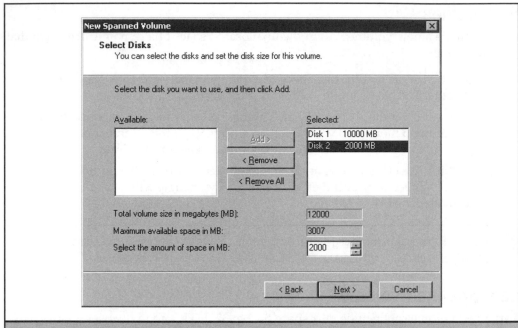

Figure 12-16. Spanned volumes can use space on multiple disks, both basic and dynamic.

CAUTION A spanned volume cannot be striped or mirrored, is not fault-tolerant, and a failure on any one disk is a failure of the entire volume.

USE THE DISTRIBUTED FILE SYSTEM

The Distributed File System (DFS) provides for the creation of a directory, called a *namespace*, that spans several file servers and allows users to easily search and locate files or folders distributed over the network. To users of DFS, files spread throughout a network that have been collected in a namespace can appear as though they are on a single server, which makes their use much easier than if they were to be accessed on their actual servers. Users need to go to only one place on the network, the namespace, to access files located in many different places. DFS also can collect, or replicate in replication groups, files and folder from across several servers for local uses such as backing up those items. DFS can be either part of a workgroup or an Active Directory domain, wherein spreading the information across several domain controllers provides a degree of fault tolerance.

There are several important reasons to use domain-based DFS. Domain-based DFS uses Active Directory to store the DFS *topology*, or configuration, providing a common interface for all server-based file handling. Also, by using Active Directory, you have automatic replication to the other domain controllers within the domain.

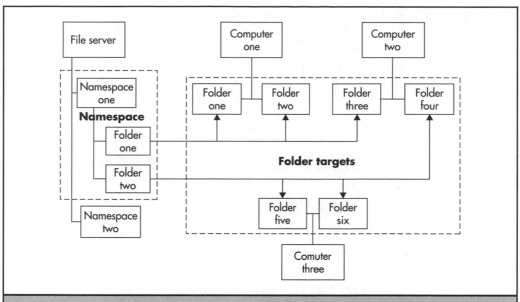

Figure 12-17.   A DFS namespace can contain a number of folder targets from a number of different computers.

You can think of a DFS namespace as a virtual parent folder that can contain virtual subfolders that contain links, like Windows shortcuts, called *folder targets* to real folders on many other computers, possibly file servers, throughout the network, as shown in Figure 12-17.

Create a Distributed File System

The DFS is a role service within File Services and must be installed. In this process you can create one or more namespaces. You then can use DFS Management to add, change, and manage namespaces, and to add and manage replication groups.

Install and Configure DFS

To add DFS to File Services and to create and populate one or more namespaces:

1. Click Start | Server Manager. Open Roles and click File Services. Scroll down the right pane until you see Role Services. Click Add Role Services.

2. In the Add Role Services Wizard, click Distributed File System and click Next.

3. Enter a name for the DFS namespace or choose to create it later. Click Next. If you have a choice between a domain-based namespace and a stand-alone namespace, read the considerations, make a choice, and click Next.

4. In Configure Namespace, click Add to add folder targets to your namespace for existing shared folders you want available there. In the Add Folder To Namespace dialog box, click Browse to select a folder target.

5. In the Browse For Shared Folders dialog box, the default server is the local server you are on. If you want shared folders from that server in your namespace, click Show Shared Folders. Select the first drive or folder in that server to be in your namespace and click OK. Enter the corresponding name to be used in the namespace and click OK.

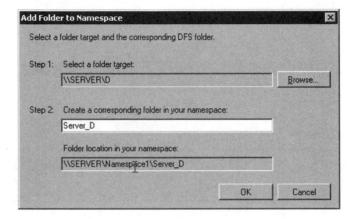

6. Repeat Steps 4 and 5 as needed to add all the shared folders to your namespace from the local and remote servers. When you have added all the folders you want to the namespace, as shown in Figure 12-18, click Next.

7. Review the warnings and informational messages, and click Install. When you are told that the installation was successful, click Close.

Start DFS Management

DFS Management can be started through either Administrative Tools or the Server Manager:

Click Start | Administrative Tools | DFS Management. In the left pane, click DFS Management.
Or, click Start | Server Manager. In the Server Manager's left pane, open Roles and File Services, and click DFS Management.
In either case, the DFS Management pane appears, as shown in Figure 12-19.

NOTE After installing DFS it may take several minutes before you will see DFS Management in the Server Manager.

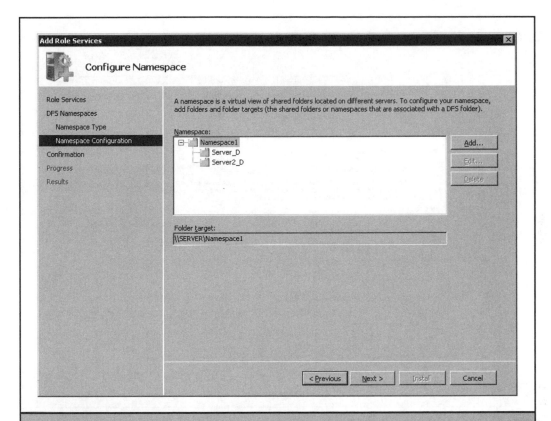

Figure 12-18.   A namespace can contain shared folders, which include disk drives, from any computer in the network.

Distributed File System Management

In DFS Management you can add a new namespace server and then new namespaces within it, or add new namespaces to the local server. Both processes duplicate that part of installing and configuring DFS. See "Install and Configure DFS" earlier in this chapter. In addition, in DFS Management you can manage existing namespaces, and create and manage replication groups.

Manage DFS Namespace

In DFS Management, you can perform a number of management functions on an existing namespace including adding and deleting folders from within the namespace, and

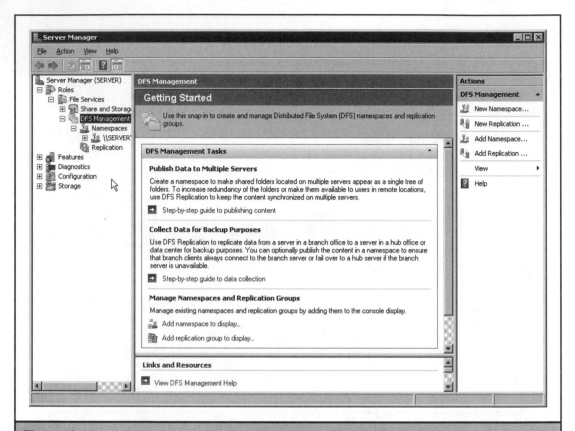

Figure 12-19. DFS Management provides a way of accessing and managing data over both a LAN and a wide area network (WAN).

adding and managing folder targets from within a folder in the namespace, as described next (the DFS pane should still be open on your screen):

1. With the DFS Manager open in Server Manager or its own window, open DFS Manager in the left pane and click Namespaces. Here you can add a new namespace server with the top Actions pane option or display another existing namespace within a domain within Active Directory.

2. Open Namespaces in the left pane, and click the server and namespace you want to work on. The folders within the namespace are displayed in the center pane, as shown in Figure 12-20. Here you can add new folders in the selected namespace with the top Actions pane option and identify folder targets for those new folders. You can also delegate management permissions for the namespace, remove it from display, and delete it.

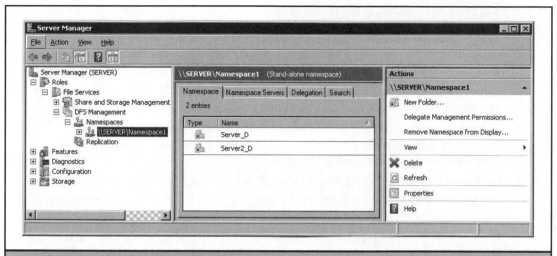

Figure 12-20.   DFS Management allows you to add, delete, and replicate namespace, namespace folders, and folder targets.

3. With a namespace selected, click one of the folders in the center pane. By right-clicking the selected folder or using the Actions pane, you can add a folder target, and replicate, move, rename, and delete namespace folders.

Manage DFS Replication

DFS Replication synchronizes data that is the same on several servers. When DFS Replication detects that this data has changed on any of the servers, it replicates just the changed blocks, not the entire files, to all the other servers. DFS Replication uses the Remote Differential Compression (RDC) protocol to determine which blocks have been changed in a file and then very quickly replicates those changes. If two or more servers change a file at the same time, DFS Replication uses a conflict resolution heuristic called "last writer wins" to choose which file will be replicated across the network. The losing files, though, are moved to a conflict folder, so they are not lost if needed.

NOTE   You must be within a domain to use replication.

To set up and use DFS Replication, you must first create a replication group, then establish a replication schedule, and finally, enable replication. The management process involves editing the group, changing the schedule, and disabling replication. Briefly look at this process in the following steps, which assume that DFS Management is open in either its own window or the server manager:

1. In the left pane, open DFS Management and click Replication. In the Actions pane, click New Replication Group. The New Replication Group Wizard will open.

2. Choose the type of replication, between multipurpose replication among a group of servers, and data collection replication between two servers, and click Next.

3. Enter the name of the replication group, enter a description if desired, and enter or browse to the domain name. Click Next. Click Add to select two or more computers to the replication group.

4. In the Select Computers dialog box, click Advanced, click Find Now, and hold down CTRL while clicking on the computers to be included, as shown in Figure 12-21. When you are finished, click OK twice, and then click Next.

5. Click OK to start the replication service. Read about the types of topology, select the one that is correct for you, and click Next. Determine if replication

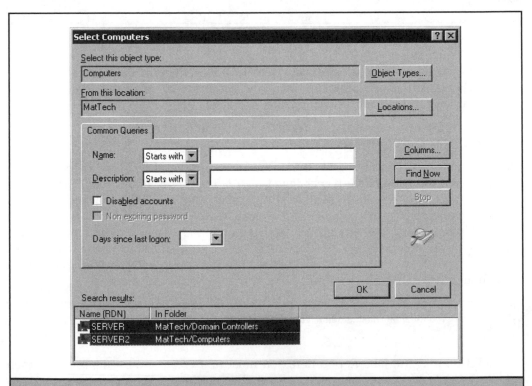

Figure 12-21.   The computers to be in the replication group must be connected within a domain forest.

is to be continuous or on a specified schedule. If the latter, click Edit Schedule, select the times to replicate, the bandwidth to use, click OK, and click Next.

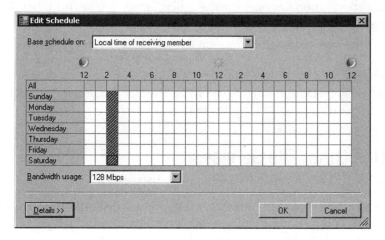

6. Select the primary member that will be the authority if two or more members contain the same information or changes. Click Next.

7. Click Add to select the folders to replicate. Click Browse, select the folder to replicate, click OK, choose how to name the folder and the permissions you want, and click OK. Repeat this step for all the folders you want replicated. When you are finished, click Next.

8. Initially, all members are disabled. Click a member and click Edit. Click Enabled, click Browse, select a path, and click OK twice. Repeat this step for all members and then click Next.

9. Review the settings you have made. If you want to make a change, click Previous. When you are ready, click Create. When you are told that the replication group has been created, click Close. You are told that there may be some delay while Active Directory replicates the configuration. Click OK.

10. Click the new replication group in the middle pane and you'll see in the Actions pane that you can add a new member, new replication folders, new connections, and a new topology. You can also create a diagnostic report, verify the topology, delegate management permissions, edit the schedule, remove the group from display, and delete the group.

Install and Use Other File Services

There are four other file services we haven't yet discussed:

▼ **File Server Resource Manager (FSRM)**, which provides the means to manage the type and quantity of information on servers and to set quotas, generate reports, and implement screens on that information.

■ **Services for Network File System (NFS)**, which implements the NFS protocol to allow the transfer of files between UNIX and Windows Server 2008 computers.

■ **Windows Search Service**, which provides improved and faster searching by clients for files on a server.

▲ **Windows Server 2003 File Services**, which provides compatibility with Windows 2000 Server and Windows Server 2003 file services by adding the File Replication Service (FRS) and the Indexing Service to Windows Server 2008.

Install Other File Services

All of these are role services that are installed from the Server Manager:

1. Click Start | Server Manager. Open Roles and click File Services in the left pane. Scroll down until you see Role Services and click Add Role Services.

2. In the Add Role Services Wizard, click the role services that you want to add (we'll look at FSRM and the Windows Search Service), and click Next.

3. Select the volumes that you want to monitor with FSRM and click Options. In the Volume Monitoring Options dialog box, specify the threshold usage of a volume at which you want to be notified and select the reports to generate (clicking a report outside of the check box provides a description of the report on the right). When you are ready, click OK and then click Next.

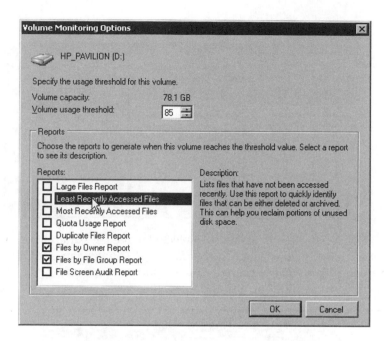

4. Select the folder in which to store the reports, or click Receive Reports By E-Mail and enter the needed information, and click Next.

5. Select the volumes that you want indexed for the Windows Search Service and click Next.

6. Review the settings you have chosen, click Previous if you want to make any changes, and then click Install. When you are told the installation was successful, click Close.

NOTE You may be told that the volumes you selected for indexing could not be added to the list to be indexed because the Windows Search Service had not been started. You can do this after the fact through the Control Panel.

Use File Server Resource Manager

FSRM can be opened from either Administrative Tools or the Server Manager.

1. Click Start | Administrative Tools | File Server Resource Manager.

   Or, click Start | Server Manager. In the Server Manager's left pane, open Roles, File Services, and Share and Storage Management, and click File Server Resource Manager.

In either case, the File Server Resource Manager window or pane appears.

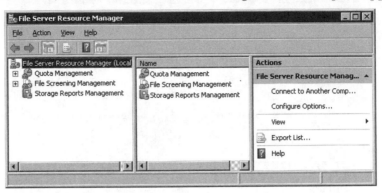

2. With File Server Resource Manager selected in the left pane, click Configure Options in the Actions pane. The File Server Resource Manager Options dialog box opens. Here you can change e-mail report settings, specify the amount of time between notification, edit and review the various reports (see Figure 12-22),

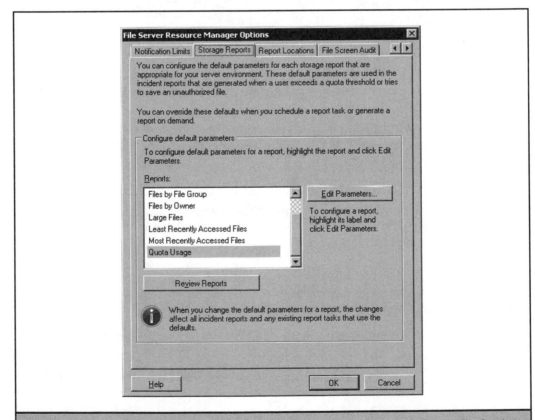

Figure 12-22. Windows Server 2008 provides a number of reports to help you manage File Services.

specify where you store the reports, and determine whether to record file screening activity. Click OK to close the File Server Resource Manager Options dialog box.

3. Double-click Quota Management and then double-click Quotas, both in the middle pane. You should see the drives you identified for quota management during installation.

4. Click one of the drives and click Create Quota in the Actions pane. In the Create Quota dialog box:

    a. Enter or browse to the path that describes the volume or folder for which you want to create a quota.

    b. Select either to create a quota only for the path specified, or to create a quota from a template for all the subfolders under the specified path by clicking Auto Apply Template.

    c. Choose either to use a quota template, which you select, or to define a custom quota, which you enter in the Quota Properties dialog box.

    d. Review the summary of your quota properties, make any needed changes, and when you are ready, click Create.

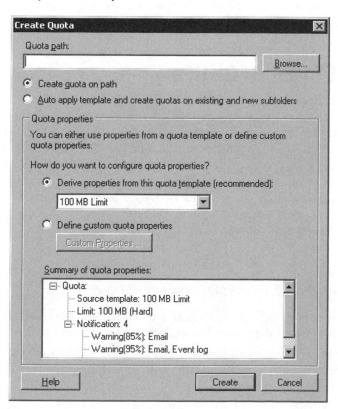

5. Click Quota Templates in the left pane to see a list of the available quotas. Double-click a template to review and edit the details of a template, or click Create Quota Template in the Actions pane to create a new one.

6. Open File Screening Management and click File Screens, both in the left pane, and click Create File Screen in the Actions pane. In the Create File Screen dialog box, enter or browse to the path on which to apply the screen, decide whether to use a file screen template or to create a new one, and click Create.

7. Click Create File Screen Exception in the Actions pane to identify a path and types of files to exclude from screening.

8. Click File Screen Templates in the left pane to get a list of the current screen templates. Right-click one of them to edit or delete that template or to create a new screen from the template. Click Create File Screen Template in the Actions pane to create a new screen template from scratch.

9. Click File Groups in the left pane to create, edit, and delete groups of file types, based on file extensions, to be used in file screens.

10. Click Storage Reports Management in the left pane to schedule a new report task, to add or remove reports from a report task, to generate a report task immediately, and to edit and delete report tasks.

WINDOWS SERVER BACKUP

Windows Server Backup is new to Windows Server 2008 and is used to blunt the impact of losing information on a volume caused by a hardware failure of a drive or a computer, or the inadvertent erasure of one or more files for whatever reason. Windows Server Backup replaces NT Backup in earlier versions of Windows Server, and, based on three separate wizards, is both faster and easier to use. You can back up an entire server or selected volumes. You can back up on another hard disk or disks, on removable disks, or on writable CDs or DVDs, but you can no longer back up to tape. Once you have created a backup of whatever data you want, you can restore that data either to the original computer and disk(s) or to others.

Types of Backup

The following are the three types of backup:

▼ **Regular or Full backup**   Copies all the files that have been selected to the backup media and marks the files as having been archived (the Archive bit is cleared).

■ **Incremental**   Copies all the files that are new or changed since the last normal or incremental backup. The Archive bit is cleared, so the files are not backed up again.

▲ **Copy**   Copies all the files that have been selected, but does not clear the Archive bit, so it does not affect normal and incremental backups.

If you just use regular backup, your backup time will be the longest, but your restore time will be least. If you use a combination of regular and incremental backup, your backups will be faster and you will use less media, but your restoration will take the longest. You need to determine which resources—backup time, restore time, or media—are most important to you. Since you probably back up frequently and restore seldom, optimizing the backup time is often the choice.

Install and Start Windows Server Backup

Windows Server Backup is not installed by default. To use it, you must install the Windows Server Backup feature in Server Manager.

1. Click Start | Server Manager. Click Features in the left pane and click Add Features on the right.

2. In the Add Features Wizard, open Windows Server Backup Features, and click Windows Server Backup. (Like many other features of Windows Server 2008, Windows Server Backup has a complete set of command-line tools that allow you to configure and operate Windows Server Backup from the command prompt. The use of command-line tools, though, is beyond the scope of this book.)

3. The Add Features Wizard pops up and tells you that the Windows Recovery Disc is required for Windows Server Backup. Click Add Required Features. Click Next and then click Install. When you are told that the installation was successful, click Close.

4. Start Windows Server Backup from the Server Manager, which should already be open, by opening Storage and clicking Windows Server Backup. Alternatively, you can start Windows Server Backup from Administrative Tools by clicking Start | Administrative Tools | Windows Server Backup. In either case, the Windows Server Backup pane or window will open. Figure 12-23 shows the Windows Server Backup pane after both a scheduled and a one-time backup have been set up.

Use Windows Server Backup

Windows Server Backup uses three wizards to:

▼ **Create a backup schedule**—Backup Schedule Wizard

■ **Do a one-time backup**—Backup Once Wizard

▲ **Do a recovery from a backup**—Recovery Wizard

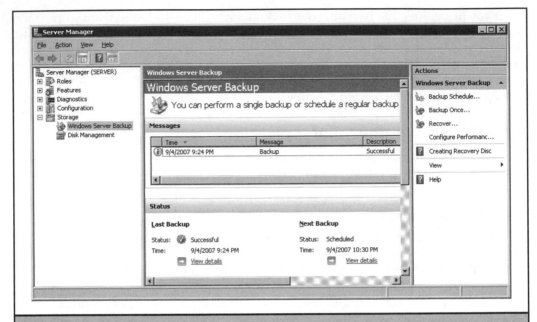

Figure 12-23. Windows Server Backup provides a simple and easy to use interface.

Schedule a Backup

The best form of backup is one that happens on a periodic or scheduled basis, so you are continuously backing up new and changed information. Prepare such a scheduled backup with the Backup Schedule Wizard (the Windows Server Backup pane or window should be open):

NOTE To do a backup, you need to know what volumes to back up, how often to do the backup, what time to do the backup, and where to store the backup. You also need to dedicate an *entire disk* (not just a volume) to the backup.

1. In the Actions pane, click Backup Schedule Wizard. Read the comments and click Next.

2. A message box opens that asks whether you want to continue without restoring the catalog of prior backups, or if this is either the first backup or you don't need to access earlier backups. Click Yes to continue; otherwise click No, click

Cancel to close the Backup Schedule Wizard, click Start | Command Prompt, click Run As Administrator, type **wbadmin restore catalog-backuptarget:** *path of latest backup*. When finished, return to Step 1.

3. Choose whether to do a full server backup or to do a custom backup where you decide which volumes to back up and click Next.

4. If you are doing a custom backup, choose the volumes to back up by clearing the check boxes of the volumes you do *not* want to back up (see Figure 12-24) and click Next. (Volumes containing an operating system must be backed up.)

5. Choose whether to back up once or more a day and the time to do the backup. Click Next. Click Show All Available Drives, select the disk on which to store the backup, click OK, again click the disk you want, and click Next. You are

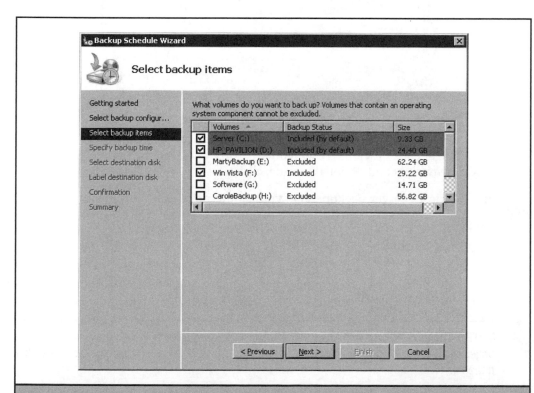

Figure 12-24.   You can choose to back up an entire server or just selected volumes.

reminded that disk(s) you have selected will be reformatted; click Yes to continue and reformat the chosen drives, or click No.

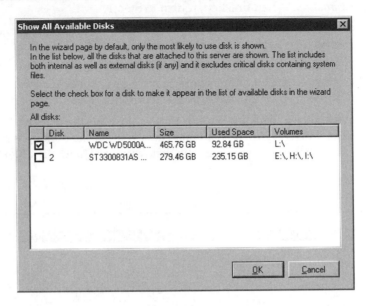

6. You are told what the label will be to identify the disk. Click Next. You are shown what the backup schedule is that you are about to create. If you want to change it, click Previous. When you are ready, click Finish. Your backup disk will be reformatted. When it is done, click Close.

In the Windows Server Backup pane, you should now see your scheduled backup, like this:

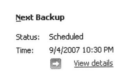

 NOTE   The drive that you will use for your backup is now dedicated to that purpose and you will no longer see it in the Windows Explorer, but it is visible in Disk Management with the label described in Step 5.

Change a Scheduled Backup

To change a scheduled backup, go back into the Backup Schedule Wizard:

1. With the Windows Server Backup pane open, click Backup Schedule Wizard in the Actions pane. The wizard opens saying a scheduled backup has been configured and asks if you want to modify or stop it, as you see in Figure 12-25.

2. If you click Modify and click Next, you are led through the same steps as you used in setting up the backup. If you click Stop and click Next, you are told that the listed backup will no longer be scheduled and that the backup disk(s) will be released. In either case, click Finish to complete the process.

3. When the backup has been either modified or stopped, click Close.

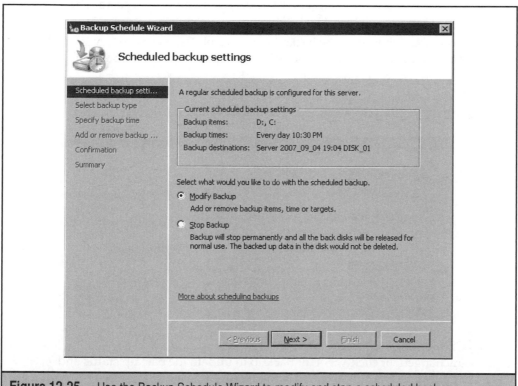

Figure 12-25.   Use the Backup Schedule Wizard to modify and stop a scheduled backup.

Do a One-Time Backup

A one-time backup can be a manual backup where you select the volumes that are to be backed up and then issue the command to do it (again assume that the Windows Server Backup pane is open):

1. In the Actions pane, click Backup Once Wizard. Choose if you want to use the options you choose for the scheduled backup in terms of the items to back up or whether you want to select different items, and then click Next.

2. A message box opens that asks whether you want to continue without restoring the catalog of prior backups, or if this is either the first backup or you don't need to access earlier backups. Click Yes to continue; otherwise click No, click Cancel to close the Backup Once Wizard, click Start | Command Prompt, click Run As Administrator, type **wbadmin restore catalog-backuptarget:** *path of latest backup*. When finished, return to Step 1.

3. Choose if you want a full server backup, or if you want a custom backup where you select the volumes. Click Next.

4. Select the volume(s) to be backed up (if Enable System Recovery is checked, then the operating system volumes must be included in the backup). Click Next.

5. Select the type of storage for the backup, between local drives or remote shared folders, and click Next. Choose the destination volume noting the amount of space required and the amount of space available. Click Next.

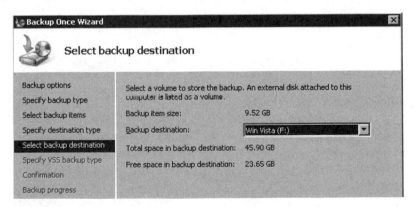

6. Click either Copy Backup to leave the backup status and application logs unchanged, or click VSS Full Backup to update the backup status and application logs. Click Next.

7. Confirm the backup settings. If needed, click Previous and make any necessary changes. When you are ready, click Backup. The backup starts by making a shadow copy of the volume(s) being backed up. Then the actual backup takes place, as you can see in Figure 12-26.

8. When the backup is complete, click Close.

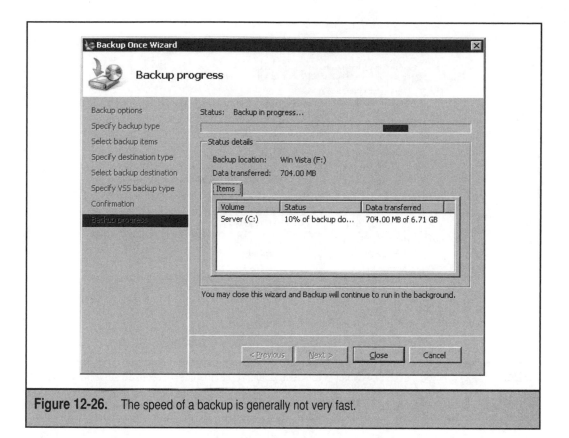

Figure 12-26.   The speed of a backup is generally not very fast.

Optimize Backup Performance

You can determine the type of backup in terms of a full, incremental, or a combination back-up in order to optimize the speed of the backup and the impact on the server workload.

1. With the Windows Server Backup pane open, click Configure Performance Settings in the Actions pane. The Optimize Backup Performance dialog box opens as shown in Figure 12-27.

2. Read the alternative settings and click the one that is correct for you. If you choose Custom, select a backup option for each volume. Click OK when you are ready.

Use the Recover Wizard

The purpose of backing up is to be able to recover data that, for whatever reason, has been lost. There are many different circumstances in which data is lost, and the loss can

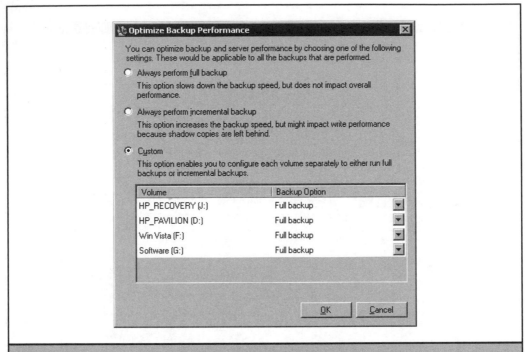

Figure 12-27. You can choose whether to speed up backup at the cost of reduced server performance, or not.

affect a single file or folder, or an entire disk. Therefore, you want to be able to recover data to fit the circumstance. Windows Server Backup can do that; see how with these steps:

1. Click Start | Administrative Tools | Windows Server Backup. The Windows Server Backup window opens. In the Actions pane, click Recovery Wizard.

2. Click whether you want to recover data from the server you are on or another server. Click Next. Select the date and time that the backup was made, as shown in Figure 12-28.

3. Click Next. Choose the objects you want to recover, files and folders, volumes, or applications, and click Next. If you choose Files And Folders, open the volumes and folders needed, and click the folders and file to recover. Hold down CTRL while selecting multiple items.

4. When you have selected all the items you want to recover, click Next. Choose the recovery destination and how you want to treat duplicate files. When ready, click Next.

5. Review your settings. Click Previous to make any desired changes and then click Recover. The recovery will take place. When you are told it has completed, click Close.

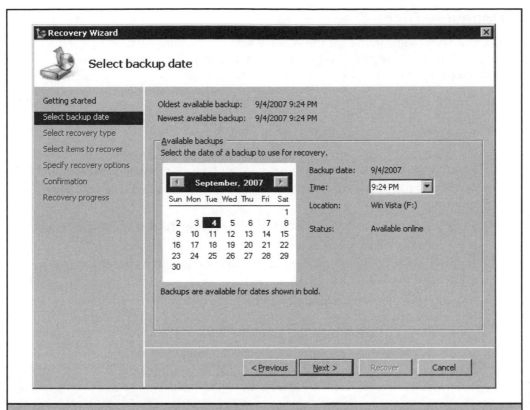

Figure 12-28.   Backup recoveries are selected based on the date and time the backup was made.

Create a Recovery Disc

If something happens to your system drive, you can use a backup you created to recover the files, but you need something to boot the computer and restore the system so it can restore the files. This "something" is a recovery disc. To create a recovery disc, you need the Windows Server 2008 installation disc or the files from that disc on a hard drive.

1. Click Start | All Programs | Maintenance | Create A Recovery Disc.

2. Select the drive where you will write the recovery disc, insert a blank disc in that drive, and click Create Disc.

3. Insert the Windows Server 2008 installation disc in the drive and click Continue. The applicable files will be read off the installation disc, and then you will be told to remove the installation disc and insert the disc to be written to.

4. Click OK. When the disc has been created, you are told how to use the recovery disc (see the next section); click Close twice.

Use a Recovery Disc

A recovery disc is a substitute for the Windows Server 2008 installation disc in its recovery mode. With a recovery disc and a system backup, you can recover from a disc failure. To use a recovery disc:

1. Put the recovery disc in its drive, restart the computer, and press ENTER to boot from the CD/DVD. The Windows Server 2008 installation will start. At the language, time, and keyboard screen, click Next.

2. On the Install screen, click Repair Your Computer. You are told that the drive is BitLocker Drive Encrypted and access is blocked. You are given a choice of loading the password from removable media (a USB key), or manually entering it.

3. Click your choice and click Next. When the Password is read, you are told the drive can be accessed. Click Finish.

4. If you have multiple operating systems on the computer, choose the one you want to recover, and click Next.

5. You next have the choice of doing a complete restore of the entire server, using a memory diagnostic tool, or opening the command prompt where you can use commands to potentially fix the problem.

6. If you choose complete restore, all the drives, including external drives and DVD, are searched for a valid backup. If you have a multiple DVD backup set, you need to have the final DVD from the set in the drive.

7. When the backup is found, click Next and follow the instructions for completing the restore.

CHAPTER 13

Setting Up and Managing Printing and Faxing

Although talk of a paperless society continues, it does not look like it will occur any time soon. As a result, the ability to transfer computer information to paper or other media is very important and a major function of Windows Server 2008. Windows Server 2008, Windows Vista Business, or Windows Vista Ultimate can serve as print servers.

NOTE Although Windows Vista Business and Ultimate can be used as print servers, they are limited to ten concurrent users and cannot support Macintosh and UNIX users, whereas Windows Server 2008 does not have a user limitation and can support Macintosh and UNIX users.

In this chapter, you'll look at what constitutes Windows Server 2008 printing, how to set it up, how to manage it, how to manage the fonts that are required for printing, and how to set up and use Print Services, a feature new to Windows Server 2008. Finally, the chapter will end with a discussion of the fax server, another new Windows Server 2008 feature.

UNDERSTAND WINDOWS SERVER 2008 PRINTING

While Windows Server 2008 can print information in a manner very similar to printing in previous versions of Windows, and many of the concepts are the same, Windows Server 2008 also has a new Print Services role with Print Server, Internet Printing, and Line Printer Daemon (LPD) Service (for UNIX) role services. Take a moment, though, and make sure you are familiar with the basic printing concepts and understand the resource requirements.

Basic Printing Concepts

It may seem obvious what a printer is, but when considering the term, you must remember to include "printing" to a file and "printing" to a fax. Also, although "printing" to a network printer does end up using a physical printing device, to the local computer this form of "printing" is just a network address. So what does "printer" mean to Windows Server 2008?

▼ **Printer** A name that refers to a set of specifications used for printing, primary among which is a hardware port, such as LPT1 or USB1, a software port, such as FILE or FAX, or a network address.

■ **Printer driver** Software that tells the computer how to accomplish the printing task desired; also part of the printer specifications.

■ **Printing device** The actual piece of hardware that does the printing. *Local printing devices* are connected to a hardware port on the computer requesting the printing; *network printing devices* are connected either to another computer or directly to the network.

▲ **Print server** The computer controlling the printing, and to which the printing device is connected.

Basic Printing Requirements

Windows Server 2008 basic printing has the following requirements that must be satisfied:

▼ One or more computers on the network set up as print servers with one or more local printing devices connected to them, or with one or more stand-alone, printers directly connected to the network.

■ The print server must be running either Windows Server 2008 or Windows Vista Business or Ultimate, but if Windows Vista Business or Ultimate is used, there is a limit of ten concurrent users, and neither Macintosh nor UNIX users on the network can use the printer.

■ The print server must have enough disk space to handle the expected print load. This varies greatly from situation to situation, so there is no good rule of thumb. Look at the size of documents that your organization normally prints and at the worst-case number of these documents that might be printed at the same time. If ten people in an office are sharing a printer and their largest print jobs are around 2MB, then 20MB is probably enough, but to be conservative, provide 50–100MB.

▲ Enough memory must be available to handle the printing load. This is a minimum of 128MB, and for a serious print load, 256MB would not be too much. Providing a fair amount of memory will ensure the best performance.

SET UP BASIC PRINTING

Setting up basic printing is done through the Control Panel:

Printers

Click Start | Control Panel, and double-click Printers.

The Printers window that opens contains an Add Printer icon that opens the Add Printer wizard. This wizard leads you through the process of setting up printers that will be available to the computer on which you are working.

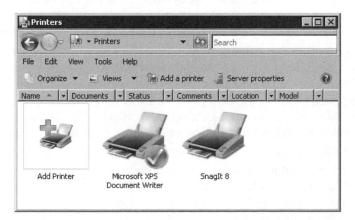

After you double-click the Add Printer icon (or click the Add A Printer task in a tasks pane), the first question asked by the Add Printer wizard is whether you want to add a local printer or to add a network printer:

▼   **Local printer**   Directly connected to the computer you are sitting at

▲   **Network printer**   Connected either to another computer on the network or directly to the network, and has been *shared*, or set up so that others can use it

Add Local Printers

To add a printer connected to the computer you are using, follow these steps (assuming that the Add Printer wizard is still open as described in the preceding section):

TIP   Before installing a local printer, make sure it is plugged into the correct connector (port) on your computer, is plugged into an electrical outlet, has a fresh ink or toner cartridge (which, along with the print heads, is properly installed), has adequate paper, and is turned on. These simple items cover most reasons for printers not working!

NOTE   If you have a printer connected to the computer by use of a Universal Serial Port, and most new printers are, Windows Server 2008 should automatically install it and you should see it in the Printers window. In that case, you should not have to use these instructions.

1. Click Add A Local Printer. The Add Printer wizard will try to detect the printer. If it is successful, the wizard tells you which printer has been found and installs it. You then are asked if you want to test the printer by printing a page. If the printer was not found, you are also told that, in which case jump to Step 3.

2. Click Yes to test the printer and click Next. The printer name, the port it is connected to, and other bits of information are presented. Click Finish. If you chose to print a test page, it will be printed. If the page printed satisfactorily, click OK to that question; otherwise, click Troubleshoot and follow the suggestions you are given. You can skip the remaining instructions in this section.

3. If the local printer you want to set up is not detected, you need to manually install it. Begin by selecting a printer port to which the printer is attached. Other than USB, which is automatically detected, this is most commonly LPT1, the first parallel port, which is also often automatically detected. If it is a serial printer, you might use COM2, because a modem is often on COM1. After choosing a port, click Next. A list of manufacturers and their printer models is presented.

4. Click the printer manufacturer's name in the left list and then select the printer model in the right list, as shown next. If your printer is not listed but you have a disk with a recent Windows driver on it, click Have Disk. If your printer is not listed and you don't have a driver, click Windows Update to connect to the Microsoft site over the Internet to see if a recent driver is available for your printer.

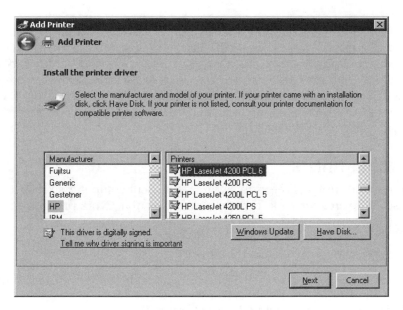

5. When you have selected your printer's manufacturer and model, click Next. If you are asked which version of the driver you want to use—the current installed driver or another—make your choice, and click Next. Accept the default or enter a printer name, indicate whether you want to use this printer as the default printer, and click Next.

6. Choose whether to share the printer, accept the default, or enter the share name. If you have chosen to share the printer, enter the printer's location and any comments and click Next. Choose whether to print a test page and click Finish.

7. If you choose to print a test page, it should be printed now. If it was printed successfully, click Close. Otherwise, click Troubleshoot Printer Problems and follow the suggestions that are presented.

When the last Add Printer wizard dialog box closes, you should see the printer that you added represented as an icon in the Printers window.

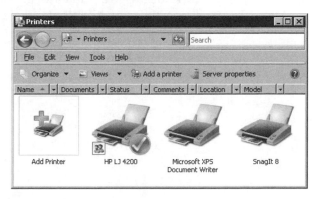

TIP   If your printer was automatically installed and a CD came with your printer, you may wonder if you should re-install the printer using the CD. Most printer drivers in Windows Server 2008 originally came from the manufacturers and have been tested by Microsoft, so they should work well. Unless the printer came out after the release of Windows Server 2008 (February 2008), the driver in Windows Server 2008 should be at least as current, if not more so than those on the CD. On the other hand, the printer's CD may provide you with access to other possible features of the printer, with software for faxing, scanning, copying, and so on.

Set Up Network Printers

Setting up network printers refers to setting up a client computer so that it can utilize printers elsewhere on a network. There are two types of network printers:

▼   Those connected to another computer

▲   Those directly connected to the network

The processes for setting up each of these are quite different from each other.

Set Up Printers Connected to Other Computers

The process of setting up access to printers connected to other computers (what is normally considered setting up a network printer) is carried out with these steps (assuming that the Add Printer wizard is still open as described under the previous heading, "Set Up Basic Printing"):

1. In the second Add Printer wizard dialog box, click Add A Network, Wireless, Or Bluetooth Printer, and click Next. Windows will search for a printer in the Active Directory if you are connected to an Active Directory, or on the network if you are in a workgroup. If you don't see the printer you want to install, click The Printer That I Want Isn't Listed.

2. The next Add Printer dialog box opens. You can add a printer by entering a unique printer name using the Universal Naming Convention (UNC, for example, \\Server1\HPLJ4550), by browsing your local network for a printer, or by entering a TCP/IP network address to a printer (depending on whether you are in an Active Directory domain, your Add Printer dialog box may look different).

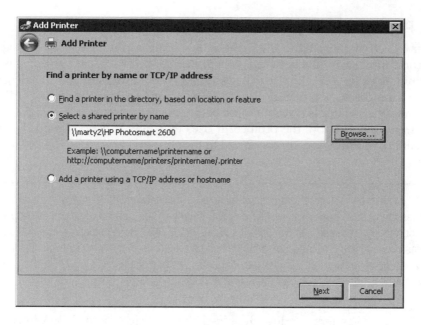

3. When you have selected a printer, click Next. Choose whether the printer you are installing is the default printer and click Next. You will be told you have successfully added the printer. If you want to test the printer, click Print A Test Page. If it prints successfully, click Close; otherwise, click Troubleshoot Printer Problems and read the potential problems and their solution. When you are ready, close the Help window, click Close, and click Finish.

Again, when you return to the Printers window, you will see an icon for the network printer. It will have a cable running beneath it to indicate that it is a network printer.

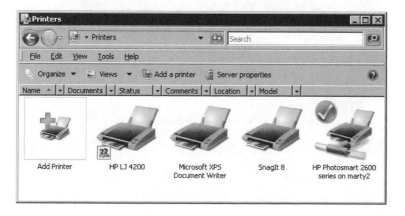

Set Up Printers Directly Connected to the Network

A printer directly connected to the network has built into it a network protocol that it uses to communicate on the network. This protocol, for most recent printers, is TCP/IP. If the printer is using TCP/IP, it may be assigned an IP address by the DHCP server (see Chapter 6 for a discussion of TCP/IP and DHCP), or an IP address may be directly assigned when the printer is set up. Before beginning the process of setting up this type of printer, you must know the protocol it uses and how it is addressed. Here are the steps to set up a printer directly connected to the network using TCP/IP and a known IP address:

TIP Most recent printers that connect directly to the network have a way of determining the IP address they have been assigned by a DHCP server on the network, and/or manually entering an IP address. For example, on HP OfficeJet 7200, 7300, 7400 and Photosmart 2570, 2600, and 2700 series printers, you press the Setup button and select Network and View Network Settings to see or print a page of settings that includes the IP address. Instead of selecting View Network Settings, if you select Advanced Setup, you can enter an IP address.

1. From the Printers window, double-click Add Printer and click Add A Network, Wireless, Or Bluetooth Printer. If the printer isn't found, click The Printer That I Want Isn't Listed.

2. Click Add A Printer Using A TCP/IP Address Or Hostname and click Next.

3. Opposite Device Type, select TCP/IP Device from the drop-down list, and enter the IP address. As you do so, you see the Port Name automatically filled in.

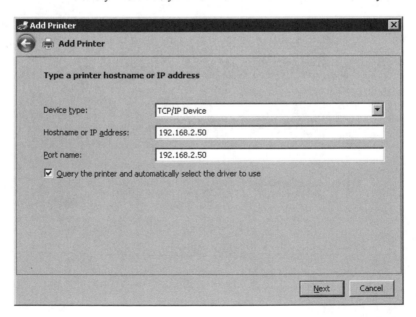

4. Click Next. The Printer Port Wizard will try to identify and set up the printer. If it is successful, you'll be told that, shown a default name, and asked if you want to use the printer as the default printer. Make your selection and click Next.

5. Decide if you want to share this printer; if so, enter a share name, location, and any comments. When all are correct, click Next.

6. You are told you have successfully added the new printer. If desired, click Print A Test Page. If it prints satisfactorily, click Close when asked; otherwise, click Troubleshoot Printer Problems, follow the suggestions that are presented, close the Help window when ready, and finally, click Close. Click Finish when the settings are the way you want them.

When you return to the Printers window, you will see your new printer, but it will not have the normal network "piping" icon making it look like it is directly connected to your computer and not on the network, like this:

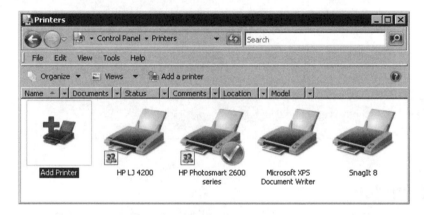

TUNE A PRINTER'S CONFIGURATION

As a general rule, the default configuration for a printer works well in most situations, so unless you have a unique situation, it is recommended that you keep the default settings. That said, it is also wise to know what your alternatives are, so look at the settings you can use to control your printer (these settings vary depending on the printer that you are configuring, so look at your printer[s] during this discussion).

A printer's settings are contained in its Properties dialog box, shown in Figure 13-1. This is accessed by opening the Printers window (click Start menu | Control Panel and double-click Printers), right-clicking the icon of the printer you want to configure, and choosing Properties. For purposes of this discussion, the tabs in the printer Properties dialog box can be grouped into printer configuration, printing configuration, and user configuration.

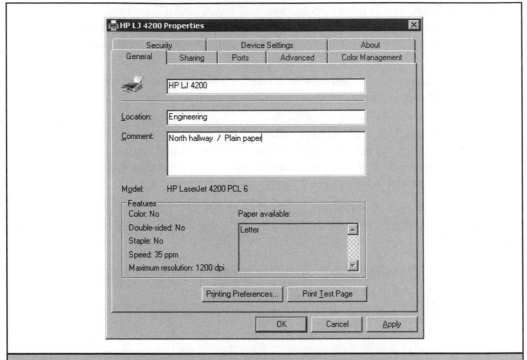

Figure 13-1. A printer is configured from its Properties dialog box.

Configure Printers

Printer configuration has to do with controlling the printer itself. On the General tab (shown in Figure 13-1), you can change the name of the printer, identify its location, and enter a comment about it. You can also set the preferences for layout, paper, and, if available, color, and print a test page. In the Ports tab, you can change the port used by the printer; add, delete, and configure ports; enable and disable bidirectional communication with the printer; and set up printer pooling. In the Device Settings tab, you can set what is loaded in each paper tray, how to handle font substitution, and what printer options are available. Your particular printer may have different or additional options, so review these tabs for your printer. Most of the printer configuration settings are self-explanatory, such as the name and location, and others are rarely changed from their initial setup, such as the port and bidirectional communication, which speeds using the printer. Several items, though, are worthy of further discussion: printer pooling, printer priority, and assigning paper trays.

Printer Pooling

Printer pooling enables you to have two or more physical printing devices assigned to one printer. The printing devices can be local or directly connected to the network, but they must share the same print driver. When print jobs are sent to the printer, Windows determines which of the physical devices is available and routes the job to that device. This eliminates the need for the user to determine which printing device is available, provides for better load sharing among printing devices, and allows the management of several devices through one printer definition.

You can set up printer pooling with these steps:

1. Install all printers as described previously in "Set Up Basic Printing."

2. In the Printers window, right-click the printer to which all work will be directed and click Properties. The printer's Properties dialog box opens.

3. Click the Ports tab and click Enable Printer Pooling.

4. Click each of the ports with a printing device that is to be in the pool, as you can see here:

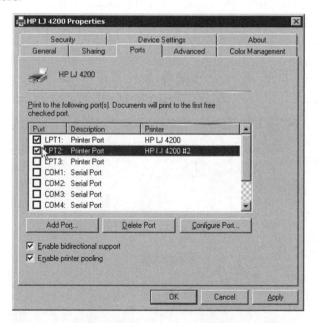

5. When all the ports are selected, click OK to close the Properties dialog box.

6. If the printer that contains the pool isn't already selected as the default printer, right-click the printer and click Set As Default Printer.

NOTE   The default printer has a check mark overlaying its icon and doesn't have the Set As Default Printer option.

Printer Priority

You can do the opposite of printer pooling by assigning several printers to one printing device. The primary reason that you would want to do this is to have two or more settings used with one device. For example, if you want to have two or more priorities automatically assigned to jobs going to a printing device, you could create two or more printers, all pointing to the same printer port and physical device, but with different priorities. Then have high-priority print jobs printed to a printer with a priority of 99, and low-priority jobs printed to a printer with a priority of 1.

Create several printers with one print device using the following steps:

1. Install all printers as previously described in "Set Up Basic Printing," except that the printers use the same port. Name each of the printers to indicate its priority. For example, "High Priority Printer" and "Low Priority Printer."

   HP LJ 4200 - High Priority   HP LJ 4200 - Low Priority

2. In the Printers window, right-click the high-priority printer and click Properties. The printer's Properties dialog box will open.

3. Click the Advanced tab, enter a priority of **99**, as shown in Figure 13-2, and click OK.

4. Similarly, right-click the other printers, click their Properties dialog box, click the Advanced tab, enter priorities of **1–98**, and click OK.

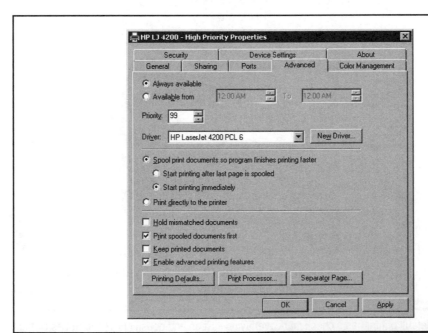

Figure 13-2. You can have different priorities for the same printer.

Jobs that are printed with the highest priority will print before jobs with a lower priority if they are in the queue at the same time.

Assign Paper Trays

Depending on your printer, it may have more than one paper tray, and as a result, you may want to put different types or sizes of paper in each tray. If you assign types and sizes of paper to trays in the printer's Properties dialog box, and a user requests a type and size of paper when printing, Windows Server 2008 automatically designates the correct paper tray for the print job. Here's how to assign types and sizes of paper to trays:

1. In the Printers window, right-click the printer whose trays you want to assign and click Properties. The printer's Properties dialog box opens.

2. Click the Device Settings tab. Open each tray and select the type and size of paper in that tray, similar to what you see in Figure 13-3.

3. When you have set the paper type and size in each tray, click OK.

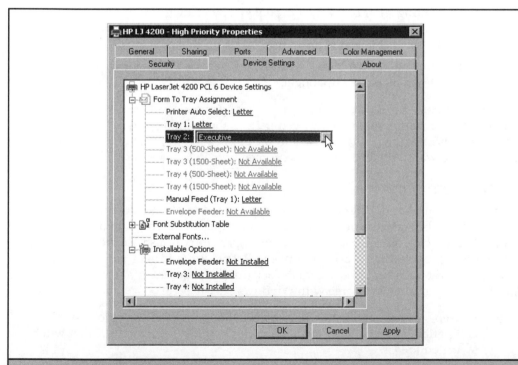

Figure 13-3.   Specific types of paper can be assigned to different trays and automatically used when called for.

Configure Printing

Printing configuration has to do with controlling the process of printing, not the printer itself or particular print jobs. Printing configuration is handled in the Advanced tab of a printer's Properties dialog box, such as the one shown previously in Figure 13-2. As stated earlier, in most cases, the default settings are appropriate and should be changed only in unique situations. Two exceptions to this are the spooling settings and using separator pages, discussed next.

Configure Spooling

In most instances, the time it takes to print a document is considerably longer than the time it takes to transfer the information from an application to the printer. The information is therefore stored on disk in a special preprint format, and then Windows, as a background task, feeds the printer as much information as it can handle. This temporary storage on disk is called *printer spooling*. In the majority of cases, you want to use printer spooling and not tie up the application waiting for the printer. However, an alternative pair of settings is available:

▼ **Start Printing After Last Page Is Spooled**   By waiting to print until the last page is spooled, the spooling finishes faster and the user gets back to the application faster, but it takes longer to finish printing.

▲ **Start Printing Immediately**   The printing will be done sooner, but the application will be tied up longer.

There is no one correct choice for this. Normally, the default Start Printing Immediately provides a happy medium between getting the printing and getting back to the application. But if you want to get back to the application in the shortest possible time, then choose to wait until the last page is spooled.

Use Separator Pages

If you have a number of different jobs on a printer, it might be worthwhile to have a separator page between them (a blank piece of paper between printed jobs), to more easily identify where one job ends and another begins. You can also use the file that creates a separator page to switch a printer between PostScript (a printer language) and PCL (Printer Control Language) on Hewlett-Packard (HP) and compatible printers. Four sample SEP separation files come with Windows Server 2008:

▼ **Pcl.sep**   Prints a separation page before the start of each print job on PCL-compatible printers. If the printer handles both PostScript and PCL, it will be switched to PCL.

■ **Pscript.sep**   Does *not* print a separation page, but printers with both PostScript and PCL will be switched to PostScript.

■ **Sysprint.sep** Prints a separation page before the start of each print job on PostScript-compatible printers.

▲ **Sysprtj.sep** The same as Sysprint.sep, but in the Japanese language.

NOTE The separation files work with HP and PostScript or compatible printers. They will not work with all printers.

If you know or have a guide to either the PCL or PostScript language (or both), you can open and modify these files (or copies of them) with any text editor, such as Notepad, to suit your particular purpose. These files are, by default, in the C:\Windows\System32 folder.

pcl.sep	4/12/2007 11:34...	SEP File
pscript.sep	4/12/2007 11:34...	SEP File
sysprint.sep	4/12/2007 11:34...	SEP File
sysprtj.sep	4/12/2007 11:34...	SEP File

Configure Users

User configuration has to do with controlling the users of a printer. When you initially set up the printer, you were asked if you wanted to share it and allow others on the network to print on it. User configuration allows you to change that decision in the Sharing tab of the printer's Properties dialog box, which turns sharing on and off, and in the Security tab of the same dialog box, where you can set the permissions for various groups of users.

NOTE Sharing and permissions are controlled by the computer to which the printer is directly connected. A printer directly connected to the network is considered to be directly connected to all computers on the network and therefore configurable by all of them, but those settings are just for that computer.

If a printer is shared, then the Security tab determines who has permission to use, control, and make changes to the printer, as you can see in Figure 13-4. The four types of permissions and the functions that they allow are as follows:

▼ **Print** Allows the user to connect to a printer to print, and to cancel, pause, resume, and restart the user's own documents.

■ **Manage Printers** Allows the user to control printer properties, including setting permissions, sharing a printer, changing printer properties, deleting a printer, and deleting all documents.

■ **Manage Documents** Allows the user to control print job functions for all documents, including canceling, pausing, resuming, and restarting other users' documents.

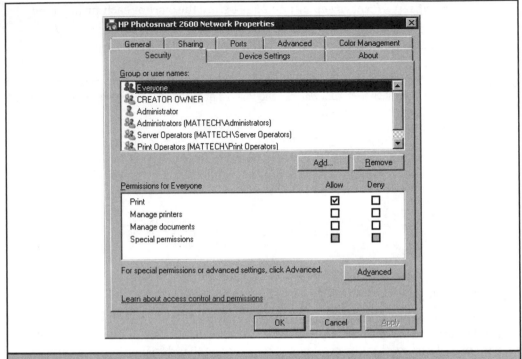

Figure 13-4.   If you share a printer, you need to determine the permissions for each group of users.

▲ **Special Permissions**   Indicates that the user has been assigned special permissions using the Advanced button and the Advanced Security Settings dialog box.

For each person or group in the Group Or User Names list, you can select the permissions that you want to give that person or group. The permission can be set in terms of allowing or denying a certain set of functions. Denying takes precedence over allowing, so if a function is denied in one place and allowed in another, it will be denied.

CAUTION   If you deny a set of functions for the Everyone group, then literally everyone will be prevented from performing those functions, even if they have been allowed elsewhere to do so.

If you want a more detailed level of permission, click Advanced in the lower portion of the Security tab. Select a particular permission entry and click Edit. This lets you select what the permission applies to and lets you further refine the permission itself, as shown here:

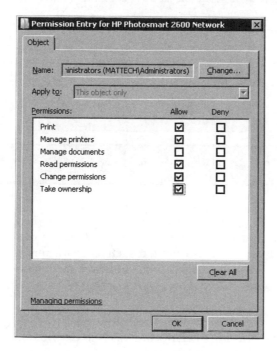

When you are done looking at permissions, close the up to three open dialog boxes.

NOTE   Chapter 15 discusses permissions in more detail.

CONTROL A PRINTER'S QUEUE

As jobs are printed by applications, they are, by default, spooled onto a disk and then fed out to the printer at whatever rate the printer can handle. If several print jobs are spooled at close to the same time, they form a queue waiting for earlier jobs to finish. Controlling this queue is an important administrative function and covers pausing and resuming printing, canceling printing, redirecting documents, and changing a document's properties. These tasks are handled in the printer's window that is similar to Figure 13-5, which is opened by double-clicking the appropriate printer in the Printers window.

Pause, Resume, and Restart Printing

As printing is taking place, a situation may occur in which you want to pause the printing. This may be caused by the printer—the need to change paper, for example—in which case you would want to pause all printing. The situation may also be caused by a document,

HP LJ 4200 - Low Priority

Printer Document View

Document Name	Status	Owner	Pages	Size	Subm
Chart of Accounts	Print...	Administrator	5	782 KB	8:31:
Chart of Accounts		Administrator	5	667 KB	8:31:
Profit and Loss		Administrator	1	20.2 KB	8:32:
Balance Sheet		Administrator	1	19.6 KB	8:32:

4 document(s) in queue

Figure 13-5.   Documents in a printer's queue can be paused, canceled, resumed, and redirected.

in which case you would want to pause only the printing of that document—for example, for some problem in the document, such as characters that cause the printer to behave erratically. In Windows Server 2008, you can pause and resume printing of all documents, and pause and resume or restart printing of a single document.

Pause and Resume Printing for All Documents

Pausing and resuming printing of all documents is in essence pausing and resuming the printer. See how that is done with these steps:

1. In the printer's window, such as the one shown in Figure 13-5, click the Printer menu and click Pause Printing. "Paused" will appear in the title bar, and if you look in the Printer menu, you will see a check mark in front of Pause Printing.

2. To resume printing, again click the Printer menu and click the checked Pause Printing. "Paused" disappears from the title bar and the check mark disappears by the Pause Printing option in the Printer menu.

Pause, Resume, and Restart Printing for a Single Document

When you want to interrupt the printing of one or more, but not all, the documents in the queue, you can do so and then either resume printing where it left off or restart from the beginning of the document. Here are the steps to do that:

1. In the printer's window, select the documents or document that you want to pause, click the Document menu, and click Pause. "Paused" will appear in the Status column opposite the document(s) you selected.

2. To resume printing where the document was paused, right-click the document, and click Resume. "Printing" will appear in the Status column opposite the document selected.

3. To restart printing at the beginning of the document, select the document and click Restart. "Restarting" and then "Printing" will appear in the Status column.

NOTE   If you want to change the order in which documents are being printed, you cannot pause the current document that is printing and have that happen. You must either complete the document that is printing or cancel it. You can use Pause to get around intermediate documents that are not currently printing. For example, suppose you want to immediately print the third document in the queue, but the first document is currently printing. You must either let the first document finish printing or cancel it. You can then pause the second document before it starts printing, and the third document will begin printing when the first document is out of the way.

Cancel Printing

Canceling printing can be done either at the printer level, which cancels all the jobs in the printer queue, or at the document level, which cancels selected documents. A canceled job is deleted from the print queue and must be restarted by the original application if that is desired. Here's how to cancel first one job and then all the jobs in the queue:

1. In the printer's window, select the job or jobs that you want to cancel. Click the Document menu and click Cancel. You are asked whether you are sure you want to cancel the selected print job(s). Click Yes. The job or jobs will disappear from the windows and no longer will be in the queue.

2. To cancel all the jobs in the queue, click the Printer menu and click Cancel All Documents. You are asked whether you are sure you want to cancel all documents. Click Yes. All jobs will disappear from the queue and the printer's window.

Redirect Documents

If you have two printers with the same print driver, you can redirect the print jobs that are in the queue for one printer to the other printer, even one across the network, where they will be printed without the user having to resubmit them. You do this by changing the port to which the printer is directed:

1. In the printer's window, click the Printer menu, click Properties, and click the Ports tab.

2. If the second printer is in the list of ports, select it and click OK to close the Properties dialog box. Otherwise, click Add Port, which opens the Printer Ports dialog box. Click Local Port and click New Port, which opens the Port Name dialog box.

3. Enter the UNC name for the printer (for example, \\Server1\HPCLJ4550) and click OK.

4. Click Close and then click Close again. The print queue will be redirected to the other printer.

Change a Document's Properties

A document in the print queue has a Properties dialog box, shown in Figure 13-6, which is opened by right-clicking the document and selecting Properties. This allows you to set the relative priority to use in printing the document from 1, the lowest, to 99, the highest; which logged-on user to notify when the document is printed; and the time of day to print the document.

Set Priority

A document printed to a printer with a default priority setting (see "Printer Priority," earlier in the chapter) is given a priority of 1, the lowest priority. If you want another document to be printed before the first one and the "first one" hasn't started printing yet, then set the second document priority to anything higher than 1 by dragging the Priority slider to the right.

Whom to Notify

The printer can notify the owner of a document of any special situations with the printing and when the document is finished printing. The owner is the logged-on user who sent the document to the printer. Sometimes it is beneficial to notify another logged-on user. You can do that by putting the logon name of the other user in the Notify text box of the document's Properties dialog box.

Set Print Time

Normally, a job is printed as soon as it reaches the top of the print queue. You can change this to a particular time frame in the document's Properties dialog box General tab (see Figure 13-6), by selecting Only From at the bottom under Schedule and then entering the time range within which you want the job printed.

This allows you to take large jobs that might clog the print queue and print them at a time when there is little or no load.

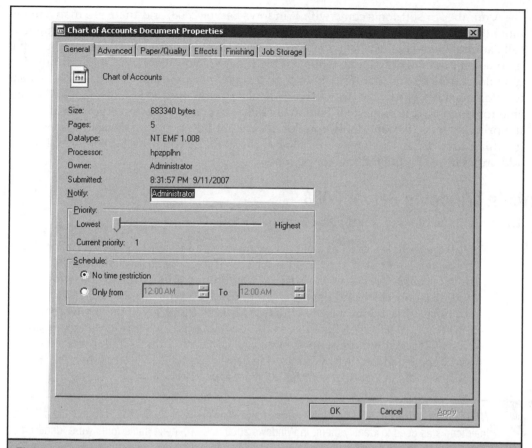

Figure 13-6.   The Properties dialog box of a document in the queue gives you a wide range of controls.

MANAGE FONTS

A *font* is a set of characters with the same design, size, weight, and style. A font is a member of a *typeface* family, all members of which have the same design. The font 12-point Arial bold italic is a member of the Arial typeface with a 12-point size, bold weight, and italic style. Systems running Windows Server 2008 have numerous fonts that you can choose from, including these:

▼   **Resident fonts**   Built into printers

■   **Cartridge fonts**   Stored in cartridges plugged into printers

▲   **Soft fonts**   Stored on a disk in the computer to which the printer is attached and downloaded to the printer when they are needed or stored on a disk in the printer

A number of soft fonts come with Windows Server 2008, and there are many, many more that you can add from other sources, including the Internet, or that are automatically added when you install an application. The font management job is to minimize the time taken downloading fonts, while having the fonts you want available. Minimizing download time means that resident and cartridge fonts are used when possible, which is automatically done by the print driver whenever a font that is both resident and available for download is requested. Font availability means that the fonts you want are on the print server's disk and fonts you don't want are not on the disk wasting space and handling time. In this section, you'll look at the fonts in Windows Server 2008, how to add and remove fonts, and how to use fonts.

Fonts in Windows Server 2008

There are three types of soft fonts in Windows Server 2008:

▼ **Outline fonts**   Stored as a set of commands that is used to draw a particular character. As a result, the fonts can be scaled to any size (and are therefore called *scalable* fonts) and can be rotated. Outline fonts are the primary fonts both used onscreen and downloaded to printers. Windows Server 2008 supports three types of outline fonts: TrueType fonts developed by Microsoft for Windows 95; OpenType fonts (also developed by Microsoft), an extension of TrueType with more shapes, like small caps, and more detail in the shapes; and Type 1 and PostScriptx fonts, developed by Adobe Systems, Inc. All the outline fonts in Windows Server 2008 are OpenType fonts.

NOTE   In Windows 95/98, Microsoft's outline fonts were identified as "TrueType fonts" and a "TT" on their icon was used to identify them. In Windows 2000 and on, these same fonts were identified as "OpenType fonts with TrueType outlines" and an "O" on their icon was used to identify them.

■ **Bitmapped fonts**   Also called *raster fonts,* these are stored as a bitmapped image for a specific size and weight, and for a specific printer. They cannot be scaled and rotated. They are included for legacy purposes and are not used in most cases. The bitmapped fonts in Windows Server 2008 have an *A* on their icon.

Fonts

▲ **Vector fonts**   Created with line segments and can be scaled and rotated. Primarily used with plotters and not onscreen or with printers.

You can view and work with the fonts in Windows Server 2008 by opening the Fonts window, shown in Figure 13-7, by clicking Start | Control Panel and double-clicking Fonts.

If you haven't installed any other fonts, or had them installed by an application, you will see the 197 fonts that are installed by Windows Server 2008. Fonts with an *O* in the icon are OpenType layout/TrueType fonts, are digitally signed, and are .ttf files.

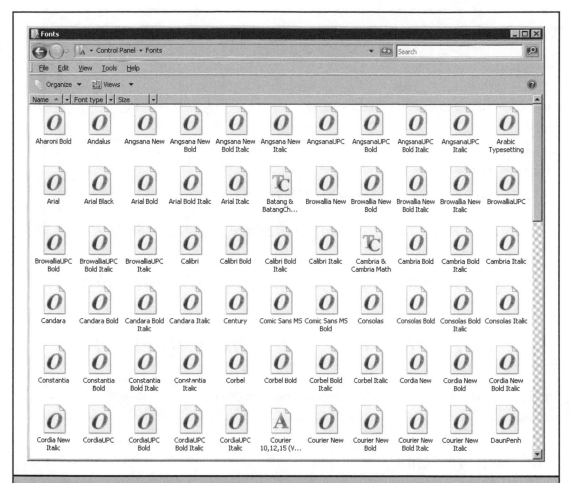

Figure 13-7.   Some of many fonts in Windows Server 2008

Fonts with an *TC* in the icon are OpenType layout/TrueType fonts, are not digitally signed, and are .ttc files. Fonts with an *A* in the icon are either bitmapped or vector fonts, are not digitally signed, and are .fon files. Older TrueType fonts that came with older versions of Windows and applications have a *TT* in the icon, are not digitally signed, and are .ttf files.

In the Fonts window, you can look at a font by double-clicking its icon. This opens a window for the font showing it in various sizes and giving some information about it, as shown in Figure 13-8. From this window, you can print the font by clicking Print. It is sometimes handy to keep a notebook with printed samples of all the fonts on a print server.

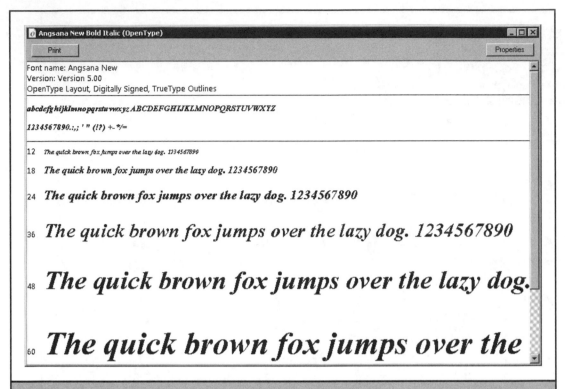

Figure 13-8. Double-clicking a font displays examples of the font in various sizes.

Add and Remove Fonts

You can add fonts to those that are installed by Windows Server 2008 with the following steps:

1. Click Start | Control Panel and double-click Fonts. The Fonts window opens, similar to the one previously shown in Figure 13-7.

2. Click the File menu and click Install New Font. Open a drive and a folder that contains the fonts you want to install (this can be a CD-ROM, a flash drive, or another hard drive on the network), like this:

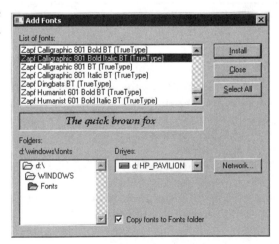

3. Select the fonts you want to install from the list (hold down SHIFT and click to select several contiguous fonts, or hold down CTRL and click to select several fonts that are not contiguous) and then click Install. When the installation is complete, click Close. The new fonts appear in the Fonts window.

You can remove fonts simply by selecting them and pressing DELETE. Alternatively, you can right-click the font(s) and click Delete. In either case, you are asked whether you are sure. Click Yes if you are. The fonts will be placed in the Recycle Bin, in case you made a mistake and want to retrieve one. If you haven't mistakenly deleted any, you can empty the Recycle Bin.

Use Fonts

Fonts are normally used or applied from within an application. For example, in Microsoft Word, you can select a line of text and then open the font drop-down list, as shown in Figure 13-9. Every application is a little different, but they all have a similar function. One nice feature of recent versions of Microsoft Word and several other recent applications is that they show what the font looks like in the list, as you can see in Figure 13-9.

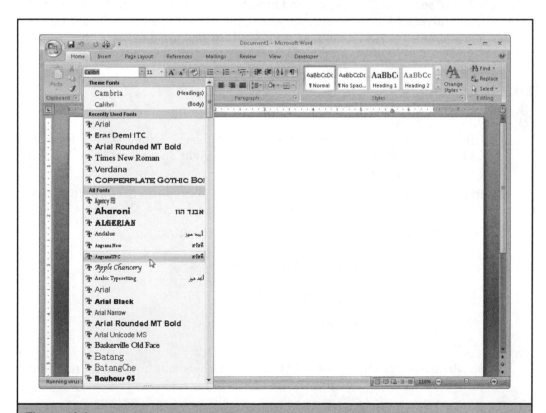

Figure 13-9. Fonts are applied in applications as shown here in Microsoft Word 2007.

Fonts used correctly can be a major asset in getting a message across, but they also can detract from a message if improperly used. Two primary rules are to not use too many fonts, and to use complementary fonts together. In a one-page document, using two typefaces should be enough (you can use bold and italic to have as many as eight fonts), and in a longer document, using three—and at most four—typefaces is appropriate. Complementary fonts are more subjective. Arial and Times Roman are generally considered complementary, as are Futura and Garamond, and Palatino and Optima. In each of these pairs, one typeface (for example, Arial) is *sans serif* (without the little tails on the ends of a character) and is used for titles and headings, while the other typeface (for example, Times Roman) is *serif* (it has the tails) and is used for the body text. There are, of course, many other options and considerations in the sophisticated use of fonts.

SET UP AND USE PRINT SERVICES

Print Services provides a centralized means to manage printing on the network, both other print servers and network printers (those connected directly to the network), as well as the local server. You can install and monitor the activity of network printers and print servers and set their permissions, priorities, and spooling configurations. You watch printer queues and redirect printing as needed. Print Services has three role services: Print Server, Internet Printing, and Line Printer Daemon (LPD) Service (for UNIX).

Install Print Services

Print Services is a role that is installed from the Server Manager.

1. Click Start | Server Manager. In the Server Manager's left pane, click Roles. Under Roles Summary, click Add Roles on the right. In the Add Roles Wizard that opens, click Next.

2. In the list of roles, click Print Services and click Next. Read the introduction to Print Services, and any of the Help articles, and then click Next.

3. Select the role services you want from the following:

   a. **Print Server**, which provides the Print Management function for multiple network printers and print servers.

   b. **LPD Service**, which allows UNIX computers to print to shared printers connected to the local server.

c. **Internet Printing**, which enables printing on the local server's shared printers using a browser and the Internet Printing Client using the Internet Printing Protocol (IPP). The Internet Printing role service also creates a web site for controlling printing on the local server.

4. If you select Internet Printing and do not have Internet Information Services (IIS) installed, the Add Role Services Required... dialog box will open and tell you that the Web Server (IIS) and several of its role services need to be installed. Click Add Required Role Services.

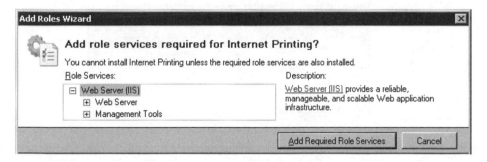

5. Click Next. If you selected Internet Printing and need to also install IIS, you can read the introduction to IIS (see Chapter 9), click Next, select the IIS role services or leave the default selection (recommended), and once more click Next.

6. You are shown the roles and role services that you have chosen to install. If this is not correct, click Previous and make the necessary corrections. When you are ready, click Install.

7. When you are told the roles and role services have been successfully installed, click Close.

NOTE   Print Management can manage a print server (a printer to which a printer is attached) running Windows 2000 or later.

Manage Printers and Printing

Print Services installs Print Management both in the Server Manager (see Figure 13-10) and in Administrative Tools. They are essentially the same, except that Print Management in the Server Manager provides management only for local printers attached to the server running Server Manager. The discussion here will be directed toward Print Management in Administrative Tools, but where it deals with the local Print Server and its printers, it applies to Print Management in Server Manager.

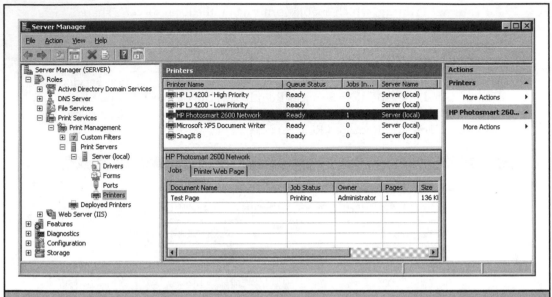

Figure 13-10. Print Management is available from both the Server Manager and Administrative Tools.

Manage Network Print Servers

As it is initially installed, Print Management manages only the local print server and its printers. To manage other print servers and their printers, the print servers must be added to Print Management. To do that:

1. Click Start | Administrative Tools | Print Management. In the left pane, right-click Print Management, and click Add/Remove Servers.

2. Type the names of one or more print servers putting commas between them, or click Browse, navigate to a server, and click Select Server. Click Add To List.

3. When you have listed all the print servers you want to manage, click OK. Open Print Servers in the left pane of Print Management and you should see all the servers you have added, like this:

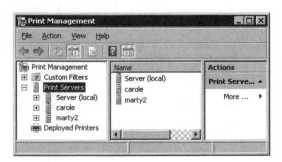

Add Printers to Print Servers

To manage printers on remote print servers, you must tell Print Management about them.

1. With Print Management open as described in the last section, right-click the server to which the printer is attached and click Add Printer.

2. In the Network Printer Installation Wizard that opens, click an installation method and click Next.

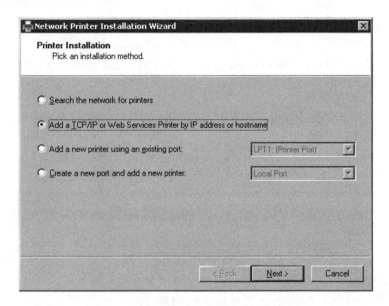

3. Click the printer you want to install and click Next. If asked, identify the driver to use and click Next. Enter the printer name and determine if you want to share the printer. If you do, enter the share name, location, and comment. Then click Next.

4. Review the printer settings that are displayed; click Back, to change anything; and then click Next. The printer and its driver are installed.

5. When you are told that the installation was successful, choose to print a test page, if desired, or install another printer. When ready, click Finish.

Manage Printing

Once you have installed the printer servers and the printers attached to them, you can select one or more printers, either within a server, or by using a filter across all servers in Print Management, and manage that printer or group of printers as described earlier in the chapter. This allows you, among other tasks, to manage sharing, to pause, resume, cancel all jobs, rename, and delete the printer.

Filters allow you to specify an attribute of a printer and select just those printers that have that attribute. Besides using filtered printers for management, you can also be alerted by e-mail or run a script when a filter selects a printer. You can use one of the four standard custom filters, shown on the right, or create a new custom filter. To create a custom filter:

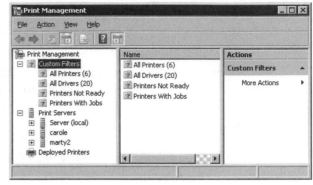

1. With Print Management open as described in "Manage Network Print Servers" earlier in this chapter, in the left pane, right-click Custom Filters and click Add New Printer Filter.

2. In the New Printer Filter Wizard that opens, type a name for the filter, enter a description, click Display The Total Number Of Printers…, and click Next.

3. Select a field, select a condition, and enter a value. Repeat this for additional criteria, as shown in Figure 13-11. When ready, click Next.

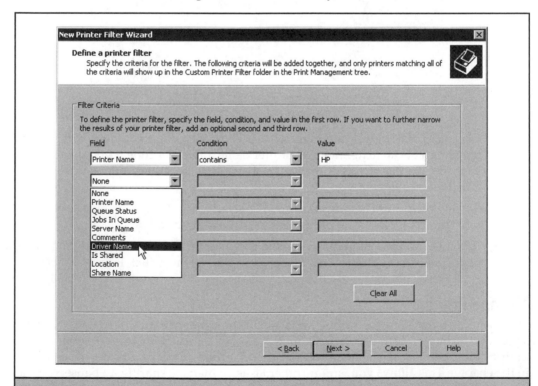

Figure 13-11.   Filters can be very specific to select a specific set of printers across a network.

4. If you wish to have an e-mail notification, click that option and enter the required information. If you wish to run a script, select that, enter or browse to where the script is stored, enter any additional arguments, and then click Finish.

Transfer a Print Load

If a printer has a large backlog of jobs and you want to offload it, maybe to speed up printing or for some other reason, you can do so with Print Management.

1. With Print Management open as described in "Manage Network Print Servers" earlier in this chapter, in the left pane, right-click the server with the load you want to shift and click Export Printers To A File.

2. In the Printer Migration wizard that opens, review the objects that will be moved and click Next. Enter a filename or click Browse to locate one for the export file and click Next. The queues and information will be exported. Click Finish.

3. Back in Print Management, in the left pane, right-click the server to which you want to transfer the load, and click Import Printers From A File. Again the Printer Migration wizard opens.

4. Enter or click Browse and locate a filename for the import file and click Next. The queues and information will be imported. Choose whether to overwrite existing printers or to import copies, and whether to list printers in the directory.

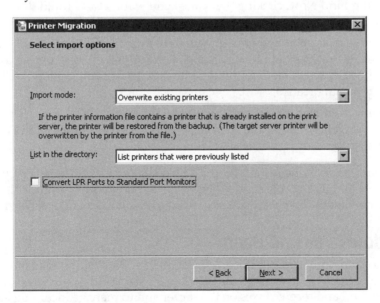

5. Click Next. The importing will take place. When you are told it has completed successfully, click Finish.

SET UP AND USE A FAX SERVER

The Fax Server provides a centralized management facility for faxing on both the local server and the network to which it is attached. With the Fax Server, you can send and receive faxes as well as manage network faxing devices, their usage, and their settings.

Install the Fax Server

The Fax Server is a server role installed from the Server Manager:

NOTE   The Fax Server requires that Print Services has already been set up. The instructions here assume that you have already installed Print Services as described earlier in this chapter.

1. Click Start | Server Manager. In the Server Manager's left pane, click Roles. Under Roles Summary, click Add Roles on the right. In the Add Roles Wizard that opens, click Next.

2. In the list of roles, click Fax Server. (If you did not install Print Services earlier in this chapter, you be told that you need to install it now. Click Add Required Role Services.) Click Next. Read the introduction to Fax Server, and any of the Help articles, and then click Next.

3. Add fax users by clicking Add, entering usernames, or clicking Advanced, clicking Find Now, clicking the names you want to add (hold down CTRL and click to select multiple names), and clicking OK twice.

4. Click Next, select whether you want only routing assistants or all fax users can access the Fax Server inbox, and click Next. If you choose routing assistants, you need to select them with the same process as used in Step 3. Click Next when you are ready.

5. Review your choices. If you want to make a change, click Previous. When you are ready, click Install, and then click Close when you are told the installation is successful.

Upon completion of the installation and possibly restarting the server, you'll see the Fax Server role and its Fax role service beneath it, as shown in Figure 13-12. The Fax role service is also available by clicking Start | Administrative Tools | Fax Service Manager.

Enable Windows Fax and Scan

Windows Fax and Scan is the fax facility in Windows Vista and is available in Windows Server 2008 after you have installed the Fax Server role. Windows Fax and Scan provides the means to send and receive faxes on the server and to manage incoming and outgoing faxes. You can both directly send a fax by scanning a document and then "faxing it" and "print" to a fax from an application like Microsoft Word. Windows Fax and Scan requires that you have a fax modem in the server and a phone line connected to it (see Chapter 8 on setting up and working with modems).

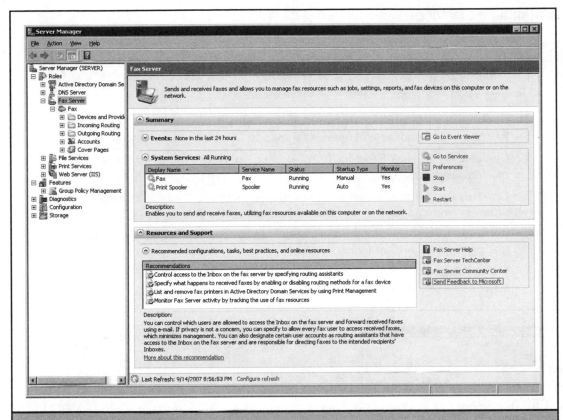

Figure 13-12. The Fax Server role provides faxing from the local server as well as management of network faxing.

Windows Fax and Scan is a Server Manager feature and is separately installed. In addition, you must install a Fax device.

Install Windows Fax and Scan

1. Click Start | Server Manager. In the left pane, click Features and on the right, click Add Features.

2. In the Features list, click Desktop Experience and click Next. Click Install and click Close when you are told the computer must be restarted, and then click Yes to restart it.

3. After resuming the installation and completing it, click Close to finish the installation.

Install a Fax Device

NOTE You can also open Windows Fax and Scan either from the Server Manager with the Fax Service Manager open, or from the Fax Service Manager window opened from Administrative Tools by clicking the Fax Console icon on the respective toolbars.

1. Click Start, click All Programs, and click Windows Fax and Scan. The Windows Fax and Scan window will open, as shown in Figure 13-13.

2. Click New Fax, click Connect To A Fax Modem, type a name for the fax modem, and click Next.

3. Choose whether the fax modem should answer incoming calls automatically or notify you and have you choose whether to answer.

4. If you get a message that the Windows Firewall has blocked some features of this program, click Unblock.

5. When Setup is done, the New Fax window will open. Continue with "Send a Fax Message" later in this chapter.

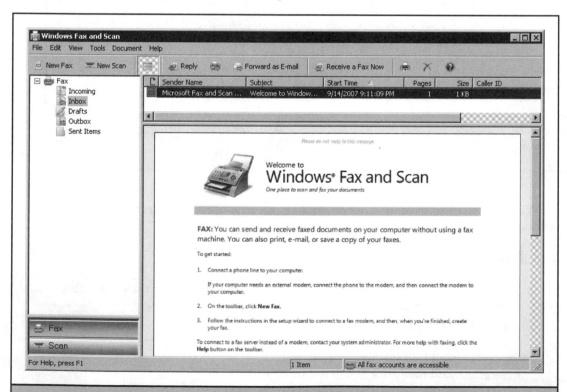

Figure 13-13. Windows Fax and Scan brings full faxing capability to Windows Server 2008.

Send and Receive Faxes

Windows Fax and Scan lets you directly send and receive faxes as you would e-mail messages; fax from a program, such as Microsoft Word, by specifying "fax" as a printer; and scan documents that are then faxed.

Send a Fax Message

To send an e-mail-type message as a fax:

1. Click Start, click All Programs, click Windows Fax and Scan, and click New Fax. After the first time you have clicked New Fax, the New Fax window opens immediately, as you can see in Figure 13-14.

2. Select a cover page if you want one (see "Create a Fax Cover Page" later in this chapter), type a phone number to be used for faxing (or click To and select one from your contacts list), and type a subject, any cover page notes, and then the message.

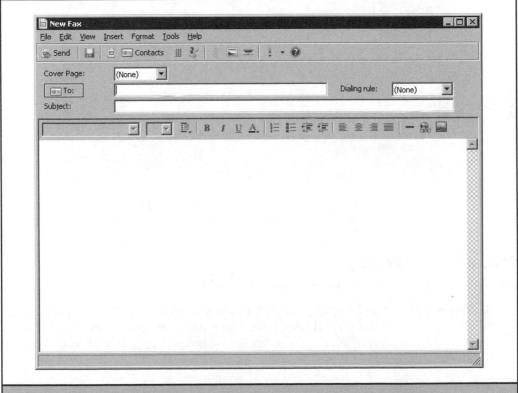

Figure 13-14. The New Fax message window looks like an e-mail message form.

3. Click Preview 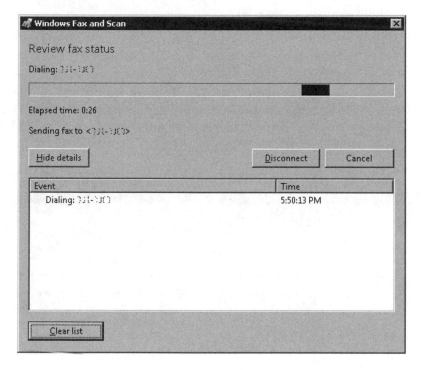 on the toolbar to look at the cover page before and/or after adding fax text. Also, you can attach documents and pictures by clicking their respective buttons on the toolbar.

4. When you are ready, click Send. The New Fax window will close, and the Review Fax Status dialog box will appear, where, if you click View Details, you can see the status of the fax being sent.

5. When the fax has been sent, you will see it in the status dialog box. When you are done, close the status dialog box and the Windows Fax and Scan window.

Send a Fax by "Printing"

Printing to a fax is as easy as any other printing method.

1. Open a document in a program such as Microsoft Word. In Word, click the File menu or Office Button and click Print. Open the printer Name drop-down list, click Fax, and click OK. The New Fax dialog box will appear with your Word document listed in the Attach box.

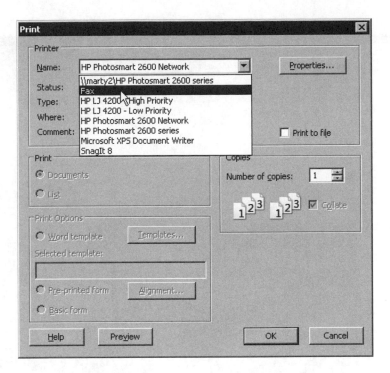

2. Follow the instructions starting at Step 2 of "Send a Fax Message." If this is the first time you have used the fax, you will first see the setup questions described in "Install a Fax Device" earlier in the chapter.

Scan and Fax a Document

To scan and fax a document (this assumes that you have a scanner attached to the server):

1. Turn on the scanner and place what you want to scan onto the scanning surface.

2. Click Start | All Programs | Windows Fax and Scan. The Windows Fax and Scan window opens.

3. Click New Scan on the toolbar. The New Scan dialog box appears. The scanner you installed should be displayed in the upper-left area. Change the scanner if you wish.

4. Choose the color, file type, and resolution you want to use, and click Preview. The image in the scanner will appear in the dialog box.

5. Adjust the margins around the page by dragging the dashed lines on the four sides. When you are ready, click Scan.

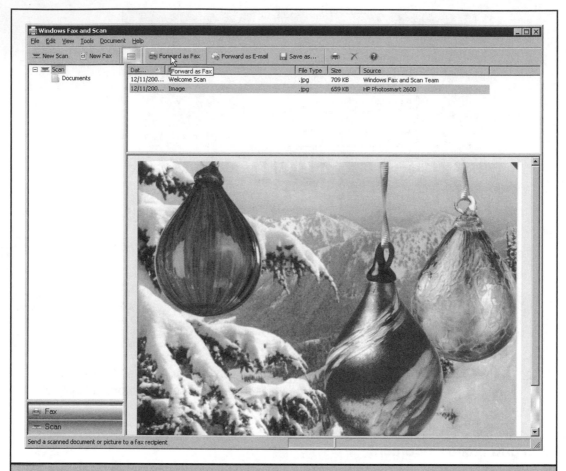

Figure 13-15. With a scanner, you can scan and fax any document.

6. The scanned image will appear in the Windows Fax and Scan window. When scanning is complete, click Forward As Fax, as shown in Figure 13-15. The New Fax message window will open with the image you scanned attached.

7. Follow the instructions starting at Step 2 of "Send a Fax Message" earlier in this chapter. If this is the first time you have used the fax, you will first see the setup questions described in "Install a Fax Device," also earlier in the chapter.

Receive a Fax

You receive faxes using the Windows Fax and Scan window. To receive a fax, you must have set up the fax as described in "Install a Fax Device" earlier in the chapter.

1. With the computer's fax modem plugged into a phone line and the fax set up, when you get any phone call, you will see a message on your screen that the phone is ringing and that you can click the message to answer the call as a fax. You can pick up the phone receiver and see if you hear the fax tone and then click the message.

2. If you chose to not be notified upon receipt of a fax (automatic receipt) in setting up the fax (see "Install a Fax Device" earlier in the chapter), you can see the status by clicking the Tools menu in the Windows Fax and Scan window and clicking Fax Status Monitor. Here, you can see when a fax comes in.

3. If you click the Ringing message, the Review Fax Status dialog box will appear. If you click View Details, you will see the fax events as they happen. When the fax has been received, you will receive a message to that effect and the Review Fax Status dialog box will also display that.

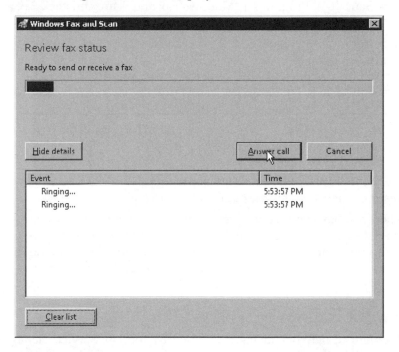

4. To see and possibly print the fax, click Start | All Programs | Windows Fax And Scan and click Fax in the lower-left corner.

5. If you open the Windows Fax and Scan window while the fax is still being received, click Incoming in the navigation pane, and watch as the fax is received.

6. When the fax has been received, click Inbox in the navigation pane, scroll through the list of faxes at the top of the subject pane, and click the fax you want to view. It will be displayed in the lower part of the subject pane.

7. With a fax selected and displayed, you can use the toolbar to reply to the fax by sending a new fax to the sender, forward the fax to one or more recipients, forward the fax as e-mail, or delete the fax. Also, you can right-click the fax image in the subject pane and, from the context menu, view, zoom, save, and print the fax.

8. When you are done, close the Windows Fax and Scan window.

Create a Fax Cover Page

Windows Server 2008 includes four fax cover pages you can use, as well as a Fax Cover Page Editor that you can use to modify one of the included covers or to create a cover page of your own. To modify an existing one:

1. Click Start | All Programs | Windows Fax and Scan, and click Fax in the lower-left corner.

2. Click the Tools menu and click Cover Pages. Click Copy, select one of the four standard cover pages, click your selection again, and click Open (Generic was selected for this illustration). Select the cover page and click Open. The cover page will open in the Fax Cover Page Editor, as shown in Figure 13-16.

CAUTION The four standard cover pages have coded fields that automatically add data. If you change them, you'll lose the auto-fill capability.

3. Use the tools on the Drawing toolbar to modify an existing cover page, thereby creating a new one of your own.

4. When you have your cover page the way you want it, click Save to save it with its existing name; or click the File menu and click Save As to give your cover page a new name. Close both the Fax Cover Page Editor and the Fax Cover Pages dialog box, as well as the Windows Fax and Scan window.

Manage Network Faxing

The management of network faxing is handled by the Fax Service Manager, which is accessed from either the Server Manager or Administrative Tools.

Click Start | Administrative Tools | Fax Service Manager.
Or, click Start | Server Manager, and open Roles and then Fax Server in the left pane.

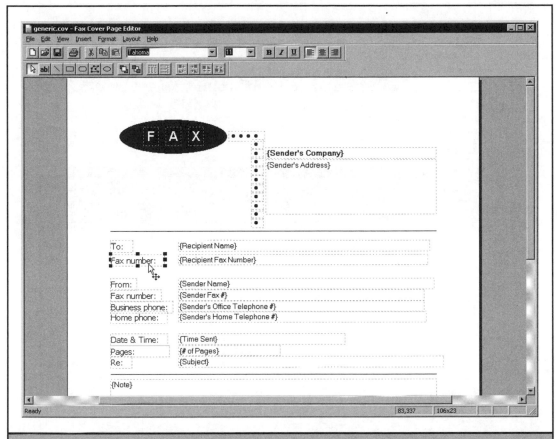

Figure 13-16. Creating your own fax cover page allows you to promote your business or activity.

In either case, open Fax in the left pane if it isn't already displayed, as shown in Figure 13-17.

Add a Fax Device

All Plug and Play fax devices are automatically recognized and installed by Windows Server 2008. To get Fax Service Manager to display the device, close and reopen the Server Manager, open Fax Server | Fax | Devices And Providers | Devices, and if needed, press F5 to refresh the view.

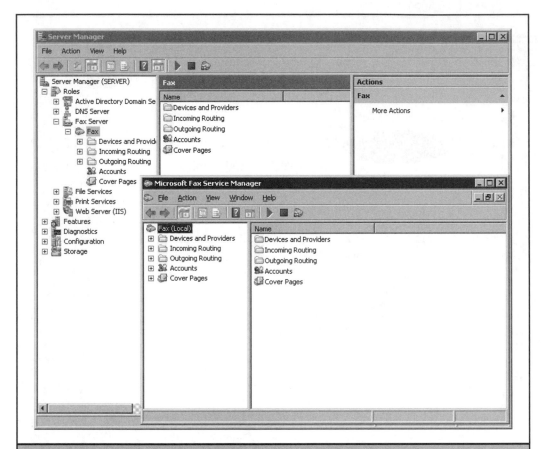

Figure 13-17.   The Fax Service Manager is "Fax" within the Fax Server or the Microsoft Fax Service Manager.

Configure a Fax Device

1. Within the Fax Service Manager, open Fax | Devices And Providers | Devices in the left pane, right-click the modem in the right or middle pane depending on which Fax Server Manager you are using, and click Properties to open the modem's Properties dialog box.

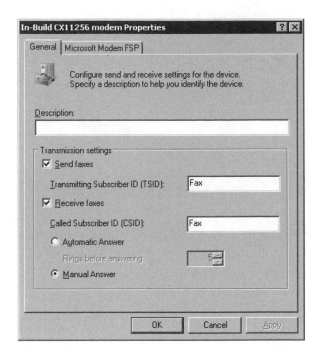

2. In the General tab, enter a description, both a transmitting and a called subscriber ID (normally the phone number), and choose between Automatic and Manual Answer.

3. In the Microsoft Modem FSP tab, you can enable adaptive answering if your modem has it.

4. After configuring the modem, click OK.

CHAPTER 14

Managing Windows Server 2008

One of Windows Server 2008's greatest strengths is the variety of management tools available to control the many facets of the operating system. The purpose of this chapter is to look at the general-purpose tools, those that are not part of setting up networking, file management, or printing. The discussion of these tools is broken into system management tools and user management tools. System management tools are those tools that facilitate running the parts of the operating system and the computer that are not discussed elsewhere. Managing computer users with their varying needs and peculiarities, both in groups and individually, is a major task and one to which Windows Server 2008 has committed considerable resources.

The area of system management has three principal facilities for managing Windows Server 2008: the Server Manager, Administrative Tools, and the Control Panel. All three have been discussed in a number of other places in this book, especially the Server Manager. Thus, in this chapter we'll focus on those areas of the Control Panel and Administrative Tools that have not been discussed.

USE THE CONTROL PANEL

The Control Panel window shown in Figure 14-1 has been a part of Windows for a long time. It is a folder that holds a number of tools that control and maintain configuration information, mainly for system hardware. Windows Server 2008 can vary a lot more than previous versions of Windows in the contents of the Control Panel due to the ability in the Server Manager to install just the roles, role services, and features that are needed. Often Control Panel tools related to specific roles are discussed with those roles. Here, we'll look at the following Control Panel tools:

TIP   In Windows Server 2008, you have a choice of two views of the Control Panel, the default Classic View and the Control Panel Home view, which is the default in Windows Vista. The Classic View, which shows all of the available tools, is generally easier to use and can save you a step or two.

▼   AutoPlay
■   Default Programs
■   Device Manager
■   Ease Of Access Center
■   Folder Options
■   Keyboard
■   Mouse
■   Regional And Language Options
■   System
▲   Taskbar And Start Menu

Figure 14-1. The default Classic View of the Control Panel shows all of the tools currently installed.

Many of the other Control Panel tools are discussed in other places in this book or are outside of its scope. Before looking at any of the specific tools, open your Control Panel and look at the tools you have available by clicking Start | Control Panel.

Because of the high variability, it is likely that you have different tools than those shown in Figure 14-1, depending on the hardware and software you have and the components of Windows Server 2008 that you have installed.

AutoPlay

AutoPlay allows you to determine what automatically happens when a piece of media (CD, DVD, memory stick, flash memory, or other object) is inserted into or attached to the computer.

AutoPlay

1. In the Control Panel, double-click AutoPlay. The AutoPlay window will open as shown in Figure 14-2.

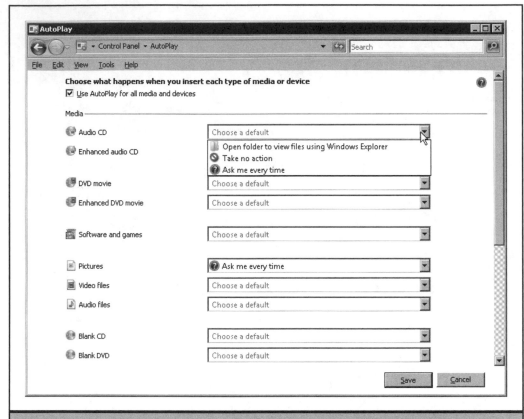

Figure 14-2. Specifying what happens on AutoPlay saves having to determine it each time.

2. For each type of media, click the down arrow to open the drop-down list, and click the action you want to take place when the media is inserted in the computer.

3. When you are finished, click Save.

NOTE If you do not make a selection for a type of media in the AutoPlay window and then insert that media, a dialog box will pop up and ask you what you want to do. In that dialog box, you can specify that you want to always take the action you are taking.

Default Programs

The Control Panel's Default Programs icon, when double-clicked, gives you a choice of opening one of three windows that, in two cases, let you specify the association between file types and programs. The third window is the AutoPlay window just described.

Default
Programs

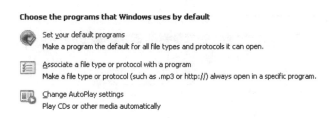

Choose the programs that Windows uses by default

Set your default programs
Make a program the default for all file types and protocols it can open.

Associate a file type or protocol with a program
Make a file type or protocol (such as .mp3 or http://) always open in a specific program.

Change AutoPlay settings
Play CDs or other media automatically

The first option, Set Your Default Programs, lets you select the program you want to use for a particular purpose and all related files. For example, you could choose to use Internet Explorer for all web browsing and for opening web-related files.

The second option, Associate A File Type Or Protocol With A Program, lets you identify the program you want to open with a particular file type. Click the file extension you want to change, click Change Program, and double-click the program you want to use.

Device Manager

Device
Manager

The Device Manager, shown in Figure 14-3, enables you to look at and configure all of your hardware in one place. You can immediately see whether you have a hardware problem; for example, the infrared transceiver in Figure 14-3 has a problem, as indicated by the exclamation point icon. You can then directly open that device by double-clicking it, and attempt to cure the problem. In many cases, the Reinstall Driver button on the General tab, which opens the Update Driver Software dialog box, will assist you. Two common problems that often can be cured are a wrong or missing driver (the case in Figure 14-3), or incorrect resources being used, often because the correct ones weren't available. If you open the Properties dialog box for a device and look at the General tab, you will get a quick device status. The Driver tab will then allow you to update, uninstall, and disable the driver, and the Details tab will give you detailed information about the device.

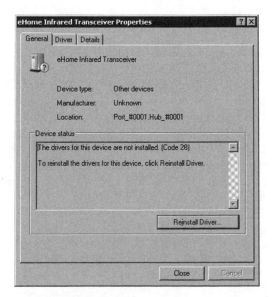

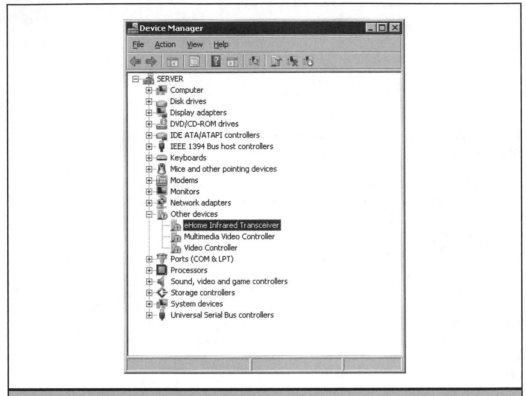

Figure 14-3. The Device Manager gives you feedback on any hardware that isn't working.

Ease Of Access Center

The Ease Of Access Center allows a user with physical limitations to more easily use Windows Server 2008. The Ease Of Access Center dialog box, shown in Figure 14-4, is opened by double-clicking Ease Of Access Center in the Control Panel. In the upper half of the window, four options are scanned by default and you simply need to press the SPACEBAR when the option you want is selected (has a rectangular outline). In the bottom half of the window are seven options that make it easier to use or replace the display, keyboard, mouse, and sound. In each window that is opened by these options, you are presented with a number of facilities that you can enable and configure to improve accessibility. Many of these facilities are repeated in several different windows. Table 14-1 summarizes these facilities and how they are turned on and off.

Ease of
Access Center

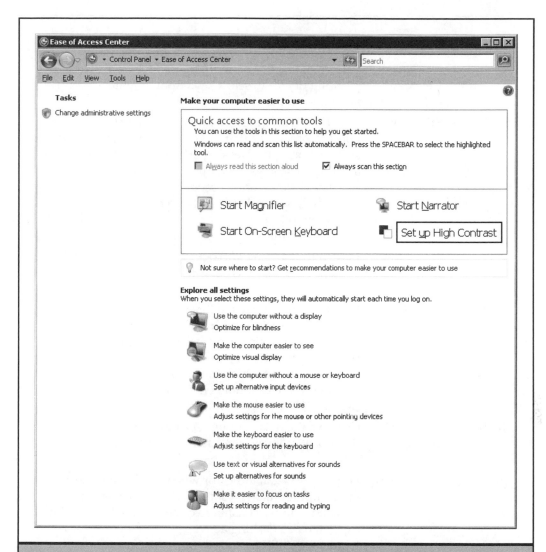

Figure 14-4.   Windows Server 2008 provides a number of ways for those with physical limitations to access the computer.

Folder Options

Folder Options in the Control Panel allows you to customize the way folders and files are displayed and handled in various Windows Server 2008 windows, including Computer and Windows Explorer. The Folder Options dialog box is opened by double-clicking Folder Options in the Control Panel; it can also be accessed by clicking the Tools menu

Area	Option	Description	Turn On or Off
Keyboard	On-Screen Keyboard	Allows the mouse or another pointing device to select keys from an image on the screen.	Ease Of Access Center.
Keyboard	StickyKeys	Enables the user to simulate the effect of pressing a pair of keys, such as CTRL-A, by pressing one key at a time. The keys SHIFT, CTRL, and ALT "stick" down until a second key is pressed, which Windows Server 2008 then interprets as the two keys pressed together.	Press either the left or right SHIFT key five times in succession.
Keyboard	ToggleKeys	Plays a tone when CAPS LOCK, NUM LOCK, or SCROLL LOCK is pressed.	Hold down NUM LOCK for five seconds.
Keyboard	FilterKeys	Enables a user to press a key twice in rapid succession and have it interpreted as a single keystroke (Bounce Keys), and also slows down the rate at which the key is repeated if the user holds it down (Repeat Keys/Slow Keys).	Hold down the right SHIFT key for eight seconds.
Keyboard	Keyboard Settings	Controls the delay before repeating, the repeat rate, and the cursor blink rate.	Ease Of Access Center.
Sound	SoundSentry	Displays a visual indicator when the computer makes a sound. The indicator can be a flashing active caption bar, a flashing active window, or a flashing desktop.	Open Ease Of Access and click Use Text Or Visual Alternatives For Sounds.
Sound	ShowSounds	Tells compatible programs to display captions when sound and speech are used.	Open Ease Of Access, click Use Text Or Visual Alternatives For Sounds, and click Turn On Text Captions For Spoken Dialog.

Table 14-1.   Tools Available in the Ease Of Access Center

Area	Option	Description	Turn On or Off
Display	Magnifier	Magnifies the area of the screen surrounding the mouse pointer.	Ease Of Access Center.
Display	Narrator	Reads the text on the screen.	Ease Of Access Center.
Display	High Contrast	Uses high-contrast colors and special fonts to make the screen easy to use.	Press together: left SHIFT-left ALT-PRINT SCREEN.
Display	Cursor Options	Changes the rate at which the cursor blinks and width of the cursor or insertion point in text.	Always on.
Mouse	Mouse Pointers	Set the color and size of mouse pointers.	Ease Of Access Center.
Mouse	MouseKeys	Enables the user to use the numeric keypad instead of the mouse to move the pointer on the screen.	Press left SHIFT-left ALT-NUM LOCK.
Mouse	Mouse Settings	Controls the double-click speed and the primary mouse button among other options.	Ease Of Access Center.

Table 14-1.   Tools Available in the Ease Of Access Center (*Continued*)

and choosing Folder Options in either Windows Explorer or Computer. The Folder Options dialog box has three tabs: General, View, and Search.

Folder Options

TIP There is one important difference between opening Folder Options from the Control Panel and opening it from Computer or Windows Explorer. From the Control Panel, it sets the default for all folders; from Computer or Windows Explorer, it sets the properties for the current open folder unless you click Apply To All Folders in the View tab.

General

The General tab allows you to choose how you want to handle three different questions:

▼ **Tasks** asks whether you want to show the task pane on the left of a window and in file folders or, alternatively, use the classic displays. This is a matter of personal choice. The task pane gives you an easy means to execute common tasks, such as copying or moving a file or folder, but it also takes up more room and can't be shown with the folder pane.

■ **Browse Folders** asks whether you want to open a new window each time a new folder is opened or to repeatedly use the same window. Opening a new window with each folder is convenient if you want to compare two folders, but it also clutters the screen. The default and most popular choice is to use the same window.

▲ **Click Items** asks whether you want to single-click, as you do in a web browser, or double-click, as you do classically in Windows, to open a folder or a file. If you choose single-click, then simply pointing on the item selects it. If you choose double-click, then single-clicking selects the item. If you are a new user, single-clicking saves you time and the confusion between single- and double-clicking. If you have been double-clicking for many years, it is hard to stop, so trying to single-click could be confusing.

View

The View tab determines how files and folders and their attributes are displayed in Windows Explorer and Computer. The Advanced Settings list has a number of settings that you can turn on or off and that are a matter of personal preference. I like to see everything, so I turn on the display of the full path in the title bar; I show hidden files; I turn off both the hiding of file extensions and the hiding of protected files. You may have other preferences. It is easy to try the different settings to see what you like by opening Folder Options in Windows Explorer. You can always return to the default settings by clicking Restore Defaults.

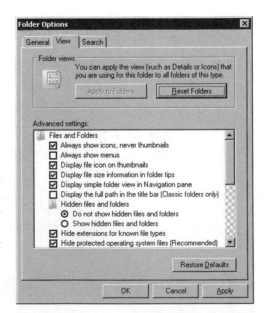

Search

The Search tab determines how searches operate and what is searched. Generally the defaults are the best middle ground between speed and a search that satisfies most needs. Using an index can speed a search, but if you turn on the role service Windows Search Service (which is off by default), it replaces indexing with its own search techniques. Natural Language Search allows you to search on a normal English phrase like "last week's finance report."

Keyboard

Keyboard in the Control Panel allows you to set the configuration of your keyboard. This is the same dialog box that can be opened from the Ease Of Access Center's keyboard settings option. The Speed tab allows you to set both how long to wait before repeating a key and how fast to do the repeating once it is started. You can click in the text box on that tab and try out your settings. Also on that tab, you can set the cursor blink rate (although the relationship between that and the keyboard is tenuous).

Keyboard

The Hardware tab shows the description of the device Windows believes you are using, and, through Properties, gives you access to the drivers that are being used with it.

Mouse

Mouse in the Control Panel allows you to set the configuration of the mouse. This is the same dialog box that can be opened from the Ease Of Access Center's mouse settings option. The Buttons tab lets you choose whether you want to use the mouse with your right or left hand. This reverses the effect of the two primary buttons on a mouse. You can also choose the speed at which a double-click is interpreted as a double-click, and you can turn on ClickLock, which lets you drag without holding down the mouse button.

Mouse

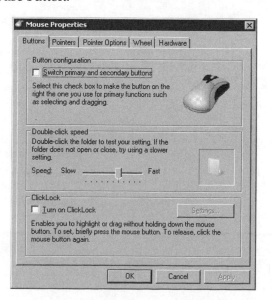

The Pointers tab lets you choose or create a scheme for how the mouse pointer looks in various situations. The Pointer Options tab lets you set how fast you want the pointer to move, whether you want the pointer to automatically go to the default button when a dialog box opens, display pointer trails as you move the mouse, hide the pointer while typing, and show the location of the pointer when the CTRL key is pressed by itself. I find this last option very handy on a laptop, where I tend to lose the pointer.

The Wheel tab (if you have a mouse with a wheel) lets you determine the degree of vertical and horizontal scrolling performed by the wheel. Like the Hardware tab in the Keyboard dialog box, the Mouse Hardware tab shows the description of the device, allows you to troubleshoot it, and, by your clicking Properties, gives you access to the drivers that are being used with it.

Regional And Language Options

Regional And Language Options, opened from the Control Panel, and shown in Figure 14-5, lets you determine how numbers, dates, currency, and time are displayed and used on your computer, as well as the languages that will be used. By choosing the primary locale, such

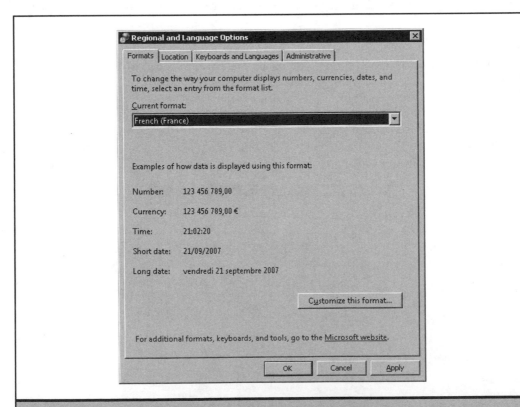

Figure 14-5.   Regional And Language Options controls how numbers, dates, time, and currency are formatted.

as French (France), all the other settings, including those for formatting numbers, currency, times, and dates, are automatically changed to the standard for that locale. You can then change the individual settings for numbers, currency, time, and so on, and customize how you want items displayed by clicking Customize This Format.

The Location tab lets you set a location used by software to determine where you are for various purposes like weather reporting. The Keyboards And Languages tab lets you select the language in which you will be typing by default and whether you want to install or uninstall supplemental language packs. The Administrative tab allows you to set the language used with programs that do not use Unicode and to copy regional and language settings to either the default user account or to system accounts.

NOTE   The custom settings for numbers, currency, time, and dates will remain set only as long as you maintain the same locale. When you change to a new locale and then change back to the original one, your custom settings will be gone, although you can use a separate profile to prevent this from occurring. See "Employ User Profiles" later in the chapter.

System

Double-clicking System in the Control Panel opens the System window shown in Figure 14-6. This can also be opened by right-clicking Computer and choosing Properties.

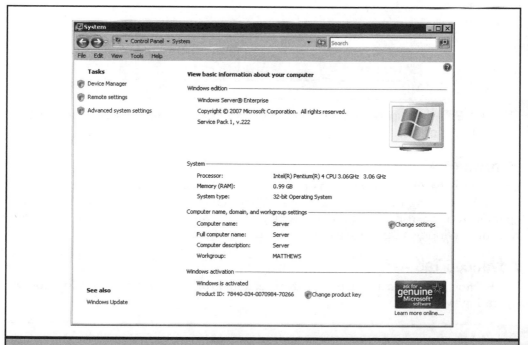

Figure 14-6.   The System window is an information screen and a gateway to other settings.

Clicking Device Manager opens the Device Manager described earlier in this chapter and shown in Figure 14-3. Clicking Remote Settings, Advanced System Settings, and Change Settings opens related tabs of the System Properties dialog box.

System

The first tab provides the ability to give the computer a description and change its name and network affiliation. Clicking Change allows you to enter a new name and to join either a domain or workgroup.

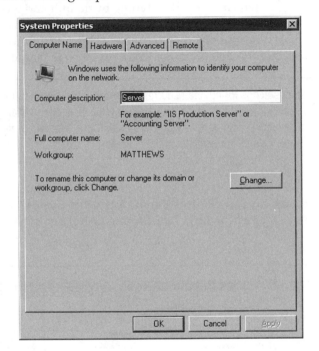

NOTE   If the computer is a domain controller, you cannot change the network name and join a different domain.

Hardware

The Hardware tab enables you to open the Device Manager, which also can be started by double-clicking Device Manager in the Control Panel and is described earlier in this chapter. You can also open the Windows Update Driver Settings dialog box, which controls how Windows Update checks for new device drivers.

Advanced Tab

The System Properties dialog box's Advanced tab provides access to the settings for two operating system features:

NOTE   You will also have a User Profiles section, which is discussed later in this chapter under "Employ User Profiles."

▼   **Performance**   Optimize performance between running applications or running background services, as is required in a file or print server; you also can identify the visual effects you want and determine the amount of disk space you want to set aside for temporary page files, the storing of memory on disk. Finally, performance options ask you how you want to use Data Execution Prevention (DEP), which prevents programs from executing code in the reserved areas of system memory. This provides protection from some security threats.

▲   **Startup and Recovery**   Select the default operating system (OS) to use on startup, how long to wait for a manual selection of that OS, and what to do on a system failure.

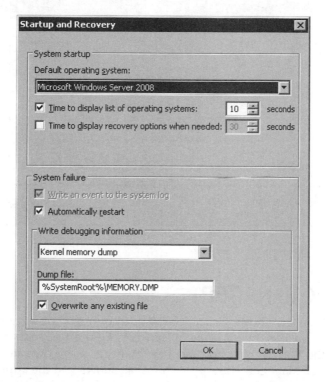

Taskbar And Start Menu

Taskbar And Start Menu Properties, shown in Figure 14-7, can be opened either from the Control Panel (where it is called "Taskbar And Start Menu") or by right-clicking a blank area of the taskbar and choosing Properties. It allows you to determine how the taskbar is displayed, what is on the taskbar, whether the most recent or the classic Start menu is used, and to customize both the look and content of the Start menu.

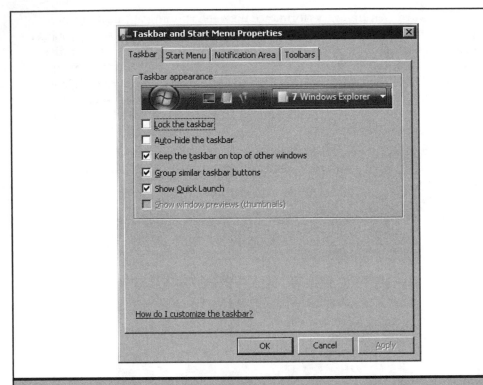

Figure 14-7.   The heavily used taskbar and Start menu should be set up for your ease of use.

USE THE TASK MANAGER

Windows Task Manager allows you to look at and control what is running in Windows Server 2008. You can start Task Manager, shown in Figure 14-8, either by right-clicking a blank area of the taskbar and choosing Task Manager or by pressing CTRL-ALT-DEL and choosing Start Task Manager. The Applications tab shows you the application tasks that are currently running and allows you to terminate a task, switch to a task, or create a new task by opening a program, folder, document, or Internet resource.

The Processes tab shows the processes that are currently loaded. These include the programs needed for the applications that are running, as well as the OS processes that are active. You can display a large amount of information for each of the processes and you can select what you want to display by choosing View | Select Columns, as shown next. After you choose the columns you want to display, you can arrange the columns by

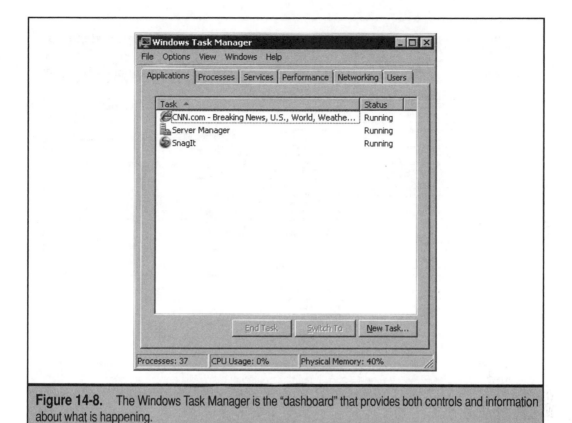

Figure 14-8. The Windows Task Manager is the "dashboard" that provides both controls and information about what is happening.

dragging the column headers, and you can sort the list by clicking the column you want sorted. You can end any process by selecting it and clicking End Process.

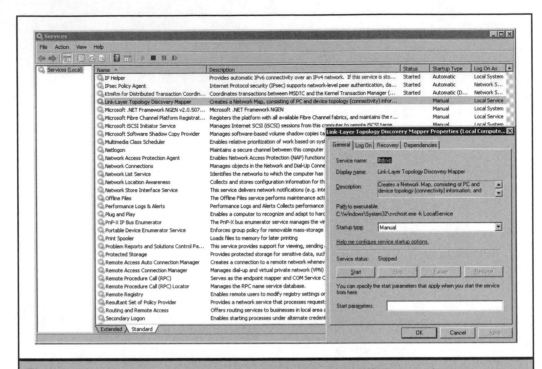

Figure 14-9. The Services window allows manual control of many Windows services.

The Services tab displays the many services available in Windows Server 2008. Clicking Services opens the Services window, which shows the services in more detail and allows you to start, stop, and set options on the services by double-clicking a service to open a Properties dialog box (see Figure 14-9).

CAUTION The majority of Windows services are automatically started and stopped by Windows itself and should only be manually started or stopped in troubleshooting situations.

The Performance tab, shown in Figure 14-10, shows you how the tasks being performed by the computer are using the CPU and memory, and what are the components of that usage. This information is particularly important in heavily used servers. You can see if either the CPU or memory (or both) is reaching its limit and what the system is doing to handle it. If you have multiple CPUs, you can see how each is being used and assign processes to particular processors by right-clicking the processes in the Processes tab. You can also set the priority of a process by right-clicking it in the Processes tab. Clicking Resource Monitor opens the Resource Monitor window, which shows disk and network usage in addition to CPU and memory.

The Networking tab shows how a particular connection to the network is being used. If there are multiple network interface cards or adapters in the computer, they will be listed at the bottom of the window and you can select the one you want to look at. The scale on the graph automatically changes to give you the most precise reading possible.

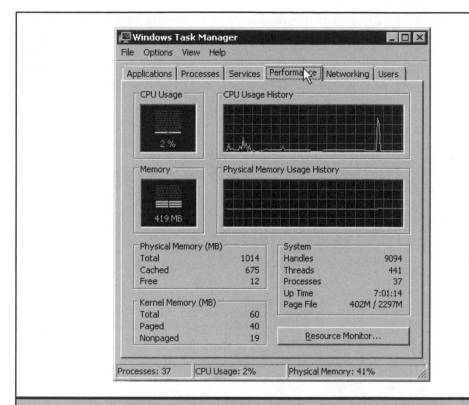

Figure 14-10.   The Performance tab can tell you when the CPU and/or memory are overloaded.

The Users tab lists the users currently logged onto the server. You can disconnect, log off, or send a message to a selected user.

USE THE MICROSOFT MANAGEMENT CONSOLE

The Microsoft Management Console, or MMC, is a shell to which you can add, and then customize, management tools that you want to use. You can create several different *consoles* containing different tools for different administrative purposes, and save these consoles as .msc files. There are two types of management tools that you can add to an MMC: stand-alone tools that are called *snap-ins* and add-on functions that are called *extensions*. Extensions work with and are available for particular snap-ins. Extensions are automatically added with some snap-ins, whereas other snap-ins require you to select the extensions. An example of a snap-in with automatic extensions is Computer Management, and one of its many extensions is the Disk Defragmenter. There are two modes in which you can create consoles: *Author* mode, in which the consoles can be added to and revised, and *User* mode, in which the console is frozen and cannot be changed. User mode also has full-access and two limited-access options.

Windows Server 2008 comes with a number of consoles already created that you have used in earlier chapters. These consoles, which I have called "windows" (because that is what they are), are located in the Administrative Tools folder (Start | Administrative Tools) and include Computer Management, Memory Diagnostics Tool, Task Scheduler, and many others. All of the built-in consoles are in User mode and cannot be changed or added to.

 NOTE   The contents of the Administrative Tools menu depend on the roles that have been installed by the Server Manager.

Create an MMC Console

A console that I have found to be handy is one to manage several remote computers on my network. In this one console, I have added Computer Management for these computers. Therefore, as the administrator on the server, I can remotely look at most of the administrative information on these computers, as you can see in Figure 14-11. Use the following instructions to create a similar console:

 NOTE   This set of steps, as mostly in this chapter, requires that you be logged on as an Administrator.

1. Click Start | Run. In the Run dialog box, type **mmc** and click OK. The MMC will open showing only a console root, the window in which you add snap-ins.

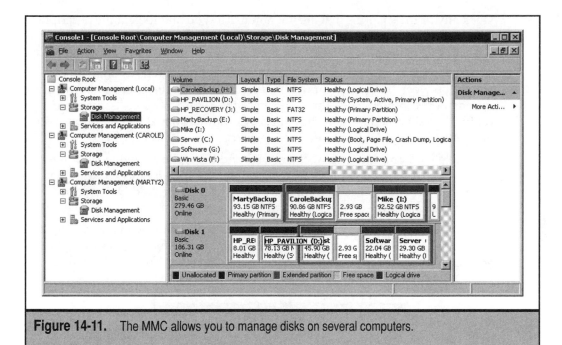

Figure 14-11.   The MMC allows you to manage disks on several computers.

2.   Click the File menu and click Add/Remove Snap-in. The Add Or Remove Snap-ins dialog box will open.

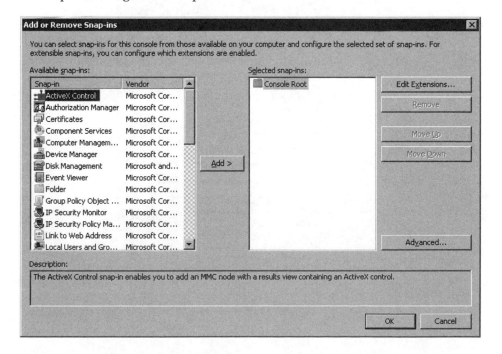

3. Click any of the snap-ins that are not familiar to you and look at the description in the lower part of the dialog box.

4. After you look at all the snap-ins that you want to, double-click Computer Management. The Computer Management dialog box opens asking you to choose between the local computer you are on and another computer. You may or may not want to include the local computer in this console. Assume you do for these instructions and click Finish. Computer Management (Local) will appear in the Add Or Remove Snap-ins dialog box.

5. Double-click Computer Management a second time, click Another Computer, browse for the other computer, and, after it is found, click Finish. Computer Management for the second computer will appear in the Add Or Remove Snap-ins dialog box.

6. Repeat Step 5 for as many computers as you want to manage in one console. In the Add Or Remove Snap-ins dialog box, select one instance of Computer Management in the right side and click Edit Extensions. The list of extensions is displayed, as shown next.

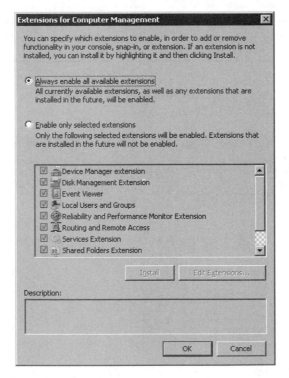

7. You can see that the default is to add all the extensions, which has been done. If you want to remove some of the extensions, click Enable Only Selected

Extensions and then uncheck the extensions you don't want (doing this once will apply to all Computer Management snap-ins).

8. After you complete all the changes you want to make to the extensions, click OK once to close the Extensions dialog box, and then click OK again to close Add Or Remove Snap-ins. You are returned to the MMC and your snap-ins appear in the left pane. Open several of the snap-ins and their extensions to get a view similar to Figure 14-11.

9. In the MMC, click the File menu and click Options to open the Options dialog box. Here, you can choose either Author mode or User mode. Look at the description of what each mode means and what each of the User mode's options means.

10. When you have chosen the mode you want to use, click OK to close the Options dialog box and return to the MMC.

11. Again click the File menu and click Save As. Enter a name that is meaningful to you and click Save. Finally, close the MMC.

Use an MMC Console

Your custom consoles are kept in the Administrative Tools folder in the Administrator area of your hard disk (C:\Users\Administrator\AppData\Roaming\Microsoft\Windows\ Start Menu\Programs\Administrative Tools). If you haven't created one or more custom consoles, you won't have an Administrative Tools folder here, but after you create your

first custom console, that folder is created and the console is automatically placed in it. This is not the same as the Administrator Tools folder containing all the built-in consoles, but when you log on as Administrator, both Administrative Tools folders will open as one from the Start menu | All Programs:

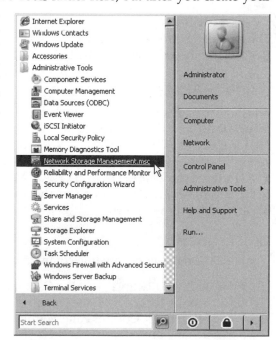

1. Click Start | All Programs | Administrative Tools | *your console* (not the Administrative Tools menu on the right side of the Start menu).

2. Open one of your remote computers and look at Storage and Disk Management.

3. After you finish seeing what you can do within your new console, close it.

EXPLORE THE REGISTRY

The Registry is the central repository of all configuration information in Windows Server 2008. It contains the settings that you make in the Server Manager, the Control Panel, in most Properties dialog boxes, and in Administrative Tools. Almost all programs get information about the local computer and current user from the Registry and write information to the Registry for the OS and other programs to use. The Registry is a complex hierarchical database that, in most circumstances, should not be directly changed. The majority of the settings in the Registry can be changed in the Server Manager, the Control Panel, Properties dialog boxes, or in Administrative Tools.

CAUTION   If you directly edit the Registry, it is very easy to make an erroneous change that will bring down the system, so you are strongly advised to directly edit the Registry only as the last alternative used in trying to change a setting.

With the preceding caution firmly in mind, it is still worthwhile understanding and looking at the Registry. Windows Server 2008's Registry Editor enables you to view the Registry, as well as to make changes to it if needed.

TIP   If you make a change to the Registry that doesn't work, you can restore the Registry to the way it was the last time the computer was started by restarting the computer and pressing F8 immediately after the startup screen. Click Last Known Good Configuration and press enter. The most recent backup of the Registry will be used to start the computer.

Start the Registry Editor by clicking Start | Run, typing **regedit**, and clicking OK. The Registry Editor will appear. Open several of the folders on the left to get a feel of the Registry, as shown in Figure 14-12.

Keys and Subtrees

The Registry consists of two primary keys, or *subtrees* (HKEY_USERS and HKEY_LOCAL_MACHINE), and three subordinate keys, also called subtrees (HKEY_CURRENT_USER, HKEY_CURRENT_CONFIG, and HKEY_CLASSES_ROOT). HKEY_CURRENT_USER is subordinate to HKEY_USERS, and HKEY_CURRENT_CONFIG and HKEY_CLASSES_ROOT are subordinate to HKEY_LOCAL_MACHINE. Each of the five subtrees is a folder in the Registry Editor, and they all are shown at the same level for ease of use. The purpose of each subtree is as follows:

HKEY_USERS

Contains the default information common to all users and is used until a user logs on.

▼ **HKEY_CURRENT_USER**   Contains the preferences, or *profile*, of the user currently logged onto the computer. This includes the desktop contents, the screen colors, Control Panel settings, and Start menu contents. The settings here take precedence over those in HKEY_LOCAL_MACHINE, where they are duplicated. Later in this chapter, under "Employ User Profiles," you'll see how to set up and manage user profiles.

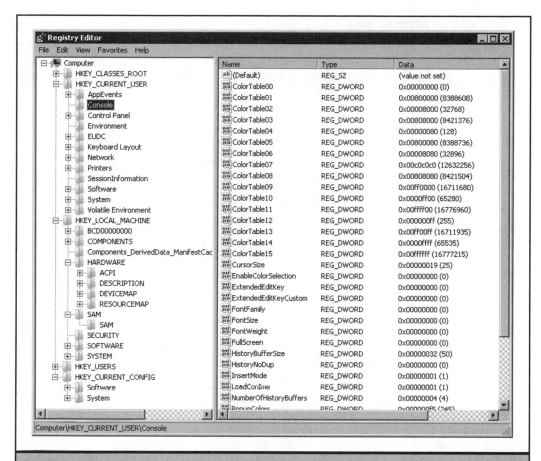

Figure 14-12.   The Registry is a database with a complex hierarchical structure.

HKEY_LOCAL_MACHINE

Contains all the computer and OS settings that are not user related. This includes the type and model of CPU; the amount of memory; the keyboard, mouse, and ports available on the hardware side; and the drivers, fonts, and settings for individual programs on the software side.

▼ **HKEY_CURRENT_CONFIG**   Contains the hardware profile for the current computer configuration. This includes the drives, ports, and drivers needed for the currently installed hardware. This is important with mobile computers and their docking stations.

▲ **HKEY_CLASSES_ROOT**   Contains the file type registration information that relates file extensions to the programs that can open them.

Keys, Subkeys, and Hives

Within each of the primary keys or subtrees are lower-level keys, and within those keys are subkeys, and within the subkeys are lower-level subkeys, and so on, for many levels. For example, Figure 14-13 shows a subkey nine levels below HKEY_LOCAL_MACHINE. You can think of keys and subkeys as folders that have folders within them and folders within those folders.

Several of the keys immediately beneath the two primary keys (HKEY_LOCAL_MACHINE and HKEY_USERS) are deep groupings of keys and subkeys. These keys (BCD, Components, SAM, Security, Software, and System), called *hives,* are stored as separate files in the C:\Windows\System32\Config folder (assuming a default installation). Each hive has at least two files, and most often three or more. The first file, without an extension, is the Registry file that contains the current Registry information. The second file, with the .log extension, is a log of changes that have been made to the Registry file. The third file, with the .sav extension, is the Last Known Good backup of the Registry (known to be good because the system was successfully started with it). The final Registry file type, with the .evt extension, tracks events as they are occurring with the Registry.

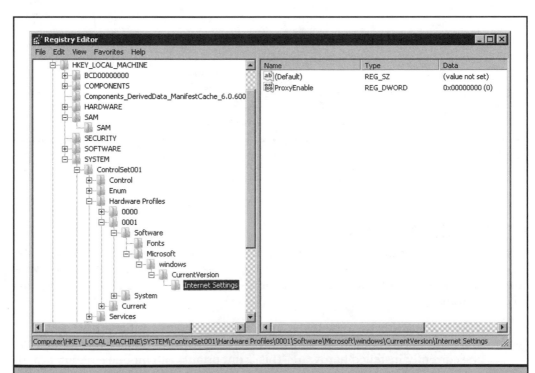

Figure 14-13.   There are often many subkeys within each key in the Registry.

NOTE   The SAM key stands for Security Account Manager. It is used for storing the username and password in stand-alone computers.

You can work with the hives to save a particular group of settings, make changes to the settings, and then either restore the original settings or add the original settings to the new ones. Here are the Registry Editor's File menu commands to do that:

▼   **Export**   Used to save a selected hive to your disk or to an external storage device. To use this command, click the hive, click the File menu, click Export, click a folder, enter a name, and click Save. A saved hive can be either restored or loaded. You can also right-click a hive and click Export to accomplish the same objective.

■   **Import**   Used to replace an existing hive in the Registry. To use this command, select the hive to be replaced, click the File menu, click Import, select a drive and folder, enter or select a name, and click Open. The restored hive will overwrite the current one.

■   **Load Hive**   Used to add a saved hive to an existing one. To use this command, select either HKEY_LOCAL_MACHINE or HKEY_USERS, click the File menu, click Load Hive, select a drive and folder, enter or select a name, and click Open. When asked, enter the name that you want to give the additional hive and click OK. A new subkey is created with the name you have given it. This can then be used by software that knows about the new name.

▲   **Unload Hive**   Used to remove a hive that has been loaded (this cannot be done if the hive was restored). Unload a loaded hive by clicking it, clicking the File menu, and choosing Unload Hive.

NOTE   You can make a complete copy of the Registry without having to identify the individual keys or hives. In the Registry Editor, click the Computer icon at the top of the Registry tree. Click the File menu, click Export, select the drive and folder in which to save the file, enter a name, and click Save.

Entries and Data Types

At the lowest level of the Registry tree, you will see a data entry in the right pane for the selected key. All data entries have three elements: a name on the left, a data type in the middle, and the data on the right. You can see two data entries on the right of Figure 14-13. The data type determines how to look at and use the data. Also, the Registry Editor has an editor for each data type. Table 14-2 provides the name of each data type, its editor, and its description.

TIP   You can automatically open the correct editor for a particular data type by double-clicking the name on the left of the data entry.

Data Type	Editor	Description
REG_BINARY	Binary	A single value that is expressed in the Registry Editor as a hexadecimal number, generally a complex number that is parsed and used to set switches
REG_DWORD	Dword	A single value that is a hexadecimal number of up to eight digits, generally a simple number such as decimal 16 or 60 or 1024
REG_SZ	String	A single string of characters, such as a filename; it can include spaces
REG_EXPAND_SZ	String	A single string of characters that contains a variable that the OS replaces with its current value when the value is requested; an example is the environment variable *Systemroot* that is replaced with the root directory of Windows Server 2008 (by default, C:\Windows)
REG_MULTI_SZ	Multi-String	Multiple strings of characters separated by spaces, commas, or other punctuation, so each string cannot contain spaces, commas, or other punctuation
REG_FULL_ RESOURCE_ DESCRIPTOR	Array	A series of hexadecimal numbers representing an array used to store a list of values

Table 14-2. Data Types Used in the Registry

WORK WITH THE BOOT PROCESS

The Windows Server 2008 startup or *boot* process is new and somewhat simpler than in Windows Server 2003. This process can be controlled and can have problems that can be addressed. As a result, it is worthwhile understanding what is taking place during booting, what you see on the screen, and what files are being used.

Steps in the Booting Process

The boot process has five major stages: preboot, boot, load, initialization, and logon. Within each of these stages, several steps take place that load and use files. In each of these stages, look at the process that is taking place, how the particular files are used, and what you see on the screen.

Preboot   Preboot is the hardware-dependent, Basic Input-Output System (BIOS)-enabled startup process. It is started either by power coming on or the system being reset. The first step is to see what hardware is available and its condition by using the power-on self test (POST) routine. Next, BIOS executes the initial program load (IPL), which locates the boot device and, if the device is a hard disk, the master boot record (MBR) is read from the first sector on the disk. Otherwise, the equivalent information is obtained from the boot device. From this information, partition information is obtained, the boot sector is read, and the Windows Boot Manager (Bootmgr.exe) is started. On the screen, you see the memory check, the identification of hardware, and the search for a boot device.

Boot   Windows Boot Manager reads the boot configuration data (BCD) and, if there is more than one boot partition, asks the user to choose a partition and its OS. If a choice is not made before the timeout, the default partition and OS is loaded. If you are booting Windows Server 2008, the Windows Boot Loader (Winload.exe) is started. If you have more than one hardware profile, you are given the option of pressing the SPACEBAR to select the hardware profile you want to use, for example, if you have a laptop that you sometimes use with a docking station. If you press the SPACEBAR, you can choose the hardware profile you want; otherwise, the default profile is used.

Load   Following the operating system and hardware profile selection, the Windows Server 2008 "splash" screen is displayed with the moving bars in the center. While this is happening, Windows Boot Loader loads the operating system kernel, the hardware abstraction layer that provides the interface between the operating system and a particular set of hardware, the Registry file, and the drivers for basic hardware devices, such as the monitor, mouse, and keyboard.

Initialization   The OS kernel is initialized and takes over from the Windows Boot Loader, bringing up the graphical display and filling the Registry with HKEY_LOCAL_MACHINE\HARDWARE key, and HKEY_LOCAL_MACHINE\SYSTEM\SELECT subkey (called the "Clone Control Set") and loads the remainder of the device drivers. Finally, the session manager is started, which executes any boot-time command files, creates a paging file for the Virtual Memory Manager, creates links to the file system that can be used by DOS commands, and finally starts the I/O subsystem to handle all I/O for Windows Server 2008.

Logon   The Windows Server 2008 graphic user interface (GUI) is started and the logon screen is displayed. After a successful logon, the necessary services are started, the Last Known Good control set is written on the basis of the Clone Control Set, and the startup programs are started.

Controlling the Boot Process

Windows Server 2008 provides the System Configuration utility (see Figure 14-14) to exercise some control of the boot process. With it you can determine the startup mode: normal, diagnostic, and selective; determine which of several operating systems is the default; what options to use; which services are enabled; and what applications are started, as well as launch a number of tools such as System Restore and the Performance Monitor.

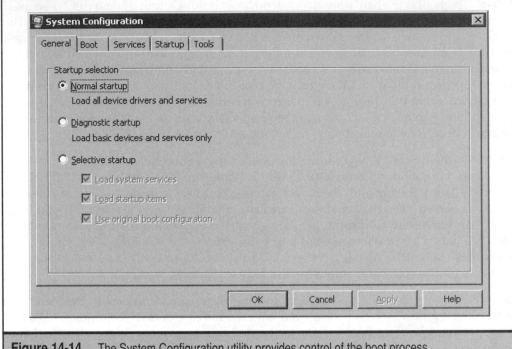

Figure 14-14. The System Configuration utility provides control of the boot process.

To start and use the System Configuration utility:

1. Click Start | Administrative Tools | System Configuration.
2. In the General tab, select the Startup mode.
3. Click the Boot tab, select the OS that will be the default, and click Set As Default.
4. Click the Services tab, review the services that are running, and uncheck any that you do not want to run the next time you boot.
5. Click the Startup tab, review the applications that are running, and uncheck any that you do not want to run the next time you boot.
6. Click the Tools tab, click the tool you want to open, and click Launch.
7. Click OK when you are finished with the System Configuration utility.

Correct Booting Problems

Numerous situations can cause a computer to not boot. To counter this fact, Windows Server 2008 has several features to help you work around the problem and to help you fix it. Among these features are:

▼   Returning to the Last Known Good Registry files

▲   Using Safe Mode and Advanced Options

Return to the Last Known Good Registry Files

If a computer doesn't successfully complete the boot process and you have just tried to install a new piece of hardware or software or have otherwise changed the Registry, the problem often is due to the Registry's trying to load a device driver that doesn't work properly, or the result of some other Registry problem. You would normally learn of this problem late in the boot process, probably in either the Initialization or Logon stages. The fastest cure for a Registry problem is to return to the last known good Registry files by following these steps:

1.   Restart the computer and press F8 immediately after the selection of a boot device. (I press F8 immediately after the initial startup screen.)

2.   Use the arrow keys to select Last Known Good Configuration and press ENTER. The Last Known Good Registry files will be used to start up Windows Server 2008.

TIP   The Last Known Good Registry files were saved the last time you successfully completed booting and logged onto Windows Server 2008.

Using the Last Known Good Configuration and Automated System Recovery are the only automated means to try to repair a problem starting Windows Server 2008. All other techniques require that you manually work on the files that are required to start Windows Server 2008.

Use Safe Mode and Other Advanced Options

Safe Mode uses only minimal default drivers to start the basic Windows Server 2008 services, with the idea that, in that mode, you can fix the problem that's preventing the full startup. You start Safe Mode with the same steps used to start Last Known Good Configuration, except that you choose one of three Safe Modes: Safe Mode, Safe Mode With Networking, and Safe Mode With Command Prompt. Basic Safe Mode does not include networking and comes up with a minimal Windows graphics interface. The second Safe Mode option adds networking capability, and the third option places you at a command prompt; otherwise, these two options are the same as Safe Mode.

As you start Safe Mode, you see a listing of the drivers as they are loaded. If the boot fails at that point, you are left looking at the last drivers that were loaded. Once you get into Windows, you might not have a mouse available, so you'll need to remember the shortcut keys for important functions, as shown in Table 14-3.

While working in Safe Mode, the System Information window is very handy, as shown in Figure 14-15. Open the System Information window by clicking Start | All Programs | Accessories | System Tools | System Information. Within System Information, opening Hardware Resources | Conflicts/Sharing, Components | Problem Devices, and Software Environment | Running Tasks is particularly valuable.

Function	Shortcut Key
Open Start menu	CTRL-ESC
Open context menu	SHIFT-F10
Close active windows	ALT-F4
Open Help	F1
Open Properties	ALT-ENTER
Search for files or folders	F3
Switch tasks	ALT-ESC
Switch programs	ALT-TAB
Switch tabs	CTRL-TAB
Turn on MouseKeys	LEFT SHIFT-LEFT ALT-NUM LOCK
Undo last operation	CTRL-Z

Table 14-3. Shortcut Keys for Use While Working in Safe Mode

In addition to Safe Mode and Last Known Good Configuration, the Advanced Options menu has the following options. These are in addition to Start Windows Normally and pressing ESC (where you are returned to the OS choices menu).

▼ **Enable Boot Logging**   Logs all the events that take place during startup in the file Ntbtlog.txt, located by default in the C:\Windows folder. The loading of all system files and drivers is logged, as shown next, so that you can see if one failed while it was being loaded. Boot logging is done in all advanced startup options except Last Known Good Configuration.

```
ntbtlog.txt - Notepad
File  Edit  Format  View  Help
 Service Pack 1, v.275 9 28 2007 21:38:13.500
Loaded driver \SystemRoot\system32\ntkrnlpa.exe
Loaded driver \SystemRoot\system32\hal.dll
Loaded driver \SystemRoot\system32\kdcom.dll
Loaded driver \SystemRoot\system32\mcupdate_GenuineIntel.dll
Loaded driver \SystemRoot\system32\PSHED.dll
Loaded driver \SystemRoot\system32\BOOTVID.dll
Loaded driver \SystemRoot\system32\CLFS.SYS
Loaded driver \SystemRoot\system32\CI.dll
Loaded driver \SystemRoot\system32\DRIVERS\sacdrv.sys
Loaded driver \SystemRoot\system32\DRIVERS\NDIS.SYS
Loaded driver \SystemRoot\system32\DRIVERS\msrpc.sys
Loaded driver \SystemRoot\system32\DRIVERS\NETIO.SYS
Loaded driver \SystemRoot\system32\drivers\wdf01000.sys
Loaded driver \SystemRoot\system32\drivers\WDFLDR.SYS
```

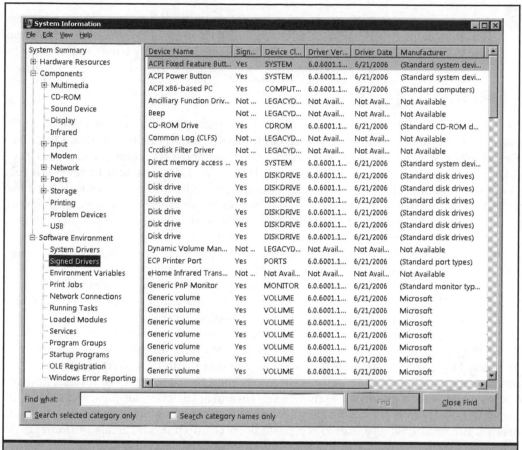

Figure 14-15. The System Information window can be useful when looking for a problem.

- **Enable Low-Resolution Video (640×480)** Sets the display for a minimal video graphic adapter (VGA) with 640×480 resolution using a known good default driver. All other drivers and capabilities are loaded normally. The VGA mode is also used in Safe Mode.

- **Directory Services Restore Mode** Restores Active Directory in domain controllers and then goes into Safe Mode, except that the mouse is available and normal video display mode is used. In computers that are not domain controllers, this option is the same as Safe Mode.

- ▲ **Debugging Mode** Turns on the debugger and then boots up into the normal configuration for the computer. This allows you to work on scripts that might be getting in the way of a proper startup.

NOTE   If you are using a 64-bit computer and the x64 version of Windows Server 2008, you will have two other Advanced Options: Disable Automatic Restart On System Failure (allows you to observe what caused the failure) and Disable Driver Signature Enforcement (lets you use unsigned drivers).

USE GROUP POLICIES

Group policies provide the means to establish the standards and guidelines that an organization wants to apply to the use of its computers. Group policies are meant to reflect the general policies of an organization and can be established hierarchically from a local computer at the lowest end, to a particular site, to a domain, and to several levels of organizational units (OUs) at the upper end. Normally, lower-level units inherit the policies of the upper-level units, although it is possible to block higher-level policies, as well as to force inheritance if desired. Group polices are divided into *user policies* that prescribe what a user can do and *computer policies* that determine what is available on a computer. User policies are independent of the computer on which the user is working and follow the user from computer to computer. When a computer is started (booted), the applicable computer group policies are loaded and stored in the Registry HKEY_LO-CAL_MACHINE. When a user logs onto a computer, the applicable user group policies are loaded and stored in the Registry HKEY_CURRENT_USER.

Group policies can be very beneficial to both an organization and the individuals in it. All the computers in an organization can automatically adjust to whichever user is currently logged on. This can include a custom desktop with a custom Start menu and a unique set of applications. Group policies can control the access to files, folders, and applications, as well as the ability to change system and application settings, and the ability to delete files and folders. Group policies can automate tasks when a computer starts up or shuts down, and when a user logs on or logs off. Group policies can also automatically store files and shortcuts in specific folders.

Create and Change Group Policies

Group policies can exist at the local computer level, the site level, the domain level, and the OU level. Although the process to create or change group policies is the same at the site, domain, and OU levels, it is sufficiently different at the local computer level to merit discussing this level separately.

Change Group Policies at the Local Computer Level

Every Windows Server 2008 computer has a single local group policy created by Setup during installation and stored by default in C:\Windows\System32\GroupPolicy. Since there can be only one local group policy, you cannot create another, although you can edit the existing one by following these instructions:

1. Click Start | Run, type **gpedit.msc**, and press ENTER or click OK. The Group Policy window will open.

2. Open several levels of the tree on the left so that you can get down to a level that shows policies and their settings on the right, as shown in Figure 14-16.

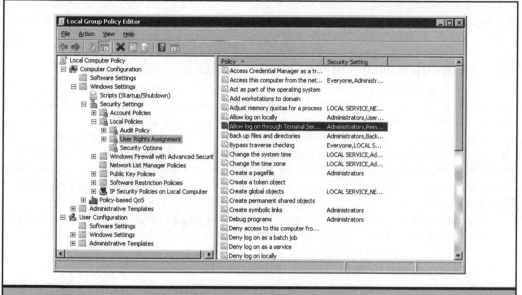

Figure 14-16.   Edit the default group policy as a start in using policies.

3. Double-click a policy to open its dialog box. Here, you can change the local policy settings by enabling or disabling it or adding or removing users or groups.

4. Add additional users or groups to a policy by clicking Add User Or Group and selecting one or more users and/or groups that you want to add.

5. Expand User Configuration | Administrative Templates | Windows Components | Internet Explorer | Internet Settings | Advanced Settings | Browsing, double-click the first setting, and then click Next Setting to review them all. You'll find that all say "Not Configured."

6. Click the Explain tab in any Properties dialog box to get a detailed description of the policy and the effects of enabling, disabling, and leaving the policy not configured.

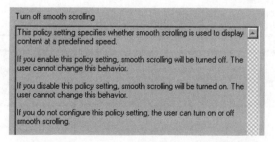

7. Make any changes that you want to make to the local computer group policies and then close the open dialog boxes and the Group Policy window.

Although group policies can be implemented at the local computer level and are by default for the computer, they are expected to be overridden at the domain or OU levels.

Review Group Policies at the Domain and OU Levels

Group policies above the local computer level are Active Directory objects and are therefore called *group policy objects (GPOs).* They are created as one object, but they are stored in two pieces: a group policy container and a group policy template. *Group policy containers (GPCs)* are stored in Active Directory and hold smaller pieces of information that change infrequently. *Group policy templates (GPTs)* are a set of folders stored by default at C:\Windows\Sysvol\Sysvol*domain name*\Policies\ and have both machine and user components, as shown in Figure 14-17. GPTs store larger pieces of information that change frequently.

You can review a GPO linked to a domain or OU by opening Group Policy Management in the Server Manager or its own MMC. See how to do this next:

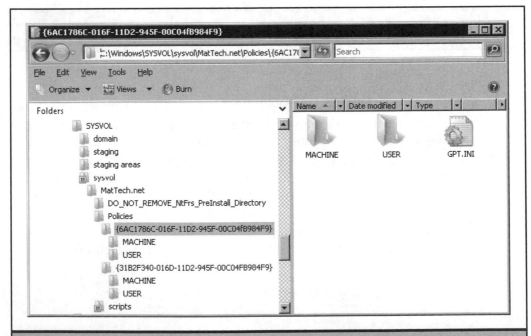

Figure 14-17. When the Active Directory Domain Services role is installed, a folder structure is set up for storing group policy templates.

CAUTION   While it is worthwhile understanding what is in the Default Domain Policy and the Default Domain Controller Policy, these are at the tip of the policy pyramid and should not be changed except when a program you install requires it.

1. Click Start | Server Manager and open Features | Group Policy Management. Or, click Start | Run and type **gpmc.msc**.
In either case, open Forest | Domains | *domain name* | Group Policy Objects and click Default Domain Policy.

2. In the right pane, click the Settings tab and click Show on the right of several of the policies to see the details, as shown in Figure 14-18 (if started from gpmc.msc).

3. In the left pane, right-click the Default Domain Policy and click Edit. The Group Policy Management Editor opens. Open, for example, Computer Configuration | Windows Settings | Security Settings | Local Policies, and click Security Options to see the detail of policies shown in Figure 14-19.

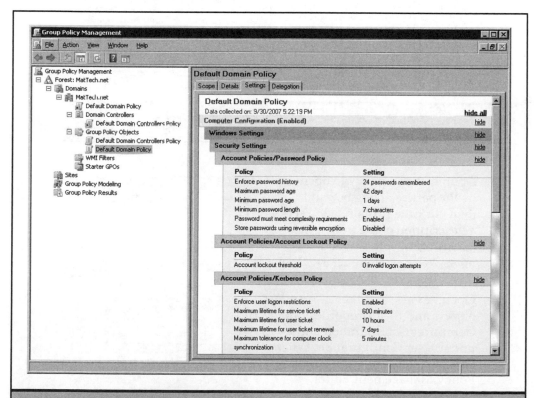

Figure 14-18.   Group policy settings can be reviewed in Group Policy Management.

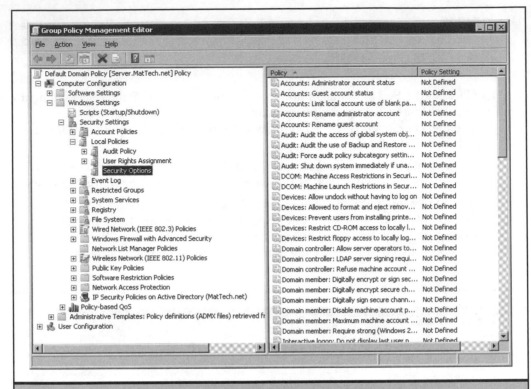

Figure 14-19. Group Policy Management can be performed at a very detailed level.

4. Double-click a policy to open its Properties dialog box and then click the Explain tab to see a description of the policy, the effects of the settings, and any notes. When you are ready, close the policy Properties dialog box.

5. Open, review, and then close other objects and their properties under Computer Configuration and then under User Configuration. When you are ready, close the Group Policy Management Editor.

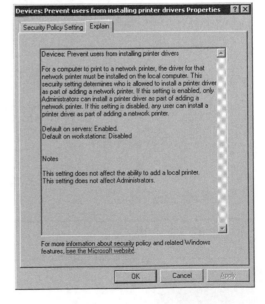

Work with Group Policy Objects

GPOs can be backed up, restored, copied, deleted, and renamed by right-clicking the GPO. You can also create a new GPO using Starter GPOs. Here's how:

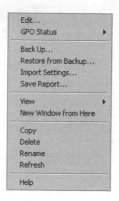

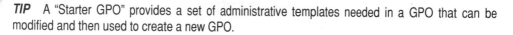

TIP   A "Starter GPO" provides a set of administrative templates needed in a GPO that can be modified and then used to create a new GPO.

1. In Group Policy Management, open Forest | Domains | *domain name* and click Starter GPOs.

2. If this is the first time you have created a Starter GPO, click Create Starter GPOs Folder.

3. In the left pane, right-click Starter GPOs and click New. Type a name for the Starter GPO, add any comments desired, and click OK.

4. In the right pane, right-click the new Starter GPO and click Edit. The Group Policy Starter GPO Editor opens.

5. Open, for example, Computer Configuration | Administrative Templates | Network | Network Connections | Windows Firewall | Domain Profile, and click one of the settings to see its description, as shown in Figure 14-20.

6. Double-click a setting to open its Properties dialog box, where you can change its settings and add comments. Click OK when you are finished.

7. Open, modify, and close as many policies and their settings as you need for your purpose. When you are ready, close the Group Policy Starter GPO Editor.

8. To create a new GPO from a Starter GPO, right-click the Starter GPO you want to use and click New GPO From Starter GPO. Type a name for the new GPO and click OK.

9. In the left pane under Group Policy Management, open Forest | Domains | *domain name* | Group Policy Objects and right-click the new GPO. In the

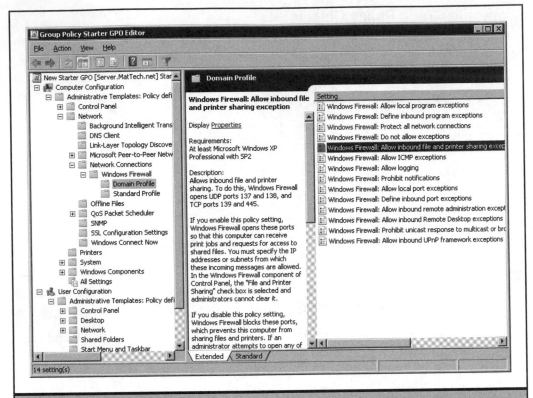

Figure 14-20. Using a Starter GPO, you can set up a GPO for a particular purpose and use it to create one or more GPOs.

context menu, you can edit and do all the other operations as you can with a default GPO.

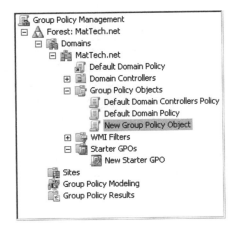

10. Once you have a GPO, you can link it to a domain, an OU, or a site by right-clicking the domain, OU, or site; clicking Link An Existing GPO; selecting the GPO; and clicking OK.

11. When you are ready, close the Group Policy Management window.

EMPLOY USER PROFILES

If you are the only user of a computer, you can tailor the desktop, Start menu, folders, network connections, Control Panel, and applications to your individual taste and needs. If several users are on the same computer, as is often the case with a server, they could potentially upset each other by making those changes. The way around this is to create a *user profile* for each user that contains individual settings for that user and that loads when the particular user logs onto the computer.

When you create a new user account and then log onto a Windows Server 2008 computer, a user profile is created automatically, and when you log off the computer, your settings are saved under that profile. When you log back on, your settings are used to reset the system to the way it was when you last logged off. When Windows Server 2008 is installed, it establishes the Default user profile that is then used as the default for all new users and saved with any changes under the user's name when the user logs off. The first user of a newly installed Windows Server 2008 is made the Administrator user and the initial settings are saved with that user. A user's profile is a set of folders stored in the Users folder on the system volume where the OS is installed. Figure 14-21 shows the folders within a user profile for a user named Administrator. In the same figure, you can see a folder for All Users and for Default, which contain files, folders, and settings applicable to all users.

There are three types of user profiles: local user profiles, roaming user profiles, and mandatory user profiles.

NOTE   The shortcuts in the Users folder list (folders with the arrows) are folders to accommodate older programs that are set up to use older versions of Windows.

Create Local User Profiles

Local user profiles are automatically created when a new user is created and logs onto the computer, and the profile is changed by the user making changes to the environment, such as changing the desktop or the Start menu. When the user logs off, any changes that were made are saved in the user's profile. This is an automatic and standard process in Windows Server 2008. A local user account, though, is limited to the computer on which it was established. If the user logs onto a different computer, a new local user profile is created on that computer. A roaming user profile eliminates the need to have a separate profile on each computer.

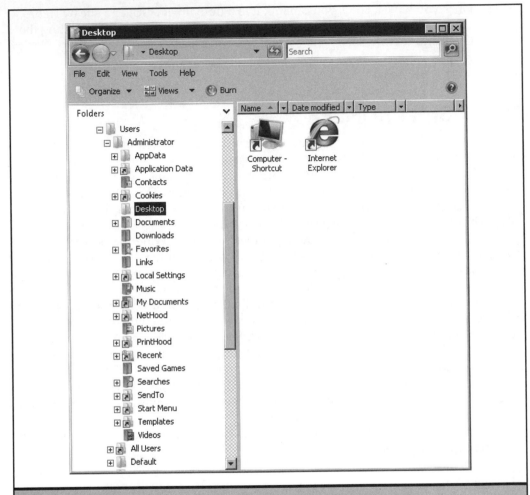

Figure 14-21. Users' profiles have a set of folders for their use of the computer.

Create Roaming User Profiles

A *roaming* user profile is set up on a server so that when you log on for the first time to a computer on the same domain as the server, you are authenticated by the server and your complete user profile is sent down to the computer, where it is saved as a local user profile. When you log off the computer, any changes that you made to the settings in the profile are saved both on the computer and on the server. The next time you log onto the computer, your profile there is compared with your profile on the server, and only the changes on the server are downloaded to the computer, thereby reducing the time to log on.

The process of creating a roaming user profile has five steps:

1. Create a folder to hold profiles.
2. Create a user account.
3. Assign the profiles folder to the user's account.
4. Create a roaming user profile.
5. Copy a profile template to a user.

Create a Profiles Folder

Roaming user profiles can be stored on any server—they do not have to be on a domain controller. In fact, because of the size of the download the first time a user signs onto a new computer, it might make sense to not store the roaming user profiles on the domain controller. There is no default folder to hold roaming profiles, so you must create one as follows:

1. Log on as Administrator to the server where you want the profiles folder to reside, and open Windows Explorer (Start | Computer).
2. Click Local Disk (C:) in the folders list. Right-click in a blank area of the right pane and click New | Folder.
3. In the new folder's name box, type the name you want to give to the folder that will hold your profiles. This should be an easily recognized name, such as "Profiles." Press ENTER.
4. Right-click the new folder and click Share. In the File Sharing dialog box, click the down arrow opposite Add, click the Everyone group, click Add, and click Share.
5. Click Done to close the File Sharing dialog box. Leave Windows Explorer open.

Create a User Account

Every user in a domain must have a user account in that domain. You have seen how to create a user account in earlier chapters (Chapters 3 and 7) and we talk about it again in Chapter 15, but as a refresher, here are the steps:

1. While still logged on as Administrator, open the Active Directory Users And Computers window (Start | Administrative Tools | Active Directory Users And Computers).
2. Open the domain within which you want to create the account; then open Users. Scan the existing users to make sure the new user is not already a user.

3. Click the Action menu and click New | User. The New Object — User dialog box will open. Enter the user's name and logon name, and click Next.

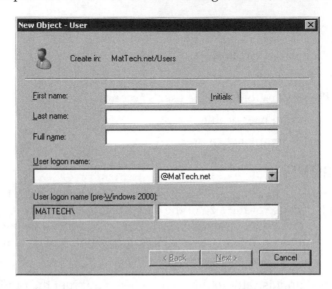

4. Enter the user's password, choose how soon the password must change, and click Next. Review the settings that you have made. If you want to change any of them, click Back and make the changes. When you are satisfied with the settings, click Finish.

For the purpose of these exercises, make several new accounts: at least one that will have a regular roaming profile and one that will be a template for a preconfigured profile. Leave the Active Directory Users And Computers window open when you are done.

Assign the Profiles Folder to a User's Account

To utilize a roaming profile, the user's account must specify that their profile is stored in the profiles folder that you established earlier. Otherwise, Windows Server 2008 will look in the Users folder of the computer the user is logging onto. The following steps show how to assign the profiles folder to a user's account:

1. In the Active Directory Users And Computers*domain name*\Users folder in which you added the new users, right-click one of the new users that you added and click Properties. The user's Properties dialog box opens.

2. Click the Profile tab. In the Profile Path text box, type *servername*\ *foldername**logonname*. For example, if the server name on which the profile is stored is Server, the folder is Profiles, and the logon name is Mike, then you would type **\\server\profiles\mike**.

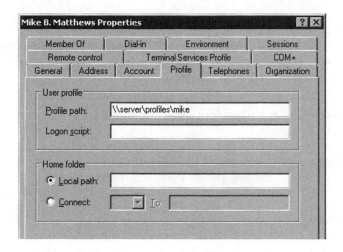

3. Close the Properties dialog box and repeat this process for the template user you created.

Create a Roaming User Profile

Once you have set up a shared folder on a server and specified in a user's account that the user's profile is in the specified folder on the server, then the actual user profile will be created and stored on the server simply by having the user log onto any computer within the network. Try this with these steps:

1. Log on one of the new users with that user's own profile to a computer in the network. Make some changes to the desktop and the Start menu, and then log off that computer.

2. Look at the folder you created on the server to hold profiles. You will see a new profiles folder named after the logon name of the user in Step 1.

3. Log on this same user to another computer in the network. The changes to the desktop and Start menu will follow you to this computer.

While the preceding technique is fine for someone you want to give free rein to in the system and who is knowledgeable about how to tailor it to his or her needs and desires, if you want to put limits on a user, or on someone who does not have a lot of knowledge about how to change the system, you want to create a template profile and then assign it to one or more users.

To build a template, simply log on the "template" user that you created to the computer you want to use for the profile, and then make the necessary changes that you want reflected in the profile. If the template will be assigned to several people, be sure that the hardware and applications are the same both among the group that will use the profile and on the computer you used to create the template.

Copy or Assign a Profile Template to a User

You can handle a template in one of two ways. You can "copy" it to create a new profile that you assign to a user, or you can assign the template as-is to several users. See how both of these are done in the following steps:

NOTE   The "copying" in this case uses a special technique and cannot use the Windows Explorer or Computer Copy command.

1. In the Active Directory Users And Computers*domain name*\\Users folder in which you added the new users, right-click the template profile you created, which I called "Roam," and click Copy. The Copy Object – User dialog box opens.

2. In the Copy Object — User dialog box, enter the name, logon name, and password for the new user.

3. Repeat Steps 1 and 2 to assign the template to several users.

4. Log on each of your new users to one or more computers and make sure they work. One possibility if the logon doesn't work is that there is a typing error in the path of the profile in the user's Properties dialog box.

Use Mandatory User Profiles

A *mandatory* user profile is a roaming user profile that cannot be changed; it is read-only. This is particularly valuable when several users are sharing the same profile. When a user logs off a computer where a mandatory profile has been used, the user's changes are not saved. The profile does not prevent the user from making changes while logged on, but the changes aren't saved. A mandatory user profile is created by taking a roaming user profile and, in the folder with the user's name, renaming the system file Ntuser.dat to Ntuser.man.

UPDATE WINDOWS SERVER 2008

When you complete installing Windows Server 2008, and periodically thereafter, you are reminded to "Stay current with automatic updates" in a little balloon in the lower right of your screen. If you choose to turn on Automatic Updates, it will automatically determine if any updates are available for Windows Server 2008, either automatically or manually download the updates over the Internet, and either automatically or manually install updates on a periodic basis. This gives you the advantage of the latest fixes from Microsoft. If you choose not to install automatic updates, you can still download and install the updates manually.

Manual Updates

To manually get and install updates, you have to open the Windows Update web site and let it scan your system to determine if updates are needed, downloading and then installing the updates. Use the following steps to do that:

1. Click Start | All Programs | Windows Update. The Windows Update window will open.

2. Click Check For Updates. You will be connected to the Internet, the Microsoft site will be checked for updates, and you will be told if there are any.

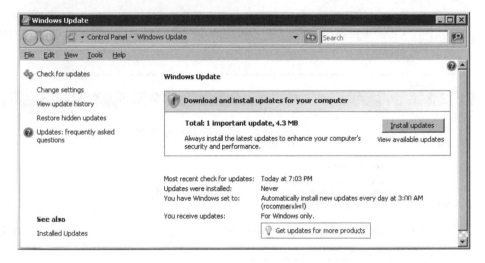

3. If you have updates that need to be or can be installed, click Install Updates.

4. Click Accept when the license agreement is displayed and then downloading will commence. When downloading is complete, the updates will automatically be installed. When the installation is complete, depending on the update, you may be told that you need to restart your computer. If asked, click OK.

5. If you don't have to restart your computer, close the Windows Update window. The updates are in place and ready to use.

Automatic Updates

If Automatic Updates is turned on, Windows goes online, goes to the Windows Update web site, and determines if there are updates you need to download. If so, Automatic Updates will, at your choice, either notify you of the update availability or just automatically download the updates. You can then choose to either automatically install the updates or just be told they have been downloaded and you can install them manually. If you choose to do all three steps (detect updates needed, download them, and install them) automatically, you can schedule a time to do it.

Turn On Automatic Updates

Automatic Updates can be turned on in two ways. Shortly after installing Windows Server 2008, you will be asked if you want to do that. This opens the Automatic Updates Setup Wizard. By following its instructions, you can turn on Automatic Updates. You can also access Automatic Updates at any time through the Control Panel. Here's how to turn on Automatic Updates in that way:

1. Click Start | Control Panel and double-click System. In the System window that opens, click Windows Update in the lower left, which is then displayed, as you saw in the last section.

2. Click Change Settings. The Change Settings window will open, as shown in Figure 14-22. Determine the amount of automation you want and click one of the three choices:

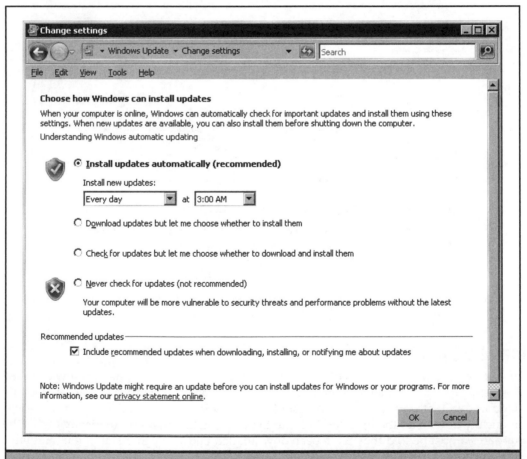

Figure 14-22.   You can select how automated you want updates to be installed to your operating system.

    a. The first choice checks to see if there are updates available, downloads them, and installs them, all automatically on a schedule you determine.

    b. The second choice automatically determines if there are updates and automatically downloads them; it then asks you before installing them.

    c. The third choice automatically determines if there are updates that are needed, then asks you before downloading them, and asks you again before installing them.

    d. The fourth choice is the manual choice where you must initiate everything.

  3. Click OK when you are finished.

Use Semiautomatic Updates

If you choose either the second or third choice, you will get a notice when updates are ready to download and/or install. When you click the icon pointed to by this balloon, the Automatic Updates dialog box opens. If you click Details, you will see the specific updates that are being proposed, along with a description of each. You can choose to download and/or install each update by clicking the check box or delay the download and/or installation. If you download and/or Install, that process will be carried out.

Maintain Automatic Updates

Once you have installed Automatic Updates, the Windows Update window shows you the most recent check for updates, the last time they were installed, what your current update settings are, lets you look at the updates that have been installed, and, as you saw earlier in this section, lets you check for new updates and change your settings.

CHAPTER 15

Controlling Windows Server 2008 Security

S ecurity is one of those topics that is so large that it is hard to get an overall picture of it. One way to try to achieve this overview is to look at the demands for security in a computer network. Once the demands are defined, you can look at how Windows Server 2008 handles the demands. Security demands include the following, which also are the major sections of this chapter:

▼ **Authenticating the user**   Knowing who is using a computer or network connection

■ **Controlling access**   Placing and maintaining limits on what a user can do

■ **Securing stored data**   Keeping stored data from being used even with access

▲ **Securing data transmission**   Keeping data in a network from being misused

Windows Server 2008 uses a multilayered approach to implementing security and provides a number of facilities that are used to handle security demands. Central to Windows Server 2008's security strategy is the use of Active Directory to store user accounts and provide authentication services, although security features are available without Active Directory. Active Directory provides a centralization of security management that is very beneficial to strong security. In each of the following sections, a security demand is further explained and the Windows Server 2008 facilities that address that demand are discussed, as are the ways to implement those facilities.

NOTE   Most sets of steps in this chapter require that you be logged on as Administrator.

AUTHENTICATE THE USER

Authentication is the process of verifying that users or objects are as they are represented to be. In its simplest form, computer user authentication entails validating a username and password against a stored entry, as is done in a stand-alone computer. In its fullest form, user authentication entails using sophisticated authentication methods to validate a potential user, possibly using a smart card or biometric device anywhere in a network against credentials in Active Directory. For objects, such as documents, programs, and messages, authentication requires using certificate validation. In Windows Server 2008, all three forms of authentication are available, and both user forms employ a single sign-on concept that allows users, once authenticated, to access other services within the local computer or the network, depending on their environment and permissions, without having to reenter their username and password.

In the normal default installation, when a Windows Server 2008 computer is started, there is a request to press CTRL-ALT-DEL. This stops all programs running on the computer except the request to enter your username and password. The purpose of stopping all programs is to prevent a Trojan horse program from capturing your username and password. If the username/password combination that is entered is not correct, you are given five opportunities to correct it, after which the computer is frozen for 30 seconds. You are then alternately given one opportunity and then five opportunities, separated by 30 seconds of inactivity, and then the pattern is repeated to correctly enter a username and password. This pattern makes it more difficult to break a password because you can't just repeatedly try a new password.

Once a username and password are entered, they must be authenticated. This can be done at either the local computer, where the user will be limited to that computer, or at a server supporting a network, possibly with Active Directory, in which case the user will have access to the network.

Local Computer User Authentication

To have a username and password accepted on a local stand-alone computer, a *user account* with that username and password must have been previously entered into the Local Users and Groups database, which is in the Security Account Manager (SAM) file of HKEY_LOCAL _MACHINE in the Registry. Here are the steps to set up a user account:

NOTE   If you are on an Active Directory domain controller, you will not have a Local Users And Groups in Computer Management. You must use Active Directory Users And Computers.

1. While logged on as an Administrator, click Start | Administrative Tools | Computer Management. The Computer Management window opens.

2. In the left pane, open System Tools | Local Users And Groups, click Users, right-click in the right pane, and click New User to open the New User dialog box.

3. Enter a username of up to 20 characters. It cannot contain just periods or spaces; it can't contain " / \ [ ] : ; | = , + * ? < > @; and leading spaces or periods are dropped.

4. Enter a full name, a description (optional), a password of up to 14 case-sensitive characters, its confirmation, and then select what the user must do with the password, as shown in Figure 15-1. A password should be at least eight characters long and be a mixture of upper- and lowercase letters, numbers, and special characters.

5. When you have successfully entered the information, click Create and then click Close. You will now be able to log off as Administrator and log on as your new user. Try that to make sure it works.

With the entry of this single username and password, the new user will be able to do anything that is within that user's level of permission on that single computer. If the computer subsequently is connected to a network, the account has to be reestablished there for the user to be able to use the network.

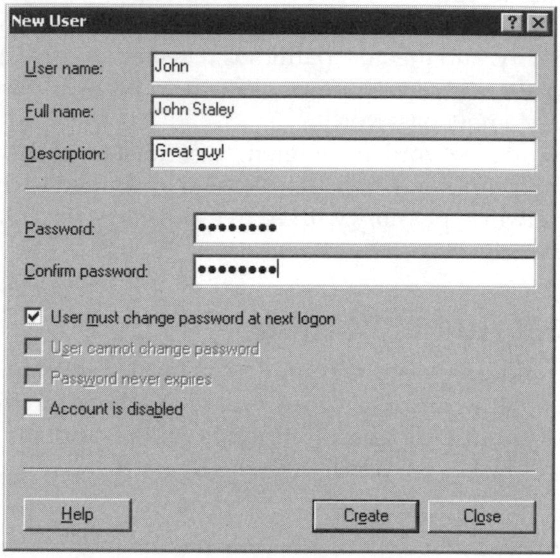

Figure 15-1.   A new user on an individual computer is entered through Computer Management.

Network User Authentication

In a network environment, user authentication can be handled by one of several methods depending on whether Active Directory is enabled. If Active Directory is not being used, then authentication is handled at a more basic level. If Active Directory is in use, then several more advanced authentication techniques are available in Windows Server 2008. If users are coming in over the Internet, they can use certificates and the Secure Sockets Layer (SSL) or Transport Layer Security (TLS) protocols for authentication. In the case of certificates, Windows Server 2008 can take an authenticated certificate and map it to a user account for integration with the rest of the system (see "Certificate Authentication," later in this chapter).

In all these methods, a user account must first be established on the server before authentication can be accomplished. Without Active Directory, the procedure for setting up a user account is exactly the same as with the local computer, discussed in the preceding section, except that it must be done on each server in the network. With Active Directory and Active Directory Certificate Services, all of which require Active Directory for full use, the procedure is a little different. Here are the steps:

1. Click Start | Administrative Tools | Active Directory Users And Computers. The Active Directory Users And Computers dialog box opens.

2. In the left pane, open the applicable domain and then the Users folder. Click the Action menu and click New | User.

3. In the New Object – User dialog box, enter the user's name and username, as you can see here, and then click Next.

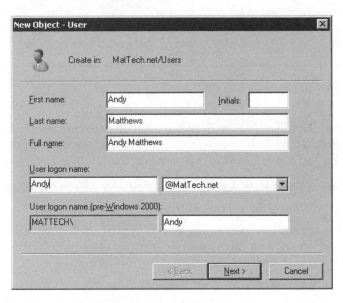

4. Enter and confirm the password, choose how you want the user to change the password, and then click Next.

5. Review your choices, use Back if you need to make any changes, and click Finish when the account is the way you want it.

By establishing this one user account in Active Directory, with the appropriate policies, the user can sign on anywhere on the network, which may extend over the Internet, and be authenticated.

Kerberos Authentication

Kerberos Version 5 is the default authentication protocol in Windows Server 2008, and Kerberos, in several versions, is the default authentication protocol over much of the Internet. This means that the same authentication routines in Windows Server 2008 can validate both a local Windows Server 2008 client and an Internet-connected UNIX client. Kerberos was originally developed by MIT for Internet authentication (http://web.mit .edu/kerberos/www/). The specification for Kerberos Version 5 is maintained by the Internet Engineering Task Force (IETF) and, along with an overview, is contained in Request for Comment 1510 (see Chapter 5 for a discussion of RFCs), which is available online at http://www.ietf.org/rfc/rfc1510.txt.

In addition to commonality with the Internet and numerous systems, Kerberos provides another major benefit to Windows Server 2008 users. In other authentication schemes, each time a user attempts to access a different network service, that service has to go to the authentication server to confirm the authenticity of the user. This doesn't mean the user has to log on again, but each service has to get its own confirmation, creating a fair amount of network traffic. That is not the case with Kerberos, which provides each user with an encrypted *ticket* with the user ID and password that network devices can use both for identity and for validity. The Kerberos ticket system also validates the network service to the user, providing mutual authentication between user and service.

NOTE The Kerberos ticket is also referred to as a service ticket or as a user ticket. They are all the same object.

Kerberos uses a Key Distribution Center (KDC) on each domain controller that stores the user accounts that have been entered into the network's Active Directory. When a user attempts to log on and use any part of the network, the following process takes place:

1. The username and password are encrypted and sent to the KDC.
2. The KDC validates the username/password combination.
3. A ticket is constructed containing the encrypted username and password plus an encryption key that can be used to transfer information between the user and any network service.
4. The ticket is returned to the user's point of logging on, where it is presented to the network service, thereby proving the authenticity of the user.
5. The ability of the service to accept and utilize the ticket proves the authenticity of the service to the user.
6. Any information transferred between the user and the service is done using the encryption key in the ticket.
7. If, while still logged onto the first network service, the user reaches out to another network service, the ticket is automatically presented to the second service, providing immediate mutual authentication and the ability to securely transfer information.

You can see in the preceding steps another major benefit to Kerberos: the inclusion of an encryption key in the ticket that allows the user and a network service to securely transfer information. This automatically solves another of the security demands, securing data transmission.

Kerberos is a very powerful means for authentication and a major asset to Windows Server 2008.

Replacements for Passwords

The weakest link in the Windows Server 2008 security scheme is probably the use of passwords. Users give their passwords to others or forget them, and passwords are stolen or just "found" in many different ways. There is nothing to tie a password to an individual. With someone's password in hand, nothing can stop you from impersonating that person on a password-protected system. Two potential replacements for passwords are smart cards and biometric devices.

Smart Cards   Smart cards are credit card–sized pieces of plastic that have a tamper-resistant electronic circuit embedded in them that permanently stores an ID, a password, a digital signature, an encryption key, or any combination of those. Smart cards require a personal identification number (PIN), so they add a second layer (smart card plus PIN in place of a password) that an impersonator would have to obtain to log onto a system. Also, smart cards can be configured to lock up after a few unsuccessful attempts to enter a PIN.

Windows Server 2008 fully supports smart cards and lets them be used to log onto a computer or network or to enable certificate-based authentication for opening documents or performing other tasks. Smart cards require a reader attached to the computer through a USB port, a PCMCIA or just "PC Card" slot, or an ExpressCard slot. With a smart-card reader, users do not have to press CTRL-ALT-DEL. They only need to insert their card, at which point they are prompted for their PIN. With a valid card and PIN, users are authenticated and allowed on the system in the same way as they would be by entering a valid username and password.

A number of smart-card readers are Plug and Play–compliant, and drivers for these devices are either included with Windows Server 2008 or available from the manufacturer. Installing them requires little more than plugging them in. With a smart-card reader installed, set up new accounts (as previously described) and then, for both new and old accounts, open the user's Properties dialog box by double-clicking a user in the Active Directory Users And Computers window (see "Network User Authentication" earlier in this chapter for directions on opening this window). In the user's Properties dialog box, click the Account tab and scroll the Account Options list and check Smart Card Is Required For Interactive Logon (if a smart card is not installed or detected by Windows Server 2008, this option may not be visible).

NOTE   In case you wondered, the PIN is encrypted and placed on the smart card when it is made. The PIN is not stored on the computer or in Active Directory.

Smart cards are particularly valuable for remote entry to a network, and they can be used by a traveling staff member with a laptop, probably using virtual private networking (VPN) over the Internet. Smart cards are also frequently used in the issuance of certificates of authenticity for documents and other objects (see the discussion of certificates later in the chapter under "Secure Data Transmission").

Biometric Devices   Smart cards do provide an added degree of security over passwords, but if someone obtains both the card and the PIN, that person is home free. The only way to be totally sure that the computer is talking to the real person is to require some physical identification of the person. This is the purpose of *biometric devices*, which identify people by physical traits, such as their voice, handprint, fingerprint, face, or eyes. Often, these devices are used with a smart card to replace the PIN. Biometric devices are now moving into the mainstream with some laptops having fingerprint readers built in. While there is nothing built into Windows Server 2008 specifically to handle them, drivers and the implementing technology are readily available. USB plug-in fingerprint scanners and their software can be purchased for less than $50. Other devices can cost several hundred to several thousand dollars for a face scanner. In the next few years, these devices will be everywhere, so, depending on your needs, you may want to keep them in mind.

Certificate Authentication

If you want to bring users into a network over the Internet, but you are concerned that sending usernames and passwords in that public way might compromise them, then you can replace them with a digital certificate. A *digital certificate* (or just "certificate") is issued by a certification authority (CA), who digitally signs it and says that the bearer is who he or she claims to be, or that an object and sender are as represented. There are both private and public CAs. An organization can be its own private CA and issue certificates to its employees, vendors, and/or customers, so that those people can be authenticated when they try to enter the organization's network. Also, a well-trusted public CA, such as VeriSign (http://www.verisign.com/), can issue a certificate to a person, object, organization, or web site. A person or organization receiving the certificate, if they trust the CA, can be reasonably certain that the presenter is as represented. Besides a certificate, most CAs provide the bearer with an encryption key in the certificate, so that secure data transmissions can occur.

To set up certificate authentication, these steps must take place:

1. The user must obtain a certificate.

2. A user account must be established for the user.

3. The certification authority must be listed in the Certificate Trust List.

4. The certificate must be mapped to the user account.

Set Up Active Directory Certificate Services   The user can obtain a certificate in several ways, one of which is through a Windows Server 2008 domain controller with Active Directory Certificate Services (AD CS) installed. AD CS is a role that must be installed in Server Manager. Here are the steps to do that:

1. Click Start | Server Manager and click Roles in the left pane. Click Add Roles to open the Add Roles Wizard dialog box. Click Next.

2. Click Active Directory Certificate Services if it isn't already checked (if it is, AD CS is already installed on this computer and you can jump to the next section). Click Next.

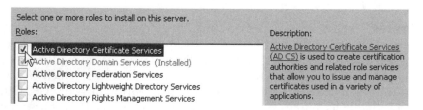

3. Read the notes and any of the Help articles you wish. Note that if you install AD CS, you will not be able to rename the computer, and then click Next.

4. Select the role services you want to use with AD CS:

    ▼ **Certification Authority** to issue and manage certificates and is required in all instances

    ■ **Certification Authority Web Enrollment** to provide a web interface to request and renew certificates

    ■ **Online Responder** to provide certificate information available in complex networks

    ▲ **Network Device Enrollment Service** to issue and manage certificates to routers and other devices without network accounts

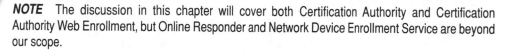

NOTE   The discussion in this chapter will cover both Certification Authority and Certification Authority Web Enrollment, but Online Responder and Network Device Enrollment Service are beyond our scope.

5. Click Next and select the type of certificate authority (CA) to be installed from the following choices:

    ▼ **Enterprise**   If this server is part of a domain, it can use Directory Service to issue and manage certificates.

    ▲ **Standalone**   If this server cannot use Directory Service to issue and manage certificates, it can still be part of a domain.

6. Click Next and select the level of CA for this server:

    ▼ **Root CA** if this is the first or only CA and will issue its own certificates

    ▲ **Subordinate CA** if this CA will get its certificates from a higher CA

7. Click Next and select whether you want to create a new private key or use an existing one.

8. Click Next and select the Cryptographic Service Provider (CSP) that you want to use to generate the private key, the hash algorithm (explained under "Challenge Handshake Authentication Protocol" in Chapter 10), and the key length, as shown in Figure 15-2. Under most circumstances, except if you are using smart cards, you want to leave the defaults. If you are using smart cards, you may need to select a CSP that is used by the smart card.

9. Click Next, accept the default or enter a name and a suffix for the CA, and click Next again. Select the validity period for certificates generated by this CA.

10. Click Next. You are shown where the certificate database and log will be stored. Once more click Next. If IIS is running, click Yes to temporarily stop Internet Information Services (IIS). If the IIS role is not installed, you can choose which role services you want installed (see Chapter 9 for more information on IIS).

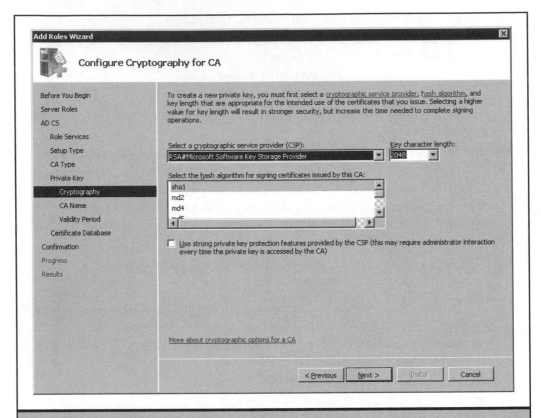

Figure 15-2.   The issuance of certificates requires a private key to sign them and then the private key is used to validate them.

11. Review the selections you have made. If you want to make changes, click Previous. When you are ready, click Install. The role(s) and role services will be installed.

12. Click Close when you are told that you have successfully completed installation. Close Server Manager. Restart the computer (even if you are not prompted).

Review the CA   Once you have installed the certification authority, you can review it with these steps:

1. Click Start | Administrative Tools | Certification Authority. In the left pane, open the new CA you just created and click Issued Certificates. You should see one or more certificates, like this (if you don't see any certificates and you restarted the computer, click Refresh in the Action menu):

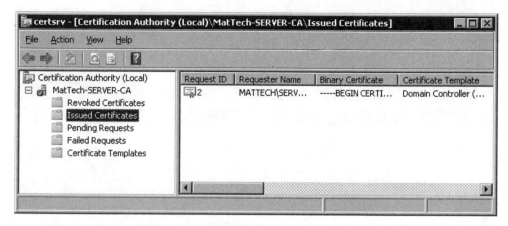

2. Double-click one of the certificates to open it, click the Details tab, and click the various fields to see the details within the open certificate. Click OK when you are done looking at the certificate.

3. Back in the Certification Authority window, click Certificate Templates in the left pane. On the right, you can see the types of certificates that are available and their intended purpose.

4. Double-click one of the templates to open its Properties dialog box. When you are finished looking at the properties, close the dialog box and the Certification Authority window.

Request a Certificate With AD CS installed, users, computers, and other services can request certificates to identify themselves. Normally, certificates are automatically given to computers and users who are known and trusted entities on the network. The certificate that was automatically created when AD CS was installed was issued to the server on which AD CS resides. It is also possible to explicitly request a certificate over either an intranet or the Internet, or on the server with AD CS.

Request a Certificate over a Web Connection Over the Internet or an intranet is the most common way that users request a certificate for their use. In doing this, the user accesses a web page that is created and maintained by AD CS. Use these steps to request a certificate over an intranet or the Internet:

1. Open your browser and enter the URL or address of the server with AD CS. The address should look something like http://*servername*/certsrv/. The page should appear as shown in Figure 15-3.

2. Click Request A Certificate and click User Certificate. If you want the user to have a smart card, click More Options, where you can select a Cryptographic Service Provider (CSP) and the request format.

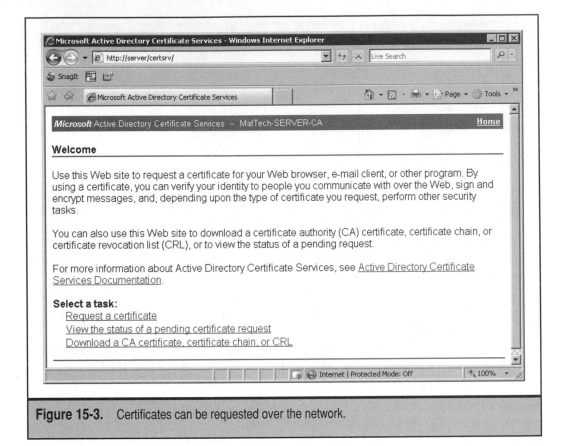

Figure 15-3. Certificates can be requested over the network.

3. Click Submit. You are told that the web site is requesting a new certificate for you and asking if you want to go ahead. Click Yes. If the user and/or computer are already known to the server, a certificate will be issued. Otherwise, you will be told that the request is pending.

4. When you see Certificate Issued, click Install This Certificate. You are told that the web site is adding a certificate to the computer and asked if you are sure you want to do that. Click Yes, given that is what you want to do. You are told that the certificate is installed and you can close your browser.

Directly Request a Certificate Directly requesting a certificate from AD CS is most commonly done for documents or other objects, or for services. It requires the Certificate console in the Microsoft Management Console (MMC). Here is how to set up the Certificate console (assuming that it hasn't been done before) and to request a certificate from it:

1. Click Start | Run, type **mmc**, and click OK. The MMC shell opens.

2. Click the File menu and click Add/Remove Snap-in. In the Add Or Remove Snap-ins dialog box, click Certificates, click Add, click My User Account for where you want to manage certificates, and click Finish.

NOTE If you choose to manage certificates for My User Account, the snap-in you create will create certificates only for you. If you choose to manage certificates for Service Account or Computer Account, you must pick a service or computer to manage, such as the web server or the local computer, and you will be able to issue certificates for the service or computer.

3. Click OK to complete the Add/Remove Snap-in process. In the console on the left, open Certificates – Current User | Personal | Certificates, as shown here:

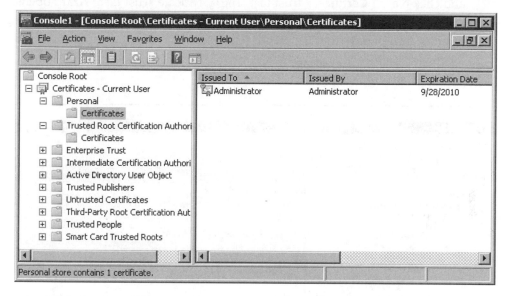

4. Click the Action menu and click All Tasks | Request New Certificate With New Key. The Certificate Enrollment wizard opens.

5. Click Next, choose a certificate type to support the purpose of the certificate you want to issue (select Administrator for at least one certificate), and click Enroll again.

6. When you are told the certificate has been enrolled, click Finish. A new certificate will be issued.

7. Close the Certificates console, click Yes to save the settings for this new console in a file named Certificates.msc, click Save, and finally close the MMC.

List Certificate Authorities To accept certificates that are presented to the network, the CA must be known to the network. This is accomplished by being listed as a trusted CA in the Certificate Trust List (CTL), which is maintained as part of the group policy.

The following steps show you how to open the group policy, which was discussed in Chapter 14, create a CTL, and make an entry into it (these steps assume that you want to work with the CTL at the domain level, but you could also do it at the local computer level and at the OU level):

1. Click Start | Server Manager and open Features | Group Policy Management | Forest | Domains | *domain name* | Group Policy Objects, as shown in Figure 15-4.

2. Right-click Default Domain Policy and click Edit. The Group Policy Management Editor window opens.

3. In the left pane, open Computer Configuration | Windows Settings | Security Settings | Public Key Policies, and click Enterprise Trust. Click the Action menu and click New | Certificate Trust List. The Certificate Trust List Wizard opens.

4. Click Next. If you so choose, enter an identifying prefix for the CTL, enter the months and/or days that it is valid, select the purposes of the CTL, and click Next.

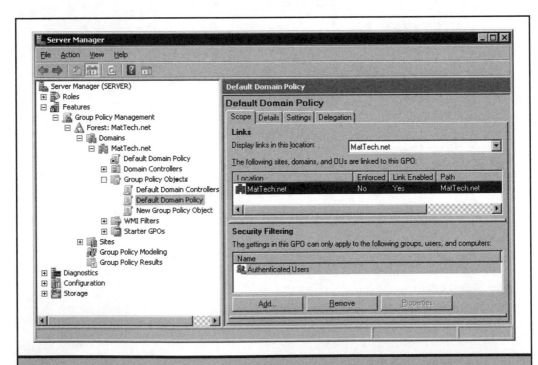

Figure 15-4. A certificate trust list can be maintained in a group policy object (GPO).

5. In the Certificates In The CTL dialog box, click Add From Store. The Select Certificate dialog box opens, in which you can select those certificates whose issuers you want to include in the CTL. Early in the list, you will find the certificates that your new CA issued as you followed the steps earlier in this chapter.

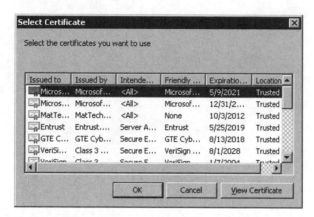

6. Double-click one of the certificates you created. When it opens, you may find that it is not trusted, even though it was created on the same computer. You are told that it must be added to the CTL to be trusted.

7. Select the certificates whose issuers you want on the CTL, holding down CTRL while selecting more than one certificate. Click OK. The new list of certificates will appear in the Certificate Trust List Wizard.

8. Click Next. You must attach a certificate, probably your own, for the purpose of a digital signature for the CTL, and the encryption key used with the signature certificate will be used with the file that contains the CTL.

NOTE   The certificate that you select for the purpose of adding the digital signature to the CTL must be created for the current user with the Administrator template, similar to the Signature certificate you created previously in "Request a Certificate."

9. Click Select From Store, select the certificate you want to use, click OK, and then click Next. If you wish, you can add a timestamp; then click Next again.

10. Enter a name that is easy to remember and a description for this CTL and click Next. Review the settings you have chosen and click Back if you need to correct something; when ready, click Finish. You will be told whether the CTL was successfully created.

11. Click OK. The new CTL appears on the right of the Group Policy Management Editor window. Double-click it. The CTL opens, and in the Trust List tab, you see a list of the certificate authorities that you have added to your CTL.

12. Click a CA. You can see some of the details behind a certificate, as shown next, and if you click View Certificate, you can see the entire certificate. Close the CTL and the Group Policy Management Editor.

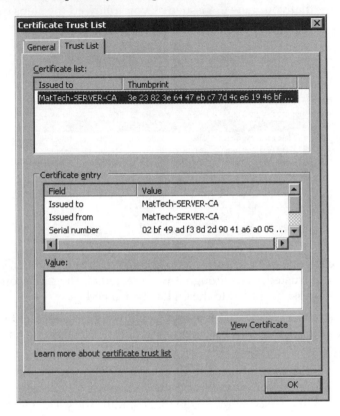

Map Certificates to User Accounts   The core of Windows Server 2008's user-oriented security are user accounts with a username and password to log on, which are the basis for the permission system that controls access to computer and network resources. Someone who comes into Windows Server 2008 with a certificate but without a username and password for a user account and the permissions that go with it cannot log on. The solution is to map or relate a certificate to a user account, so that someone who presents an acceptable certificate will be attached to a user account and given the permissions he or she would acquire by logging on with a username and password. Windows Server 2008 does certificate mapping in two ways: through Active Directory Domain Services and through Internet Information Services (IIS). Also, mapping can be done from one certificate to one user account (one-to-one mapping) or from several certificates to one account (many-to-one mapping). Mapping through IIS was discussed in Chapter 9.

Certificate mapping through Active Directory Domain Services can be done with the following steps:

1. Click Start | Administrative Tools | Active Directory Users And Computers.

2. Click the View menu and click Advanced Features (if it is not already checked).

3. In the left pane, open the domain with the user account to which you want to map, and then click Users.

4. In the list of users on the right, select the user account to which a certificate will be mapped.

5. Click the Action menu, click Name Mappings (if you don't see it, redo Step 2) to open the Security Identity Mapping dialog box, click the X.509 Certificates tab, and click Add to open the Add Certificate dialog box.

6. Search for and identify, or type, the path and name of the certificate that you want to use, and then click Open. Often the certificates, which have the extension .cer, are in the C:\Windows\System32\Certsrv folder.

7. If you don't find a CER file, you may need to export one from the MMC Certificates console. To do so, click Start | Run, type **mmc**, and press ENTER. Then click the File menu, click Open, select the Certificates.msc file, click Open, open Console Root | Certificates – Current User | Personal | Certificates, and select the certificate to use.

8. Click the Action menu; click All Tasks | Export; click Next; click No, Do Not Export The Private Key; click Next; accept the default DER Encoded Binary format; click Next; enter a useful filename; browse to where you want it stored; click Next; click Finish; and click OK when told that the export was successful. Close the Certificates console.

9. Double-click the certificate you will use, and it is displayed in a second Add Certificate dialog box.

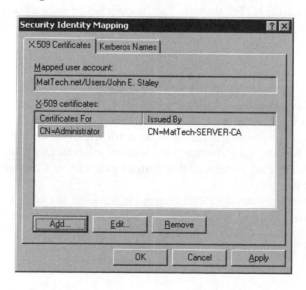

10. If you want one-to-one mapping, both Use Issuer For Alternate Security Identity and Use Subject For Alternate Security Identity should be checked (Use Issuer For Alternate Security Identity is always checked by default and is grayed in most instances, so you can't change it). If you want many-to-one mapping only, Use Issuer For Alternate Security Identity should be checked.

11. Click OK. The certificate is displayed again in the Security Identity Mapping dialog box; click OK again. Close the Active Directory Users And Computers window.

Now, when a user presents this certificate, she or he will be mapped to the related user account and given the permissions that are associated with it.

CONTROL ACCESS

User accounts identify people and allow them to log onto a computer and possibly to a network. What they can then do depends both on the permissions given to them or given to groups to which they belong, and on the ownership of the object they want to use. Windows Server 2008, when using the New Technology File System (NTFS), allows an administrator to assign various levels of permission to use an object (a file, a folder, a disk drive, a printer), as well as to assign ownership and the rights of ownership. (You cannot do this with the FAT or FAT32 file system.)

When you initially install Windows Server 2008, most files, folders, disk drives, and printers withhold permission from most users except for administrators to do most tasks with these objects. You can change the default permission rather quickly by using a property called *inheritance* that says all files, subfolders, and files in subfolders automatically inherit (take on) the permissions of their parent folder. Every file, folder, and other object in Windows Server 2008 NTFS, though, has its own set of *security descriptors* that are attached to it when it is created, and with the proper permission, these security descriptors can be individually changed.

Ownership

Initially, all permissions are granted by the creator of an object or by an administrator. The creator of an object is called its *owner*. The owner of an object has the right to grant and deny permission, as well as the right to grant the Take Ownership permission to others, allowing them to take ownership. An administrator can take over ownership from someone else, but an administrator cannot grant others ownership to objects the administrator did not create.

You can check the ownership and change it through the object's Properties dialog box. For a file or folder, open the Properties dialog box through Windows Explorer and see how you would change the ownership with these steps:

1. Click Start | Computer. In the pane on the left, drag Folders to the top of the pane; open the disk and folders necessary to see in the right pane the folder or file that you want to look at or change the ownership for.

2. In the right pane, right-click the subject folder or file and click Properties.

3. In the Properties dialog box, click the Security tab and then click Advanced. The Advanced Security Settings dialog box opens.

4. Click the Owner tab, in which you can see who the current owner is and the people to whom the ownership can be transferred. When you are finished, click OK twice to close the two dialog boxes still open. Also close the Windows Explorer.

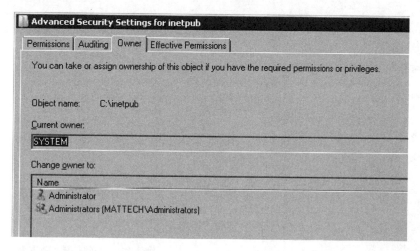

Giving permission to take ownership is described in "Permissions" later in this chapter.

Groups

Groups, or *group accounts*, are collections of user accounts and can have permissions assigned to them just like user accounts. Most permissions are granted to groups, not individuals, and then individuals are made members of the groups. It is therefore important that you have a set of groups that handles both the mix of people in your organization and the mix of permissions that you want to establish. A number of standard groups with preassigned permissions are built into Windows Server 2008, but you can create your own groups, and you can assign users to any of these.

Look at the groups that are a standard part of Windows Server 2008 and see what permissions they contain, and then create your own if you need to. As with user accounts, you look at groups differently depending on whether you are on a stand-alone server or on an Active Directory domain controller.

Groups in Stand-Alone Servers and Workstations

To view and add groups in stand-alone servers or workstations, you need to use the Computer Management window, as follows:

1. Click Start | Administrative Tools | Computer Management.

2. In the left pane, open System Tools | Local Users And Groups, and double-click Groups. The list of built-in groups will be displayed, like this:

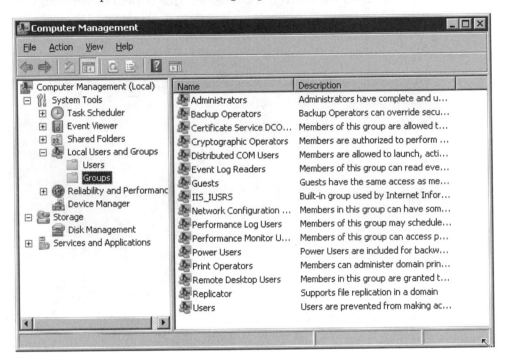

3. Double-click a few groups to open their respective Properties dialog boxes, in which you can see the members of each group.

4. Click the Action menu and click New Group. The New Group dialog box opens.

5. Enter a group name of up to 256 upper- or lowercase characters. It cannot contain just periods or just spaces; it can't contain " / \ [ ] : ; | = , + * ? < > @; and leading spaces or periods are dropped. Enter the description of what the group can uniquely do, and click Add. The Select Users dialog box opens.

6. Click Advanced, enter a username and password if asked, click Find Now, hold down CTRL, and select the users that you want to include in the group. Click OK. When you have selected all you want to include, click OK. Your new group should look similar to this:

7. When your group is the way you want it, click Create and then click Close. The new group will appear in the list on the right of the Computer Management window. Close that window when you are ready.

Groups in Active Directory Domain Controllers

To view and add groups in an Active Directory domain controller, you need to use the Active Directory Users And Computers window. Within that window, you will find two sets of groups: those in the Builtin folder, which are similar to what you saw in the stand-alone server, and those in the Users folders, which are created by Active Directory. The Builtin groups are limited to the local domain (called a *domain local scope*), while the Users groups can be either domain-limited or not limited (called a *global scope*). Look at both sets of groups and add a new group to Users with the following steps:

1. Click Start | Administrative Tools | Active Directory Users And Computers. The Active Directory Users And Computers window opens.

2. In the left pane, open the domain in which you want to work, and then open the Builtin folder. You will see a list of groups that has many of the same groups that you saw on the stand-alone server.

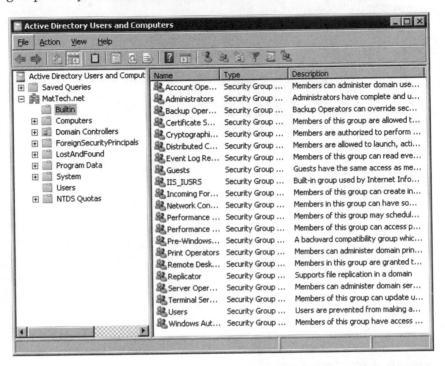

3. Click Users in the left pane. You will see a mixture of users and groups, but a different set of groups that are supporting Active Directory and network operations.

4. Click the View menu and click Filter Options. Click Show Only The Following Types Of Objects, click Groups, as shown next, and click OK. Once again, open the Users folder, and your Active Directory Users And Computers window should look similar to Figure 15-5.

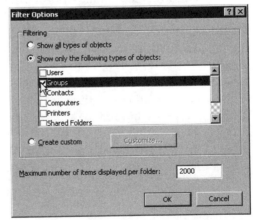

5. Double-click several of the groups to open them. They contain substantially more information than the groups on the stand-alone servers and workstations.

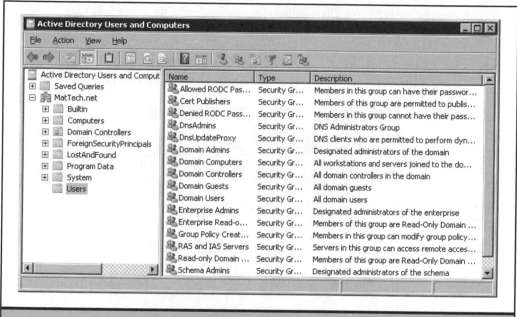

Figure 15-5.   Active Directory provides a number of standard groups that can be used.

6. While Users is still selected in the left pane, click the Action menu and click New | Group. The New Object – Group dialog box opens.

7. Enter a Group name of up to 256 characters. It cannot contain just periods or just spaces, and leading spaces or periods are dropped. Notice that the pre–Windows 2000 name is automatically filled in for you. Only the first 20 characters of this name will be used, so if you want, you can enter your own short group name in this field.

8. Choose the group scope. Here are the scope choices:

   ▼ **Domain Local**   Can contain users and global or universal groups from any Windows Server 2008 or Windows NT domain, but their permissions are limited to the current domain

   ■ **Global**   Can contain users and global groups only from the current domain, but they can be given permissions in any domain

   ▲ **Universal**   Can contain users and global or universal groups from any Windows Server 2008 domain, and they can be given permission in any domain, but they are limited to distribution groups

9. Choose a group type. Distribution groups are used for e-mail and fax distribution, whereas security groups are used to assign permission. Click OK when you are done.

10. Right-click your new group and click Properties. The Properties dialog box opens. Enter a description and e-mail address, as shown here:

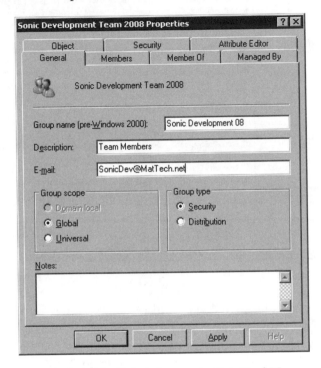

11. Click Members, click Add, click Advanced, click Find Now, and then hold CTRL and select the user accounts that you want included in the group. When you are done, click OK twice. Look at the other tabs and make any necessary changes. The Security tab is discussed in the next section.

12. When you have completed the group the way you want it, click OK, and close Active Directory Users And Computers.

Permissions

Permissions authorize a user or a group to perform some function on an object. Objects, such as files, folders, disks, and printers, have a set of permissions associated with them that can be assigned to users and groups. The specific permissions depend on the object, but all objects have at least two permissions: Read, and either Modify or Change. Permissions are initially set in one of three ways:

▼ The application or process that creates an object can set its permissions upon creation.

- If the object allows the inheritance of permissions and they were not set upon creation, a parent object can propagate permissions to the object. For example, a parent folder can propagate its permissions to a subfolder it contains.

▲ If neither the creator nor the parent sets the permissions for an object, then the Windows Server 2008 system defaults will do it.

Once an object is created, its permissions can be changed by its owner, by an administrator, and by anybody else who has been given the permission to change permissions. The following sections look at the default permissions for three commonly used objects—folders, shares, and files—and at how those defaults are changed.

Folder Permissions

Folder permissions are set in the Security tab of the folder's Properties dialog box, shown in Figure 15-6. You can click this tab and change the permissions with these steps:

1. Click Start | Computer. Windows Explorer opens.

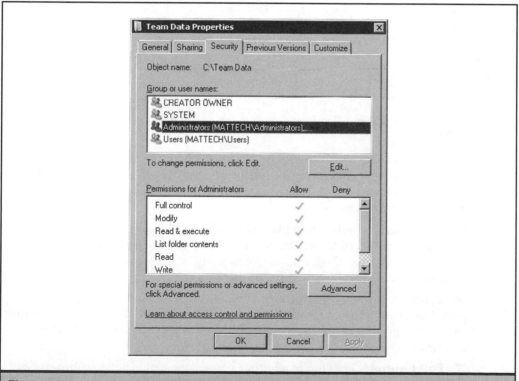

Figure 15-6. A set of default permissions is automatically set for each object in Windows Server 2008.

2. In the Folders pane on the left, open the boot drive, right-click in a blank area of the right pane, and click New | Folder. Type a name for the new folder and press ENTER.

3. Right-click the new folder and click Properties. In the Properties dialog box, click the Security tab. You should see a dialog box similar to Figure 15-6.

You can see that with a default installation of Windows Server 2008, four groups are available to be given permissions. Two of these groups are domain groups (Administrators and Users groups), and two are system groups, one for internal operating system (OS) functions (System group), and one representing the owner or creator of the object. If you click each group and look at its permissions, you can see that Administrators and System have permission for everything, Users have limited permissions, and the Creator Owner has no permissions. All of the permissions that are shown here are grayed, meaning that they are inherited from a parent object (the root folder in this case) and have not been set specifically for this object.

NOTE   The default permissions in Windows Server 2003 and 2008 are substantially different than those in Windows 2000 and earlier versions of Windows NT, where the Everyone group had full permission to do everything in all but a few of the OS folders. Windows Server 2003 and 2008 start out with the opposite philosophy, where only Administrators have permission to do everything, and Users (everyone else) have limited permission. This is an intentional tightening of security on the part of Microsoft.

Add New Permissions

To add new permissions:

1. Click Edit in the middle of the Security tab to open the Permissions dialog box. Click Add.

2. In the Select Users, Computers, Or Groups dialog box, click Advanced, click Find Now, double-click a single user, group, and/or computer to whom you want to grant permission, or hold CTRL while clicking several objects and then click OK. Click OK once more.

   If you selected the new group that you created earlier in the Groups section to be added here, as I did, you will see that group automatically picked up the same permissions as those for the Users group because the new group you created is automatically a member of that group.

3. Select one of the new users, groups, or computers that will be given permissions, and then click Allow for the permissions that you want that entity to have, or click Deny to specifically exclude a permission. The tasks that can be performed with each permission are as follows:

   ▼ **Full Control**   The sum of all other permissions, plus delete subfolders, change permissions, and take ownership.

   ■ **Modify**   The sum of the Read & Execute and the Write permissions, plus the delete folder permission.

- **Read & Execute** The same as List Folder Contents, but inherited by both folders and files.

- **List Folder Contents** Read permission, plus view the list of subfolders and files in a folder, as well as execute files, and move through folders to reach other files and folders, where the user may not have permission to access the intervening folders (inherited only by folders).

- **Read** View the contents of subfolders and files in the folder, as well as view the folder's attributes (Archive, Hidden, Read-Only), ownership, and permissions.

- **Write** Make subfolders and files inside the folder, plus view the ownership and permissions for the folder and change its attributes.

- ▲ **Special Permissions** Detail permissions that are contained in the other six permissions.

4. After selecting the permissions that you want to use, click OK and then click Advanced. The Advanced Security Settings dialog box opens, as shown in Figure 15-7. Notice that the majority of the permissions are inherited and

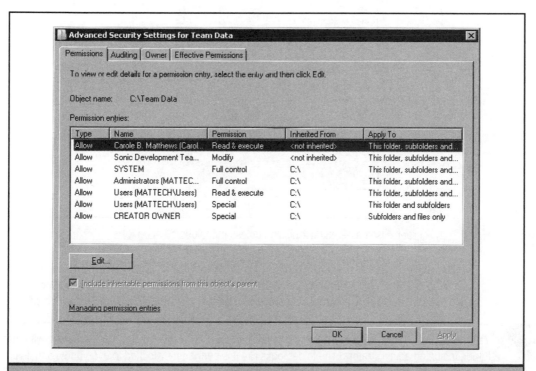

Figure 15-7. Detail permissions behind folder permissions can be viewed in the Advanced Security Settings dialog box.

that the Creator Owner here is shown as having Special permission. This seeming inconsistency is due to the original parent permission being applied to subfolders and files only.

5. Select a user or group and click Edit twice. The Permission Entry dialog box appears, as shown next. This contains a more detailed level of permissions, called Special Permissions, which are contained within the primary permissions described in Step 3. The Special Permissions that are granted by each primary permission are shown in Table 15-1.

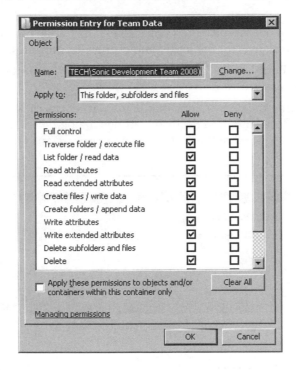

 NOTE   Synchronize isn't a default permission unless the folder is set up for it.

6. Make any changes that you want to the detail permissions, check the check box at the bottom if you want the permission to be propagated to the subfolders and files of this folder, and click OK four times to close all open dialog boxes.

 TIP   Denying everyone the Full Control permission prevents anybody from doing anything with the folder, including administrators. The folder looks like it is permanently locked to everybody, and if you try to delete it, for example, you will be denied access. An administrator, though, can still go in and change the permissions to something more reasonable and then the folder can be deleted.

Special Permission		Primary Permission				
	Read	Write	List Folder Contents	Read & Execute	Modify	Full Control
Transverse Folder/ Execute File			Yes	Yes	Yes	Yes
List Folder/Read Data	Yes		Yes	Yes	Yes	Yes
Read Attributes	Yes		Yes	Yes	Yes	Yes
Read Extended Attributes	Yes		Yes	Yes	Yes	Yes
Create Files/Write Data		Yes			Yes	Yes
Create Folders/ Append Data		Yes			Yes	Yes
Write Attributes		Yes			Yes	Yes
Write Extended Attributes		Yes			Yes	Yes
Delete Subfolders and Files						Yes
Delete					Yes	Yes
Read Permissions	Yes	Yes	Yes	Yes	Yes	Yes
Change Permissions						Yes
Take Ownership						Yes
Synchronize	Yes	Yes	Yes	Yes	Yes	Yes

Table 15-1. Special Permissions Granted by Primary Permissions for Folders

Share Permission

Shares are shared folders, and for those who do not own or administer the folders, a slightly different set of permissions exists. As with regular folders, shared folder permissions are set in the Security tab of the folder's Properties dialog box. The first three of the standard groups look the same, but Users now have more permissions, although they are still limited and cannot add or change the permissions. An administrator can open this dialog box and change the permissions in the same way as he or she could with unshared folders.

File Permissions

File permissions are set in the Security tab of the file's Properties dialog box, shown next. As you can see, it is very similar to folder permissions except they are limited to files. This means that the List Folder Contents permission is no longer available, and definitions of the individual permissions change slightly.

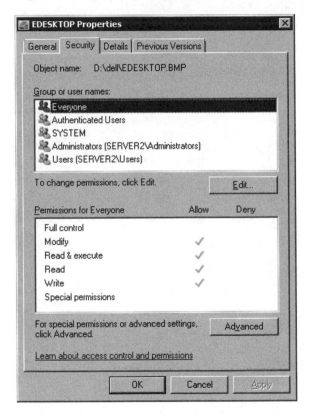

▼ **Full Control**   The sum of all other permissions, plus change permissions and take ownership.

■ **Modify**   The sum of the Read & Execute and the Write permissions, plus delete and modify the file.

■ **Read & Execute**   The Read permissions, plus execute applications.

■ **Read**   View the contents of the file as well as view its attributes (Archive, Hidden, Read-Only), permissions, and ownership.

■ **Write**   Write to the file, plus view the file's permissions and ownership, and change its attributes.

▲ **Special Permissions**   Unique permissions that have been set for named users or groups as described in the Advanced Security Settings dialog box.

SECURE STORED DATA

User authentication puts a lock on the outside doors of the computer, and controlling access puts locks on the inside doors, but if someone breaks through or gets around those barriers, the data inside is available to anyone who wants it. For example, someone may take a disk drive and access it with another operating system, or steal a laptop and methodically break through the passwords. Or, much simpler and more common, an employee either purposefully gets or mistakenly is given access to data that employee should not have and decides to misuse it.

The answer to all of these scenarios is to make the data itself unusable without a key. This is done by encrypting a file, a folder, or the whole disk so that no matter how it is accessed, by another operating system or a low-level utility, it is encrypted and cannot be read without the key, and the key is itself encrypted so that it is exceptionally difficult to obtain and use.

File and Folder Encryption

File and folder encryption has been built into Windows Server 2008 NTFS and is called the *Encrypting File System (EFS)*. Once EFS is turned on for a file or a folder, only the person who encrypted the file or folder will be able to read it, with the exception that a specially appointed administrator will have a recovery key to access the file or folder. For the person who encrypted the file, accessing it requires no additional steps, and the file is re-encrypted every time it is saved. All of the encrypting and decrypting is done behind the scenes and is not obvious to the user.

NOTE   Neither system files or folders, nor compressed files or folders can be encrypted. You can decompress a compressed file or folder and then encrypt it.

The Encryption Process

The actual encryption of a file or folder is done with a *symmetric encryption key,* which is the same for both encryption and decryption and is very fast. The symmetric encryption key (also called a *secret key*) is itself encrypted using the file owner's public key that is contained in his or her EFS certificate. (See "Understand Private/Public Key Encryption," later in this chapter.) Therefore, the owner with her or his private key matching the public key is the only one who can open the encrypted file—except for the recovery administrator. When the file is created or re-created and a symmetric key is made, the key is actually encrypted twice, once for the owner and once for the recovery administrator. Then if the need arises, the recovery administrator can use his or her private key to decrypt the file.

The encrypted symmetric key is stored as a part of the file. When an application requests the file, NTFS goes and gets it, sees that the file is encrypted, and calls EFS. EFS works with the security protocols to authenticate the user, use his or her private key to decrypt the file, and pass an unencrypted file to the calling application, all in the background, without any outward sign that it is taking place. The encryption and decryption routines are so fast that on most computers that can run Windows Server 2008, you seldom notice the added time.

TIP Because many applications save temporary and secondary files during normal execution, it is recommended that folders rather than files be the encrypting container. If an application is then told to store all files in that folder where all files are automatically encrypted upon saving, security is improved.

Encryption Considerations

Several requirements must be met to use file and folder encryption:

▼ Windows 2000 or later NTFS must be in use. Any other file system, whether Windows NT 4 NTFS or FAT, will not work with EFS.

■ AD CS should be installed and running either on a stand-alone computer or within a domain. If AD CS is not running, EFS will issue its own certificates, but these are considered "not trusted" by Windows Server 2008.

■ The user of the file or folder must have an EFS certificate. If one does not exist, it is automatically created.

▲ There must be one or more certificated recovery agent administrators. If one does not exist, a default administrator is automatically appointed and a certificate is issued. The default administrator on a stand-alone computer is the local administrator, while in a domain, it is the domain administrator on the first domain controller that is installed.

Recovery Agent Administrators The reason for requiring a recovery agent administrator is shown by the situation in which someone leaves an organization, maybe through an accident, and his or her encrypted files are needed. Another situation is one in which a disgruntled employee encrypts shared files before leaving the organization. EFS is disabled without a recovery agent, so that files cannot be encrypted without a means to decrypt them. Several recovery agents may be assigned to an EFS file or folder, but there must be at least one. For each recovery agent, as well as the user, a copy of the symmetric encrypting key encrypted with the person's public key is stored with the encrypted file. Whoever decrypts the file reveals only the data and not any of the other keys.

Copy and Move EFS Files
Copying and moving EFS files and folders has special significance. Here are the rules:

▼ If you copy or move an unencrypted file or folder to an encrypted folder, the item copied will be encrypted.

■ Copying or moving encrypted files or folders to another file system, such as Windows NT 4 NTFS or Windows 98 FAT32, removes the encryption, although only the owner or recovery agent can do this. Everyone else will be denied access.

▲ Backing up encrypted files or folders with Windows Server 2008 Backup leaves the items encrypted.

TIP When you back up encrypted data, make sure that both the user and the recovery agent keys are also backed up, which can be done with AD CS.

Use File and Folder Encryption

The actual process of encrypting a file or folder is very easy; you simply turn on the Encrypted attribute. Given that there is a certificated recovery agent administrator and that the user turning on the encryption has an EFS certificate, there is very little else to do. Look at the full process, including the certification, in the next sections.

Create EFS Certificates

Earlier in this chapter, under "Certificate Authentication," there is a discussion of setting up AD CS and requesting a certificate. The following steps show specifically how to request an EFS Recovery Agent certificate:

1. While logged on as the administrator who will be the recovery agent, open the MMC by opening the Start menu, clicking Run, typing **mmc**, and clicking OK.

2. In the Console, click the File menu, click Open, and double-click your Certificates console. In the left pane, open Console Root | Certificates – Current User | Personal | Certificates.

3. Click the Action menu and click All Tasks | Request New Certificate. The Certificate Enrollment wizard opens. Click Next.

4. Select EFS Recovery Agent as the certificate template as shown next, click Enroll, and click Finish.

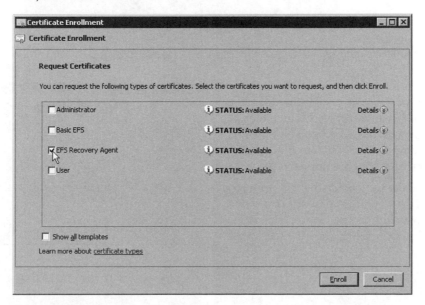

5. Close the MMC.

Encrypt a File and a Folder

Encryption of either files or folders can be done from Windows Explorer or from the command prompt.

NOTE The encrypted files and folders are displayed in green in Windows Explorer.

Encrypt a File from Windows Explorer Here are the steps to encrypt a file from Windows Explorer:

1. Click Start | Computer. In the folders tree on the left, open the drive and folders necessary to display on the right the file you want to encrypt.

2. Right-click the file and click Properties. In the General tab, click Advanced. The Advanced Attributes dialog box opens.

3. Click Encrypt Contents To Secure Data.

4. Click OK twice. You get an Encryption Warning that the file is not in an encrypted folder, which means that when you edit the file, temporary or backup files might be created that are not encrypted.

5. Make the choice that is correct for you. If you don't want to see this warning in the future, click Always Encrypt Only The File. Click OK.

TIP   To unencrypt a file or a folder, simply follow the same steps used to encrypt it and remove the check mark in front of Encrypt Contents To Secure Data. You, of course, must be either the person who originally encrypted the file or folder, or a recovery agent.

Encrypt a Folder from Windows Explorer   Encrypting a folder from Windows Explorer is very similar, as you can see in these steps:

1. Open Windows Explorer and display in the right pane the folder you want to encrypt.

2. Right-click the folder and click Properties. In the General tab, click Advanced. The Advanced Attributes dialog box opens.

3. Click Encrypt Contents To Secure Data and click OK twice. The Confirm Attribute Changes dialog box opens.

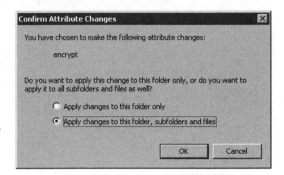

4. You are asked whether you want to apply the encryption to this folder only or to the folder, its files, and its subfolders. If you choose This Folder Only, *existing* files and folders in the folder being encrypted will *not* be encrypted, while files and folders created or copied to the encrypted folder after the fact will be encrypted. If you choose This Folder, Subfolders And Files, existing files and folders, as well as those created or copied in the future, will be encrypted.

5. Choose the settings that are correct for you and click OK.

CAUTION   If you choose Apply Changes To This Folder, Subfolders And Files for a shared folder that has files or subfolders belonging to others, you will encrypt those files and subfolders with your key, and the owners will not be able to use their property.

Test File Encryption

So what happens when someone tries to access an encrypted file? Try it yourself. Log off and log back on as a different user and then try to open the file. It looks as if it's going to open, and then a little message appears:

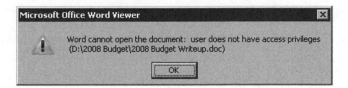

The actual message varies depending on the application you are using to try to open the file. If access is appropriate, the recovery agent administrator can solve the problem.

Okay, what about copying the file to a non–Windows Server 2008 NTFS file system, such as a Windows 98 FAT32 machine on the network? The file is no longer encrypted when you do that, correct? Again try it, first while logged on as the one who encrypted the file. Everything will work as it is supposed to—the file will be copied and will no longer be encrypted. Then log off and log back on again as someone else and try copying the file. Once more it looks as if it's going to work, and then another little message appears:

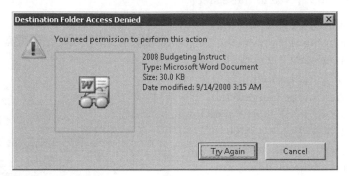

Drive Encryption with BitLocker

Windows Vista and Windows Server 2008 have a new feature called BitLocker Drive Encryption. BitLocker encrypts the entire drive or volume on which Windows is installed (and on Windows Server 2008 additional volumes or drives can also be encrypted), so if the computer is stolen, lost, or the drive taken from the computer, information on that drive would be protected. BitLocker requires that a USB device, such as a flash drive, be inserted that contains a key used to start the computer or resume from hibernation (we'll call this a "USB key"). If the computer has a Trusted Platform Module (TPM) version 1.2, a hardware component, BitLocker will additionally verify the integrity of the system when it starts, make the use of the USB key optional, and allow the use of a personal identification number (PIN) as another alternative. If BitLocker with TPM finds that the system integrity has been compromised beginning with the initial boot files, or that the drive is no longer in the original computer, the system will lock down and not start. At that point a BitLocker recovery process can be started. BitLocker therefore has four authentication modes:

▼ BitLocker by itself requiring a USB key

■ BitLocker with TPM and no authentication component

■ BitLocker with TPM and a USB key

▲ BitLocker with TPM and a PIN

BitLocker is all but transparent to use; other than plugging in the USB key or entering a PIN, there is no evidence BitLocker is in use. Should BitLocker lock down the system whether due to a security breach or a hardware failure, the recovery process is easily implemented by someone with the appropriate recovery key, generally on a USB device, or with a recovery password.

BitLocker Installation

On Windows Server 2008, BitLocker is not installed and must be installed as a feature from Server Manager.

1.   Click Start | Server Manager. Click Features in the left pane and click Add Features in the right pane. The Add Features Wizard will open.

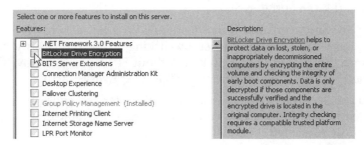

2.   Click BitLocker Drive Encryption, click Next, and then click Install.

3.   Click Close and click Yes to restart the computer. Upon restarting, the installation will resume. When you are told that installation was successful, click Close.

BitLocker Setup and Control

BitLocker is set up and controlled through the BitLocker control panel. If the computer you are setting up does not have TPM, you need to first change a group policy to allow using a USB key in place of TPM. If you think you have TPM (you will be told very quickly if you don't), you can skip the first three steps in the following series.

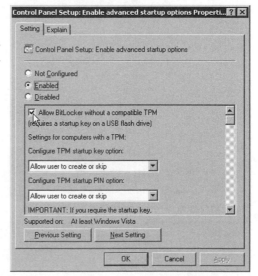

1.   If you are going to use a USB key for the key, insert it. Then click Start | Run, type **gpedit.msc**, and press ENTER to open the Local Group Policy Editor.

2.   In the left pane, open Computer Configuration | Administrative Templates | Windows Components | BitLocker Drive Encryption. In the right pane, double-click Control Panel Setup: Enable Advanced Startup Options to open the dialog box of that name.

3.   Click Enabled and assure that there is a check mark beside Allow BitLocker Without A Compatible TPM. Click it if it isn't checked, click OK, and close the Local Group Policy Editor.

4. Click Start | Control Panel and double-click BitLocker Drive Encryption.

BitLocker Drive Encryption

5. In the BitLocker Drive Encryption window that opens, click Turn On BitLocker under the System drive, as shown in Figure 15-8. You are asked if you really want to use BitLocker Drive Encryption on a server since it reduces performance and is only needed if the server is in an unsecured location (like an outlying office).

6. If you do want to go ahead, click Continue With BitLocker Drive Encryption. If you have TPM, you can choose, by clicking, to use BitLocker without a key, require a PIN, or require a USB key. Without TPM, you only have the choice of, and need to click, Require Startup USB Key At Every Startup.

7. If you choose to use a PIN, you are asked to enter and confirm your PIN. If you choose to use a USB key and you have several removable drives, click the drive from those presented. In either case, click Save.

8. You are asked where you want to store the recovery password and told that it is recommended that the password be stored in several places. I recommend

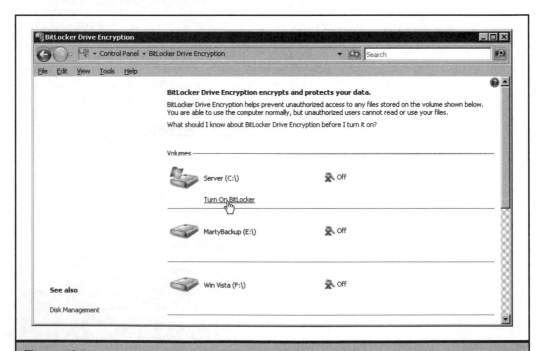

Figure 15-8. You must first enable BitLocker on the System drive, after which you can encrypt the remaining drives on the server.

that at a minimum you store it on a USB key and on a hard drive rather than storing any on the computer you are encrypting (because if the computer is stolen, the thief has the key). Click an option and then repeat to save or print the key as many times as you wish.

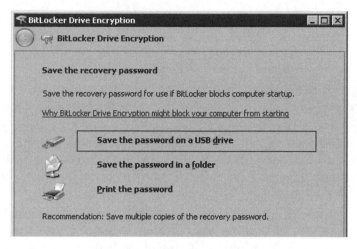

9. Click Next. You are told that the encryption is about to start and given the option to run a system check to see if the keys you have stored are all available. It is strongly recommended that you do the check. Click Continue.

10. Make sure the USB key is plugged in and click Restart Now. After restarting, you should see a balloon message from a system tray icon saying the "BitLocker Drive Encryption Is *xx*% Complete." If you reopen the BitLocker control panel, you'll see that the drive encryption is in process.

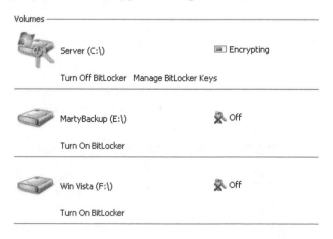

Use a Computer with BitLocker

Using a computer with BitLocker is not much different than using one without it, except that unless you have TPM, you must plug in the USB key before starting the computer. There are several logistical issues to keep in mind:

▼   If you create, copy, or move a file on or to a BitLocker drive or volume, it will be automatically encrypted, but will remain so only on that drive. Given that the system is started with the USB key, a PIN, or TPM, the file will be available in the same way it was before installing BitLocker.

■   If you copy or move a file from the BitLocker drive or volume to another unencrypted drive, the file will automatically be unencrypted on the second drive.

■   If you share files on the BitLocker drive, other users with appropriate permission will be able to see and use the files as they could on a non-BitLocker drive. The files will remain encrypted on the BitLocker drive, but the user will be able, with the correct permission, to copy the file to an unencrypted drive where the file will be unencrypted.

▲   If the computer you are working on has TPM and you have installed BitLocker, when it starts up, it looks for any condition that might represent that someone has been trying to hack into it. This might be changes to the startup files, disk errors, or changes to the Basic Input/Output System (BIOS). When TPM with BitLocker sees any of these conditions, it will lock the system and prevent it from starting. The same items that TPM/BitLocker look at can be affected by hardware failure, which can cause the system to lock up. With the recovery key, though, the system can be easily unlocked.

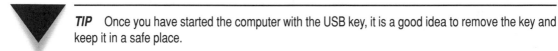

TIP   Once you have started the computer with the USB key, it is a good idea to remove the key and keep it in a safe place.

You can temporarily disable BitLocker or turn it off altogether by clicking Turn Off BitLocker in the BitLocker Drive Encryption control panel. Disabling the drive lets the system be restarted without the key, as you might want to do to upgrade the system, change the BIOS, or to change any of the startup files, but the drive remains encrypted and uses a plain text key that has been stored on the computer. Turning off BitLocker decrypts the drive, which can take some time.

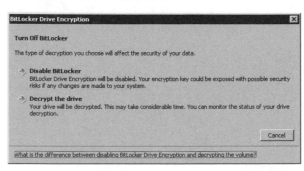

You can duplicate either the startup key or the recovery password by clicking Manage BitLocker Keys in the BitLocker Drive Encryption control panel. When you click Duplicate The Recovery Password, the same Save The Recovery Password dialog box opens that you saw earlier, and you can save a copy of the recovery password on another USB key, in a folder on a hard drive, or print it. If you click Duplicate The Startup Key, you can choose another USB key on which to save it.

BitLocker Recovery

If the USB key is not present or the system locks down for some other reason, you get a message that BitLocker has prevented the system from starting and that you should either insert a USB key (it can be one with the startup key or one with the recovery password) and press ESC to reboot, or you should press ENTER to see a screen where you can enter the recovery password. If you don't have a numeric keypad, you can use the function keys as numbers (F1=1, F2=2, F10=0, and so on). Once you have entered the correct password, the boot process automatically continues.

UNDERSTAND PRIVATE/PUBLIC KEY ENCRYPTION

Several encryption schemes for securing data transmission are in current use: private key encryption, public key encryption, and combinations of the two. The set of these three schemes and the technology and standards or protocols that surround them collectively is known as the *public key infrastructure (PKI)*. In Windows Server 2008, PKI is an integral part of the operating system, especially in Active Directory. Windows Server 2008 has implemented all three encryption key schemes and fully supports them with AD CS.

Private Key Encryption

Private key encryption, or *symmetric cryptography* (which is also what is used with file and folder encryption, as previously discussed), is relatively old and uses a single key to both encrypt and decrypt a message. This means that the key itself must be transferred from sender to receiver. If this is done over the phone, the Internet, or even a courier service, an unauthorized person simply needs to intercept the key transfer to get hold of the key and decrypt the message. Private key encryption, though, has a major benefit in that it is much faster (as much as 1,000 times faster) than the alternatives. Private key schemes are therefore valuable in situations where you do not have to transfer the key or can do so with security—for example, for personal use such as data encryption, as just discussed, or sending information to someone that you first meet face to face. Several private key encryption schemes are available with Windows Server 2008 for exchanging information. If you are transferring information among Windows Server 2008 and Windows Vista computers, Advanced Encryption Standard (AES) 128 will be used by default using a key 128 bits long. Within the same versions of Windows, AES-192 and AES-256 are also available with respectively longer keys. For exchanges with older versions of Windows and other operating systems, the default is to use 3DES (three-step encryption using the Data Encryption Standard). The older DES using a 56-bit key is no longer felt to be secure.

Public Key Encryption

Public key encryption, or *asymmetric cryptography,* which was developed in the mid-1970s, uses a pair of keys—a public key and a private key. The public key is publicly known and transferred, and is used to encrypt a message. The private key never leaves its creator and is used to decrypt the message. For two people to use this technique, each generates both a public key and a private key, and then they openly exchange public keys, not caring who gets a copy of it. Each person encrypts their message to the other by using the other person's public key, and then sends the message. The message can be decrypted and read only by using the private key held by the recipient. The public and private keys use a mathematical algorithm that relates them to the encrypted message. By use of other mathematical algorithms, it is fairly easy to generate key pairs, but with only the public key, it is extremely difficult to generate the private key. The process of public key encryption is relatively slow compared with private key encryption. Public key encryption is best in open environments where the sender and recipient do not know each other.

Combined Public and Private Key Encryption

Most encryption on the Internet actually is a combination of public and private key encryption methods. The most common combination, Secure Sockets Layer (SSL), was developed by Netscape to go between HTTP and TCP/IP. SSL provides a highly secure and very fast means of both encryption and authentication.

Recall that private key encryption is very fast but has the problem of transferring the key, whereas public key encryption is very secure but slow. If you were to begin a secure transmission by using a public key to encrypt and send a private key, you could then securely use the private key to quickly send any amount of data you wanted. This is how SSL works. It uses a public key to send a randomly chosen private key, and in so doing sets up a "secure socket" through which any amount of data can be quickly encrypted, sent, and decrypted. After the SSL header has transferred the private key, all information transferred in both directions during a given session—including the URL, any request for a user ID and password, all HTTP web information, and any data entered on a form—is automatically encrypted by the sender and automatically decrypted by the recipient.

Several versions of SSL exist, with SSL version 3 being the one currently in common use. SSL 3 is both more secure than, and offers improved authentication over, earlier versions.

Another combination of public and private key methods is Transport Layer Security (TLS), which is an open security standard similar to SSL 3. TLS, which was drafted by the Internet Engineering Task Force (IETF), uses different encryption algorithms than SSL. Otherwise, TSL is very similar to SSL and even has an option to revert to SSL if necessary. Both SSL 3 and TLS have been proposed to the World Wide Web Consortium (W3C) standards committee as security standards.

Encryption Keys and Certificates

The PKI in Windows Server 2008 and in general use on the Internet depends on digital certificates to issue, authenticate, and maintain encryption keys. (See "Certificate Authentication," earlier in this chapter, for a discussion of certificates and how to issue and use them.) To get an encryption key, you get a certificate, of which the key is a part. To authenticate the key, you use the certificate that it is a part of. The key is stored in a certificate, which is the means by which keys are maintained in an organization. AD CS in Windows Server 2008 provides all of these services.

NOTE   Windows Server 2008 includes a feature called Cryptography Next Generation (CNG) that interfaces with the PKI to allow the creation and use of custom cryptography algorithms. The use of this, though, is beyond the scope of this book.

SECURE DATA TRANSMISSION

The discussion so far in this chapter has dealt with securing computers and their contents and has been silent about securing the transmission of data among computers, using e-mail or otherwise transferring information either within a LAN directly or using an intranet or the Internet. Yet the need to extend a network to outlying parts of an organization and to customers and suppliers is very real and requires secure data transmission. Securing data transmission means the encryption of the information being transmitted so that it cannot be read and misused by those not meant to read it. Encrypting information is probably as old as the human race and has really blossomed with the advent of computers. Data encryption has become so sophisticated that the U.S. government, worried that it won't be able to decrypt the data (can you imagine that!), hasn't until a few years ago allowed the better technology to be exported (everyone was getting it over the Internet anyway).

Implement Data Transmission Security

You may be thinking that SSL and TLS sound great, but also sound complex to use. In fact, both are easy to use, either across the Internet or internally in a LAN.

Implement Secure Internet and Intranet Transmissions

To implement secure Internet and intranet transmissions, you need a web server that supports SSL or TLS, such as Microsoft IIS 7, plus a supporting web browser, such as Microsoft Internet Explorer 7, both of which are included in Windows Server 2008. From the browser, to visit a web site that has implemented SSL or TSL, you simply need to begin the URL with *https://* rather than http:// (see Chapter 9 on IIS for details on how to implement secure web sites). SSL will then kick in, and without your even being aware that it's happening, the browser and server decide which encryption algorithm to use to transfer a private key, and then use that key and the chosen private key encryption scheme to encrypt and decrypt all the rest of the data during that session.

Once you are connected using SSL, your browser will indicate that a secure connection is established. IE7 displays a padlock icon to the right of the address bar.

NOTE Even though the combination of public and private encryption is relatively fast, it is still significantly slower than no encryption. For that reason, it is recommended that you use SSL only when you send sensitive information, such as financial or credit card data, and not for an entire web site.

Implement Secure LAN Transmission

Although SSL can be used within a LAN and in an intranet, it requires a security server (which function IIS fulfills) and can get in the way of applications that are working across a LAN. The answer to this is *Internet Protocol Security (IPSec)*, which works between any two computers over a network to supply encrypted transmission of information without a security server and without getting in the way of applications. IPSec is a part of IP and works at the third (Network) layer, below any applications, and therefore seldom interferes with them (see the discussion of networking layers in "The OSI Model" in Chapter 5).

The IPSec Process IPSec is almost totally automated, and once group policies are established for its operation, network users don't realize that their network communication is taking place securely. The process for establishing and carrying out IPSec is as follows:

1. Domain or local computer policies are established that specify what network traffic needs to be secure and how that security will be handled.

2. Based on the policies, IPSec establishes a set of filters to determine which network packets require secure transmission.

3. When IPSec receives from a sending application a series of network packets that require secure transmission, the sending computer passes this fact to the receiving computer. The two computers exchange credentials and authenticate each other according to IPSec policies.

4. Given authentication, the two computers work out an algorithm whereby each computer can generate the same private key without having to transmit the key over the network, again according to IPSec policies.

5. The sending computer uses the private key to encrypt the packets it is transmitting, digitally signs them so that the receiving computer knows who is sending the packets, and then transmits the packets.

6. The receiving computer authenticates the digital signature and then uses the key to decrypt the packets and send them on to the receiving application.

Set Up IPSec To set up and use IPSec, you need to only establish or revise default IPSec policies. You can do that through the IP Security snap-in to the MMC with these steps:

1. Click Start | Run, type **mmc**, and press ENTER. The MMC shell opens.

2. Click the File menu, click Add/Remove Snap-in, scroll down, and double-click IP Security Policy Management.

3. Select whether you want to manage security policy for the local computer, the AD domain this computer is a member of, another AD domain, or another computer (I'm using a domain in this example), and click Finish.

4. If it is open, close the Add Standalone Snap-in dialog box and click OK to close the Add Or Remove Snap-ins dialog box. Open the Console Root and click IP Security Policies On Active Directory, so that your MMC looks like this:

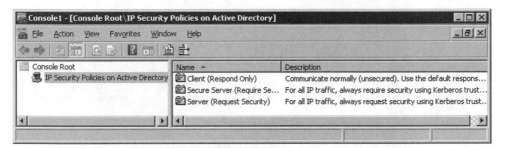

5. Right-click Secure Server and click Properties. In the Rules tab, you will see a list of IP Security Rules, as shown here:

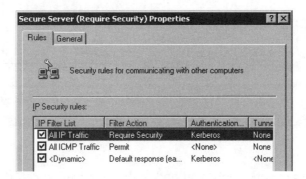

6. Select the All IP Traffic rule and click Edit. The Edit Rule Properties dialog box opens. Look at each of the tabs and then return to the Filter Action tab.

7. Click Require Security and click Edit, which displays a list of security methods similar to the list in Figure 15-9. You can select each of these and click Edit again to select the particular security method you want for a given situation.

8. When you are done, click OK twice and then click Close twice to return to the IPSec console, where you can also click the Close button, answering Yes to save the console settings with the name IPSec.

You can see that the Windows Server 2008 IPSec default is to require security on all IP traffic. This is a safe default; your data will be better protected. The negative side of this default is that the security negotiation between the computers, encrypting and decrypting the data, and the extra bits to transmit, all take time. It also uses a lot more

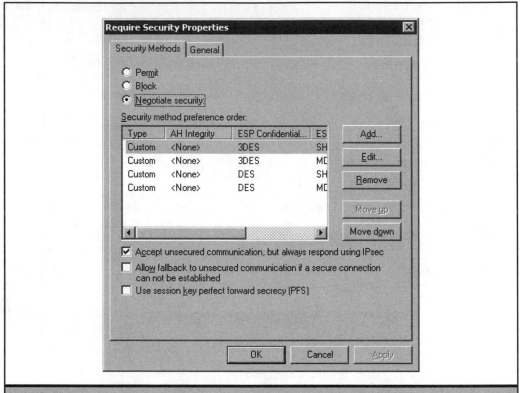

Figure 15-9.   Windows Server 2008 gives many options in specifying the level of security used.

bandwidth on the network. Only you and your organization can determine which is more important—time and bandwidth, or security. The point is that Windows Server 2008 gives you the choice, enabling you to make the determination of which networking aspect has a higher priority.

INDEX

B

C

G

H

▼ M

Q

R

X

Y

Z